The Art of Dress

The Art of Dress

FASHION IN ENGLAND AND FRANCE 1750 to 1820

Aileen Ribeiro

Yale University Press
New Haven & London

Designed by Gillian Malpass
Set in Linotron Bembo by Best-set Typesetter Ltd., Hong Kong
Printed in Singapore by C.S. Graphics PTE Ltd

Library of Congress Cataloging-in-Publication Data

Ribeiro, Aileen, 1944–
The art of dress: fashion in England and France 1750 to 1820 /
Aileen Ribeiro.
Includes bibliographical references and index.
ISBN 0-300-06287-7
1. Costume – England – History – 18th century.   2. Costume –
France – History – 18th century.   3. Costume in art.   4. Costume
– England – History – 19th century.   5. Costume – France –
History – 19th century
I. Title. GT736.R53   1995
391\.00942\09033–dc20 94-35347
CIP

A catalogue record for this book is available from
The British Library

Frontispiece: A. Labille-Guillard, *Self-portrait with Two Pupils* (detail), 1785.
The Metropolitan Museum of Art, New York.
Gift of Julia A. Berwind, 1953

Endpapers: T. Gainsborough (attr.), studies of shoes.
Courtauld Institute Galleries, Witt Collection.
Photo: Caroline Cook, Courtauld Institute of Art

To Stella Mary Newton
with love and gratitude

Contents

1   Boucher, *Madame de Pompadour* (detail of pl. 55).

Acknowledgements

I am indebted to the many art galleries, museums, libraries,
and private owners listed in this book, both for their help and advice,
and for providing photographs of works of art in their collections.
I am grateful to Her Majesty the Queen for access to the
clothing accounts of Georve IV in the Royal Archives;
to Georges Vigne, curator of the Musée Ingres at Montauban,
for the opportunity to make an extensive study of the Ingres drawings there;
and to Miriam Stewart of the Fogg Art Museum, Harvard University,
for making available the David sketchbooks deposited there.
I wish to acknowledge the help given by the staffs of the
British Library, the Departments of Prints and Drawings, and of
Manuscripts at the British Museum, the Prints and Drawings Department
at the Victoria and Albert Museum, the Archive of the National Portrait Gallery,
the Bibliothèque Nationale, the Lewis Walpole Library at Farmington,
and the Society of Antiquaries.
I would especially like to thank the staff at the Yale Center
for British Art, New Haven, for making my stay there during a
brief Visiting Fellowship, such an enjoyable and profitable experience.
I am grateful, for their helpful comments and advice, to
Brian Allen, Hugh Belsey, Valerie Cumming, Joanna Marschner,
Shelley Tobin and Penelope Ruddock.
At the Courtauld Institute, I would like again to pay tribute to the
customary help and efficiency of the staffs of the Libraries,
the Photographic Department, and the Photographic Survey of
Private Collections.
Last, but certainly not least, I would like to record my gratitude to
my editor Gillian Malpass for her commitment and professionalism
in the realising of this book.

2 David, *Coronation of Napoleon* (detail of pl. 162).

Introduction

Truth and History: The Meaning of Dress in Art, 1750–1820

Boswell asked Dr Johnson what he thought about portraits.
He agreed in thinking them valuable in families.
I wished to know which he preferred,
fine portraits or those of which the merit is resemblance.
Johnson: 'Sir, their chief excellence is being like.'
Boswell: 'Are you of that opinion as to the portraits
of ancestors whom one has never seen?'
Johnson: 'It then becomes of more consequence that they should
be like; and I would have them in the dress of the times,
which makes a piece of history . . . Truth, sir,
is of the greatest value in these things.'
(James Boswell, *Journal of a Tour of the Hebrides*, 1785)

The human figure cannot be understood merely through the
observation of its surface; the interior must be laid bare,
the parts must be separated, the connexions perceived, the differences noted,
action and reaction observed, the hidden, constant, fundamental
elements of the phenomena impressed on the mind . . . A glance at
the surface of a living being confuses the observer;
here, as elsewhere, we may adduce the true proverb
'We see only what we know' . . .
perfect observation really depends on knowledge.
(Goethe, Introduction to *Propyläen*, 1798)

3 Copley, *Mrs Thomas Gage* (detail of pl. 239).

The Nature of Dress

Dress is the most fleeting of the arts, a prey to the arbitrary dictates of novelty and the attacks of critics, subject to endless speculation – and quite meaningless out of historical context. It is, on the other hand, the only art that relates so closely to the narrative of our lives, both as individuals and in relation to the wider world; for clothing is simultaneously intensely personal (a reflection of our self-image) and, as fashion, it is, in the words of Louis XIV, 'the mirror of history'.

Clothes distinguish humanity from the other animals and defend us 'from the Inclemencies and Vicissitudes of Climate and Season, and hide those Parts which Delicacy and the Interests of Society require to be hidden', as one early philosopher of dress expressed it in 1792.[1] But as soon as dress had achieved the basic necessities of warmth and modesty, it began to attract censure precisely because the notion of morality is such a variable. Dress, as an art so closely linked to the body, so revelatory of conscious or unconscious sexuality, is constantly liable to hostile interpretation.

The history of dress is often seen as an area impervious to reason and analysis. The traditional Judaeo-Christian notion of the sinfulness of certain aspects of dress might be played down nowadays, but many people would agree with the feminist viewpoint of Mary Wollstonecraft that 'an air of fashion is but a badge of slavery', that too great an interest in self-adornment implies a diminution of the intellect and a mind disposed to frivolity. Again, from *A Vindication of the Rights of Woman* (1792) we read: 'The air of fashion which many young people are so eager to attain, always strikes me like the studied attitudes of some modern prints, copied with tasteless servility after the antique; the soul is left out, and none of the parts are tied together by what may properly be termed character'.[2]

These comments have a relevance to the choice of costume in portrait painting in any age. Mary Wollstonecraft's views are also a rewording of the medieval belief that too great a concentration on worldly things demeans human spirituality. It is the futility of fashion in the face of the inevitability of death – the medieval notion of the Dance of Death – that still persists throughout the period covered by this book, in art as well as in literature. Robert Dighton's *Life and Death Contrasted, or An Essay on Man and Woman* (pl. 4) is just such an attack on the fashions and on fashionable pursuits.[3]

What enraged critics of dress (artists and writers) – as it still does today – was the perpetual restlessness of fashion, its urgent imperative towards the new and its hedonistic consumerism. Oscar Wilde noted, only half tongue-in-cheek, that fashion was 'a form of

ugliness so intolerable that we have to alter it every six months', but his attempts to popularise a more aesthetic costume than that of his own time met with as little success as the efforts of the dress reformers of the late eighteenth century (among whom might be included Jacques-Louis David) in the promotion of 'timeless' clothing.

Dress reformers are usually moved by considerations of ideology, aesthetics or health; practicalities (and sometimes details) are often lost in the grand overall plan. Walter Vaughan's *Essay Philosophical and Medical concerning Modern Clothing* (1792), for example, aimed ambitiously to 'investigate the Causes of Dress, to prove that the Common Mode of clothing not only alters the natural form of our Bodies, but also produces Inability, Disease and Death'; his concern was to remove dress from the 'Trumpery of the Milliner and the Apparatus of the Toilette' by proposing 'a Clothing suitable to every Age, Sex, Constitution and Country' – a complete impossibility.[4] In an age of reason, however, it was a firmly held belief that costume ought to be more rational, to be less indebted to the bizarre and to break away from the artificial conventions of society. 'Nos habits sont de fer', exclaimed a contemporary of Wollstonecraft and Vaughan, 'ils sont l'invention des siècles barbares et gothiques. Il faut que vous brisiez aussi ces fers, si vous voulez devenir libres et heureux'.[5]

How to break the manacles of fashion occupied the minds of dress reformers, artists and critics particularly in the eighteenth century; the early years of the nineteenth century saw a considerable simplification of dress for both men and women, and attacks on fashionable costume are far less strident than earlier. The general artistic preference for the simple and natural as against the formal and artificial can be seen in Daniel Chodowiecki's *Natur und Afectation* (pl. 5); the absurdly over-dressed couple on the right (the woman in particular is barely able to walk under the weight of her vast wig and towering headdress, and with her wide, hooped skirt), are contrasted with the simplicity of the couple unconstrained by clothing (other than the merest drapery) and unaffected by notions of false modesty.

A dislike of fashion as inimical to a state of nature drew much of its inspiration from Rousseau, whose *Discours sur les sciences et les arts* (1750) elaborated on the theory that Art (that is, all the arts of 'civilised' living, including dress) acted as a corrupting force on manners and thought. For Rousseau, fashion corrupted virtue and masked vice; 'l'homme du monde est tout entier dans son masque; ce qu'il est n'est rien, ce qu'il paraît est tout pour lui'.[6] Here is the essence of the Romantic credo, the claim of the individual to be important in his own right, and not to be judged on outward appearance only. Allan Ramsay's portrait

4 R. Dighton, *Life and Death Contrasted, or An Essay on Man and Woman, c.*1784. Pen and ink and watercolour. Sale, Sotheby's, London, 23 February 1978, lot 37.

3

of Rousseau of 1766 (pl. 6) shows the philosopher in his famous 'Armenian' costume, consisting of fur-lined gown and hat. In its ease of movement and element of the exotic it conforms perfectly to the eighteenth-century ideal of the 'artistic' costume; Rousseau's disciple, Louis-Sébastien Mercier, claimed that 'l'habillement orientale est fait pour la taille humaine'.[7] Here, we are meant to see a man of progressive ideas depicted in costume above the vagaries of high fashion. But with Rousseau nothing is ever what it appears, for this costume was adopted by him in the early 1760s, when a urinary complaint necessitated the wearing of loose clothing. Rousseau records that it was on the advice of an Armenian tailor that he wore this outfit (which is not specifically Armenian, but one of many variants of the loose fur-trimmed gowns, oriental in origin, but widely worn in central Europe and the Russian empire). Rousseau claims in his *Confessions* that he never wore any other costume, which is certainly not true, as on formal occasions he conformed to the conventions of society. His sense of martyrdom must have been increased by

the fact that he was sometimes attacked in the streets wearing what Lady Sarah Lennox described as his 'very silly . . . pellisse & fur cap'.[8] The painting was the subject of a famous quarrel between Rousseau and the Scottish philosopher and historian David Hume; Rousseau, morbidly sensitive and touchy, came to dislike Ramsay's portrait, claiming it made him look like 'un Cyclope affreux'.

Such controversies only added to the legend of the great (but sometimes misunderstood) philosopher, not just as the man who set out the virtues of the common people in an age of aristocracy, but as one whose writings liberated men, women and children from the dictates of an artificial society and the clothing that symbolised such slavery. On Rousseau's tomb at Ermenonville (which became a place of pilgrimage after his death in 1778) visitors could see the image of a number of naked children burning women's whale-bone stays and children's swaddling clothes,[9] a reference particularly to his *Emile* (1762), a pioneering work on the upbringing of children.

One visitor to Ermenonville in the summer of

1788 was John Villiers, Earl of Clarendon. Having made his pilgrimage to the tomb (where the inscription read 'Ici repose l'homme de la nature et de la vérité') it is clear from Villiers's account that one of his main purposes was to search out 'some relics of this great man'. 'Every incident, the most trivial, becomes dignified and interesting when it relates to such a man; and circumstances of this kind, such as the apparel he wore . . . are particularly attractive as impressing ideas of personality'. One of the villagers, Villiers relates, 'brought down a pair of shoes that Rousseau used to wear; the soles and heels were of wood, and the other parts matted with reed and lined with hair . . .'; these had been worn at the time of Rousseau's death and were brought out almost as religious objects to be venerated by distinguished visitors.[10]

The Romantic cult of relics – often clothing – that belonged to great men is one that might be smiled at now, but which is understandable; to touch something that has been in bodily contact with one of our heroes can be a moving experience and an intimate and tangible link with the past. In the same vein, the artist Pierre-Nolasque Bergeret recalled seeing at Isabey's a number of garments that had belonged to Napoleon; 'il nous faisait voir toutes les reliques impériales qu'il possédait, telles que le costume complet que portait Napoléon Bonaparte à la bataille de Marengo, l'habit qu'il portait à l'hôtel des Invalides le jour de la première distribution des croix d'honneur.'[11]

Surviving costume is an essential component in the study of the history of dress, not just with regard to the clothing of famous people, but as evidence of the lives of our ancestors. Walking in Monmouth Street in London (famous for its second-hand clothes shops throughout this period) Thomas Carlyle conjured up 'the whole Pageant of Existence' on seeing, with a kind of pleasurable melancholy, the sartorial relics of the recent past:

What still dignity dwells in a Suit of Cast Clothes! How meekly it bears its honours. No haughty looks, no scornful gesture; silent and serene it fronts the world, neither demanding worship nor afraid to miss it. The Hat still carries the physiognomy of its Head; but the vanity and the stupidity . . . are gone. The Coat-arm is stretched out but not to strike; the Breeches in modest simplicity depend at ease and now at last have a graceful flow; the Waistcoat hides no evil passion, no riotous desire; hunger or thirst now dwells not in it. Thus all is purged from the grossness of Sense, from the carking cares and foul vices of the World; and rides there, on its Clothes-horse . . .[12]

Carlyle's fanciful musing on old clothes (from his cumbersome metaphorical work *Sartor Resartus* of 1833–4, an attack on materialism in the guise of a discussion on clothing, the 'adventitious trappings' of society) underlines the limitations of the surviving object. Clothes, however splendid the craftsmanship and luxury, are basically a commodity and cannot have the emotional impact of art or literature. From a study of surviving dress we can understand cut and construction, we can appreciate qualities of design; but we cannot gain perceptual knowledge. Clothing is full of signs, sometimes contradictory; it is often ambiguous and lends itself to disguise and role-playing. To contradict Mr Gradgrind, the *facts* which can be gleaned (from surving costume) are not enough in any consideration of the nature of dress; more complex allusions and emotions should concern us, especially when considering the various ways in which dress is depicted in art. This book is, therefore, not so much about a history of dress as about the ways in which fashion acts as a link between life and art.

It has been persuasively if controversially argued by the art historian Anne Hollander, that 'the history of dress . . . has no real substance other than in images of clothes'. She develops the theory that, since costume is inextricably bound up with the human image, when represented in art it becomes in itself a form of visual art. 'It is pictorial art that dress most resembles, and to which it is inescapably bound, in its changing vision'.[13] Certainly the history of dress in some respects is not unlike the history of art at a very simplistic level – a cycle of dissatisfaction with the status quo,

6   A. Ramsay, *Jean-Jacques Rousseau*, 1766. Oil on canvas. National Gallery of Scotland, Edinburgh.

reaction, invention and change fuelling the creative impulse. In addition, the idea of the *Zeitgeist*, albeit currently unfashionable, has its attractions, although the unity of various forms of art seems clearer in some periods, such as that under discussion, than at other times. Furthermore, styles of dress can – with caution – be linked to art-historical terms as reflections of prevailing artistic impulses. Carlyle was particularly attracted to architectural analogies; 'in all his Modes and habilatory endeavours, an Architectural Idea will be found lurking; his Body and the Cloth are the site and materials whereon and whereby his beautiful edifice of a Person is to be built', and, he continues, the resulting types of dress can be 'Grecian, Gothic, Later-Gothic, or altogether Modern and Anglo-Dandiacal'.[14]

While accepting the Hollander thesis that the representation of garments in art gives them the *gravitas* they might not have in real life, it is important to record the fact that the clothes themselves are the starting point for both artist and sitter. In analysing dress in art, we have mentally to reconstruct it through knowledge of surviving garments, calculating how it might or might not work on the body as depicted by the transforming hand of the artist; this then has to be linked with other contemporary visual, literary and documentary material. Most of the dress seen in fashionable portraiture before our own century was expensive and complicated to put on: the choice of what costume to wear was crucial to both artist and sitter. The ephemeral but vital arts of the tailor, dressmaker and hairdresser were essential in producing the finished and living figure immortalised by painters and sculptors, as the following tribute to the 'artists' of fashion indicates:

> . . . the marble, however finely polished, however elegantly and naturally compleated, is but a statue still. The painter, though an Apelles, leaves you only a figure without motion; nor can all his tints, his dyes, and his touches make that picture move. But when life and motion are added to the painter's beauty and the sculptor's grace, surely then the artist is invited to make the most splendid display of his taste and judgement; and though his work will decay like the most compact posey culled with judgement and arranged with taste, yet he will have the satisfaction of a temporary fame . . .'[15]

The Art of Dress

It is, perhaps, a paradox that dress achieves immortality through the portrait, that the canvas gives it a vitality that cannot be achieved in the half-light of a museum existence. A portrait suggests a precise mo-

ment in history, and often the costume is so important to the image that it transfixes the sitter in a kind of time-warp. An example of this is the simple white silk bodice and skirt in which Queen Henrietta Maria was depicted by van Dyck in the 1630s; it is hard to remember that she lived through the Interregnum and into the Restoration, for the popular image of her is fixed before the Civil War. Again, the Empress Eugénie of France ('born to be a dressmaker' in Florence Nightingale's waspish comment) brings to mind the frothy tulle ball-gowns created by Worth and painted by Winterhalter in the late 1850s and 1860s; we do not think of her living until 1920 in a world in which dress and behaviour were light years away from the luxury of the Second Empire. In the period covered by this book, an obvious example of the perfect harmony created between sitter, dress and artist is Boucher's portrait of Madame de Pompadour (1759; pl. 7), a riot of curvilinear forms in the shape of a Rococo *robe à la française*, of peachy-pink taffeta.

Such happy alliances resulted not from accident but from hard work, Goethe knew how difficult the portrait painter's job was:

> They are supposed to incorporate into their portrait everyone's feelings towards the subject, everyone's likes and dislikes; they are supposed to show not merely how they see a particular person, but how everyone would see him. I am not surprised when such artists gradually grow insensitive, indifferent and self-willed.[16]

The ideal portrait, claimed Goethe in his novel *Elective Affinities* (1809), revealed the history and character of the sitter. Baudelaire echoed this, stating that a portrait should be like a dramatised biography, demanding 'immense intelligence' from the artist, who also had to be an actor 'whose duty is to adopt any character and any costume'.[17]

The fusion of character, likeness and costume (often thought of as irreconcilable elements) was the mark of a great artist, and even then not always easy to achieve with originality and imagination at a time when portraiture enjoyed hitherto unheard-of popularity. The first sentence of William Combe's *Poetical Epistle to Sir Joshua Reynolds* of 1777 begins 'This seems to be a Portrait-painting Age', and he gives the reasons for this as 'the increase of Sentiment' and 'that spirit of Luxury which pervades all ranks and professions of men'.[18] Fuseli, in his *Lectures on Painting*, published in 1820, lamented the increase in portraiture which he attributed to the levelling of society by 'liberty and commerce'; it was no longer the 'exclusive property of princes, or a tribute to beauty, prowess, genius, talent and distinguished character', but open to all as 'a kind of family calendar'. Present-day portraiture, he claimed, was a conspiracy between artist and sitter to produce only 'external likeness; that deeper, nobler aim, the personification of character, is neither required, nor, if obtained, recognised'.[19]

The portrait was both public, in the sense of being subject to the conventions of society, and private, in the sense of being painted for the intimate contemplation of family and loved ones. It was of its time and yet timeless in its claim on posterity; it could represent reality in dress or it could express fantasy. Whatever the final image, the artist had to resolve the dilemma of depicting the likeness of the sitter, including his costume, and yet show his own imagination and inspiration – otherwise the portrait became a mere mechanical likeness. Some society artists opted for the easy life in their emphasis on likeness above all, which pleased an undiscriminating clientele of the kind described in Edith Wharton's novel *The Custom of the Country* (1913):

> Not one of the number was troubled by any personal theory of art; all they asked of a portrait was that the costume should be sufficiently 'lifelike', and the flesh not too much so; and a long experience of idealizing flesh and realizing dress fabrics had enabled Mr Popple to meet both demands.[20]

Wharton is here poking fun at both artist and sitters – Edwardian ladies with much money and little taste – but it holds true for society portrait painters in any age. The sway of fashion and the idealised face of the moment as seen through the eyes of a society artist served to present women as decorative objects, a factor particularly present in portraits in the mid-eighteenth century; by the end of the century female dress was considerably simpler in style and fabric, and as a consequence more emphasis could be given to character, although rarely without some slight obeisance towards contemporary notions of beauty. For women usually had their portraits painted in their youth and at the height of their beauty, when they were very conscious of the part played in their appearance by dress and hairstyles. Men, on the other hand, could be painted at various stages in their lives and careers; active in the world of affairs, their portraits showed them in Protean guise, as warriors, statesmen, professionals, as well as in the costume of rank and status. As Goethe noted: 'A man's fairest memorial is . . . his own portrait . . . It is the best text to the music of his life.'[21] Less influenced by the vagaries of fashionable portrait painting, less subject to sartorial flights of fancy, men could more readily be painted at ease, and with greater individuality than was allowed to women.

The costume worn by the sitter is an essential element in any portrait, but surprisingly little is known about the processes of choice. Who chose the costume and why? Did sitters expect a literal rendition

of their appearance? What part, if any, did sitters play in the selection of pose and costume when a drapery painter was involved? Most sitters were probably content to accept the dictates of the artist, particularly a fashionable society artist; but there must also have been clients strong-willed enough to have definite ideas on how they wished to be represented. The subject of costume in painting has been largely ignored by art historians; this may be because of ignorance or a resentment at the intrusion of dress into the painterly process, a dislike of the 'busyness' of clothing in what Rilke calls the 'stillness of pictures'. But dress cannot be ignored, particularly in portraiture.

Some general comments can be made about artists' studios of the period. Fashionable artists had elegant

7 F. Boucher, *Madame de Pompadour*, 1759. Oil on canvas. Wallace Collection, London.

waiting-rooms and studios hung with portraits and collections of engravings after their own and others' works; these provided inspiration for the sitter and advertisement for the artist. Artists such as Boucher and Fragonard had built up connoisseurs' collections of *objets d'art*; David's studio contained furniture in the classical style, casts after the antique and even tunics and togas. History painting was at the top of the hierarchy of the fine arts and it was more acceptable for an artist to be painted in the process of such work than it was to be observed in the painting of portraits in modern dress. It is relatively rare to find depictions of studios where a clothed sitter is visible on the easel alongside his presence in the flesh. Often the canvas is hidden from view, as in Hayman's *Self-*

portrait with Grosvenor Bedford of about 1750 (pl. 8). Here, there is a clear demarcation between the formal appearance of the sitter in his grey suit, gold-trimmed white waistcoat, powdered bob wig and hat held somewhat awkwardly under his arm as polite convention dictated, and the informal frock-suit of the artist who, in contrast to his client, wears his own hair.

The contrast between contemporary costume and the pretentiousness of the poses and attributes adopted by fashionable artists, can be enjoyed in Henry William Bunbury's affectionate satire on Reynolds, *A Family Piece* of c.1781 (pl. 9). A portly city merchant wearing a large 'physical' wig (very old-fashioned by this time) sits next to his wife whose modish hairstyle, ribboned cap and *décolletage* would have been thought inappropriate for her age and station in life. Their child, as a yawning Cupid, finds the process of sitting to an artist as tedious as did the many adults who were motivated more by duty than by vanity.

One way of lessening the boredom involved in sittings was to use the services of the drapery painter, a practice shrouded in some mystery, as it was not in the interests of the fashionable artist to reveal precisely how much of his own work was on the canvas. The drapery painter, stated *The London Tradesman* (1747), 'is employed in dressing the Figures after the Painter has finished the Face, given the Figure its proper Attitude, and drawn the Out-lines of the Dress or Drapery'.[22] Some of these 'painter taylors', as Hogarth called them, earned considerable sums of money, the most famous among them being the Fleming Joseph van Aken, who, according to Vertue, excelled in the painting of 'silks, sattins, velvets, embroiderys'. Van Aken worked for a number of artists, including Ramsay, Hudson, Knapton and Dandridge; Vertue noted that he 'puts them so much on a Level that its very difficult to know one hand from another'.[23] Such a drapery painter would have had a considerable say in the pose and costume of a portrait when the artist was too busy, too lazy or too unimaginative to think up new ideas for himself. Thomas Hudson, for example, relied on van Aken's services (and those of his younger brother Alexander, who took over from him after his death in 1749) to produce slick conventional portraits with stereotyped poses and costume. Hudson's *Unknown Gentleman* and *Unknown Lady* of 1750 (pls 10, 11) are typical of this genre. The man is a good example of what Horace Walpole described as this artist's 'fair tyed wigs, blue velvet coats and white satin waistcoats, which he bestowed liberally on his customers';[24] the wife, or fiancée, is depicted in another type of conventional costume, less high fashion than an imaginary mixture of contemporary dress with references to van Dyck and Kneller.[25]

Hudson was Reynolds's teacher, and thus the practice of using drapery painters was perpetuated. In a

10 (far left) T. Hudson, *Unknown Gentleman*, 1750. Oil on canvas. Dulwich Picture Gallery, London.

11 T. Hudson, *Unknown Lady*, 1750. Oil on canvas. Dulwich Picture Gallery, London.

letter to Elizabeth Montagu of 1761, Lord Bath wrote:

> I have discovered a secret by being often at Mr Reynolds', that I fancy he is sorry I should know. I find that none of these great Painters finish any of their Pictures themselves. The same Person (but who he is I know not) works for Ramsey, Reynolds, and another called Hudson, my Picture will not come from that Person till Thursday night, and on Fryday it will be totally finished and ready to send home.[26]

The reference here is probably to Peter Toms, who worked for a number of fashionable artists, including Reynolds, Cotes and Ramsay, and it appears the practice of drapery painting went on into the 1760s,[27] after which it gradually declined, although busy artists with royal and aristocratic clients found it necessary to use the services of studio assistants. Such assistants or pupils working in the studio of the artist were under his direct control and less likely to make mistakes over the costume, as Toms apparently once did, adding an 'elaborate dress of state' to the head of one of Reynolds's sitters although she had requested a 'rural habit'.[28]

Many artists both in England and France used either dolls or full-sized lay figures to help with pose and costume; these were generally of wood or cork and sometimes with moveable brass joints. Some of these small androgynous dolls with male and female wardrobes have survived, for example the sculptor Louis-François Roubiliac's articulated figure at the Museum of London.[29] Another survival is the artist Ann Whytell's small (about 11½ inches high) wooden figure, with its large wardrobe and box dated 1769 (pl. 12).[30] The costume comprises underwear, fashionable dress and wigs of human hair for both sexes, and for a man, Vandyke and hussar outfits. There are also two hussar costumes and other small items of dress which belonged to the lay figure used by the artist Arthur Devis (in the Harris Museum and Art Gallery, Preston). Dolls were also used by Hayman, Gravelot and Gainsborough, among others; there are far fewer references to their use by artists in France, although in the inventory of Louis-Michel van Loo's effects (made after he died in 1771) are listed 'des mannequins et leurs habits, des étoffes de satin et de taffetas de différentes couleurs'.[31]

Besides dolls, or complementary to them, were life-sized lay figures on which drapery or actual costume could be arranged. James Northcote records the use of the lay figure in Reynolds's studio; in 1772 he refers to his work on a portrait of the Duke of Cumberland in Garter robes 'which I paint from the Duke's own robes put on upon the layman'.[32] Grand and elaborate costume of this kind necessitated far more time than the noble owners had at their disposal, and of course it had to be accurate. How meticulous the depiction of such clothes could be can be seen in the useful (and fairly rare) conjunction of portrait and surviving costume; Reynolds painted Lord Middleton (1761–2) in the coronation robes of a baron (pl. 13); red velvet

12 S. Hennequin, wooden lay figure and clothes; the property of the artist Ann Whytell, 1769. Los Angeles County Museum of Art. Gift of Elsie De Wolfe Foundation.

surcoat and mantle with two powderings (rows) of 'ermine' (actually black bristle tails) on white 'miniver' (really rabbit – a frequent economy in the eighteenth century due to the expense of pure northern squirrel, or miniver). Lord Middleton's robes still exist, as does his suit, which consists of red velvet breeches and a sumptuous sleeved waistcoat of glittering golden brocaded silk, probably French. The accuracy and detail of Reynolds's painting (of the flowered silk coat in particular) may be seen when comparing it to the original, still in superb condition, on loan to the Museum of Costume in Nottingham (pl. 14).

Paradoxically, this type of costume appealed to many artists more than everyday fashionable dress, for it was, in a sense, timeless (or at least hallowed by tradition), and the grandeur of a sweeping mantle

offered not only dramatic possibilities, but the opportunity to demonstrate skill in the handling of luxury fabrics.

Any professional or occupational costume indicative of status had to be painted exactly, according to *The Artist's Repository and Drawing Magazine* of 1784–6, but even so such draperies 'ought to have noble, large and majestic folds; their movements being slow, grave and orderly, possessing a dignity corresponding to the situation of the wearer'.[33] On the other hand, when painting everyday fashions, the artist, while maintaining 'an evident distinction and peculiarity of character' with regard to textiles, was in no way a 'draper or merchant', and he 'need not paint his laces precisely to a Brussels pattern . . .'[34] When an artist did paint the details of costume precisely, copied from the

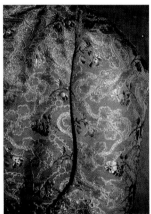

14 Detail of coat worn by Lord Middleton at the coronation of George III. Brocaded silk. City of Nottingham Museums, Museum of Costume and Textiles. Lord Middleton

13 J. Reynolds, *Francis Willoughby, 3rd Baron Middleton*, 1761–2. Oil on canvas. The Lord Middleton.

sitter, this sometimes occasioned comment. In 1751 Peter Manigault from Charleston wrote apropos of his portrait by Ramsay: 'The Drapery is all taken from my own Clothes, & the very Flowers in the lace, upon the Hat, are taken from a Hat of my own . . .'[35]

Ramsay was particularly expert in the appreciation of female toilettes, and almost certainly offered tactful suggestions to his sitters regarding colours, choice of accessories and other matters. He was fairly unusual for an eighteenth-century British artist in his use of detailed preparatory drawings for his portraits. A letter to Walpole about the painting of his nieces Laura (the Hon. Mrs Keppel) and Charlotte (Lady Huntingtower) in 1765 'begs Mrs Capel may come dressed in the manner she proposes to be painted, as he wants to make a sketch of her attitude upon paper, as he has already done to Lady Huntingtower'.[36] In fact the painting (which once hung at Strawberry Hill, and is now in a private collection in the United States) is not particularly successful either in dress or pose, and the sitters seem stilted and nervous in relation to each other (Ramsay's intimate style is best suited to the single portrait), but the letter indicates the care the artist took over the costume. Often his drawings have notes on the costume and show different arrangements of dress and accessories from those in the finished portraits, although never far removed from the original.

Ramsay may have learnt the usefulness of such drawings from French artists, as the practice was more common in France than in Britain. Artists such as Nattier made preparatory drawings of their sitters in informal dress, even the grandest of ladies, and then worked them up to a formal portrait. His drawing of Madame Henriette de France (Caen, Musée des Beaux-Arts) shows one of the homely daughters of Louis XV wearing a plain *sacque* gown with front fastening and playing a base viol, as she does in the finished portrait at Versailles (1754) but wearing court dress, the *grand habit* with its stiff, boned bodice, huge hoop and train.

Drawing from the life gave a greater sense of vivacity to the sitter and obviated the need for dolls or lay figures which could produce rather rigid poses, and sometimes – in the hands of a less than expert artist – an awkwardness between the costume and its wearer. Drawings were particularly important for catching the immediacy of feminine fashions, the most famous and detailed being those of Ingres, which are such a wonderful source for the historian of dress. It is well known that Ingres 'enhanced' the dress of his sitters by using fashion plates, which were easily accessible sources, especially for his beautifully detailed portrait drawings.[37] Painted portraits took much longer and sometimes the dress and pose changed as the artist had second thoughts. Artistic genius, as Proust knew, could take liberties with a sitter's pose, costume and even face:

All that artificial harmony which a woman has succeeding in imposing upon her features, the persistence of which she oversees in her mirror every day before going out, relying on the angle of her hat, the smoothness of her hair, the vivacity of her expression, to ensure its continuity, that harmony the keen eye of the great painter instantly destroys, substituting for it a rearrangement of the woman's features such as will satisfy a certain pictorial ideal of femininity which he carries in his head.[38]

This may explain why in the work of many great artists – artists as different as Hogarth and Boucher, Lawrence and Ingres – the faces, particularly of the female sitters, look curiously alike, and yet at the same time they have the stamp of their own character and the intelligence of the artist.

The business of sitting for a portrait was a co-operative venture between artist and sitter, and it often took some time before the perfect costume could be selected. When William Hickey wanted a portrait of his mistress Charlotte Barry in 1781, he chose the fashionable artist Richard Cosway to paint her. She had two sittings, her hair arranged by 'Freschini . . . in the most fashionable and elegant style' (we are not told what her dress was) and on a further visit to see the progress of the portrait, 'not with any idea of her then sitting again, she being in riding habit', Cosway was so impressed by her appearance, with her hat off 'and some of her curls having blown loose', that he 'rubbed out the elegantly arranged hair, and drew her exactly as she then sat before me'.[39]

If this is an example of an accidental but successful choice of dress, then Lady Hester Newdigate's experience with Romney a few years later is an example of a more protracted and probably more stressful encounter between artist and sitter. In 1790 Lady Hester went up to London to be painted by Romney who had written to her 'to dress myself in white Sattin before I come to him today; I have no such thing in town, must get my head dress'd in haste & . . . borrow a Gown which I shall not be able to get into . . .' Two days later she managed to obtain such a gown but there were clearly problems either with the costume or the pose. Two years later, however, Lady Hester wrote to her husband that 'my Picture is certainly much improv'd. All seem Satisfy'd with it. I have reason to be so, for it is handsomer than ever I was in my life'.[40] The finished portrait (pl. 15) shows the sitter in a kind of compromise costume, a short-sleeved white muslin gown over a white satin underdress; it relates both to the fashion and to the kind of

15 G. Romney, *Lady Hester Newdigate*, 1790–2. Oil on canvas. Private Collection.

books tend to have surprisingly little information on the clothing worn by clients.[42]

The element of flattery was a constant, especially with portraits of those women who prided themselves on their sense of fashion. A considerable number of English sitters wished to keep abreast of changing styles by having their portraits brought up to date, particularly the hairstyles, always the most sensitive barometer of style. For example, in *Mrs Abington as the Comic Muse* Reynolds painted the fashionable actress in about 1768 (Waddesdon Manor, Bucks), but some five years later altered the hair to the new modish height; similar alterations to the hair appear in Hayman's portrait of Mrs Hoadly (pl. 212) and in Cotes's portrait of the Countess of Donegall, *c.*1766 (ex-Dunbrody) where the head was repainted, possibly by Gainsborough, in the 1780s.[43] The paradox of these portraits is that the costume is often 'timeless' or vaguely historical, and thus forms an odd contrast to the ultra-fashionable hairstyles.

16 J. Opie, *Frances Dillon, Lady Jerningham*, *c.*1800. Oil on canvas. Private Collection.

generalised 'classical' dress that Romney was keen to promote.

It is, perhaps, rather more successful as a costume than that seen in John Opie's *Frances Dillon, Lady Jerningham* of *c.*1800 (pl. 16): 'I sat for the fourth time to Opie', she wrote to her daughter, dressed '*d'après le Breste*, in Black Velvet and gold fringe, my French veil over my hair leaving out the Cap underneath. Everybody finds it very like, and I believe it is so – only with 10 or 13 years taken off, so that it will do for Posterity. I don't dislike the flattery, as it makes a decent Picture'.[41] The Dillons were an old Catholic family with long-established French connections and the dress in this portrait was probably one owned by the sitter and slightly adapted by the artist. These two portraits by Romney and Opie are fairly rare instances of discussion about the dress in a portrait that can be linked to known paintings. It is worth noting that the information comes from the sitters and not from the artists, for the latter on the whole were reluctant to commit themselves to a discussion of individual portraits, preferring – where they mention dress at all – to discuss theory rather than practice; surviving sitter

This feeling that portraiture had to be up to date – even to the absurd lengths of altering portraits of ancestors – is made fun of in Smollett's novel *Peregrine Pickle* (1751), where a country squire tries to modernise his family portraits by van Dyck by employing 'a painter vellow from London to clap decent perriwigs upon their skulls at the rate of vive shillings a head'. Smollett wants his readers to share with him the joke that, far from finding the costume of van Dyck old-fashioned, it was now the vogue to be painted in this dress.

A portrait is not merely a mechanical image, it is the likeness of the sitter and his or her character seen through the temperament of the artist, whose views on costume condition the finished work and often reflect the opinions of contemporary critics writing about art and dress. The eighteenth century inherited the Renaissance belief that art should strive to depict perfection and that some rational solution had to be arrived at in the relation of costume to character. To some extent the French Revolution blew away many of the established rules about taste in art so dear to the eighteenth century; a consensus was no longer a desirable thing in itself and by the early nineteenth century dress had changed quite radically to accommodate artistic aesthetics of simplicity, form and function.

★　　★　　★

Critics and artists were agreed that attitudes towards dress, both in art and in life, differed in France and England. It is necessary to look only at the great *Encyclopédie* to note the importance of dress in French society; the volumes contain a fund of information on fashion, from manufacture to consumption, as well as discussing the role of costume in manners and behaviour. As the American critic Susan Sontag puts it: 'French culture . . . allows a link between ideas of vanguard art and of fashion. The French have never shared the Anglo-American conviction that makes the fashionable the opposite of the serious.'[44] It is precisely because of this that the French felt free to paint the details of dress, whereas the English were more wary in their attitude towards fashion, expressing a preference for the general over the specific. Hazlitt, in his critical writings on art, felt that English artists such as Reynolds were too generalised in their portraits, too prone to equate perfection of form with spiritual poverty; English art was 'Gothic and unfinished', whereas French art was 'dry, hard and minute'. More poetically, Baudelaire claimed that there were two ways of understanding portraiture, 'as history and as fiction'. In the first category he placed such artists as David and Ingres, 'whose aim is to set forth the contours and the modelling of the subject faithfully, severely and minutely' with their characteristic attitudes. The second method of painting was to 'transform the portrait into a picture . . . a poem full of space and reverie . . . there the imagination has a greater part to play'; among such artists he includes Reynolds and Lawrence, perhaps over-emphasising their poetic content and ignoring the way in which social position is revealed in their portraits.[45]

While English art is prone to escapism in the pursuit of moral elevation, French portraits depict the real and the particular in dress, although critics sometimes disapproved and occasionally the artists grumbled at the sartorial whims of their sitters. Vigée-Lebrun, for example, had trouble with some of her royal and aristocratic sitters over their choice of dress, particularly, as she recalled in her memoirs, Caroline Murat, Queen of Naples, who changed both dress and hairstyle from day to day during the time her portrait was being painted, creating a great deal of additional work for the artist. Although Vigée-Lebrun tried to persuade her sitters to wear simplified costume, it was – unlike the versions seen in contemporary English painting – real dress, high fashion. Her memoirs, written in old age, disparage (too much) the fashions of the *ancien régime* and exaggerate her own importance as an innovator: 'As I greatly disliked the style of dress worn by the women at that time, I did my best to make it a little more picturesque, and whenever I obtained the confidence of my models, I delighted in draping them after my fancy'. In advance of fashion, she claims, she suggested her sitters should wear large shawls so that she could 'imitate the beautiful style of the draperies of Raphael and Domenichino'.[46] While painting portraits, Vigée-Lebrun preferred to wear the fashionable simple chemise gown of the 1780s (except at Versailles where full, formal dress had to be worn) and she is so dressed in a number of her self-portraits, including her *Self-portrait in a Straw Hat* of 1782 (pl. 17). This work pays homage to Rubens's portrait of Susanna Fourment known as the '*Chapeau de Paille*' (although it is a black beaver hat, and not straw); and both paintings are now in the National Gallery, London. Vigée-Lebrun's costume consists of a pink silk chemise gown, with fringed white muslin collar and cuffs, reminiscent of early seventeenth-century styles; the black silk scarf echoes the gauzy drapery of the Rubens portrait, and the straw hat (part of the contemporary pastoral mode) is trimmed with wild flowers and an ostrich plume. Such a costume, although with obvious historical references, is real dress, unlike the more 'classical' or 'timeless' white gowns which, for example, Angelica Kauffman uses for her self-portraits, her impersonations of the various muses and her mythological heroines.

Vigée-Lebrun's self-portrait might be usefully compared with that of her rival Adélaïde Labille-Guiard of 1785 (pl. 18), who is shown at her easel with two of her pupils. Can she really have painted wearing this very fashionable satin gown, a style known as a *robe à l'anglaise*, or is it to be seen as a tribute to her status as an important artist with court connections? It is slightly ironic that she depicts herself wearing semi-formal costume typical of the *ancien régime*, whereas her political sympathies lay with the opponents of the court; Vigée-Lebrun, on the other hand, an artist totally identified with the monarchy, is shown in the simpler style of dress which came to be linked with the progressive aspirations of the French Revolution.

Intelligent critics in the eighteenth century accepted the importance of fashion to the French economy and society, but worried how far it inhibited moves to make people more rational and equal. This is one of the concerns discussed in the *Encyclopédie* under the aegis of Diderot[47] whose interest in dress extended to his role as art critic of the Salons. On first reading, his opposition to fashionable dress in portraiture is uncompromising; from his review of the Salon of 1767: 'Il n'y a point de tableau de grand maître qu'on dégradât en habillant les personnages, en les coëffant à la française.' People so dressed, he claims, are like dolls; how absurd is the clothing of a man of fashion – 'ces bas, ces souliers, cette culotte, cette veste, cet habit, ce chapeau, ce col, ces jarretières, cette chemise; c'est une friperie', and as for that of women, 'la dépouille d'une femme serait une boutique entière'.[48]

Mercier in his *Tableau de Paris* talks in a similar but more general way about the problem of the public display of portraits which can mean nothing to those who do not know the sitters:

What are we to make of these financiers, these middle-men, these unknown countesses, these indolent marquises . . . as long as the brush sells itself to idle opulence, to mincing coquetterie, to snobbish fatuousness, the portrait should remain in the boudoir; it should never affront the vision of the public. . . .[49]

Critics concurred in the view that the character of the sitter ought to be represented in a portrait as well as the costume; ideally the two elements should complement each other, particularly with regard to men's portraiture. Diderot realised that in the real world, however, the classical drapery that he admired in art was not practical, and in any case both in art and life too great a subservience to the antique diminished the importance of Nature, that indefinable Holy Grail of artist and critic alike. His solution was to suggest a kind of negligence in the portrait with regard to dress, to subdue the element of fashion. 'Il n'y aurait rien de si ridicule qu'un homme peint en habit neuf au sortir de chez son tailleur', stated Diderot; old, familiar costume not only allows the sitter to relax, but also in itself reveals character.

D'ailleurs, il y a dans un habit vieux une multitude infinie de petits accidents intéressants, de la poudre, des boutons manquants, et tout ce qui tient de l'user; tous ces accidents rendus réveillent autant d'idées et servent à lier les différentes parties de l'ajustement; il faut de la poudre pour lier la perruque avec l'habit.[50]

There are never missing buttons in portraits (this would perhaps be too slovenly) but it is common to see hair powder on the shoulders of men's coats.

It was Diderot's opinion that old clothes were not only comfortable in themselves but added a touch of the picturesque. In a famous passage rejecting a stiff new *robe de chambre* offered by Madame Geoffrin which made him feel like a dummy, he eulogises his old gown: 'Elle était faite à moi; j'étais fait à elle. Elle moulait tous les plis de mon corps sans le gêner; j'étais pittoresque et beau . . .'[51] This is not the gown seen in Louis-Michel van Loo's portrait of Diderot exhibited at the 1767 Salon (pl. 19) which was of lustrous shot silk; it was a studio property and turns up in other

17 E.-L. Vigée-Lebrun, *Self-portrait in a Straw Hat*, 1782. Oil on canvas. National Gallery, London.

18   A. Labille-Guiard, *Self-portrait with Two Pupils, Mademoiselle Marie-Gabrielle Capet and Mademoiselle Carreaux de Rosemond*, 1785. Oil on canvas. The Metropolitan Museum of Art, New York. Gift of Julia A. Berwind, 1953.

19 (facing page) L.-M. Vanloo, *Denis Diderot, c.*1767. Oil on canvas. Louvre, Paris. (Photo: © Réunion des musées nationaux)

20 W. Hogarth, *Self-portrait with Pug*, 1745. Oil on canvas. Tate Gallery, London.

works by van Loo, including his self-portrait of 1763 (Château de Versailles). In spite of the apparent negligence, albeit elegant, of the sitter's image, Diderot disliked the portrait, claiming the pose was affected and the gown too luxurious, giving him the look of a minister of state rather than a philosopher. Furthermore, he did not like being painted without a wig which he customarily wore, which is rather perverse considering his violent and published objections to the wig.[52]

Powdered wigs, identified as artificial, against Nature, as destroyers of character (all epithets applied to them by Diderot and other critics), were however an essential part of masculine formal attire until the French Revolution, and even beyond. Perhaps by lessening individuality they contributed to the sense of order and uniformity that played such an important role in French costume, but which allowed for some diversity, some *esprit* in life and portraiture. Establishing the boundaries of acceptable variety in dress and appearance occupied the minds of both artist and critic in the eighteenth century.

In spite of the fashionability of the noble savage from the 1760s onwards[53] it was generally accepted that, in Balzac's words, 'qui dit homme dans la civilization, dit homme habillé'. But what constituted the most beautiful in terms of clothing? Was it to be seen in fashionable contemporary costume, the Baudelairean notion that in the hands of a great artist

the eternal can be distilled from the transitory? Or should it be searched for in modes hallowed by antiquity and the Old Masters?

Hogarth had the idea that beauty could be found and identified it as a gently curving serpentine line which stood for Nature against deformity and extremes. In his *Self-portrait with Pug* of 1745 (pl. 20), such a line appears on the palette resting next to the volumes of Shakespeare, Swift and Milton. His costume is fashionably artistic, a red morning gown over a black waistcoat and on his head a red velvet cap edged with fur, trimmed with a gold tassel. X-rays reveal that his first thought was to portray himself in wig and white cravat, but he may have felt that a more exotic costume better suited the image of the theorist and critic. A few years later he published his *Analysis of Beauty* (1753) which aimed to lay out 'the Principles of personal Beauty and Deportment'. Most of his comments on dress refer to women; this is not surprising when it is considered how far the prevailing Rococo style conformed to his own curved line; 'the beauty of intricacy', he claims, 'lies in contriving winding shapes', and the irregular and asymmetrical aspects of costume please him best, provided they are not taken to extremes. Women, 'when they are at liberty to make what shapes they please in ornamenting their persons, those of the best taste choose the irregular as the more engaging . . . so a single feather, flower or jewel is generally placed on one side of the head, or, if even put in front, it is turn'd awry to avoid formality'.[54]

The illustration from *The Analysis of Beauty* (pl. 21) depicts the statuary yard of Hogarth's friend John Cheere at Hyde Park Corner; it contains a mixture of classical sculptures and modern art objects, all of which demonstrate points in the author's argument, as do the figures round the border. The images juxtapose the ideal with the deformed – the statue of Antinous (fig. 7) next to a fashionable dancing-master (fig. 2); the *Apollo Belvedere* (fig. 8) next to a Roman general (fig. 14) 'dress'd by a modern tailor and peruke-maker, for a tragedy', and probably intended to represent the actor James Quin, famed for his bombastic style in antique tragic roles. Above the scene, at the top of the border, is a serpentine line wound round a cone (fig. 20) which is referred to in the discussion of the stays (figs 1–7 along the bottom of the border (pl. 22)) of which figure 4 (centre) is the ideal. 'Every whale-bone of a good stay must be made to bend in this manner', stated Hogarth, and the whole garment should be 'truly a shell of well-varied contents'; he goes on to say that if a lace at the top of the stays at the back were brought round and down to the 'bottom peak of the stomacher, it would form such a perfect, precise, serpentine line, as has been shewn round the cone, figure 20'.[55] At the time

Hogarth wrote, the stomacher he refers to, was a stiffened inverted triangular panel which filled in the open bodice of the dress and was placed over the stays. The stays (or corset) were essential for a woman's deportment and for the perfect, taut line of mid-eighteenth century dress; as Hogarth indicates, they were not to be too curved or too straight, but to show a happy medium. Later on, at the end of the century the stiffly whaleboned stays came, like the

powdered wig, to be synonymous with artifice and, under the influence of a new aesthetic linked to dress reform, hygiene and the promotion of a 'natural' image, they were largely discarded when the high-waisted Neoclassical styles in costume appeared.

Hogarth was perhaps too absolutist in his notion that there was just one type or line of beauty which could be applied to all the arts including dress, and a few years later Allan Ramsay published his *Dialogue on*

21 W. Hogarth, *The Analysis of Beauty*, 1753, plate 1. Engraving. British Museum.

22 Hogarth, *The Analysis of Beauty* (detail of pl. 21).

19

Taste (1755) proposing the relativity of beauty, its individual nature. 'A very little sedate reflection must convince a man of sense that there is no standard of female beauty to which all the various degrees of it may be referred'.[56] But Ramsay was a man of his time, placing importance on the correct manners and costume of his sitters and far more at home (perhaps this is due to the French influence on his work) with contemporary dress than with the kind of fanciful clothing that artistic fashion and the whims of his sitters sometimes dictated. His best portraits involve a detailed but not slavish attention to dress, 'the pleasure that arises from the discovery of truth and the just relation of things'.[57]

His fashionable portrait practice gave Ramsay a thorough understanding of the nature of fashion, which he described as 'habit formed upon caprice' and promoted through a process of imitation. In his *Dialogue on Taste* there is a long passage devoted to the way in which fashion works, which he defines as a process of innovation at the top of society which then moves down through the social scale. As an example he suggests that if 'a man of ordinary rank' were to start a fashion for triangular cuffs to his coat 'when the mode is square, there is no doubt he will meet with many to despise, but none to imitate him'. However, if a man of rank were to take up this fashion and have it made in a rich fabric such as velvet, 'the triangle will then be found to meet with a quite different reception . . . and will soon become an object of imitation', all other cuffs being regarded as 'detestable'.[58] Ramsay's argument has more force than might at first be appreciated, for triangular cuffs would have been considered absurd in the context of masculine clothing, and he is making a point about the arbitrary nature of fashion: that it can, as Boswell pointed out in his essay *On Imitation* (1780), 'make what is of itself ugly or disagreeable, become artificially beautiful or pleasing'.[59]

Ramsay's ideas were further developed by the Revd Archibald Alison in his *Essays on the Nature and Principles of Taste*, published in 1790. While accepting the idea of fashion as imitation through a process of association (fashion = taste and elegance), Alison deplores the notion that a man of intelligence should concern himself with such matters. Unlike Ramsay, who was a stylish man and valued the importance of costume both in his portrait practice and in its own right as one of the foundations of society, Alison tends to play down the role of dress, except for urging the advisability of a unity of colouring to produce an artistic, harmonious effect. Costume, particularly for men at the time Alison is writing, had undergone a sea-change from the bright colours of Ramsay's mid-eighteenth century *Dialogue on Taste* to darker, more sober hues, such as 'the Colours of a glass Bottle, of a dead Leaf, of Clay . . .'[60] or, for those of a more conventional cast of mind, dark blue and black.

Alison's comments should be viewed in the light of the overriding influence of English fashions on men's dress, whereas Ramsay painted many of his sitters in the French styles (in both senses of the word) at the beginning of the period. One of the elements of this style is – in the hands of a great artist – an ability to make magic from the prosaic reality of dress. Attention has already been drawn to Baudelaire's perceptive comments on the differences between French and English portraits, the former noted for a faithful and severe rendering of costume and character. 'Faithful' and 'severe' are words particularly appropriate in considering the work of David, both with regard to his history paintings and his portraits (see Chapters 2 and 3). While his artistic imagination created the pose, the tangible reality of the clothing was necessary to aid the creative process and as a factual record, particularly for official portraits. The diary of Joseph Farington records a visit to the artist's studio in 1802, where he saw the famous painting of *Bonaparte Crossing the Alps*, painted in 1800 (of which there are five versions) and he noted: 'David does not trust to his Memory in painting, but has always, if possible, an object before him for every part of his picture. The cloaths of Bonoparte – the Horse furniture &c – were laid in different parts of the room.'[61] David, in fact borrowed the costume (a general's blue and red uniform and leather breeches) that Napoleon had worn at the battle of Marengo (1800) to which he added a cloak, possibly a studio prop, for extra dramatic effect.[62]

The dramatic possibilities of costume can also be seen in David's self-portrait of 1794 (pl. 23) painted shortly after his release from prison. Less overtly fashionable than the smart caped redingote seen in the Uffizi *Self-portrait* of 1791, the loose greyish-brown coat (called a *houppelande* after the name of a loose, medieval gown), of this painting is still stylish and practical. For someone with such proselytising zeal over the introduction of a national, Republican costume (see Chapter 3), his own taste, like that of Robespierre, was for conventional and fashionable dress. According to Miette de Villars: 'David était toujours très soigné dans sa mise . . . son goût recherché pour la toilette ne se démentit jamais, même au plus fort de la révolution'. While his fellow terrorists wore *bonnets rouges* and *carmagnoles* (working-class jackets associated with the *sans-culottes*) 'il travaillait, lui, le conventionnel, en manchettes et habit de velours, peignant sans faire une seule tache à ses vêtements'. When his pupils cleaned their palettes on their clothes, he reproved them, saying 'il faut s'habituer de bonne heure à peindre proprement'.[63]

David's pupil Ingres lived and worked in a period

23   J.-L. David, *Self-portrait*, 1794. Oil on canvas. Louvre, Paris. (Photo: © Réunion des musées nationaux)

when men's clothes were a sober foil to the increasingly lavish toilettes of the Empire and Restoration. It is therefore unsurprising that art historians have compared his portraits of women unfavourably with those of David in his prime, dwelling as they do on the details of costume and accessories; Norman Bryson, for example, claims that Ingres was corrupted by success, in thrall to his couturier's instincts and turned women into *objets de luxe*.[64] There is certainly a glossy quality in Ingres's painted portraits, quite different from the delicacy of the pencil portraits which can be appreciated for their linear qualities and where the costume intrudes less upon the susceptibilities of the art historian. But the dwelling on personal adornment, the love of luxury objects, is not (*pace* Bryson) exclusive to the new early nineteenth-century bourgeoisie, but an inherited and particularly French appreciation. It must also be admitted that fashions towards the end of the period under discussion certainly were fussier and more ornamented, less appealing to the eye than the relative simplicities of female dress of the late eighteenth-century; it is for this reason, rather than any 'romantic' notion, that David's heart and soul were no longer so engaged, that his paintings in exile are commonly not as highly thought of as those of his earlier career, which were often inspired by political ideology.

The history of art during the period – and particularly in the eighteenth century – is full of the sound of artists protesting at their enslavement to the demands of fashionable portraiture. 'Maudits portraits! ils m'empêchent toujours de marcher aux grandes choses',[65] exclaimed Ingres, excusing his failure to produce more history paintings; other artists, for example Gainsborough, expressed a wish to paint landscapes. Even artists who, like Reynolds, flourished in the social world inseparable from portrait painting, had to justify their achievements with reference to intellectual theory. Jonathan Richardson's famous *Essay on the Theory of Painting* (1715) summarises the virtues of generalised costume against the claims of high fashion in portraiture. To Richardson's mind, 'the great Business of Painting is to relate a History or Fable'; thus the 'Antique Taste' should be paramount, and artists should not paint 'the Habits of their own Times'.[66] Even when the artist has to paint portraits in contemporary costume, 'Lace, Embroidery, Gold and Jewels must be sparingly employ'd. Nor are Flower'd Silks so much us'd by the best Masters as Plain; nor these so much as Stuffs or fine Cloth'.[67] In spite of the patterned silks in fashion (and those surviving in museum collections), if early eighteenth-century portraits were the sole source material for the history of dress, it would be easy to assume (erroneously) that men and women wore fairly plain garments with little ornamentation. Furthermore, as Richardson remarks, most

portrait painters developed a kind of anti-fashion, what he calls an 'Arbitrary Loose Dress', which is familiar from the almost identikit portraits of Kneller and his school. Hogarth's *Analysis of Beauty* pours scorn on this practice; artists, in order to achieve the 'Pictoresque', he says,

have contrived a dress wholly at their disposal call[ed] drapery (to exercise all the principles of beauty upon but such dresses never could be wore, they would have been so incommodious nor would they have been at all agreable if the folds were stir'd or seen in any other view than just as in their Pictures) as often the Dress of the Times belonging the story they have painted are not known . . .[68]

In spite of such comments as this (and Hogarth, as so often, was quite prepared to be alone in his unfashionable opinions) drapery painting remained an adjunct of fashionable female portraiture until well into the second half of the century. It was sometimes combined with elements of historical costume, the combination aiming to be both 'timeless' and of past times; it could serve both for portraiture and history painting. The often odd mixtures of dress – for elements of contemporary costume inevitably crept in – are satirised in Oliver Goldsmith's novel *The Vicar of Wakefield* (1766), where the Primrose family decides to be painted 'in one large historical family piece':

My wife desired to be represented as Venus, and the painter was requested not to be too frugal of his diamonds in her stomacher and hair. Her two little ones were to be as Cupids by her side; while I, in my gown and band, was to present her with my books on the Whistonian controversy. Olivia would be drawn as an Amazon, dressed in a green joseph, richly laced with gold, and a whip in her hand. Sophia was to be a shepherdess, with as many sheep as the painter could put in for nothing; and Moses was to be dressed out with a hat and white feather.[69]

Goldsmith probably had in mind the kind of loosely draped gowns painted by his friend Reynolds, for the depiction of Mrs Primrose as a classical goddess and Sophia in Arcadian costume; contemporary dress was represented by the clerical (Dr Primrose) and riding dress (Olivia's 'green joseph'). Some sixty years later such a concept would be considered even more amusing, and so Rowlandson wants us to see it in his illustration to the novel, *The Family Picture* (pl. 25) which was published in 1817; the feeling of the story remains but with contemporary touches of fashion.

It was Reynolds, the greatest theoretician among English artists, who championed the notion that a grand historical style could be incorporated into portraiture. Friends like Dr Johnson were depicted in quasi-classical drapery that summoned up the virtues of antiquity and served to avoid what Reynolds called the 'whimsical capricious forms' of fashion. The bulk and heavy folds of drapery added *gravitas* to portraits and set off the face and character of the sitter. The portrait of *Laurence Sterne* (1760; pl. 24), shows the clerical author (the first two volumes of *Tristram Shandy* had just appeared) in his black Geneva gown over a double-breasted cassock, his preacher's scarf partly concealing the white lawn bands at his neck; the whole costume enhances the slightly diabolical appearance of the sitter. An equally clever use of real costume can be seen in Reynolds's *Self-portrait as DCL* of the late 1770s (pl. 26). The academic dress with its historical and traditional elements reminds the viewer of the sitter's status and achievements, but also of his place in the story of great art; the red silk gown echoes that worn by Venetian senators as painted, say, by Titian or Veronese and the black velvet cap recollects that worn by Rembrandt. As a fashionable artist Reynolds had to be expert in painting dress and accessories, and his early career proved this; although his sitter books contain little information on costume,[70] there is no doubt that the final choice in the portrait was his, and he had complete control over the draperies, whether his or those painted by his assistants or pupils.

During the 1760s Reynolds evolved his theories on the 'general' as opposed to the 'particular' in dress,

and these were eventually published in the *Discourses*. One of these theories involved the impropriety of incorporating contemporary styles and fabrics into historical paintings, which Reynolds discusses in the *Fifth Discourse* (1772): '. . . if the draperies were like cloth or silk of our manufacture, if the landskip had the appearance of a modern view, how ridiculous would Apollo appear instead of the sun, or an old Man with an Urn to represent a river or a lake.'[71] Reynolds may not have wanted, say, a nymph to represent an aspect of nature, but he *did* wish that his female sitters could sometimes resemble nymphs in their dress. No doubt it was with this in mind that he painted *Three Ladies Adorning a Term of Hymen* (1773; pl. 28); the daughters of Sir William Montgomery appear in loose gowns that are faintly classical in style, although their hair is arranged in contemporary fashion. Here there is no sense of any particular fabric being depicted in the dress, for as Reynolds had remarked in the *Fourth Discourse* (1771), 'it is the inferior stile that marks the variety of stuffs'.[72]

According to Reynolds's pupil James Northcote, his master was not really interested in dress; he 'would throw a piece of muslin over the back of a chair in order to see the character of it, but seldom troubled himself to do more'.[73] This helps to explain the anatomical distortions in some of his female portraits, as well as their appearance as mere bundles of drapery, during the 1770s (see, for example, his *Mrs Carnac*, pl. 238) Reynolds's beliefs that too much individuality destroyed portraiture inevitably clashed with some sitters' views that their costume should be depicted realistically. Edward Dayes noted how Reynolds struggled 'with the hydra Fashion', and Leslie and Taylor recalled how the 'late Duchess Dowager of Rutland told Mr. F. Grant R.A. that Sir Joshua made

25 T. Rowlandson, *The Vicar of Wakefield: The Family Picture*, 1817. Watercolour and pen over pencil on wove paper. Yale Center for British Art, New Haven, CT. Paul Mellon Collection.

24 J. Reynolds, *Laurence Sterne*, 1760. Oil on canvas. National Portrait Gallery, London.

her try on eleven different dresses before he painted her "in that bedgown". No doubt the "bedgown" was the dress with the least marked character about it, the nearest to that "generalised" drapery which Reynolds's theory required him to seek, though his natural inclination or the happy obstinacy of the ladies forced him, in many cases, to paint the fashions of the times.'[74]

The portrait of the Duchess was destroyed by fire in 1816, but a mezzotint by Valentine Green of 1780 shows her in just such a 'bedgown', a simple dress with cross-over front, a sash at the waist and with an ermine-lined cloak. The costume is not unlike one of Reynolds's much earlier and more successful efforts in this genre, his portrait of one of the great beauties of the day, *Elizabeth Gunning, Duchess of Hamilton and Argyll*, of about 1760 (pl. 27); the Duchess leans against a sculpted plinth with a relief of the Judgement

of Paris and there is a further reference to Venus in the white doves. Here again is the bedgown, the simple informality of which is echoed in the unloosed chignon with tresses flowing over her shoulder; she wears a simplified version of the coronation kirtle

with its scallopped sleeves, and leans on the red velvet coronation mantle with its four rows of ermine tails identifying her status as duchess. Hazlitt found such portraits too affected, too imbued with their own sense of vanity or the artist's 'fanciful theory'; 'they have not the look of individual nature, nor have they, to compensate the want of this, either peculiar elegance of form, refinement of expression, delicacy of complexion, or gracefulness of manner.'[75] The critic's views here were conditioned by the very different aesthetic of his own time, with its greater emphasis on the simplicity of the actual dress and a more natural manner. In his last years, during the 1780s, Reynolds having proved the possibilities and the limits of the Grand Style in dress, returned to painting the fashions, which by then were gradually moving towards the modest simplicity they were to reach in the early nineteenth century.

Reynolds is often regarded as diametrically opposed to his great rival Gainsborough, and in some ways this is true; the latter was uninterested in theories and aesthetics, not a good organiser and certainly not the social animal that Reynolds was. Against the notion of Reynolds as an Establishment artist is the general post-Romantic preference for the apparent spontaneity of Gainsborough, although he was far from being the untutored and instinctive artist now found attractive. While portraits by Reynolds are always corporeal, even when the costume is very fanciful, those by Gainsborough, especially in his later years, look insubstantial and romantically hazy, the costume

28 (above) J. Reynolds, *Three Ladies Adorning a Term of Hymen*, 1773. Oil on canvas. Tate Gallery, London.

27 J. Reynolds, *Elizabeth Gunning, Duchess of Hamilton and Argyll*, c.1760. Oil on canvas. Lady Lever Art Gallery, Port Sunlight.

26 (facing page) J. Reynolds, *Self-portrait as DCL*, late 1770s. Oil on canvas. Royal Academy, London.

25

often merging into the landscape. James Dallaway noted that Gainsborough was 'the only painter of this country who attempted the thin brilliant manner of Vandyck, and his likenesses are attained more by the indecision, than the precision of his outline'.[76] His letters tell us that he aimed in painting to make the heart dance and to portray 'modern truth', but it is not quite clear what the latter phrase means; inner truth, in the sense of character, is often not revealed and Gainsborough was happy enough to paint 'fancied dress' in spite of his strictures on the subject when discussing the work of Reynolds.

In this context the famous dispute over the Lady Dartmouth portraits is often quoted. In 1769 Gainsborough painted Lady Dartmouth, but the portrait was disliked and returned, eliciting the injured response from the artist: 'had I painted Lady Dartmouth's Picture, dressed as her Ladyship goes, no fault (more than in my Painting in General) would have been found with it'. In a further letter to Lord Dartmouth in 1771 Gainsborough comments on the 'amazing Effect of Dress' in portraiture and offers to paint another portrait dressed '(contrary I know to Lady Dartmouth's taste) in the modern way . . .' Two portraits of the sitter exist, the first (pl. 29) shows an unflattering image of a plump lady in an imaginary costume consisting of a white dress under a red gown with ermine edging and scallopped sleeves (a reference here, as in Reynolds's *Duchess of Hamilton and Argyll*, to peeresses' coronation robes). Lord Dartmouth complained that his wife looked too 'large', but Gainsborough argued that the 'fancied dress' worn

by Lady Dartmouth detracted from the likeness, 'the principal beauty and intention of a Portrait'.[77] The second portrait of Lady Dartmouth (pl. 30) – a slimmer, but not particularly appealing image – shows the higher hairstyle of the early 1770s and a wrapping gown held in at the waist with a fringed sash. This is also an imaginary costume, not unlike that worn by Gainsborough's *Lady Ligonier*, 1771 (San Marino, CA, Huntington Library and Art Gallery) described as a 'graceful' 'fancied dress'.[78] Did the Dartmouths ignore Gainsborough's advice on the 'unluckiness of fancied dresses'? Did the artist change his mind? Or is there another portrait of the sitter in a costume more related to high fashion?

As Dallaway noted above, Gainsborough was notorious for the 'indecision' of his portraits, something that particularly affected his depiction of costume. Leslie and Taylor comment that 'Gainsborough . . . painted his ladies with a certain generalising management of their actual dresses'[79] and this is especially obvious in his 'impressionistic' hatched portraits of the 1770s and 1780s, where the clothing and the pale powdered hair almost blend into the foliage of the landscape. The *Countess of Chesterfield* (*c.*1778; pl. 31), for example, is a good example of how the artist subordinates the details of the dress (a fashionable *robe à l'anglaise*) and the sparkling silk shawl to the overall conception of the romantic image.

This sense of 'editing' the costume in a portrait (a peculiarly English concept) can be seen throughout the period, but most notably in the eighteenth century when theory demanded purity of line over details of dress and the tactility of fabrics. Romney, too (see pl. 15, *Lady Newdigate*) mixed real and fancy dress to produce the desired effect, to give the feel of the fashion without the minutiae of its details. The *Memoirs of the Life and Works of George Romney* compiled by his son (a vindication of the artist's real desire to be a poetic and heroic painter) claims that Romney influenced public taste 'in expelling from the empire of fashion the long and shapeless waist; and in introducing a more simple and graceful mode of dress, approaching nearer to the Grecian'.[80] This, according to Romney's son was a return 'to nature and truth', but it was also in line with moves towards classical simplicity in dress during the 1780s and 1790s which made his contributions to the costume in a portrait more acceptable to the sitter, and perhaps resulted in a more coherent and attractive image than was sometimes achieved by Reynolds.

Reynolds in his later life seems to have had some reservations about the 'Painters imaginary dress' and a rejected manuscript note for his *Tenth Discourse* (1780) seems to accept 'that people . . . appear more pleasing more agreable in the dress of the times . . .'[81] But with regard to sculpture he felt, like Diderot, that the use of contemporary costume was inimical to intellectual contemplation. In the three-dimensional form of sculpture character and expression can be a tactile experience as well as one of sight and mind, and most

critics united in believing that contemporary costume (and especially the wig) hindered the true appreciation of a statue or sculpted bust. One critic at the 1783 Salon commented on the exhibition of famous historical figures (*grands hommes*) of French history and literature:

> Convenons d'abord que rien n'est plus ingrat, pour la sculpture sur-tout, que notre costume. Le génie de l'artiste doit se glacer à la vue des formes bizarres de nos habillemens . . .
>
> Sous la toge des anciens, à travers leur cuirasse, nous suivons toutes les formes de leur corps; mais qu'est-ce qui reconnaîtra le plus beau torse, lorsqu'il sera enveloppé d'un juste-au-corps et d'une veste?[82]

By the early nineteenth century, under the aegis of the Neoclassical movement in all the arts, especially in France, antique nudity or the simplest of draperies were the vogue in heroic sculpture. In a conversation with Napoleon, the sculptor Canova articulated the prevailing theory on costume:

> God himself would be unable to do something fine if He tried to portray His Majesty dressed . . . in his French breeches and boots. The language of the sculptor, I resumed, requires the sublime and either the nude or that style of drapery that is proper to our art . . . we sculptors cannot clothe our statues in modern costume . . .[83]

In England, more pragmatic and less impressed with theory, the arguments were not so clear-cut. In 1795 Farington recorded the discussions over the costume to be given to a proposed statue of Lord Cornwallis to be erected in Madras; 'whether [it] should be in a modern dress or as has been generally the custom in the habit of a Roman'. Benjamin West believed that it should be in contemporary costume, as it would be 'an Historical record', and

> that the prejudice in favor of representing Moderns in Ancient dresses was an absurdity. – That Sir Joshua Reynolds in his opinion had judged ill in accustoming himself to dress his women in fancied drapery and wd. have rendered them more interesting to posterity had He followed their fancies and described them in the fashion of their day . . .

The sculptors John Bacon and Thomas Banks disagreed, claiming that modern dress was 'unpicturesque' and that 'in 20 years when the fashion had varied it would appear disgusting'. Farington, in his role as peacemaker proposed a compromise; Cornwallis should be depicted in 'his robe of Peerage which might be so managed as to conceal or break the lines of our formal dress', and this was accepted.[84] The statue, by Banks, unveiled in 1800 (Madras, Fort

31 T. Gainsborough, *Anne, Countess of Chesterfield*, c.1778. Oil on canvas. Collection of the J. Paul Getty Museum, Malibu, California.

St George Museum) shows Cornwallis full-length in military uniform under his peer's parliamentary robe, which is draped to reveal the insignia of the Order of the Garter.

By the early nineteenth century the pendulum had swung against the use of classical drapery for statues. The antiquarian John Carter found 'the roman mode of habiliment' in sculpture 'false to national Custom, appearing ridiculous to us who live and to a succeeding generation',[85] and the poet Southey attacked 'unhappy statues half-naked'. Southey was referring in particular to heroic statuary in St Paul's Cathedral, such as Flaxman's monument to Lord Howe (1803) where the admiral in his uniform (with the ribbon of the Order of the Bath put on the wrong way!) is surrounded by figures *à l'antique*,[86] an incongruity that many critics found displeasing. But there was no real dispute over the importance of classical art in the history of taste and its impact on such applied arts as dress. James Dallaway is typical of many commentators in his praise of the seductive charms of Greek art, especially statuary which 'is and will ever be, the rule of precision, grace and grandeur, because it presents the most perfect representation possible of the human form'.[87] Richard Payne Knight added in

his *Analytical Inquiry into the Principles of Taste* (1805) that 'the precious remains of Grecian sculpture' were fixed canons of perfect taste which inspired standards of 'elegance in the human form, and the modes of adorning it'. His theory – certainly not a new one – was that the costume of Periclean Athens had produced a timeless perfection in dress, whose 'permanency and unvaried simplicity' was a perpetual reproach to contemporary costume.[88]

Payne Knight's references are to female costume, for it was felt that by the end of the eighteenth century male dress had achieved a kind of sober permanence. This may be one of the explanations behind Robert Fagan's curious portrait, *The Artist and his Wife*, of 1803 (pl. 32); the artist's conventional costume – dark blue coat with brass buttons, cream waistcoat and starched cravat – is a startling contrast to the semi-nudity of his wife, her breasts further emphasised by a girdle which holds in place the flimsy classical shift. Its romantic freedom of expression raises the question as to whether Fagan knew the mysterious portrait of the Fontainebleau School of Henry IV's mistress, *Gabrielle d'Estrées and one of her Sisters* (Paris, Louvre), both women naked to the waist in a linen-draped bath, one fingering the nipple of the other. Whatever the impulse behind Fagan's portrait of himself and his wife, it is clearly for private contemplation. The mixture of the proper with the improper, the real with the fanciful (although the artist's wife may have posed for him in this 'costume') is Romantic in its originality and composition.

The French Revolution changed the whole cultural milieu; all the arts, including dress, claimed a new obeisance to the dictates of nature and truth, even if classical authority was used to reinforce their arguments. But in the eighteenth century the limitations of nature as the inspiration of art and dress were understood; 'l'homme ne peut laisser à son corps la forme que lui a donné la nature', was Jean-Nicolas Démeunier's comment in his important philosophical work *L'Esprit des usages et des coutumes des differens peuples* of 1776.[89] And was it not (*pace* van Loo's famous portrait of Diderot discussed above) just as much a conceit to be painted in a state of careful negligence, as to be depicted fresh from the tailor? The portrait is an artificial construct, as is costume. In the interplay between the artist, the sitter and the dress there can be no honesty. Portraits can be attempts at reality or they can be examples of the creative impulse in terms of fanciful, historical and 'timeless' costume – never truly imaginative in the sense of inventing dress, for the contemporary sartorial aesthetic cannot escape the artist whatever his ideological aspirations. Given the close link between art and dress in the painterly process this Introduction has attempted to establish, the first half of this book will look at the changes in fashion from 1750 to 1820, and the second section will discuss the ways in which artists, writers, men and women, co-operated to produce a distinctive vision of the past, inseparable from the present.

England and France, 1750–1820

It can be argued that from 1750 to 1820 there were more dramatic changes in politics and society than any before the present century. The political upheavals resulting from the French Revolution and the economic implications of the industrialisation of Europe changed peoples' lives – the way they thought, the way they lived and the way they dressed.

In society and in dress there was a change from the importance of consensus to a new emphasis on the individual, from the traditional certainties of the *ancien régime* to a novel sense of experimentation; in short to modernity. For much of the eighteenth century, high society was homogeneous in taste and manners, and any sense of individuality subordinated to the general taste to produce a unity of culture. Men and women were to be considered in their social context, in relation to others; emphasis on outward appearance as an indication of status was approved – it was the triumph of form over feeling. Only in the 1780s does the veneer begin to crack, with a growing contempt for old values fostered by the ideas of the *philosophes*, but without any sense of the implications of the new revolutionary thought. During that decade also, there was a growing equation between the rigidity (in every sense) of formal fashion and an increasingly unfashionable ultra-conservatism in politics.

Until then the details of dress in itself and its role as an essential and binding force in society were undisputed. 'Dress is a very foolish thing', commented Lord Chesterfield, 'and yet it is a very foolish thing for a man not to be well dressed according to his rank and way of life'. Boswell found, in an essay 'On Luxury' in the *London Magazine* (1778), that 'dress has a great deal of influence on the mind. Every one has felt himself more disposed to decorum and propriety and courtesy and other good qualities when genteelly dressed, than when in slovenly apparel'.[90] It was the 'slovenly apparel', the adoption of informal English styles in dress, particularly for men, which, according to some French critics helped to inculcate revolutionary beliefs. The comte de Ségur was not alone in his view that a widespread decline in standards of dress and behaviour in aristocratic circles and at court fuelled disrespect for the monarchy and ultimately for the whole system based on caste:

Chez les Français principalement où tout semble fait pour occuper plus les yeux que la pensée, les formes, les habillements, les habitudes influent plus qu'autre part sur les moeurs; et dans un pays où tout est prestige, l'éclat est une source de respect, et l'étiquette la sauve-garde de la puissance.[91]

By the time Ségur had published these words in 1803, society had changed radically in France, and all over Europe the costume of men and women had altered in line with the new revolutionary precepts: simple, unadorned styles influenced by the 'progressive' and ideologically sound fashions of English country clothing (for men) and the austere but elegant modes of antiquity (for women). The details of these changes are recorded later in this book, but it is worth noting here how startling they appeared to contemporaries and how romantically remote the pre-revolutionary world appeared in the early nineteenth century. When Elizabeth Inchbald edited Hannah Cowley's popular comedy *The Belle's Stratagem* (1781) for the *British Theatre* in 1808, she commented in her introduction:

... the mention of powder worn by the ladies, their silk gowns and other long exploded fashions together with the hero's having in Paris 'danced with the Queen of France at a masquerade', gives a certain sensation to the reader which seems to place the work on the honourable list of ancient dramas.[92]

Visiting Versailles, a popular English pursuit once Anglo-French hostilities were over, 'one cannot fancy any one living in those rooms or walking in those gardens without hoops and Henri quatre plumes. If one could but people them properly for a couple of hours, what a delightful recollection it would be'.[93]

For two countries so close geographically, England and France had developed different political, social and cultural systems; they were also rivals as colonial powers and trading nations. Any tentative approaches from one country to another were hampered by traditional prejudice and established rivalries, although at the upper levels of society there were many cultural links and intellectual contacts.[94] One of these contacts was through fashion which, ever since the time of Louis XIV, had been virtually a French monopoly, although from the middle of the eighteenth century more informal English styles, and especially those for men, became important as they were linked with a more 'democratic' political system. By the middle of the century the two main fashion impulses in Europe were those of France and England. The relationship between the two countries was seen as a kind of marriage – perhaps one of convenience in the eighteenth-century sense – somewhat uneasy at times, but the two styles, being so different, were seen as complementary. The Leipzig *Journal für Fabrik, Manufaktur und Handlung* of June 1806 discusses the differences between England and France in terms of fashion, as a striking and easily verifiable analogy. English fashions are simple, functional and efficiently produced through the medium of new technology; French fashions captivate by their elaborate styles and elegance. England is admired for her intellect as shown in her superiority with regard to masculine costume; France receives praise for her 'feminine' skills at presentation.[95]

Attitudes to dress also differed. In England there was a feeling that dress had to be correct and suitable for the occasion; in the words of Mrs Delany, 'the vanity and impertinence of dress is always to be avoided' and the goal was 'a decent compliance with the fashion'.[96] English novels, perceptive analyses of the subtle nuances of society, single out those, in the words of Carlyle, 'whose trade, office and existence consists in the wearing of clothes', as unworthy of serious consideration. Thus, Fanny Burney's heroines think that conversation about dress is vulgar and 'showy' and Jane Austen's characters are too high-minded to think fashion an interesting topic for intelligent women.[97]

Contrast this with the situation in France where intelligent and informed discussion of dress was one of the 'douceurs de vivre' of French society; salon culture could embrace the latest modes in dress design alongside those in literature and philosophy. So deeply entwined was the appreciation of all details of dress and accessories in French society that it was particularly worrying to perceptive critics when, from the 1780s, this French hegemony in taste seemed threatened by the carelessness of English styles. The uniform luxury of formal French dress was shattered by the French Revolution, and a sense of the unity of the *tout ensemble* gave way to a new emphasis on the disparate elements of dress, a kind of deliberate disharmony. It was ironic that the writer Madame de Genlis who, through her contacts with the Orléans circle, had done so much to promote revolutionary ways of thought, should in her old age regret the lost civilisation of the *ancien régime*, the days regulated by the type of dress suitable for different occasions and the pleasure gained by the way that subtleties of costume and well-chosen accessories revealed the finer shades of social distinctions. With the new world of the nineteenth century the sense of dress as a public pursuit vanished, to be replaced by an almost selfish concentration on the private person and at the same time a democratic emphasis on the sameness of dress for virtually all occasions, the abolition of a hierarchy of dress appropriate for each age and class.[98]

Many commentators sensed that the impact of the French Revolution and the subsequent upheavals in society and politics could be seen in the fragmented nature of the costume they saw around them. Admittedly, the English viewpoint was sometimes one of almost jingoistic superiority, as witness John Scott's *Visit to Paris in 1814*:

There is no feeling for moral symmetry in the French; something unfinished, or irregular, or inconsistent, starts forth among their finest exhibitions. The nicest of the beaux shall have a bad hat, or mended boots, or his skin peeping through his shirt, or something wild or poor about him.[99]

Scott admits to being puzzled by the French inability to grasp the concept of the 'gentleman' in dress, that amalgam of understated and sober elegance, that triumph of tailoring and perfection of accessories that was the prevailing influence on masculine wear throughout Europe. It was as though the French, the defeated nation, were unable or unwilling to abide by the rules of the new order, that overtly male world which war and commerce had done so much to bring about.

In the same way in which national differences in politics and society were revealed through fashion and portraiture, so also did the English and French diverge in their attitudes towards the past. In both countries a renewed interest in history gathered momentum from the middle of the eighteenth century, at the same time that the first serious books on the history of costume were published. As one eminent French cultural historian puts it: 'La naissance de l'histoire du costume baigne dans le renouveau romantique de l'intérêt pour le passé'.[100] The most elevated expression of this interest in the past was in history painting, which (again) took different forms in England and France. In England there was a greater sense of history than of art, an inclination towards antiquarianism rather than the visual depiction of the past. The preference was for themes from the late medieval and early modern periods in history, a kind of picturesque 'proto-Romanticism' that reflected English interest in the masquerade and influenced all the arts including dress. Interest in the classical past was not widely evident in history painting; 'a serious and deep understanding of antiquity, and what it had to offer, did not penetrate beyond a very small coterie of artists and patrons'.[101] With no state support for art in England and native indifference to the concept of grand generalised historical themes and allegory, the cultural climate encouraged the private and the individual at the expense of the public, both in art and life. In English history painting – as in the English theatre – there was no particular respect for the unity and uniformity of costume that was more evident in French history painting and on the stage, particularly during the late eighteenth century.

State patronage of the arts in France helped to promote the role of the history painter, who had been an essential part of cultural propaganda since the time of Louis XIV. The dramatic unities of the French theatre and a sense of visual coherence (including more attention to the details of historic dress) influenced history painting, particularly of subjects taken from classical antiquity, during the second half of the eighteenth century. The idea of the past being invoked to explain the present was particularly relevant during the revolutionary years when an explicit link was made between the heroism of antiquity and the stirring events taking place in France. Classical styles influenced all the arts in France during these years, including the theatre, interior design and fashion. The most popular themes in the arts when French revolutionary fervour was at its height were Roman; from the time that society re-established itself under the Directory, a softer, more sensual Grecian style was in vogue.

So dominant was the classical taste all over Europe, particularly in the applied arts, that by the early nineteenth century even England had succumbed to some extent, although there was not the same devotion to antiquity in dress. The English had always, in any case, preferred the more recent past – the Tudor and Stuart periods – to inspire national sentiment and as source material for the theatre, portraiture and dress. France also, under the Empire and the Restoration discovered a new interest in the medieval and Renaissance periods, and le style troubadour began to appear in painting and in costume. Classical themes were too closely identified with revolutionary republicanism to sit easily in a renewed monarchical system, and although they did not disappear after the establishment of the Empire, they were somewhat marginalised when the current taste was for patriotic and princely ideas. Fashion, too, in the second decade of the nineteenth century, particularly for women, reflected in its styles and fabrics a growing trend – almost a retrogression – to ancien-régime luxury. The past, however, is a foreign country and can never be recaptured; post-revolutionary French society was bourgeois, with private rather than public taste, and preferred the more intimate scale of painting in le style troubadour to the intellectual demands of large history paintings à l'antique, more suited to a public arena.

While a case can be made out for the discussion of fashion as an Anglo-French enterprise, a theme that forms the first half of this book, the two countries had more profound differences in their attitudes to the past, which were created by their political and cultural rivalries. These differing (but occasionally complementary) attitudes demand a chapter on each country, England and France; these chapters form the second half of this study. It is important, however, not to be too insistent on a compartmentalised view of history; in many respects fashion and fancy dress (that is, dress of, or conditioned by, the past) are closely linked and sometimes interchangeable.

I

The Fabric of Society:
Fashion from 1750 to 1789

Mode: Coutume, usage, manière de s'habiller, de s'ajuster,
en un mot, tout ce qui sert à la parure & au luxe;
ainsi la mode peut être considerée politiquement & philosophiquement.
(D. de Jaucourt, *Encyclopédie*, x, 1765)

Fashion may be considered in general as the custom of the great.
It is the dress, the furniture, the language, the manners of the great world,
which constitute what is called the Fashion in each of these articles,
and which the rest of mankind are in such haste to adopt,
after their example.
(A. Alison, *Of the Nature of the Emotions of Sublimity and Beauty*, 1790)

33   Batoni, *Sir Henry Warkin Dashwood* (detail of pl. 48).

It can hardly be said that any sense of *entente cordiale* existed between England and France in the period covered by this book; even at times when there were no overt hostilities in Europe, Anglo-French relations were dominated by the threat of war and colonial rivalry. At the cultural and social level, Anglo-French attitudes were a complex blend of envy, bafflement and traditional distrust, although at the upper reaches of society in both countries there were exchanges in artistic and intellectual matters.

The relationship between France and England during the second half of the eighteenth century is revealed in fashion and the ways in which it is portrayed. To begin with, it is possible to make some very general statements on the ways in which uniformity and individualism, conflicting forces in society and in clothing, were linked respectively to France and England. Under Louis XIV the French had established the splendours of formal costume at court, the expensive and lavishly trimmed *grand habit* for women and for men the *habit à la française*. The English, who had a less court-centred society and greater social mobility, were associated with more 'egalitarian' styles in dress, with simpler fashions and more practical fabrics; imitation of aspects of working-class clothing for men, as an example, were noted from the middle of the eighteenth century.[1]

These national differences were revealed also in the type of portraiture in the two countries, the French preference being for indoor scenes that could demonstrate the luxury and taste of the sitter both in his or her surroundings and in dress; the English, on the other hand, liked to be portrayed in the open air, on their estates, in the countryside. These different attitudes were further emphasised by the choice of dress in portraiture, the French in formal costume and the English in the more functional styles that outdoor life demanded. Of course this is something of an oversimplification, for the French were sometimes depicted *en déshabillé*, as in François-Hubert Drouais's *Group Portrait* of 1756 (pl. 35), but this is informality of the most lavish kind, with a concentration on the beautiful fabrics of the costume. The woman in the process of dressing – the toilette was an essential part of upper-class refinement in dress – wears a dull-gold dress with a stomacher trimmed with lilac bows; her white linen powdering mantle indicates that her hair has just been completed, but she still has to choose what accessories and jewellery to wear from the box at her feet. The little girl, whose hair is also powdered, wears a dress of lustrous blue satin, and her father's outfit consists of a superb brocade dressing-gown and matching waistcoat (the silk is a late 'bizarre' style, that is with a pattern based on exotic and fantastic designs), with red knee-breeches.

As a contrast, Joseph Wright's *Mr and Mrs Thomas*

Coltman (*c*.1770; pl. 34) shows a scene of similar intimacy, but out of doors. The recently married couple are depicted in riding costume; Thomas Coltman wears a lightweight summer frock-coat over a blue waistcoat trimmed with silver twist *à la hussar*, leather breeches and boots. His wife Mary sits sidesaddle in a red riding habit (red was a popular colour for riding habits as it was for the hooded cloak – 'little red riding hood' – which women and girls often wore in the country); her waistcoat, like her husband's, is trimmed with braid, as is her beige hat decorated with ostrich feathers. Not all English sitters appear in their portraits in this kind of stylish occupational costume; some Englishwomen, in particular, attracted comment by being depicted in incongruously elaborate dress in a landscape, but it is still true to say that, on the whole, relatively informal costume was *de rigueur* in English art.

35 F.-H. Drouais, *Group Portrait*, 1756. Oil on canvas. National Gallery of Art, Washington, Samuel H. Kress Collection.

34 J. Wright, *Mr and Mrs Thomas Coltman*, *c*.1770. Oil on canvas. National Gallery, London.

The sense of being in harmony with nature which is so evident in Wright's portrait, ran counter to the urbanity and indoors living at which the French excelled. They 'have very little turn for conversing with nature . . .' stated Philip Thicknesse in his *Useful Hints to Those who make the Tour of France* (1768), 'A large town, fine cloaths, cards, assemblies and theatres are the amusements of seven-eighths of the French who have not their bread to get'; no 'Frenchman of fortune and fashion . . . lives the life of what we call a country gentleman'.[2]

Most English visitors to France took with them their prejudices as mental baggage, and found them on the whole to be confirmed, although some were more tolerant than others. The Revd John Andrews in his *Account of the Character and Manners of the French* (1770) points out the main differences between the dress and way of living of the English and the French, and is prepared to accept the superiority of the latter in some respects. The French, he found, were particularly fond of what he calls 'exterior Marks of Grandeur . . . Swords and full Dresses . . . magnificently apparelled as if they were going to Court', but he also noted that because a growing number of Frenchmen had travelled to England, where clothing was simpler, it was possible to see 'People of Fashion . . . walking in Undress on a Morning in the streets of Paris, who formerly would have thought it beneath their Dignity'.[3] Andrews makes a rather exaggerated distinction between the English nobility and gentry who have 'a more political turn of mind . . . ever engaging them in perpetual scenes of serious Business', which is reflected in their sober and practical clothing; and the French, who had an incurable addiction to 'gallantry and dissipation', and were too devoted to dress.[4] 'Dress', according to Thicknesse, 'is an essential and most important consideration with everybody in France' . . . 'a piece of state policy to prevent their employing their intellectual faculties'.[5] No doubt this was a slighting reference to the interest expressed by men in their clothing, which Andrews described as a 'needless Diversion'.

Most visitors, however, were captivated by the dress and the manners of women in France. Even Andrews, who was startled at the way in which Frenchmen dedicated to women 'almost their whole Time, whereas the English allow them but a moderate Share of their Company and Attention', was impressed by their wit, intelligence and elegance. 'Whatever they devise relative to the Ornament and setting off of their Persons, is generally thought agreeable and becoming'.[6] How Frenchwomen achieved this sense of what the following century described as *chic*, was a mystery to Englishmen, for they were not regarded as handsome, nor, as Andrews pointed out, did they have the lithe figures formed by the 'bodily exercises such as Walking [and] Riding' which Englishwomen enjoyed. One explanation provided by Lord Hertford, English ambassador to France, in a letter to Horace Walpole in 1763, was that they 'wore' better; 'even the homely ladies, after they have passed the first bloom of youth, are so much better dressed and ornamented that it requires a close inspection not to think them pretty.'[7]

The cultivation of the *tout ensemble* – the costume, accessories and the wit to wear them with style – derived from court and salon society in the late seventeenth century, had by the mid-eighteenth century spread to all women with any pretension to good breeding. There was a sense of the subtleties and the nuances of existence expressed in the right choice of dress; there was all the time in the world for the leisured games of life, walking, dancing, conversation and the elaborate ritual of dressing. Clothes, most of all, expressed personal taste and public luxury in just the way that Henry James's terrible Madame Merle in *The Portrait of a Lady* (1881) phrases it: 'I know a large part of myself is the clothes I choose to wear. I've a great respect for *things*. One's self for other people – is one's expression of one's self; and one's house, one's furniture, one's garments, the books one reads, the company one keeps – these things are all expressive.' Madame Merle (whose cynical and manipulative nature is in direct descent from the marquise de Merteuil in Laclos's *Les Liaisons Dangereuses*) is described by James in a way appropriate to *ancien-régime* society; she was 'too perfectly the social animal that man and woman are supposed to be . . . she existed only in her relations, direct or indirect, with her fellow mortals'.

As Thicknesse puts it, there was among people of fashion 'an ease and good-breeding which is very captivating, and not easily obtained, but by being bred up . . . from an early age; the whole body must be formed for it, as in dancing, while there is the pliability of youth; and where there is, as in France, a constant, early and intimate correspondence between the two sexes'.[8] Aided by the perfect deportment taught by the dancing-master – 'pour se présenter en compagnie & en faire l'agrément'[9] – and by the correct clothing for each occasion chosen with taste and skill, French men and women in high society acted out their roles with the precision and grace of a minuet.

The *Monument du Costume*, a series of plates by Jean-Michel Moreau (Moreau le Jeune) with text by Retif de la Bretonne, was published in 1789 and sums up the essence of life for the privileged few on the eve of the French Revolution. Plates 36 and 37 are from this series which portrays the lives of a 'jeune femme de bon ton', and a cavalier *à la mode*. '*N'ayez pas peur ma bonne Amie*' (published originally in 1776) shows

the fashionable young lady, Céphise, lying on a sofa, having announced her pregnancy. Suitably, she is dressed in a stylish *déshabillé*, a jacket and skirt, and is clearly adhering to the fashionable advice to avoid the wearing of boned stays in this condition. At this level of society, the birth of a hoped-for heir was very important and the declaration of pregnancy was a social and public event. Thus, the seated visitors are dressed in the height of fashion, the formal *robe à la française* with its elegant back drapery and worn over hoops. A young abbé offers his good wishes, his hand to his ruffled shirt frill and the fashionable *chapeau-bras* under his arm; only his clerical bands distinguish his calling. Such young abbés (often the younger sons of the nobility) were fashionable fixtures in society boudoirs; 'there is no Lady of any Distinction', remarked Andrews, '. . . whose Toilet is not honoured with some clerical Attendant'.[10]

La Sortie de l'Opéra (1778) shows a newly married ducal pair leaving the theatre dressed with the richly trimmed formality that their status demanded; for him the embroidered silk habit *à la française*, powdered bag wig and sword, and for her the vast hooped *décollétée robe à la française*. This is a public occasion, so the couple are officially together in their grandest clothes, but already embarking on diverging private lives

which were the hallmark of *ancien-régime* aristocratic marriages and which gave credence to accusations of hypocrisy and artifice, leitmotifs of *Les Liaisons dangereuses* (1782), which, perhaps wrongly, we see with the virtue of hindsight as a savage indictment of what Madame Merle calls 'the old, old world'.

Perceptive French critics and many English visitors to France noted a disturbing sense of corruption in the higher levels of society, something emphasised by the marginalising of the aristocracy as a caste cut off from the rest of the nation. A French historian has noted the paradox of the situation of the nobility, 'to be at one and the same time the official élite of the kingdom, and a body of rejects, seen as alien, useless and harmful'.[11] The huge court culture at Versailles (which also served to cut the king off from his people and from Paris) in lieu of any real participation in politics, encouraged 'an extraordinarily sensitive feeling for the status and importance that should be attributed to a person in society on the basis of his bearing, speech, manner or appearance'.[12] English travellers to the French court admired the surface grandeur – the palaces, the entertainments, the glittering costume – but some, like Walpole, sensed decay, an unhealthy persistence in the meaningless charade of much court ceremonial and a gradual collapse of the

36 (above left) J.-M. Moreau (after), '*N'ayez pas peur ma bonne Amie*', 1776. Engraving. Private Collection.

37 J.-M. Moreau (after), *La Sortie de l'Opéra*, 1778. Engraving. Private Collection.

infrastructure so laboriously erected by Louis XIV; 'parade and poverty' was Walpole's summing up.

It is a cliché, but none the less true for all that, that in England there were fewer glaring gulfs between the classes; a greater sartorial freedom produced – depending on the viewpoint – a kind of social anarchy, or a refreshing individualism. The former view was more prevalent, with levelling in fashion attacked as socially confusing; a typical comment is that made by an English critic in 1767: 'In England the several ranks of men slide into each other almost imperceptibly, and a spirit of equality runs through every part of the constitution. Hence arises a strong emulation in all the several stations and conditions to vie with each other . . . In such a state as this, fashion must have uncontrolled sway.'[13] A few writers, such as Bernard de Mandeville in his *Fable of the Bees* (1714) accepted that the democratisation or wider availability of fashion would benefit the economy, and thereby promote the development of new technology, but it is likely that the majority of men, certainly in the mid-eighteenth century, felt uneasy at the social implications of a levelling down in dress, some even advocating the re-introduction of sumptuary legislation.[14]

Foreign visitors to England often confessed themselves puzzled by the conflicting signals sent out by clothing; dress then, as now, was a social minefield with unwritten rules. In 1785 a German visitor, in *A View of England towards the Close of the Eighteenth Century* admitted to being confused: '. . . to guess at the rank in life of those who appear in the streets or in public places, is a difficult matter. The rich man dresses frequently as if he had but a small income, and he, whose circumstances are very narrow, is desirous of being supposed to be in affluence'.[15] This claim, that dress served to confuse station in life, was also made by countless English critics, with less validity, for it was as clear then as it is today that native perception and interpretation of class through the way in which clothes were worn, as well as the garments themselves, was as sharp as ever.

By the time that Wendeborn (the German writer quoted above) was visiting England, the process of fashion consumption had speeded up, even among those whom he calls 'in a middling station of life', who needed at least three suits a year (the word 'suit' was used in the eighteenth century to mean complete outfits plus accessories, for men and women). While acknowledging that fashion increased 'the pride, the wants and the cares of families', he also pointed out that the pursuit of the latest styles helped the economy of the nation.[16] By this time the fashions, under the aegis of the dominant middle classes, were relatively sober and simple, based on fine quality English woollen materials that had long been produced, and on such new fabrics as cotton, whose manufacture

was beginning to be vastly expanded and diversified through the technological innovations of the period. This kind of dress played an important part in what Peter Earle in *The Making of the English Middle Class* (1989) calls the 'bourgeois culture that was destined to become the dominant national culture'.[17] But this only happened gradually and unevenly and was not totally confirmed until the end of the eighteenth century, for French fashions remained for some time entrenched in the top levels of society, particularly for women. A quick look at the English language during the second half of the eighteenth century shows how many French words relating to dress, textiles and manners had been incorporated: *etiquette* (1750); *fête* (1754); *rouge* (1753); *ennui* (1758); *monde*, i.e. society (1765); *passé* (1775); *chignon* (1783); *bandeau* (1790), and so on.

New styles were generally thought to emanate from Paris, and perhaps it was only half tongue-in-cheek that Walpole cautioned Henry Seymour Conway in 1759 on his return from abroad:

You are so thoughtless in your dress that I cannot help giving you a little warning against your return. Remember, everybody that comes from abroad is sensed to come from France, and whatever they wear at their first appearance immediately grows the fashion. Now if, as is very likely, you should through inadvertence change hats with the master of a Dutch smack, Offley will be upon the watch, will conclude you took your pattern from M. de Bareil, and a week's time we shall all be equipped like Dutch skippers.[18]

London was the obvious conduit for French fashions; when, in Goldsmith's play *She Stoops to Conquer* (1773) Tony Lumpkin is asked if Marlow and Hastings are Londoners, the reply is: 'I believe they may – they look woundily like Frenchmen', which would have provoked an appreciative guffaw from a patriotic audience convinced that foreign styles were being imported at the expense of native manufactures. In 1745 the Anti-Gallican Association was founded 'to oppose the insidious arts of the French Nation' and to discourage 'the introduction of French modes'. Such anti-French feeling waxed and waned according to the state of war between the two countries, but never disappeared, as can be seen in the work of English caricaturists throughout the period, Bunbury's *Englishman at Paris, 1767* (pl. 38) points out the contrast (from an English point of view) between the bluff Englishman in the foreground with his sturdy greatcoat and the effete, over-refined Frenchman in his chaise, attended by a foppish servant who has a huge fur muff. Another contrast is made between the hairdresser on the left with his large club wig and parasol and the peasant on the right with jacket, sabots and loose baggy trousers – the *sans-culotte* of the future. In Paris in 1765 William Cole noted 'all the world got into Muffs; some so ridiculously large & unweildy as to oblige them to have a Sort of Belt of the same Skin come over one shoulder, as the Order of the Garter is worn, to support their Enormity: this is the constant Method of the Parisian Coachmen . . .' He also noted the dislike of hats among fashionable Frenchmen, 'for Fear of discomposing their well adjusted Hair', and remarked on 'a new & most troublesome Invention . . . a Parasol or Umbrella of Silk, which opens by Springs & covers them in the Summer from the Sun, & in the Winter from the Rain'.[19] Some years later while in France, the artist George Romney also remarked on the continuing fashion for muffs and for the hat ('chappo Bras') to be carried under the arm; he preferred the English way of wearing the hat on the head, for it threw 'the face into half shadow'.[20]

Caricatures of the national differences between the French and the English were furthered not just in the visual arts but in the theatre and via travellers' tales. Louis-Sébastien Mercier, who visited England in 1780, commented on well-established stereotypes: 'A Paris, on pense qu'un François ne peut traverser une rue sans être insulté; que chaque Anglois est féroce et mange de la chair toute crue. A Londres, ils croyent que tous les François ont un corps maigre, ventre plat, portent une grande bourse, une longue epée, et surtout ne se nourissent guère que de grenouilles'.[21] English and French writers advised their nationals to avoid unpleasantness when travelling abroad by adopting the fashion of the host country. An anonymous English naval officer, compiling a *Gentleman's Guide in his Tour through France* (*c.*1768), advised men to wear uniforms if possible, but otherwise to dress 'à la mode de France' in 'lac'd coat, silk stockings, powder'd hair and lac'd ruffles'.[22] Some twenty years later the author of *Le Parisien à Londres, ou avis aux Français qui vont en Angleterre* commented that the people of London would remark adversely on French formal costume, and that it would be tactful for his countrymen to avoid wearing the *habit à la française*, sword and *chapeau-bras*.[23] However, by this time the fashionable young Frenchman would have been unlikely to be so formally dressed, having adopted the kind of English costume so disapproved of by Jean-Antoine Rigoley de Juvigny (*De la Décadence des lettres et des moeurs depuis les Grecs et les Romains jusqu'à nos jours*, 1787) – styles more redolent of the stable, he thought, than of the salon; young Frenchmen had all taken to wearing skimpy frock-coats, thick cravats, hats with the brim over their eyes and a whip or a cane in the hand.[24] Dire results for French civilisation were predicted, in just the same way that on the other side of the Channel, '. . . having a French hairdresser might be the precursor of a Bastille in Hyde Park'.[25]

38 H. W. Bunbury, *Englishman at Paris, 1767*. Pen and watercolour. Formerly Bowood, present whereabouts unknown.

It has already been noted that the part of the body most sensitive to changes in dress is the head and in the demonology of French vices the hairdresser ranked high in English estimation. In an anonymous caricature published in 1784, '*Changez moi cette Tête*' (pl. 39) women flock to change their *démodée* head-dresses (*têtes*) for more up-to-date versions; the scene looks oddly like a waxworks (was the artist familiar with the famous wax museum in Paris run by Marie Grosholtz, later Madame Tussaud?), and there is a macabre premonition of the removal of heads by the guillotine in the French Revolution. In the mid-eighteenth century, the wig summed up the essence of French elegance and civility for a man of taste; there was an art in the choice of the most flattering style, the exact placing of the curls (buckles, in English, from the French *boucles*) which was far less appreciated in England. Sterne's *A Sentimental Journey* (1768) records a visit to the barber in Paris to have his wig 'set' (this had to be done at regular intervals, to keep it in shape) but the man refused to have 'anything to do with my wig':

I had nothing to do but to take one ready made of his own recommendation.

–But, I fear, friend! said I, this buckle won't stand.

–You may immerge it, replied he, into the Ocean, and it will stand.

–What a great scale is everything upon in this city, thought I – the utmost stretch of an English periwig-maker's ideas could have gone no further than to have dipped it into a pail of water. – what difference! 'tis like time to eternity.[26]

Changez moi cette Tête.

Vive la faribole,
Parir en est l'école,
Une seule palote,
Y change le gout,

Dans ce pays frivole,
Pour un mot l'on rafole,
Et l'on cabriole,
En chantant par tout,
Changez moi cette Tête, Tête d'ancien gout

Aujourd'hui la frisure,
Demain c'est la ceinture,
Toujours nouvelle allure,
On vous pousse à bout,

Une Vieille en guenille,
Aux dépens de sa fille,
Veut être gentille,
Et passer par-tout,
Changez moi cette Tête, Tête de Hibou,

Pub. by H. Humphrey Jan.ry.19.1784 N.o 51. New Bond Street .

The perfect matching of wig to face can be seen in Jean-Baptiste Perroneau's portrait of Jacques Cazotte of c.1760 (pl. 40), depicting a style known as *à la mousquetaire*, according to Beaumont's *Enciclopédie perruquière* of 1757. The diagonal side curls echo the lines of the face, captured slightly smiling, full of that sense of *esprit* which, as Stendhal remarked, was so characteristic of eighteenth-century France, a lost art, 'de faire naître le rire de l'âme et de donner des jouissances délicieuses par des mots imprévus'.[27] In spite of the view of Diderot and other critics that the wig produced a bland uniformity of visage, in the hands of a sensitive artist and with that passion for physiognomy which is also one of the traits of the century, the character shows through. Cazotte, a writer of verse, romantic novels and oriental tales, wears a comfortably loose suit of salmon-pink silk lined with white; the fine Flemish lace of his shirt-frill is thrown into prominence by the black silk ribbon brought round under his chin from the wig bow at the back, and the matching lace of his ruffles is shown off by the characteristic eighteenth-century gesture of inserting the hand through the waistcoat buttons.

A similar gesture can be seen in Hudson's *Sir Henry Oxenden* (pl. 41), painted around 1755 to celebrate his marriage. He wears the kind of figured silk more often seen in costume collections than in portraits, where the play of light on plain fabrics was, on the whole, preferred by artists; plate 42 is a study for costume attributed to Hudson showing how the clothes and the stance produce the curves which are so typical of eighteenth-century dress. *The Rudiments of Genteel Behavior* of 1737 by a dancing-master, François Nivelon, aimed to produce for its readers 'a graceful Attitude, an agreeable Motion, an Easy Air' if they followed his instructions. The rubric to the first plate, *Standing* (pl. 43) instructs men to hold their head erect and the shoulders not drawn back too much, otherwise 'the Chest will appear too prominent, the Arms stiff and lame, and the Back hollow, which will intirely spoil the true Proportion'. The arms were to be easy, not too close to the sides, and the right hand must 'place itself in the Waistcoat easy and genteel, as this Figure is represented'. Within this conventional pose, the results could be startlingly different, as can be seen when comparing the relaxed image of Cazotte with his *vif* expression, and the loose but brilliant handling of the paint, with the glossy and meticulous depiction of the details of the costume in Hudson's *Oxenden* who shows to the world his public face, but little personality.

Both men are almost certainly wearing French silks,

for by the late seventeenth century the French silk industry was the most important in Europe; it ranged from the production of very expensive and complicated brocaded silks (which were mainly used at court and on formal occasions) to the light taffetas that were popular for women's dress in the 1780s and 1790s. It was the mercers who sold the best silks (and the finest woollen cloths) and who acted as catalysts for the fashion industry; they were the middlemen between the manufacturer and the customer, transmitting the caprices of court and society to the silk industry, based in Lyons. Mercier, was, as usual, perceptive in his definition: fashionable mercers 'sont des créateurs, des intermédiares, des magiciens des signes sociaux, et leur commerce peut s'étendre par tout l'univers'.[28] One of the most important and influential mercers in Paris was the firm of Barbier et Tetard, in the faubourg Saint-Martin, who supplied silks and other fine fabrics to the French court and aristocracy, and to foreign customers too. The mercers' guild was the third largest in size, but the first in terms of prestige and Barbier was one of its most prominent members; 'Il y a des nouveautés chez Barbier qu'on ne voit point ailleurs', commented the *Encyclopédie* in its entry under 'Nouveauté'.[29] From the Barbier Letters (London, Victoria and Albert Museum), which cover the second half of the eighteenth century, it is clear how much the customers of the firm relied on his knowledge of the fashions; they required advice as to the most popular colours, the types of embroidery that might suit the formal *habit à la française*, the best kind of linings, and so on. Tailors and *couturières* dealt directly with Barbier, and it is possible that such people were available on the premises to give advice on the amounts of fabric needed, to cut out the materials and sometimes to make them up.[30]

It was only in the last quarter of the eighteenth century that the status of the mercer in the determining of fashion styles, began to be challenged by the tailor and the *modiste*; this coincided with the gradual eclipse of the expensive and lavishly trimmed patterned stuffs (except on exceptionally formal occasions) which could hide a multitude of sins in their assemblage into garments, by simpler styles in plainer fabrics where poor seams could not be hidden by embroidery and where fit was increasingly important. This was particularly the case with regard to men's clothing.

The first important treatise on tailoring was published in 1769 by a Parisian master-tailor, F.-A. de Garsault. *L'Art du tailleur* describes, with the aid of diagrams, the making of the main garments in a man's wardrobe and how to measure the customer. The absence of earlier works is explained by the fact that relatively few changes in style had taken place in menswear since the French established their hegemony in this field – 'l'habit complet français, et on peut dire européen' is the author's comment on the way in which the *habit à la française* had been adopted all over Europe. A sign of the times, however, was the appearance of the greatcoat or redingote, which de Garsault describes as 'espèce de manteau pris des Anglais qui le nomment Ridinchood'.[31]

The most characteristic item of male wear in the period was the coat; known from the late seventeenth century as a *justaucorps* because it was tailored close to the body, it had by the mid-eighteenth century assumed the name of *habit* in France. The *habit à la française* was the most formal version of the coat, made of expensive fabrics and usually trimmed with braid or embroidery. By about 1750 the heaviness of the coat with its heavily reinforced side pleats had begun to diminish and the coat fronts curved away from mid-chest. Fabrics at their most luxurious can be seen in Drouais's portrait of the Comte de Vaudreuil of 1758 (pl. 44), aide-de-camp to the prince de Soubise during the Seven Years War. De Vaudreuil stands in front of a map of Germany, where many of the campaigns took place (the armour at his feet is another reference to his military career), and he points to Santo Domingo in the West Indies, where he was born. His blue velvet coat is lined with squirrel, as is his waistcoat of brocade with its heavy festoons of gold and silver lace. His wig is of a style known as *aile de pigeon*, and the ends of the black silk ribbon which ties the wig bag in place, are brought round to the front to fasten in a bow at the neck. On the chair behind him lie his three-cornered black hat and a pair of soft leather gloves which seem to have a life of their own, retaining the shape of the wearer's hands

– gloves were frequently the most expressive of accessories.

Fur was used in the most subtle of ways in the eighteenth-century. Rarely used in western Europe with the fur outside, it lined coats[32] and mantles, its softness acting as a luxurious foil to the silk garments. Such opulence appealed less to the more austere British, and most of the fur-lined coats seen in their portraits refer to foreign travels, most often painted on the Grand Tour. In Pompeo Batoni's portrait of John Scott (1774; London, National Gallery), the sitter wears a coat of blue silk trimmed with silver twist and lined with the most splendid sable; it seems likely that

44 F.-H. Drouais, *Joseph-Hyacinthe François de Paule de Rigaud, comte de Vaudreuil*, 1758. Oil on canvas. National Gallery, London.

45 T. Gainsborough, *Sir
Edward Turner*, 1762. Oil on
canvas. Wolverhampton Art
Gallery and Museum.

– as with many of Batoni's clients – such an outfit would have been purchased in Italy.

It is worth comparing the expensive but restrained elegance of the comte de Vaudreuil's costume (where the coat and breeches match and the waistcoat forms a contrast) to the fussy outfit depicted in Gainsborough's *Sir Edward Turner* (1762; pl. 45). Turner had recently come into a fortune and must have spent a considerable amount on this suit of French silk, grey brocaded in white, black and gold; attractive enough as a pattern, the effect in a three-piece costume is of an *embarras de richesse*. Such suits survive in museum collections, but it is rare to see them in portraits – even Hudson's *Sir Henry Oxenden* has only his coat and waistcoat of figured silk, the breeches are of blue velvet. It would be interesting to know what Gainsborough thought of his sitter's somewhat *nouveau-riche* taste in costume, but he has painted him in a stylish enough pose, his legs crossed at the ankles in the conventional manner for full-length portraits.

During the following decade the coat became tighter, cut narrower across the back and with the side fronts showing a more pronounced curve. Such a style was more suited to the young and slim than to the portly and middle-aged, such as Gainsborough's *Matthew Hale* (pl. 46) which must date from the early 1770s. The lack of tucks and darts in tailoring caused problems of fit more noticeable in such plain materials as the greenish-blue velvet in this portrait; the coat fits badly over the chest and shoulders, and crossing the legs was not easy because of the open-scissor shape of the breeches and their diminishing amount of fabric. Although Hale's portrait includes the accoutrements of a gentleman, the snuff-box and the sword, the gesture of holding the leg at the ankle was not one that would have been recognised by dancing masters, who taught deportment as well as dance steps to polite society.

During the 1770s *embonpoint* was increasingly out of fashion as the macaronis in England and their counterparts in France, the *élégants*, promoted a slimmer silhouette with short, tight-fitting coats and breeches almost reaching to the calf. The sartorial absurdities of the macaronis with their towering wigs and tiny hats might only have been a footnote in the history of dress had their styles not coincided with the first generation of English caricaturists: their images ridiculing these fashions were on sale at the print shops in London and helped to further the move towards a more tailored and streamlined appearance.[33] The bright colours favoured by the macaronis (possibly originating from the *élégants*) have been seen as an attempt to counter the growing sobriety in men's clothing during the 1770s. Although this trend has sometimes been exaggerated (and Englishmen con-

tinued to wear such colours as red on some occasions, as their portraits evince) it is true to say that simplicity and sobriety in clothing was more usual from the 1770s and even more so in the following decade, when the coat curved away radically at the sides, eventually forming 'swallow' tails at the back.

In the landscape settings that English artists painted into their portraits, the disparity between formal costume and the outdoors (where such clothing would not have been worn) was sometimes remarked upon. When Gainsborough painted Captain William Wade (pl. 47) – the portrait was exhibited at the Royal Academy in 1771 – he depicted him in full dress, a red silk suit and a waistcoat of gold satin embroidered in multi-coloured silk, which the artist has painted with glistening touches of paint; the effect has to be

46 T. Gainsborough *Matthew Hale*, early 1770s. Oil on canvas. Birmingham City Art Gallery.

47 T. Gainsborough, *Captain William Wade*, 1771. Oil on canvas. Victoria Art Gallery, Bath City Council.

of protocol at the Assembly Rooms, regulating the conduct of visitors, precedence at dances, and other tasks; it was an important job, demanding tact as well as the most polished social graces, for Bath was the most fashionable watering-place in the eighteenth century. It is thus appropriate that Wade stands in his elegant costume, hand on hip in a pose ratified by the dancing-master; Gainsborough seems also to have borrowed from van Dyck's *James Stuart, Duke of Lennox* then at Wilton House (now New York, Metropolitan Museum of Art). However, when the portrait was first painted, there was criticism that Wade looked out of place in the countryside in this quintessentially urban, formal costume, and Gainsborough then painted in a balustrade suggesting the terrace of a grand house.

Gainsborough's *Captain Wade* is a fairly rare example of an English sitter looking totally at home in his high, powdered bag wig and superb formal silk suit. Even in this context, however, a touch of the countryside has crept in with the bouquet of fresh flowers with their uneven stems pushed through the buttonholes of his coat: a sense of *rus in urbe* was never far away even in the grandest English images. On the whole, however, if the evidence of portraits is correct, Englishmen felt more at home in less formal attire, in the frock-coats and frock-suits which feature so prominently in their painted images during the second half of the eighteenth century. Compared to the high incidence of formal patterned suits existing in costume collections (which were kept even when out of date because of the expense of the silk) frock-coats survive less frequently because – presumably – they were worn out and thought not worth preserving because of their cheaper fabrics.

The frock was originally a sporting and country coat, without such cumbersome features of full dress as the heavy stiffened cuffs and flared skirts. It had a small turned-down collar and drastically reduced side pleats, or none at all; the cuff was either the small round type or slit for ease in movement. Made of woollen cloth or wool and silk mixtures in such sober colours as brown, buff, blue and green, it became a staple of the wardrobe of the affluent Englishman during the later eighteenth century. English tourists took the style with them to Italy and had the garment made up in lightweight silk; it was a more comfortable costume in a hot climate than full dress. Batoni's somewhat unflattering portrait of Sir Henry Watkin Dashwood (*c*.1768; pl. 48) shows him in a blue silk frock-suit trimmed with silver braid and matching buttons; in accordance with the relative informality of the costume, he wears his own, unpowdered hair instead of a wig. Unusually, Batoni has not included the Roman setting or antique marbles that usually feature in his portraits of Englishmen on the Grand

appreciated from a distance, and represents the *essence* of embroidery rather than minute attention to all the details of the stitches and design. Wade was elected Master of Ceremonies at Bath in 1769 and resigned in 1777 because of his adultery – not for nothing was he known as the 'Bath Adonis'; round his neck he wears the ribbon and badge of his office. He was in charge

48 P. Batoni, *Sir Henry Watkin Dashwood*, *c*.1768. Oil on canvas. Courtesy of P. & D. Colnaghi & Co. Ltd, London.

Tour (see pl. 216) and which testify to the educational element behind their travels, even if this was more evident in the breach than in the observance. This was clearly the view of the anonymous author of *Fashion. A Poem*, of 1775:

These are our Men of Fashion; − True,
Europe they saw − it saw them too.
To foreign climes, unpolish'd sent,
They come − as wisely as they went.
What learnt they for their vast expence?
− Oh! they can ride, and dance and fence −
And nothing else save such devices?
− Yes − they import their dress and vices.[34]

So much had men's clothing in England undergone a sea-change during the 1770s, that when William Hickey returned to London from India in 1780, his wardrobe needed a complete overhaul, as it was far too bright and richly trimmed to be *à la mode*, especially for someone who confessed that he 'always had a tendency to be a beau'. He sold his clothes in Monmouth Street in London, obtaining only one-seventh of what he had originally paid for them, but kept one suit of velvet and two others 'least ornamented with lace'. Frock-coats now made up the main part of his new outfits, the tailor he consulted advising the following:

a dark green with gold binding, dark brown with the same, a plain blue, and for half-dress a Bon de Paris with gold frogs, all of which he spoke as being much worn and of the highest ton. I bespoke the four suits accordingly. My next calls were at Rymers for boots, Wagner for hats, and Williams of Bond

Street for leather breeches. In three days I was to come forth a proper 'Bond Street lounger', a description of person then just coming into vogue.[35]

At about the same time that Hickey was ordering his new clothes, the same spirit of modernity in dress can be seen in Wright's portrait of Sir Brooke Boothby (1781; pl. 49). Communing somewhat uneasily with Nature (in a pose that is, in its own way, as artificial as that of Gainsborough's *Captain Wade*), the sitter manhandles a copy of the autobiographical *Rousseau. Juge de Jean Jacques* which he had published in 1780. The portrait has been seen, both in pose and in dress, as influenced by late Elizabethan and Jacobean melancholy, but while the full-length reclining figure might recall such images as Isaac Oliver's *Edward Herbert, 1st Baron Herbert of Cherbury* (*c.*1610–15; Powis Castle, Powys),[36] the costume is certainly not indicative of a melancholic *déshabillé*, but a definite statement of high fashion. Boothby wears a light-brown cloth frock-suit; both coat and waistcoat are double-breasted, and the latter is cut fashionably short across the waist, allowing the long slim breeches to be seen. So slim-fitting is the coat that it no longer covers the thighs, and the sleeves are so modishly tight that they have to be unbuttoned at the wrist to aid movement of the arm. There is a new emphasis on plain linen, unadorned with lace, in the revival of the cravat which is here tied in a loose bow, and for the shirt ruffle. The English fondness for fine-quality linen was catered for by the numbers of specialist shops in the main cities of the kingdom, and in Oxford Street in London which was famous for its shops selling a wide range of cottons and linens, and was particularly admired by foreign visitors in the 1780s.[37]

An emphasis on good, clean linen in England was a sign of national pride and was often compared to the state of affairs in France where, it was felt, surface splendour masked private squalor. Walpole, in Paris in 1765, wished 'there was less whisk [whist] and somewhat more cleanliness'; and a few years later the author of *The Gentleman's Guide in His Tour through France* found men's costume to be a sham, for the 'lac'd ruffles . . . are often tack'd upon either false sleeves, or a shirt as course [sic] as a hop sack'.[38] Visitors to France were advised to take as much linen as they could, and to avoid, if possible, the services of the laundresses who were reputed the worst in Europe.

A German visitor to England in the 1780s summarised the main elements of the dress of Englishmen: '. . . the English still wear plain broadcloth, both in summer and winter; but it is of the finest kind . . . in general, even those of the middling class wear very excellent linen, and change it daily. The fineness of

49 J. Wright, *Sir Brooke Boothby*, 1781. Oil on canvas. Tate Gallery, London.

the shirt and stockings, a good hat and the best shoes, distinguish a man in opulent circumstances'.[39]

The 'good hat' by this time might be one of a number of styles, for the tyranny of the universal three-cornered black hat (made ideally of beaver which made the best felts[40]) began to be eroded during the later eighteenth century, under the romantic impulse towards individuality in dress. During the 1780s, round hats with uncocked brims (Sir Brooke Boothby, for example, wears a dashing style known as a 'wide-awake') largely replaced the cocked three-cornered hat which became the preserve of the conservative and old-fashioned. At court and at formal assemblies another style of *chapeau-bras* was carried under the arm, a hat with the crown folded between two crescent-shaped brims, a version of the formal *bicorne* with its brim turned up high in front and behind.

In contemporary comments made on the dress of Englishmen there is a new sense that the 1780s were a transitional period, when the old certainties – emphasis on the total effect and the suit in particular – begin to give way to the breaking-up of costume structures, a new stress laid on the individual components, and especially on the accessories of costume, such as the headwear and footwear. In France during the 1780s, a decade of Anglomania, when, according to the *Cabinet des Modes* (15 May 1786), it was increasingly rare to to see 'habits à la Françoise, avec le chapeau sous le bras, & l'epée au côté', the streets of Paris were full of young men copying English dress – 'C'est aujourd'hui un ton parmi la jeunesse de copier l'Anglois dans son habillement', remarked Mercier in his *Tableau de Paris* (1782–8). In a famous passage he urged his fellow-countrymen to return to their lace and their formal silk coats in the French style, and no longer to wear caped redingotes or greatcoats, the straight English suit, and above all to avoid wearing the hat on the head (as distinct from being carried under the arm), thick stockings, starched cravat and short hair.[41] The equation of wearing one's own hair with anti-social and even revolutionary tendencies was easily made by those to whom the powdered wig (or at least the hair pomaded and powdered) symbolised traditional values. During the Gordon Riots in London in 1780, the mob attacked peers on their way to the House of Lords in order to – in Walpole's word – 'diswig' them, which in many cases they succeeded in doing.

During the 1770s many Frenchmen had adopted the English frock-coat under the name of the *frac*, or *fraque*; it differed from the original in that it was usually made of silk or mixed materials, had trimming and decoration, and was cut in variety of styles, for example with a sloping shawl collar instead of the small round collar. Gradually, in spite of such critics as Mercier, other English garments such as redingotes, leather breeches and boots were assimilated into the French male wardrobe. One of the promoters of English fashions (which also included horse-racing and gentlemen's clubs) was Philippe, duc d'Orléans, a friend of the Prince of Wales; both men were at the centre of opposition to court policies and Orléans, in particular, used costume to focus attention on his political sympathies.

It is one of the ironies of the late eighteenth century that as France moved towards revolution, the court had already begun to economise, both in its ceremonies and entertainments, and in costume. Louis XVI, unlike his predecessors, was not interested in clothes and although on formal occasions he was dressed in the court *habit à la française* or the splendid costume of the premier French order of chivalry, the Saint-Esprit, commentators both hostile and friendly, noted that he looked ill at ease in full dress and at state events. His fellow-monarch George III solved the problem of how to adapt the current simplicity in male dress (his own personal preference chimed well with this) to a sense of the exclusivity proper to royalty, by the invention of the Windsor uniform by 1778. This was blue with red collar and cuffs, and trimmed with gold braid. The king was painted in it by Gainsborough and other artists, and depicted wearing it in caricatures and in commemorative items. It was 'his preferred style of dress in the last thirty years of his active reign', a perfect symbol of his attitude to his clothes 'which owed little to fashion but a great deal to order, familiarity and comfort.'[42]

In the choice of colour for the Windsor uniform, however, George III was following fashion even if his most direct inspiration might have come from military costume. Shades of blue were popular for frocks and greatcoats, as a Russian visitor N.M. Karamzin noted in 1790: '. . . dark blue is the favourite colour of the English . . . of fifty persons whom one meets in the streets of London, at least twenty are dressed in dark blue coats.'[43] In his portrait by William Hoare, of the late 1770s (pl. 50), the writer Christopher Anstey wears a dark blue frock-suit as befits a man who made a name for himself with his gentle satire in poetic form on dress and manners in *The New Bath Guide* (1766); his costume is modestly stylish but not over-fashionable. A man of his age, in his fifties, would be more comfortable with certain styles of his youth, like the lace shirt-frill and sleeve ruffles, than with the plain linen seen in Wright's portrait of Boothby. Anstey's hair is a compromise between the powdered wig and the unadorned locks; it is his own hair frizzed and powdered. Carl Philipp Moritz, travelling in England in 1782 noted that Englishmen had their hair 'dressed and curled with irons, to give the head a large bushy appearance, and half their backs are covered

wears in Gainsborough's '*The Morning Walk*' at the National Gallery, London. It is hard to say if the prevailing Anglomania influencing fashion in France during the 1780s produced a similar vogue for black costume for men. J.F. Sobry in his *Discours sur les principaux usages de la nation françoise* (1786) claimed that black was not only an official and clerical colour, but had been adopted by some middle-class Frenchmen; 'la couleur noire est celle qui domine le plus parmi les habits des François; et il faut convenir que cela ne contraste pas peu avec la gaiété naturelle à notre nation.'[45] As Sobry stated, black was the colour worn by 'les gens d'Eglise' and 'les gens de justice'; it was also worn by the *noblesse de robe*, who held the main administrative and judicial offices in the kingdom. A member of this relatively new nobility, Charles-Alexandre de Calonne was painted by Vigée-Lebrun in 1784 (pl. 51); he was chief finance minister to Louis XVI, a position underlined by the fact that his hand holds a letter to the king and rests on a draft edict for the reorganisation of France's national debt. He wears the costume of his rank, a wonderful glossy black satin suit; the lace (appropriate for formal wear at court) is delicate French needle-lace and the glittering star and blue moiré ribbon (*cordon bleu*) indicate that he holds the order of the Saint-Esprit. A heavily curled lawyer's wig was an essential part of this official costume and the artist had to paint it in spite of her declared abhorrence of wigs; this opinion of hers made it all the more absurd, she states in her memoirs, that she should be accused of having an affair with Calonne.

Although the majority of the illustrations chosen in this section on men's dress concentrate on the formality that dominates *ancien-régime* fashion, it is only right to point out that by the 1780s, there seem to be an increasing number of men painted at their ease, with a relaxed informality of costume. Again, there is a process of selection at work, for certain garments had not as yet made it to the artist's studio; the greatcoat or redingote, for example, although a very popular item of men's wear both in France and England as evidenced by contemporary comment and through the pages of the fashion magazines, did not attract artistic attention until a later date. On the whole clothes had to be fairly well established before being painted in what was intended to be a permanent record; artists were wary of depicting fashions that might just be a passing whim.

The loose morning-gown or dressing-gown, on the other hand, had a long tradition in portraiture; such gowns were both stylish (as worn by the unknown gentleman in Drouais's *Group Portrait*, 1756; pl. 35) and comfortable, as Diderot claimed his old *robe de chambre* was. Such gowns were colourful, exotic, and – because they had been part of the masculine ward-

50 W. Hoare, *Christopher Anstey and his Daughter*, c.1779. Oil on canvas. National Portrait Gallery, London.

51 E.-L. Vigée-Lebrun, *Charles-Alexandre de Calonne*, 1784. Oil on canvas. The Royal Collection, © 1994 Her Majesty Queen Elizabeth II.

with powder'.[44] Anstey's daughter is dressed in a simple white frock (the word, somewhat confusingly, begins to be applied to the dress of young girls, as it also refers to the long gown worn by small boys before they were 'breeched'); this is the type of dress which anticipates the Neoclassical style taken up by women during the last years of the eighteenth century. Children in England were noted for what Moritz describes as the 'free, easy and natural' appearance of their hair which was, as Mary Anstey's indicates, a contrast to the towering feathered coiffure of the fashionable doll she holds out.

'If you wish to be full drest, you wear black' in England, says Moritz and by the time he is writing, formal costume would be a frock-suit, the old style of coat being, according to the *Fashionable Magazine* of 1786, 'too antiquated for any other place than court'. A black silk velvet frock-suit is what William Hallett

52   J.-L. David, *Alphonse Leroy*, 1783. Oil on canvas. Musée Fabre, Montpellier.

robe since the seventeenth-century – they could be regarded as 'timeless', and were thus appropriate wear for artists, philosophers and writers (see van Loo's portrait of Diderot, pl. 19). Their practicality made them attractive to scientists, doctors and a wide range of professional men. David's portrait of Dr Alphonse Leroy (1783; pl. 52) shows the sitter in a padded shot-silk morning gown, worn over a white waistcoat, white shirt and loosely tied cravat. It was customary for professional men to work dressed in this way – a gown over shirt, waistcoat and breeches – in the morning, before meeting colleagues, clients and other visitors. Leroy's own hair straggles from under a striped silk scarf arranged as a kind of turban; such headdresses, either lightweight unstructured styles such as this, or the warmer velvet caps often trimmed with fur, such as Hogarth wears in his *Self-portrait* (pl.

20) kept the head warm when the hair was cut very short to accommodate a wig, or before the hair was formally dressed for the day.

Painted in the same year as Dr Leroy, Jacob More's *Self-portrait* (pl. 53) is a wonderfully direct image of an artist at work, with a much more convincing relationship with nature than in Wright's *Boothby*; More was a landscape artist, so this is not altogether surprising. Painted for the artists' gallery of self-portraits at the Uffizi, More's self-image links the worlds of the *ancien régime* and early Romanticism. His clothes are conventional enough (except for the buff felt round hat trimmed with gold braid) but it is rare to see a man discard his coat and reveal himself in his waistcoat, the shorter back of which was not designed to be seen. No doubt he welcomed the chance to experiment in the painting of what was normally hidden, including the wide crumpled linen shirt-sleeves with their dropped shoulder seam. Appropriately for an Italian setting, More's suit is of lightweight silk, the striped and embroidered waistcoat, buff-coloured breeches fastened at the knee with diamond-paste buckles, and a frock-coat with braided tassels and loops and the same tight buttoned sleeves as seen in Wright's portrait of Boothby. Finally, it is worth noting how More's receding hairline draws attention to his face and his direct gaze. Altogether a modern image as the baggage of the old world (in a Carlylean sense) is set aside to prepare for the new.

★   ★   ★

Turning to women's dress in the mid-eighteenth century, it is difficult not to be captivated by the way in which the elements of the Rococo style were absorbed with such ease into dress in France by the 1730s; it had a more modest impact on Englishwomen's costume. It was a style characterised by wit and fantasy, by playful ornamentation, asymmetry and three-dimensional decoration; at its heart was a *horror vacui*, and by the middle of the eighteenth century critics such as the Abbé Leblanc in his *Lettres* (1751), compared its confusion of forms unfavourably with the noble simplicity of the Greeks.[46]

In terms of costume, the new style exemplified every fantasy about the essence of the feminine; everything undulates and curves, from the tightly curled hairstyles (a popular style was named *tête de mouton*, like a sheep's fleece) decorated with a tiny, frivolous headdress called a *pompon* (a few flowers, a scrap of lace, a glittering *tremblant* jewelled ornament which shivered as the wearer moved) to the dress itself, usually a *sacque* or a *robe à la française* with floating back drapery, and trimmed with ribbons and flowers in serpentine curves. With the aid of small hoops or hip pads, the silhouette formed a graceful pyramid.

Both in art and in dress, François Boucher was the presiding genius of the Rococo, particularly in his portraits of the marquise de Pompadour painted during the 1750s. Perhaps the most famous of these is that dated 1756 (pl. 55) where she is depicted in a superb dress of green silk taffeta decorated with lace and pink rose garlands; the bodice of the gown has a row of ribbon bows (*échelle*: ladder) of pink and silver striped silk, the same fabric used for her shoes. When it was exhibited at the Salon of 1757, Baron Melchior Grimm complained that the dress was 'surchargé d'ornements, de pompons et de toutes sortes de fanfreluches', and certainly in lesser hands such a costume might have turned out too overwhelming; here, allied to the marquise's own sense of refinement, it is the perfect visualisation of the Goncourts' belief that

the prime object of Rococo painting was to delight the eye. Never had the roundness of women's bodies been celebrated as it was in Rococo portraiture, where the fashion lead was taken by Madame de Pompadour. As one contemporary remembered: 'Très-bien faite, elle avait le visage rond, tous les traits réguliers, un teint magnifique, la main at les bras superbes, des yeux plus jolis que grands, mais d'un feu, d'un spirituel, d'un brillant que je n'ai vu à aucune femme. Elle était arrondie dans toutes ses formes, comme dans tous ses mouvements'.[47]

Boucher, as Madame de Pompadour remarked, was not especially good at likenesses, but this mattered less than the representation of a somewhat idealised face and the overall decorative effect of the portrait. Renoir claimed that Boucher was the artist who best

53 J. More, *Self-portrait*, 1783. Oil on canvas. Uffizi, Florence.

understood the female figure; indeed it is clear that he loved the female body and painted it as an *objet de luxe*. The sweetness and eroticism of Boucher's portraits – even the *embarras de richesse* of the costume – no longer, perhaps, appeal, but it is still difficult to understand how such art could have so enraged Diderot. His review of the Salon of 1765 includes the famous attack on what he sees as Boucher's artifice and affectation; looking at his portraits the critic can see only 'toujours le rouge, les mouches, les pompons, et toutes les fanfioles de la toilette'.[48] For Diderot, such portraits were little more than fashion plates and deserved only hostile consideration. He was one of the critics arguing for a higher moral tone to be taken in painting, a demand that was to be fulfilled by Neoclassicism which from the mid-eighteenth century swept over all the arts, eventually reaching dress by the end of the century, and which resulted in 'moderation', straighter lines, and greater purity of form in costume.

Rococo, a style associated with absolutism and hedonism, was never assimilated in England to the same extent as it was in France. Of course its influence can be seen in painting, by artists who had been to France or who were aware of developments in art across the Channel – Hogarth's Line of Beauty, after all, celebrates the asymmetrical curve; it can be seen in some of the applied arts, including silk design; and even in interiors, where is often takes the form of a playful *chinoiserie*; but it only appears in the mainstream of art, architecture and grand interiors in muted form; it was not in England, as in France, 'le goût moderne' or 'le goût du siècle'. As already noted, fashion styles for women came from France, and therefore the Rococo did make some impact, particularly in the 1760s, but never with the same *joie de vivre*, the same whole-hearted enthusiasm, as in France. The dress itself is less decorated, more subdued, as can be seen in comparing plates 7 and 55 with Gainsborough's *Ann Ford, Mrs Philip Thicknesse* (1760; pl. 54). The artist has given the sitter a witty, convoluted 'rococo' pose, a study in diagonals, which echoes her white satin *sacque* dress trimmed with pleated ribbon applied in serpentine curves. On seeing the portrait, Mrs Delany found it 'a most extraordinary figure, handsome and bold, but I should be very sorry to have anyone I loved set forth in such a manner'.[49] What precisely did she mean? The dress is modest, conventional and attractive. She might have disliked the 'unfeminine' challenging turn of the head, but it is much more likely that she found the legs crossed in this way somewhat disturbing, for this was a masculine pose; women's stays were pointed and boned down the front in a way that impeded women from bending too far forward, and made crossing the legs, except at the ankles, slightly uncomfortable.

The way in which the stays flattened the bust and helped to promote the erect posture which Mrs Delany admired (but not in Mrs Thicknesse's portrait, for her body is only just saved from slouching by the carriage of the head and the invisible support of the corset) can be seen in the more conventional image of *Susanna Beckford* by Reynolds (1756; pl. 56). Painted shortly after her marriage, she wears a turquoise watered-silk dress, a *sacque* or *robe à la française*; it is trimmed with waving lines of ruched ribbon on the bodice and down the sides of the open gown, and her lace is the fashionable blonde or silk lace which catches the light, as does the skirt with its pattern of wavy lines caused during the finishing process of making moiré silk. Such watered silks in the popular blue colour occur in many portraits during the 1750s and 1760s; these include Gainsborough's *Lady Innes* (*c*.1757; New York, Frick Collection) where the sitter's lace is also of blonde, and Zoffany's *Queen Charlotte* (*c*.1766; Bath, Holburne Museum), in which the Queen, like Susanna Beckford, wears a pair of matching bracelets.

As a young painter of society sitters, Reynolds ably demonstrated his virtuoso skill in the depiction of costume and fabrics during the 1750s. The *London Magazine* for July 1755 gave this *Advice to a Painter*:

54   T. Gainsborough, *Ann Ford, Mrs Philip Thicknesse*, 1760. Oil on canvas. Cincinnati Art Museum. Bequest of Mrs Mary M. Emery.

55 (facing page)   F. Boucher, *Madame de Pompadour*, 1756. Oil on Canvas. Alte Pinakothek, Munich.

56 J. Reynolds, *Susanna Beckford*, 1756. Oil on canvas. Tate Gallery, London.

Let her cap be mighty small,
Bigger, just, than none at all;
Pretty, like her sense; and little;
Like her beauty, frail and brittle . . .
Dress with art the graceful sack;
Ornament it well with gimping,
Flounces, furbelows and crimping;
Let of ruffles many a row,
Guard her elbows white as snow;
Knots below and knots above,
Emblems of the tyes of love.

This is a useful, if cynical, summary of the fashion knowledge that a society artist had to learn if he was to succeed; the anonymous author of this verse would perhaps have agreed with Diderot that a concentration on the minutiae of dress only served to show up the mindless vanity of the sitter.

In England a sense of restrained good breeding had to come through in portraiture even if this resulted in the lack of expression evident in Susanna Beckford's face. The ideal Englishwoman, declares Jean-André Rouquet in his *The Present State of the Arts in England* (1755):

. . . must have a fine white skin, a light complexion, a face rather oval than round, a nose somewhat longish, but of a fine turn and like the antiques, her eyes large and not so sparkling as melting; her mouth graceful, without a smile, but rather of a pouting turn, which gives it at once both grace and dignity; her hair clean and without

57 F. Boucher, *Madame de Pompadour*, 1758. Oil on canvas. Courtesy of the Fogg Art Museum, Harvard University Art Museums. Bequest of Charles E. Dunlap.

powder . . . her shape tall and erect, her neck long and easy, her shoulders square and flat, plump rising breasts . . . This is what the English painters have often occasion to represent.[50]

The French and English had somewhat differing views about the ideal female face, which were reflected in portraiture. As we have seen, the French liked a round face, the English an oval; according to Philip Thicknesse, 'a short round face is esteemed the most beautiful in France. The long oval Madonna face, which we admire, is called by the French, le visage de mouton'.[51] In France, a distinctive personal charm was preferred to regular beauty, a vivacity heightened by the use of cosmetics. Rouge, in particular, was much worn in France, for it was thought to give brightness to the eyes and it was necessary to give colour to a face which was artificially whitened and where the hair was powdered.

'The Face is the chief Seat of Beauty' declared the author of *Abdeker, or The Art of preserving Beauty* (1754) and it became, in France a canvas on which to paint a perfect complexion. In Boucher's portrait of Madame de Pompadour of 1758 (pl. 57), the marquise is putting the finishing touches to her face by rouging her cheeks; a swansdown powder puff lies by her mirror, and she holds a patch-box in her hand. Invented in the seventeenth century to cover pimples, the beauty potential of patches was soon realised, and a whole language of sexual dalliance evolved as to the placing of the patches on face and bosom; because of this element of overt coquetry and because – even in

France – the aim of cosmetics was to achieve a heightened naturalism, patches do not appear in portraits (although of course they are satirised in caricatures; see pl. 83).

Madame de Pompadour reveals how the art of make-up was as much a joyful ritual as dressing formally for the day; the pink and white of her dress complements the colours in her complexion. From the fresh flowers on her dressing-room table, she has chosen blue to form a hair ornament (*pompon*) and on her wrist, tactfully much in evidence, is a pearl bracelet with a cameo portrait of Louis XV (the other bracelet to the pair had a portrait of Henry IV). Eighteenth-century make-up was not just gilding the lily, it had the practical benefits of remedying a defective diet and covering the ravages of illness.[52] Works like *Abdeker* included recipes to whiten the complexion and to soften the skin, for the aim of an English beauty was a refined pallor with just a touch of (natural) pink on the cheeks. Society ladies in their portraits lack vivacity; it is only when artists paint their sitters as friends, like Reynolds's *Nelly O'Brien* (London, Wallace Collection) or *Mrs Abington as Miss Prue* (pl. 67); or when Gainsborough paints Ann Ford, the wife of his first biographer Philip Thicknesse, (pl. 54) that we see character on an equal footing with fashion.

Henry Fielding's heroine Sophia Western in *Tom Jones* (1749) has a complexion with 'rather more of the lily than the rose', and this remained the aim of English beauties; rouge was rarely worn, even when, from the later 1760s some women took to powdering their hair, with the result that they often look vapid and unresponsive in their portraits.[53] During the Seven Years War (1756–63) English fashion magazines urged their readers to boycott such French fashions as the *tête de mouton* hairstyles, but presumably, like all such advice, it was ignored. In Scotland there were old-established close links with France; ladies there, said one visitor to Edinburgh, 'do not so readily adopt any trifling fashion from London. They conform themselves much more to the manners and taste of Paris, with which they have as constant a communication as with England'.[54] On the slender evidence available it is hard to know how true this is, but looking at portraits by Ramsay, for example, it is clear that he infused his sitters with a sense of French grace and style which brought out their best points with a quiet delicacy that owed much to his treatment of the fabrics of dress. In his portrait of Martha, Countess of Elgin (*c*.1763–4; pl. 58) the strong features of the sitter are thrown into focus by her dark hair and the exquisite details of the dress, painted in a flickering and hazy style. The dress is a soft pink silk, the buttoning front bodice of the same silk, ruched; she wears a 'necklace' of pink ribbon, her *pompon* is of pink and white flowers and at her breast is a pink

58 A. Ramsay, *Martha, Countess of Elgin, c.*1763–4. Oil on canvas. In the collection of the Earl of Elgin, KT.

rose, probably kept fresh in a tiny bosom bottle filled with water and pinned inside the top of her gown. The pink and white of her dress and hair ornaments are contrasted with the black lace mantle and the lustrous dark fur of the sable muff.

In 1766 Lady Susan Lennox wrote to her friend Lady Susan Fox Strangways that '. . . the french dress is coming into fashion', and she then proceded to describe it. Hair was now to be cut and curled and then powdered; no cap was to be worn but 'only *little, little* flowers dab'd in on the left side', and a black or white feather with a diamond feather-jewel. Round the neck there could be 'a broad puff'd ribbon Collier with a tippet ruff or only a little black handkerchief very narrow over the shoulders'.[55] This might be a description of Lady Elgin, especially as Lady Susan then notes that the fashionable bodice is a 'compère', that is, the front-buttoning style which we see in the Ramsay portrait. The most characteristic part of French dress, however, was the *sacque* or *robe à la française*, originally in the early eighteenth century a loose flowing gown, known as a *robe volante*; tightened up by the 1730s, but still with the characteristic back drapery, it entered the wardrobe of the fashionable English lady. By the middle of the century it was the dress worn on most formal occasions by the French and the English. It took the form of an open gown, that is completely open down the front, with the breast area being filled in with a separate stomacher piece, and worn with a matching skirt known as a petticoat. Surviving examples, portraits and contemporary references indicate how elaborately

trimmed such *sacques* could be, using ribbons, flowers, padded silk puffs, lace, and embroidery.

In most of the portraits discussed, the sitters are posed so that it is difficult to see the graceful line of the flowing silk at the back, which can sometimes look like bundled drapery, as in Gainsborough's *Mrs Thicknesse*. Turning to a lesser artist is often a better way to see the more precise details of dress, and Henry Pickering's *'Eleanor Frances Dixie'* of the mid-1750s (pl. 59)[56] shows the crisp folds of the *sacque* falling from the shoulders. The dress is of an English Spitalfields silk with its typical, naturalistic floral design on an off-white ground; the low neckline is covered by a fine lawn kerchief edged with lace and kept in place with a blue ribbon bow. The same ribbon trims her fine straw hat and the white linen cap she wears underneath, as was the custom. Her complexion seems little aided by art, but the long kid gloves were necessary to keep the arms and hands white, as were the hat and the scarf to keep the sun off face and bosom. Englishwomen were known for their love of exercise (note how in their portraits they are seen walking in the countryside, whereas their French sisters are, more often than not, depicted seated indoors); moderately vigorous activity plus tight-lacing (for which the English were famous) produced the good figure admired by such visitors as the French lawyer Pierre-Jean Grosley: '. . . a good shape is the most striking article of English beauty, from which it is almost inseparable'.[57]

One of the last portraits of Madame de Pompadour, finished after her death, is that by Drouais (pl. 60) of 1763–4. She, too, is depicted in a beautiful flowered silk, but a painted one, probably imported from the East; the marquise was a patron of the Compagnie des Indes Orientales and such painted silks from China entered Europe via the company's Indian depots. Diderot's opinion of this costume is not known, but would doubtless have been unflattering; at the Salon of 1759, apropos of a portrait of the marquise by van Loo (now lost) in a 'robe de satin en fleurs', he grumbled: 'Je n'aime point en peinture les étoffes à fleurs. Elles n'ont ni simplicité ni noblesse . . . Quelqu' habile qui fût un artiste, il ne feroit jamais un beau tableau d'un parterre, ni un beau vêtement d'une robbe à fleurs . . .'[58]

Diderot goes on to exclaim at the amount of space such a hooped dress would occupy – 'imaginer l'espace que ce panier à guirlandes doit occuper . . .' – but the size of the hoops in fashionable dress was modest when compared to those worn under court dress. Court dress, the *grand habit*, consisted of a heavily whaleboned bodice with layers of lace sleeves, *manchettes*, a huge hooped skirt and a long train which it was very difficult to manoeuvre, especially when stepping backwards and curtseying, as royal protocol

dictated; those being presented at court required the services of the dancing-master to teach them the correct and graceful movements. Such a nerve-wracking occasion demanded a great deal of preparation, and Walpole's correspondence records Lady Hertford's anxiety in 1763 when, as wife to the English ambassador, she was presented to the French royal family. Sensibly, as Lord Hertford wrote to Walpole, she decided to take the advice of the duchesse de Nivernois (wife of the French ambassador to England, 1761–3) who ordered for her the magnificent Lyons brocade which she wears in her portrait by Alexandre Roslin of 1765 (pl. 61). Seated with her vast hoops billowing out at the sides, Lady Hertford looks some-

60 F.-H. Drouais, *Madame de Pompadour*, 1764. Oil on canvas. National Gallery, London.

59 H. Pickering, *'Eleanor Frances Dixie'*, c.1755. Oil on canvas. City of Nottingham Museums, Castle Museum and Art Gallery.

61 (facing page) A. Roslin,
Isabella, Countess of Hertford,
1765. Oil on canvas.
Hunterian Collection,
University of Glasgow.

62 T. Gainsborough, *Queen
Charlotte*, 1781. Oil on canvas.
The Royal Collection, ©
1994 Her Majesty Queen
Elizabeth II.

what overwhelmed by her grand costume – the rigidly curled and powdered coiffure, the black lace lappets (long streamers pinned to the headdress) and matching shoulder mantle which was *de rigueur* on such occasions, the brightly coloured flowered silk, and the glittering diamonds which she wears as earrings, necklace and for stomacher ornaments. 'Of the superior worth of Diamonds over all other Jewels' was the heading of a chapter in a treatise by a well-known jeweller;[59] such stones 'being the most beautiful and valuable of all' were 'the chief ornament of great and distinguished personages'. Extensively faceted in the brilliant cut to produce a depth and fire in their appearance, they looked best in candlelight, complementing the gold and silver of fine brocaded silks.

It is very rare to see a portrait of a non-royal sitter wearing court dress, for, however wonderful an assemblage of luxury fabrics and accessories, it was increasingly seen to be absurdly archaic (in essence it dated from the 1670s), over-elaborate and removed from contemporary fashion, which, during the second half of the eighteenth century, was moving towards simpler styles. The huge hoops and the large patterns of the dress fabric, often with attendant trimmings, made women appear – in the words of Elizabeth Montagu – like state beds on castors. From the 1770s hoops disappeared from fashion, but they were retained for court wear, making the disparity between court and everyday fashion even greater. John Villiers noted at Versailles on the eve of the French Revolution how ridiculous court dress appeared; ' . . . their long trains, as they walked through the courts, were supported by pages, and their monstrous hoops, rising on each side, seemed destined to defend their ears from the never-ending nonsense and impertinence of their beaux'.[60] By the time of this comment, in 1788, the *grand habit* was no longer worn except for court presentations, royal state occasions and for the ceremonies of the order of the Saint-Esprit. For other court events and ceremonies the *grande robe à la française* or *robe parée*, worn over a medium-sized hoop, replaced the *grand habit* on the orders of Marie-Antoinette. Such *toilettes de cérémonie* can be seen in Moreau's illustrations to the *Monument du costume* (pls 36 and 37).

In England, too, by the late 1770s the *robe à la française* was worn on all except the most formal occasions at the English court; it retained the treble silk (and lace) ruffles of the elbow-length sleeves which were no longer worn in ordinary dress and it was worn over a large hoop. This is what Queen Charlotte wears in her portrait by Gainsborough of 1781 (pl. 62). The artist has risen to the challenge of representing what might be regarded as an absurd sartorial confection, without overwhelming the sitter. The *sacque* is made of gold-spangled silk gauze over

white silk, flounced and furbelowed and trimmed with tasselled bunches of gold lace. It could easily look ridiculous, but the dignity of the Queen and the consummate ability of the artist to transmute the yardages of fabric (about twenty yards would be needed) into a coherent whole, makes the portrait into one of the most compelling images of monarchy. Gainsborough was lucky in the Queen's choice of fabric for her court dress, being the kind of hazy material (cobwebby gauze) that could blend in with her powdered hair, the lace and flowers in her headdress, and the landscape in the background. No artist, other than Goya, has succeeded so well in the depiction of these fragile and misty fabrics, so much a part of fashion from the last years of the eighteenth century.

Queen Charlotte was never a beauty; on her arrival in England in 1761 Walpole noted that she was rather plain and pale, but that she 'looks sensible and is genteel.' Initially reluctant to wear powder, it had become part of her public persona by the time of Gainsborough's portrait, the high-piled hairstyle that fashion demanded during the 1770s and 1780s suiting her formal style. The fact that court dress was deliberately kept behind current fashions suited a traditional and conservative queen such as Queen Charlotte, but not a stylish queen such as Marie-Antoinette who was so associated with the latest modes. Even when the French queen was painted in her *grand habit* early in her reign by a sympathetic artist such as Vigée-Lebrun, she looks awkward in the cumbersomely draped *panier*; both sitter and artist were better suited to collaborating in portraits where (as in pl. 82). Marie-Antoinette is shown in the up-to-date outfits created by her famous modiste, Rose Bertin.

The style and appearance of the *robe à la française* depended on the wearing of a hoop to create the desired cone-like form, and to allow the material at the back to flow out in an elegant fan shape. From the 1750s, however, some adventurous ladies had begun to abandon their hoops, which caused the problem of how to cope with the surplus drapery. Mrs Delany noted of a famous beauty, Lady Coventry, in 1754 that she wore 'a black silk sack, made for a large hoop, which she wore without any, and it trailed a yard on the ground'.[60] By the early 1760s Oliver Goldsmith in *The Citizen of the World* was sarcastically commenting on the English ladies who had 'laid their hoops aside', resulting in the back drapery being dragged along the ground. Gainsborough's *Lady Alston* (pl. 63) which must date from the early 1760s, shows how the problem was resolved – by bundling the drapery under the arm. Lady Alston's costume is a cream silk sack, worn with a stomacher bodice and matching petticoat of sea-green ruched silk; the puck-

63 T. Gainsborough, *Lady Alston*, c. 1761–2. Oil on canvas. Louvre, Paris. (Photo: © Réunion des musées nationaux)

ering of the silk on the skirt gives a slightly quilted look, and added a little bulk to produce the rounded appearance which the hoop had helped to sustain for so long.

A new fashion aesthetic evolves quite slowly over a period of time, as the eye gets used to the possibilities of a novel look. When hoops disappeared it was still felt that dress needed fullness and bounce at the hips, and this was provided by side-pads or by gathering the fabric of the gown up at the back and sides, or both. This is seen in the costume study by Gainsborough (pl. 64) which shows a woman in the tight-fitting English gown known as a nightgown, which, as the name implies, began life as an informal garment, but which was stylish everyday wear by the mid-eighteenth century. Depending on the fabric, trimming and accessories, it could be informal (undress) or semi-formal (full-dress), and it became increasingly popular during the 1760s as the *sacque* receded into formal life. The nightgown was a dress for walking in, part of that fashion for 'agreeable negligence' which Grosley noted in Englishwomen's costume in the 1760s, when they were seen in the morning in St James's Park in 'a short gown, a long white apron, and a hat . . .'[62]

Drawn from the life (the model is possibly one of his daughters) this study may also be related to Gainsborough's *Mary, Countess Howe* (pl. 65) of the

early 1760s.[63] Lady Howe wears an English nightgown – 'tight-bodied' was the contemporary name for the way in which the fabric of the bodice is drawn so tautly over the torso. The fabric is pink lutestring (or lustring), a summer season taffeta with a glossy sheen; Gainsborough loved to paint this shimmering silk whose colour changed in different lights. He also responded, as noted, to the difficulties created by gauzy, transparent fabrics when one colour or tone is often overlaid with another. In the portrait of Lady

65   T. Gainsborough, *Mary, Countess Howe*, early 1760s. Oil on canvas. The Iveagh Bequest, Kenwood.

64   T. Gainsborough, costume drawing, *c.* 1760–2. Black and white chalk. British Museum, London.

Howe he captures the intrinsic nature of the fine floating materials of the sleeve ruffles, apron and kerchief crossed over the bosom, but without defining precisely what they are, whether lace-edged silk gauze or fine embroidered muslin. It does not particularly matter, for the *tout ensemble* delights the eye, as it also serves to demonstrate the genteel art of deportment, how to manage yards of expensive silk and gossamer-fine accessories with grace. Yes, of course the influence of van Dyck can be seen here with regard to the pose; his full-length portrait of Elizabeth Howard, Countess of Peterborough (L.G. Stopford Sackville Collection) is a possible source. And Lady Howe's gesture of one gloved hand holding the other glove may derive from van Dyck's *Anne Carr, Countess of Bedford* (Petworth House, W. Sussex). But it might also be tentatively remarked that full-length poses for women were limited by their fashionable costume and it was quite difficult to walk in high-heeled shoes with no support arch. The hand resting on the hip and curved inwards is elegant in a Vandyckian way, but might the arm held akimbo have also aided the balance? It is worth noting, too, how many full-

length female sitters are supported by pillars or plinths (admittedly not just a pose restricted to women – but see pls 7, 15 and 27) such as Ramsay's *Lady Louisa Conolly*, 1759 (pl. 66). Again, Lady Louisa wears a wonderful pink lutestring dress, but of a rather more formal type than the nightgown worn by Lady Howe; it is trimmed with large winding furbelows on the skirt, and on the bodice with rows of green ribbon. More precise than Lady Howe's portrait with regard to the details of dress, it is somehow too exact; it is as though the costume wears the sitter, an impression accentuated by the head being too small for the body. Gainsborough, more than any other English artist in

the eighteenth century, expresses movement in the costume and pose of his sitters, who seem in harmony with the landscape around them. Ramsay, on the other hand, prefers repose, and it is perhaps no accident that his most beautiful and perceptive portraits are of women seated half-length; Lady Conolly's costume is a wonderful *tour de force* in terms of attention to detail and the crispness of the silk, but the pose is stiff and the background looks like a painted backdrop.

Pink was the eighteenth-century colour *par excellence* for women's dress; in different shades, from peachy pink, coral pink, sugar pink and a dark pink, in portraits and in surviving costume, it testifies to the popularity of a colour which suited most women, flattering and warming their complexions. It is one of the colours of carnations, Queen Charlotte's favourite flower, and of hyacinths, Madame de Pompadour's favourites; there was also a dusky pink named after the marquise which was popular for Sèvres china. Pink was especially in vogue during the period from the 1740s until into the 1770s, and Reynolds's *Mrs Abington as Miss Prue* in 1771 (pl. 67) shows the fashionable actress wearing not the costume of Congreve's 1695 play, *Love for Love*, but stylish contemporary dress, a pink silk nightgown trimmed with net and lace flounces and a white apron (although not as fine as that worn by Lady Howe). Both women wear wide black silk bracelets; these emphasised the whiteness of the skin and drew attention to the elegant gestures of the hands, particularly useful for an actress. Mrs Abington, however, as Reynolds has

66 A. Ramsay, *Lady Lousia Conolly*, 1759. Oil on canvas. Private Collection.

67 J. Reynolds, *Mrs Abington as Miss Prue in Congreve's 'Love for Love'*, 1771. Oil on canvas. Yale Center for British Art, New Haven, CT. Paul Mellon Collection.

painted her in her character as a wanton ingénue, seems about to suck her thumb with a kind of sexual coquetry which appealed to the artist (who liked the company of sexy, witty women) but which would have made Mrs Delany feel slightly affronted.

Mrs Abington excelled in roles from Restoration and contemporary comedy, which required a profound knowledge of social graces and the costume which was appropriate. She seems to have acted as a kind of fashion consultant,

> constantly employed in driving about the capital to give her advice concerning the modes and fashions of the day. She is called in like a physician, and recompensed as if she were an artist. There never is a marriage or ball in which she is not consulted . . . As she never appears on the stage but in the most elegant dress, her taste is sure to be copied by all the ladies who happen to be spectators.[64]

William Barker credited her with the introduction of a relaxed informality in dress; she has 'introduced that species of dress consonant to every idea of natural elegance, in which the body is left to that freedom so congenial to common sense . . .', and which advanced an ideal of deportment far from the artifice promoted by the dancing-masters who 'teach their pupils to walk in curved lines'.[65]

Curved lines, then, which had reached their apogee with the Rococo in the middle decades of the eighteenth century, were on their way out by the 1770s, to be replaced by simpler, more natural styles, even though Barker does not go into details as to what these might be as popularised by Mrs Abington, who, at least in her portrait by Reynolds, looks prettily curved. In fact, although curves in the form of three-dimensional Rococo trimmings were passé by this time, there was a new feeling that dress with its softly rounded forms, should reflect the female body beneath; it could thus claim to be more 'natural'. Dress began to be released from the formal, triangular constraints of the mid-eighteenth century (as typified, for example, in Ramsay's *Lady Conolly*) and turned into a variety of less formal styles which could be worn in different ways,

A convenient simplification has been made so far between the formal robe *à la française* with its flowing back drapery, and the less formal English nightgown with its tight-fitting bodice and modest ornamentation. All kinds of stereotypes have been written into the fondness of the French for loose gowns and the English preference for being tightly laced (strait-laced), even when wearing the robe *à la française*. However, during the 1770s the French began to adopt a number of English styles, such as the close-bodied gown which they named a robe *à l'anglaise*. At

first the robe *à la française* was easily turned into a robe *à l'anglaise* by sewing down the back pleats, and thus forming a continuous line from the bodice into the skirt. During the 1780s there was a complete division of bodice and skirt at the waist; the skirt was set with tiny pleats into the bodice with particular fullness at the hips to help create (with the aid of hip pads or side rumps) the bounce and movement that characterises dress in this decade. Another way to create the fashionable bulk at the back and sides of the dress was to kilt up the overskirt by means of interior or exterior loops, buttons or tassels to form swags of material. This style had originated during the 1770s and was known as *à la polonaise*; a good example can be seen in Moreau's *Sortie de l'Opéra* (pl. 37) where in the centre right the back view of a fashionable theatre-goer shows such a festooned draping of the overgown.[66] The swags could be arranged to suit the taste of the wearer for it was a versatile style, which went well with the light floating silk taffetas of the 1770s and the layers of silk gauze and muslin of the 1780s. Gainsborough's *The Mall* (1783; pl. 68) shows some of the ways in which the dresses are looped up to form diaphanous puff-balls, or else allowed to trail on the ground. Walpole well described the painting as 'all a-flutter like a lady's fan', as a group of fashionable ladies and their self-effacing escorts parade in their finery in the Mall in St James's Park, which was the place to see and be seen, to gossip and to show off new clothes between twelve and two, especially on a Sunday. Madame Roland, visiting London in 1784, noted the dress in detail: women wore

> in general, white gowns of very fine muslin made exactly like those which we have borrowed from them, but generally drawn up in festoons by strings that pass underneath the train of the gown, and suspend it a little above the skirt of the petticoat; they all have large or small caps under the hat; the latter is very diversified in its form, and often overloaded with a quantity of ribbons . . .

Such women tended, she says, to be middle class, whereas those of the upper class, with aristocratic disdain for practicality, wore gowns which were 'longer and always trailing'.[67] It seems likely that for this scene, Gainsborough used small dressed dolls; W.T. Whitley states that the artist William Collins possessed a little model of a woman 'dressed by the great painter's hand'[68] which may have been used for some of the fashion-plate figures that people this *jeu d'esprit*.

In her comment, Madame Roland refers to the style of dress which the French had borrowed from the English, the robe *à l'anglaise*, and of which the *polonaise* was a variant – indeed the newly established fashion magazines list many names for this type of

gown, some called after famous society ladies, such as the Duchess of Devonshire. The *robe à l'anglaise* could be quite formal – what the *Encyclopédie méthodique* (1785) called 'un grand négligé' – with an open bodice fastening over a kind of stomacher front, and with elbow-length sleeves. It could be worn with a closed front-fastening bodice or (and this was particularly fashionable in the 1780s) it could have a bodice that closed at the top of the central front and then sloped away at the sides leaving a triangular gap to be filled in by a false 'waistcoat' or 'vest'; it was always worn as an open gown, with the skirt either matching or contrasting.

In the 1780s one of the most popular variations on the *robe à l'anglaise* was the redingote, which the French had adapted from the English greatcoat or riding coat; this had long tight sleeves to the wrist and echoed masculine styles in its caped collar and double-breasted fastening or false waistcoat front. Various views of this fashionable dress can be seen in an engraving by Louis Le Coeur of *The Palais Royal Garden Walk* (1787; pl. 69), as can the vast ribboned hats which feature so prominently in French and English women's costume during this decade. The Palais Royal was originally a large garden owned by the duc d'Orléans, who had it enclosed and remodelled during the 1780s, installing cafés and shops which sold, as John Villiers noted in 1788, 'everything

68 T. Gainsborough, *The Mall*, 1783. Oil on canvas. Copyright the Frick Collection, New York.

69   L. Le Coeur after C.-L.
Desrais, *The Palais Royal
Garden Walk*, 1787.
Engraving. Bibliothèque
Nationale, Paris.

that is rich, brilliant and beautiful'. Like the Mall in St James's Park, it was one of the places for the fashionable world to gather.

Comparing plates 68 and 69 there seems at first to be a curious reversal of the usual fashion allegiances during the 1780s, when the English style appears to be based on a soft, downy femininity, and that of the French more reliant on a harder, more tailored line as part of their Anglomania. But in both images there is a process of selection at work, which serves, almost to the extent of caricature, to pick out and exaggerate certain styles. Gainsborough was possibly inspired by fashion plates to select the type of fluffy, layered, gauzy costume which harmonised best with the hazy foliage of his landscape; Claude-Louis Desrais (after whose work *The Palais Royal Garden Walk* was engraved) was a well-known fashion artist, whose concern was to promote the latest styles invented by the *modistes*, such as the redingotes and the elaborate headdresses seen here.

On the whole it would appear that fashionable Frenchwomen were less inclined than their English counterparts to be portrayed in the more obviously masculine, structured garments such as the riding habits in which many English ladies are painted during the 1780s. The greatcoat could be converted into the chic redingote, but the French were not accustomed to see women wearing riding habits as a walking costume, which was the case in England – it was too obviously a *sportif*, masculine garment. Even in England there were grumbles that greatcoat-dresses and riding habits, along with the new low-heeled shoes, gave women more freedom of movement to indulge in swaggering masculine deportment. *The*

Gentleman's Magazine for February 1781 has some 'Remarks on the Rage of the Ladies for the Military Dress', in which women are criticised for their propensity, even in summer, for wearing 'cloth riding habits instead of their cool chintzes'. Some women, the author claims, have even taken to masculine or military hairstyles and hats; he instances one who wore 'a whisking queue', another 'a greasy braid' and one in 'a vast hat with a cockade'. Furthermore, the satire continues, one woman had even been sighted in 'a pair of tight leathern breeches' from which she pulled a watch 'and returned it to its place with a most officer-like air'.[69] During the 1780s there was war (against America) and the threat of war (from France which had sided with the rebellious colonies) and a heightened sense of military alertness which resulted in the formation of a number of militia regiments. Visiting local militia camps to watch the men drilling and to be entertained by the officers became a fashionable pastime, and many women had habits made in the colours of their husband's regiments.

Francis Wheatley's portrait of Mrs Stevens (pl. 70) shows the sitter in a riding habit, comprising jacket and skirt of mole-coloured wool, worn with a striped silk waistcoat with large revers, a masculine shirt with pleated ruffle and a plain cravat knotted in a bow at the neck. The coat is so tight across the chest by this date (*c.*1790) that it can only fasten edge to edge with hooks and eyes; this is true also of men's formal dress at this period when the coat slopes sharply away from mid-torso. On the ledge on which Mrs Stevens rests her arm is a black hat edged with gold braid and trimmed with black ostrich feathers. It is a restrained and stylish ensemble, with little touches to lighten the

70 (facing page left)   F. Wheatley, *Mrs Stevens*, *c.*1790. Oil on canvas. Yale Center for British Art, New Haven, CT. Paul Mellon Collection.

austerity: the tiny jewelled stick-pin in the frilled jabot, the gold watch hanging at the waist from a ribbon and the silver buttons on the jacket, one of which (on the sleeve) the sitter has forgotten to do up. The muted colour of the costume is in line with fashionable trends during the 1780s for the outdoor wear for both sexes. Betsy Sheridan in 1785 noted that for women's riding habits the most popular colour was 'pitch . . . a sort of blackish green', but that also 'dark blues are very general – indeed all dark colours are fashionable, cambrick frills and white waistcoats. Rather large yellow buttons. The most fashionable Hat a large black beaver with gold Braid . . .'[70]

By the 1770s other jacket and skirt styles were to be seen in the wardrobe of a fashionable woman, both in France and in England. Some of these jackets derived from the costume of working-class women, first taken up by the bourgeoisie in France and then by the upper classes; they were shortened, tightened and given a variety of fashionable names such as *caraco* or *pierrot*. Instead of the wool and wool and linen mixtures of working-class jackets and bodices, the new fashionable styles were made of silk or cotton. In England, too, various types of jacket were popular forms of fashionable undress, and there is a rare, early depiction of such an outfit in Reynolds's *Sophia Pelham*, exhibited at the Royal Academy in 1774 (pl.

71). Described by the *Public Advertiser* as 'Mrs Pelham, whole length, in a flowered muslin Brunswick dress, feeding her poultry', the sitter is shown in a thigh-length jacket with an upper sleeve edged with ruched cotton and a pink ribbon, a matching skirt with a large hem flounce and a bodice tying with pink ribbon at the neck. Her fine lawn apron is caught up

71 (above) J. Reynolds, *Sophia Pelham*, 1774. Oil on canvas. The Earl of Yarborough.

century the amount and the variety of cotton textiles increased enormously.[71]

Not until the very end of the century did the French cotton industry radically increase its output, and this – for political reasons – was more towards the cheaper, printed fabrics than the light, fragile muslins. These were imported from India (F.-A. de Garsault in his *L'Art de la lingerie*, 1771, said that the majority came from Bengal and Pondicherry) and from England, even during times of war. De Garsault's treatise (one of a series of such works dealing with the arts and crafts and published by the Paris Académie des Sciences) lists the huge amount of linen – the term encompasses all kinds of linens and cottons – which people of fashion required, 'tant pour la nécessité que pour la propreté, & même pour le luxe'. The cult of *déshabillé* was well established in France, and Joseph-Siffred Duplessis's *Madame de Saint-Maurice* (1776; pl. 72) shows a stylish *negligé du matin*. Admired for its truthfulness – both in capturing the honest likeness of the sitter and in the quality of the fabrics – when it was exhibited at the Salon in 1777, it is a useful portrait for the dress historian in the precision of the details of such an informal costume. Madame de Saint-Maurice wears an embroidered muslin front-buttoning bodice and short gown; the skirt, also of embroidered muslin, has an under-petticoat of pink silk, a colour that is picked up in the ribbons of the jacket and at the bosom. It is a good example of a portrait where the artist is totally in harmony with the sitter's wish to be represented in the relative simplicity of an informal *toilette*.

The growing predominance of white as a colour for fashionable dress, particularly during the 1780s, is reflected in the portraiture of the time. White satin and taffeta reflected the light and produced brilliant highlights; layers of silk gauze and muslin either on their own or over pastel-coloured opaque silks could achieve more subtle effects. Styles in dress that were less decorated than in previous decades appealed more to artists, including Reynolds, who seems, during the 1780s, to recover his interest in painting female fashions. His portrait of the Waldegrave sisters of 1781 (pl. 73) is a study in sisterly unity and domestic virtue. Dressed in white silk *polonaise* dresses over muslin skirts, with lace-trimmed fichus over their shoulders, the filmy costumes echo the pale grey of their powdered hair. From left to right, Maria holds a skein of silk, which Laura winds on to a card, and Horatia embroiders muslin on her tambour frame. The embroidered bag on the table would have contained sewing impedimenta (silks, cards, needles, scissors, etc.) and was to become a fashion accessory in its own right at the very end of the century, the forerunner of the handbag.

The style of dress which was to have the most

72 J.-S. Duplessis, *Madame de Saint-Maurice*, 1776. Oil on canvas. The Metropolitan Museum of Art, New York. Bequest of James A. Aborn, 1968.

with her basket as she holds it against her waist to scatter the grain. It is a pretty pastoral image, the artist happy to paint the simplicity of real dress when it suited the mood. With the growing mood towards simplicity in dress during the second half of the eighteenth century, fabrics such as cotton became newly fashionable. In England cotton textiles had been banned in 1721 with the aim of protecting the English silk industry – legislation aimed mainly at the popular printed Indian calicoes. Like all such laws, they were circumvented by the rich and influential, and contemporary letters and diaries, as well as surviving samples in scrapbooks, indicate that calicoes continued to be worn; in any case, the law excluded the Indian muslins which began to be very popular for fashionable wear from the 1760s. In 1774 the law banning the importation of all cotton fabrics was lifted, and this gave greater impetus to domestic manufacture; during the last quarter of the eighteenth profound influence on future developments in the Neoclassical period, was the *chemise à la reine*, which derived its name from the costume worn in a controversial portrait of Queen Marie-Antoinette exhibited at the Salon of 1783 (pl. 74). The origins of this dress may lie in the simple cotton dresses, *robes à la créole*, favoured by French ladies in the West Indies and brought to France during the 1770s. Vigée-Lebrun first saw the Queen wearing a chemise gown at Marly in the mid-1770s, and she wore this kind of dress when pregnant with her first child in 1778. It was comfortable and flattering, a simple tube of muslin pulled on over the head (a radical departure from the established form of dress which women stepped into, like a coat, and which had a number of constituent parts); the chemise fastened with a drawstring at the neck and there was sometimes a double falling collar, as in the Vigée-Lebrun portrait. To the modern eye the dress is modest and flattering, in line with established moves towards greater simplicity in costume during the 1780s, but the fact that it was based on the shape and fabric of a woman's shift caused consternation when seen in a portrait of the Queen, and Vigée-Lebrun's painting was removed from the Salon. The next year the dress appeared in the *Gallerie des Modes* as the *chemise à la reine* with a double collar, tied with ribbon at the neck, but open down the front. The only chemise gown thought to exist in a British museum (at the Gallery of English Costume in Manchester), dates from the mid- to late 1780s and is also open down the front; it is of white figured muslin with slots in the plain muslin sleeves so they can be gathered up into puffs, as in the Vigée-Lebrun portrait of Marie-Antoinette.

It is one of the minor ironies of history that this style of dress which, in a more structured form, became the famous Neoclassical chemise as worn by famous Directoire beauties, was first made popular by

74 E.-L. Vigée-Lebrun (after), *Queen Marie-Antoinette*, *c*.1783. Oil on canvas. National Gallery of Art, Washington. Timken Collection.

Marie-Antoinette. The *Correspondance secrète, politique et littéraire* in September 1779 attributed the popularity of the style to the Queen's fondness for the pastoral life: 'Parées de chapeaux de paille unis & comme de simples Bergères, Sa Majesté, Madame la Comtesse d'Artois, Madame la Comtesse Jules de Polignac passent les beaux momens du jour en promenades champêtres dans le bois, dans les prairies'.[72]

In 1784 the Duchess of Devonshire, one of the great leaders of fashion in England, attended a concert 'in one of the muslin chemises with fine lace that the Queen of France gave me'[73] and the style, as the fashion magazines and countless letters and diaries record, became all the rage. Lady Jerningham wrote to her daughter Charlotte in 1786 on the immense popularity of white muslin dresses which 'are certainly the prettyest at your age, and are wore entirely here by the young people with sashes...'.[74] Two such dresses can be seen in plate 75, Angelica Kauffman's *Lady Elizabeth Foster* (1786), and in plate 76, Rowlandson's *Mrs Abington*. Lady Betty, the great friend of the Duchess of Devonshire (and of the Duke whom she eventually married) was painted in Naples, with the island of Ischia in the background. It is one of the most charming of all eighteenth-century portraits, the Leghorn straw hat, edged and trimmed in black silk and decorated with black and white feathers, acting as a frame for the face. According to the German J.W. Archenholz, 'the most elegant part of an Englishwoman's apparel is her hat, which is usually adorned with ribbands and feathers'.[75]

73 J. Reynolds, *The Ladies Waldegrave*, 1781. Oil on canvas. National Gallery of Scotland, Edinburgh.

75 A. Kauffman, *Lady Elizabeth Foster*, 1786. Oil on canvas. National Trust, Ickworth.

bum rolls and starched kerchiefs (which the French called *fichus menteurs* for they falsely increased the size of the bosom), which is such a staple in the work of Rowlandson and other social satirists, was just the latest way of distorting the female body. Such artificial aids to 'beauty' were picked up by the caricaturists who, coincidentally, flourished during the 1770s and 1780s, when some of the fashions were at their most exaggerated.

Nathaniel Dance's *The Introduction*, of the late 1770s (pl. 77) gives some idea of the ways in which dress and hairstyles were seen as out of all proportion to each other and to the natural shape of the body. The slim figure of the young man is quite insignificant in comparison to the two fearsome ladies with their tightly boned bodices, wide circumference of skirt (formed by hoops, side rumps and bum rolls) and towering hairstyles decorated with lace, flowers and feathers.

To reach such heights, hair was padded out with a variety of substances – false hair, cotton wool and horsehair were just some of the pleasanter materials, according to the caricaturists – and then powdered and ornamented. Feathers were particularly popular, a fashion in England set by the Duchess of Devonshire and in France by Marie-Antoinette, although her mother the Empress Maria Theresa disapproved, saying it was a style worn by actresses and not fit for a Queen of France. In the spring of 1775 the German scientist and critic Georg Christoph Lichtenberg noted his first sight of feathers in London, 'four, five or six big ostrich feathers, white, blue, red and black together; they quiver at the slightest movement';[76] by

76 (above) T. Rowlandson, *Mrs Abington Reclining on a Couch, c.* 1786–7. Pencil, wash and watercolour. Yale Center for British Art, New Haven, CT. Paul Mellon Collection.

77 N. Dance, *The Introduction, c.*1778–9. Pencil. Yale Center for British Art, New Haven, CT. Paul Mellon Collection.

The white cotton chemise gown which Lady Betty wears, with its double frilled collar and waist sash, is similar to that worn by Mrs Abington, although the latter's sleeves are slightly longer, and the pattern of pale blue stripes over part of the dress indicates a printed muslin. But Rowlandson's portrait of the now plump, middle-aged actress, which dates from the later 1780s, is distinctly less flattering than Kauffman's image of Lady Betty Foster to modern eyes. The rounded female figure of the 1780s, aided by hip pads, the following year Mrs Delany thought that women's headdresses were like the Tower of Babel, stretching to the sky.

A number of critics thought it surprising that artists had not influenced the appearance of women's hair. In spite of the claim by the *Town and Country Magazine* in 1779 that Reynolds had been instrumental in persuading women to be painted in less elaborate and more classical hairstyles,[77] this was not apparent to Sophie von la Roche when she visited England in 1786. She did 'not find the general taste in pompous hair-dressing . . . at all pretty and graceful. Perhaps the fact that I had pictured English women like the originals of Reynolds' pictures, nobly and simply attired with Greek coiffure, accounts for this'.[78]

The most comprehensive criticism of women's hair was made in William Barker's *Treatise on the Principles of Hair-Dressing*, (?1780) in which the 'Deformities of Modern Hair-dressing are pointed out, and an elegant and natural Plan recommended, upon Hogarth's immortal System of Beauty'. The author's main thesis is that, as the body is rounded, so should dress and hairstyles be; straight lines were to be avoided, whether in the shape of stays or in hair where 'the oval is lengthened to a risible stretch'. He urged women to follow 'the works of an Angelica Kauffman, Sir J. Reynolds, Cipriani, &c, pointing out the quintescence of elegance in a style diametrically opposite to the depraved taste of the present day', but most of all they should look at Hogarth's 'admirable Analysis of Beauty' for its praiseworthy abhorrence of straight lines, if they 'mean to attain to elegance of dress and deportment'.[79]

By the time that Barker was composing his treatise, around 1780, female fashions were beginning to move away from the styles that Dance had exaggerated in *The Introduction* – the tightly laced bodice, the skirt like a decorated lampshade and the soaring hairstyle – to a softer silhouette, albeit one which might appear too rounded for Hogarth, whose particular fondness was for a shallower curve. Two paintings by Gainsborough indicate the directions in which women's fashion were progressing during the 1780s. His portrait of the actress Sarah Siddons (pl. 78) of *c*.1783–5 shows her in a blue and white striped wrapping gown, tied at the waist with a blue silk sash; she holds a fox-fur muff and the same fur edges her yellow silk mantle. Her striking features, particularly her long nose, are emphasised by the stylish angle of the black beaver hat trimmed with ribbon and ostrich feathers; Walpole noted of her appearance in 1782 that she was handsome, with a good figure, but 'neither nose or chin [are] according to the Greek standard'. Walpole also disliked the style of gown she wears, called a levite (the name derived from the

quasi-'oriental' stage costume customarily worn in Racine's *Athalie* by the Jewish priestesses) which he claimed was like 'a man's nightgown bound round with a belt'. Such wrapping-gowns had been popular throughout the eighteenth century as informal indoor dress, and adapted by a number of artists as a kind of 'timeless' costume parallel to the dressing-gowns worn by men. The most fashionable modiste, Rose Bertin, popularised the levite gown, which she supplied to her clients, including Marie-Antoinette. Sarah Siddons, in her portrait by Gainsborough, clearly realises the dramatic effect of the contrast between the softly draped style of the dress and the crisp pattern of the plain blue stripes on a white ground.

Whereas Mrs Siddons is portrayed in a real costume, an ensemble of her own choosing, Lady Sheffield in her portrait by Gainsborough (pl. 80) of 1785, shows the artist's preference for blending elements of

78 T. Gainsborough, *Sarah Siddons*, *c*.1783–5. Oil on canvas. National Gallery, London.

Both Gainsborough portraits demonstrate the importance of headwear during the 1780s; the more flattened but equally frizzed hairstyles of that decade were better able to accommodate hats than those of the 1770s when hair was so high. Mrs Siddons's hat is a structured affair; that of Lady Sheffield is more akin to the softer silk and ribbon confections that were the forte of the French *marchandes de modes*. These were called *poufs* (they were often as large as a small padded couch) and provided fertile grounds for the imagination of the modistes in their use of allusions, both personal and in relation to the wider world. A *pouf aux sentiments*, for example, could relate to the wearer and her interests in a form of truly personalised millinery; the *Correspondance secrète* stated solemnly that if, say, the English widow of an admiral were to order a hat from Beaulard (a fashionable designer): '...le marchand porta deux jours après à l'étrangère un bonnet qui fit l'admiration de tous les cercles. Des bouillons de gaze y représentoient parfaitement une mer agitée, mille brimborions différens imitoient des vaisseaux, une flotte complette &c.'[80] Sometimes headwear served to comment on fashionable crazes and topical events; there were *poufs* inspired by the rage for ballooning, by popular plays like Beaumarchais's *Marriage of Figaro*, by French victories

79 (above) Gainsborough, *Lady Sheffield* (detail of pl. 80).

80 T. Gainsborough, *Sophia Charlotte, Lady Sheffield*, 1785. Oil on canvas. The Alice Trust, Waddesdon Manor.

fantasy into fashionable dress. The gown is a pale yellow silk *robe à l'anglaise*, with a trailing overskirt; Gainsborough has added to the dress a central ribbon bow, pearls twining round the arms and edging the top of the bodice, and a gauzy Vandyke collar – all slightly fanciful touches which nonetheless fit well with contemporary fashion. Vandyckian poses (Lady Sheffield's is derived from the portrait of Elizabeth Howard, Countess of Peterborough (L.G. Stopford Sackville), reversed, and van Dyck dress with its soft lace, natural waistline and softly muted colours, found an appreciative echo in the fashions of the 1780s. The hat, a concoction of satin, ribbons and pearls, also shows the influence of van Dyck in the spiky, pointed appliquéd silk on the underside of the brim (pl. 79). Such a decorative feature, known as Vandyking or Vandykes, was a popular motif in women's dress and accessories during the later eighteenth century.

in the American War of Independence and by the storming of the Bastille.

Many of these *poufs à la circonstance* (i.e. with topical allusions) were created by Rose Bertin, who was particularly expert in catching the fleeting whims of fashion and who supplied the aristocracy and crowned heads of Europe, including the Queen of France. Introduced to Marie-Antoinette, then Dauphine, in the early 1770s, she soon became an essential part of the Queen's establishment, visiting Versailles twice a week to advise and consult on the royal wardrobe. Under Bertin's tutelage, the not especially beautiful Queen (the Habsburg jaw and prominent nose were a bit heavy for eighteenth-century taste) became a woman of supreme elegance. According to Vigée-Lebrun, the Queen had a wonderful transparent complexion, superb arms and a grace in deportment which was unrivalled. Her preference for simpler styles in dress has already been noted with regard to the famous *chemise à la reine* as depicted by Vigée-Lebrun. An equally refined image can be seen in Lie-Louis Perin-Salbreux's portrait of 1782 (pl. 81), once thought to be Marie-Antoinette, but now identified as her sister Marie-Caroline, Queen of Naples and the Two Sicilies. The Queen is portrayed in a morning costume of white satin, the lustrous folds of the silk falling over the arm of her chair as she sits, book in hand, leaning on a fine secretaire. Fresh roses in her hair complement the mood of relaxed informality in the costume which was appropriate to the private nature of the portrait.

Public portraits of the French Queen were a different matter and the correct balance had to be achieved between the sitter as a royal personage, and – especially in an age of *sensibilité* – as a royal mother. In 1785 the Swedish artist Adolf-Ulrik Wertmüller painted a group of the *Queen, the Dauphin and Madame Royale* in the English Garden at the Petit Trianon at Versailles. The painting (in the Nationalmuseum, Stockholm) shows the Queen stylishly dressed in a *robe à la turque* (a version of the *robe à l'anglaise*) of brown silk over white, and a *pouf* of ribbons and feathers by Bertin; the little Dauphin, clutching his mother's skirt, wears a silk skeleton suit (an English style comprising a jacket and trousers, buttoned together at the waist) with the badge and ribbon of the Saint-Esprit, and his sister appears in a muslin chemise gown over a blue slip.

The painting was not well received for reasons that are somewhat obscure, the main one being that it was too casual. In spite of the fact that there was no impropriety in the costume of the royal group, critics possibly felt that the poses of the figures were too relaxed and informal, that Marie-Antoinette was depicted more as *mère de famille* than as queen and mother of her people. A portrait was called for where

the Queen was to be represented showing her children to the Nation, a grandiose and typically French concept; the resulting commission was Vigée-Lebrun's *Marie-Antoinette and her Three Children* of 1786 (pl. 82). The Queen wears a red velvet *robe à l'anglaise* trimmed with sable and a matching *pouf* decorated with white silk, ostrich feathers and an egret (heron) plume; her costume is trimmed with the royal French lace, *point d'Alençon*, which also features in the dress of her children, Madame Royale, the Dauphin (again in the fashionable skeleton suit with the insignia of the Saint-Esprit) and the baby duc de Normandie on his mother's lap. Marie-Antoinette's fashionable costume was probably a Bertin creation; as the most prominent *modiste* to the Queen, her taste was trusted to help produce an image of elegant

81   L.-L. Perin-Salbreux, *Marie-Caroline of Austria, Queen of Naples*, 1782. Oil on canvas. Private Collection.

regality; with the clever touch for which she was famous, Bertin's dress for her royal patron was based on the ancient French royal colours, white, red and black. It was a sense of the appropriate allusion, allied to a skill in the decoration of costume, that was the forte of the *marchandes de modes*. In 1776, almost one hundred years after women were officially established as *couturières*, the complementary profession of *modiste* was recognised. In a period when the basic styles of dress did not undergo radical change, decoration – ribbons, flounces, lace, flowers, etc. – became all-important. Hitherto in the shadow of the fashionable mercers, the new corporation of *marchandes de modes, plumassières et fleuristes* (their full title) far outshone the *couturières* whose work, in theory, they were supposed to supplement. The *Encyclopédie méthodique* (1785) described the role of the *marchande de modes*:

celle qui dispose & vend tous les petits objets qui servent à la parure . . . Le taffetas, la gaze, la blonde, les dentelles, les agrémens, les rubans de toutes espèces, les fleurs, les plumes &c sont les matières qu'elle emploie . . . Son art n'est pas de fabriquer aucune chose; il consiste à former ingénieusement des résultats nouveaux, des ornemens variés & gracieux de toutes les productions légères des autres arts . . .[81]

Like the publisher of prints, the *modiste* had to be up to the minute in catching the public mood; she had to be skilled in the nuances of colours, the exact placing of lace and ribbons to be both witty and flattering. In the rage for novelty which is the main guiding force of fashion, the *modiste* (and to a lesser degree, her English equivalent, the milliner) cast her net wide for inspiration – which she might find in sources as varied as politics, courtly pastimes, fashionable literature, pastoral paintings and the romance of the past. French fashions, claimed Mercier, were an art form – 'art chéri, triomphant, qui dans ce siècle a reçu des honneurs, des distinctions' – which had entered the palaces of kings and the houses of the nobility; 'tout ce qui concerne la parure a été adopté avec une espèce de fureur par toutes les femmes de l'Europe'.[82] *Modistes* such as Bertin, with an international clientele, were largely responsible for the acceleration of fashion change at the very top of society, but their designs would not have had maximum exposure (thus furthering the progress of the modes among the slightly less elevated levels of upper-class society) without the aid of the fashion magazines, which during the last quarter of the eighteenth century gradually replaced travelling dressed dolls as a medium of information on dress.[83]

It is perhaps no accident that writing about fashion, both at a fairly superficial journalistic level and at a deeper philosophical level, began to intensify during the second half of the eighteenth century. Dress, which has always of course been a visible part of the modern world, seems to gain more credence from this time onwards, as it responds to the quickening pace of political, social and cultural change. The Barthesian thesis (in his *Système de la mode*, 1967) that fashion *is* only the language of fashion, in written form, has some element of truth in it, particularly during the last quarter of the century with the outpouring of publications devoted to dress. Some, like the *Monument du costume* (1789) both admired and criticised contemporary dress with a kind of philosophical detachment. Others purported only to describe the latest styles, aware that their writings could only be ephemeral. And a third category claimed to incorporate some educational content; the aim of the *Lady's Magazine*, for example, was 'to combine amusement with instruction, to convey useful information, to register remarkable events, and especially to afford a Repository for the productions of Female Genius', in other words the creations of the dressmakers, although these are very rarely named.

Both in France and England there were occasional, random publications on fashion throughout the eighteenth century, but only from the 1770s can the regular appearance of information on dress be noted, firstly with the rather prosaic *Lady's Magazine* from 1770, and then the comprehensive and beautifully illustrated *Gallerie des modes et costumes français* from 1778 to 1787 which used the services of such artists as Claude-Louis Desrais and François-Louis-Joseph Watteau. The idea behind the *Gallerie* was to produce a permanent record of the most elegant French fashions, although, curiously, only two costume designers are mentioned, the court tailor P.-N. Sarrazin and Rose Bertin. The liveliness of the attitudes in the plates in this publication must have been the result of close collaboration between the artists and the tailors and *modistes*.[84]

Cheaper fashion magazines were published for a wider market, and the *Cabinet des modes*, which began in 1785 was the most important of these; in the following year, reflecting the prevailing Anglomania, it turned into the *Magasin des modes nouvelles françaises et anglaises*. Published every two weeks, the *Cabinet des modes* was able to communicate a wide range of styles as French fashion became more eclectic; it noted how the very names of fashion indicated diverse influences – the *robes à l'anglaise, à la polonaise, à la turque*, and so on. It is probably to this magazine that Mercier refers in his *Tableau de Paris*, when talking of the *marchandes de modes*:

Elles ont dans l'imagination des resources inépuisables pour varier le goût de la parure: un journal fait exprès rend compte de tous ces

no better, being 'Decoys for the Unwary' and their shops 'Places for Assignations'.[86] Here, the milliners are advertisements for their own wares, such as the large lace, gauze and muslin caps and the folded kerchiefs; one woman sews a ruched silk muff which would complement the fashionable rounded headdress. By the 1780s pretty printed cottons were part of the wardrobe of many up-to-date women (see the seated milliner on the left), but were still too informal to be represented in portraits.

As noted, artists preferred to paint plain fabrics for the costume in their portraits as they were less fussy, less distracting from the character of the sitter. Plain fabrics could range from the highly luxurious velvet and sable as worn by Marie-Antoinette in plate 82, to the simple muslin in the same artist's portrait of the Queen in plate 74. Furthermore, they tested the skills of the artist far more than the meticulous rendering of a repeat pattern could do. But again, compared to what women actually owned, what is depicted in portraits is a selection of garments and fabrics that appealed to the artist's eye.

In Lawrence's portrait of Eliza Farren (1790; pl. 84), the artist has combined the luxury of fur with the simplicity of muslin, to produce a stunning image of a stylish sitter. Lawrence seems to have had a particular feel for textiles which evoked in him an emotional response; he is the only English artist who can be compared with Ingres in his rendering of the different qualities of fabrics. It seems, according to his biographers, that even as a young man he felt able to suggest a choice of clothes to his sitters, including Queen Charlotte who was famously not amused at her bareheaded image now in the National Gallery.

Eliza Farren also looks bare-headed, although a glimpse of a fashionable white bandeau can be seen on the crown of her head. She wears a white muslin chemise gown which trails on the ground, but the portrait is dominated by a white satin hooded mantle trimmed with fox and a vast fox muff also lined with white satin; the blue silk ribbon on the muff is an inspired touch. Lawrence was upset by some critics who carped about the supposed inconsistencies between the bare arms (hardly visible) and the fur-trimmed cloak, and between the cloak and the summer landscape. Edmund Burke consoled the artist, saying 'Never mind what little critics say, for painters' proprieties are always best'.[87]

The author of *Woman, Sketches of the History, Genius, Disposition, Accomplishments, Customs and Importance of the Fair Sex* (1790) also seems to be on Lawrence's side: 'It is wrong to believe that cold climates should prevent people from wearing thin dresses; by means of furred cloaks, which may be used in the open air, one may wear an under-dress of the lightest stuff possible'.[88] In any case, Eliza Farren, an

ajustements variés qui changent non seulement pour la cour, la ville, ou la campagne, mais encore pour le salon, le cabinet, le boudoir, les chaises longues . . .[85]

Given the importance of the *marchandes de modes* in France and the milliners in England with regard to the outfitting of fashionable ladies, it is not surprising that the smartest women (in every sense of the word) were attracted to the profession. Their shops and workshops were in the centre of town, in the most fashionable areas, and, inevitably due to their often exalted clientele, became centres of gossip and assignation. Attractive girls were employed to entice the customer and to give advice on the latest styles and accessories. Such centres of fashion and gossip were sure also to attract men-about-town, as can be seen in Robert Dighton's *A Morning Ramble; or The Milliner's Shop* of *c*.1782 (pl. 83). Two such men, dressed in frock-coats and carrying canes (a fashionable accessory which had long replaced the swords of an earlier period) pay court to the young milliners with badinage and the offer of a visit to the masquerade. The caricaturist's view that the transactions here are more likely to be of a personal mercenary kind than the ordering of fashion accessories echoes the comments made earlier in the century in *The London Tradesman* (1747): 'A young Coxcomb no sooner is Master of an Estate, and a small Share of Brains, but he affects to deal with the most noted Milliner . . .'; the latter fare

84 T. Lawrence, *Eliza Farren, later Countess of Derby*, 1790. Oil on canvas. The Metropolitan Museum of Art, New York. Bequest of Edward S. Harkness, 1940.

actress specialising in contemporary roles (which she took on after the retirement of Mrs Abington in 1782), had a sense of what was appropriate and refined in dress; Lawrence would not have wished to diverge from the reality of this costume with its contrasts of textures, the painting of which is a tribute to his virtuoso ability. Later in his career, according to Allan Cunningham, the artist 'became a master of softening down the geometrical lines and the manifold points of modern dress into something like elegance'.[89] Although Lawrence did not generalise the costume in his portraits as Reynolds and Gainsborough had done, he did slightly mellow the sometimes exaggerated female fashions of the 1820s. There was no need to do that in 1790, for dress at the beginning of the French Revolution was really (after a number of false starts) approaching the elegant simplicity that so many artists desired.

2

Painters of Modern Life: Fashion from 1789 to 1820

How times are changed. When they had nothing better to attend to,
the fashionable Parisians were correctness itself in all that pertained to the toilette,
and were therefore thought a frivolous people;
but now they have something of more importance than dress to occupy them,
and the light airy character that was usually given them
will have no foundation in truth.
(Arthur Young, *Travels in France,* 1789)

Toute la distinction des conditions, nuance si essentielle au bonheur d'aujourd'hui,
est presque dans la manière de porter les vêtements.
(Stendhal, *Histoire de la peinture en Italie,* 1817)

The ideas of natural equality and the Manchester steam engines
together have, like a double battery levelled the high towers and
artificial structures of fashion in dress.
(William Hazlitt, *On Fashion,* 1818)

In terms of dress, the year 1789 is an arbitrary date, for the French Revolution did not initiate any dramatic change in fashion. What it did do was to act as a catalyst for the move towards the simpler and more 'democratic' styles in dress which have been noted during the 1780s. In some ways fashion could be seen to act as a Trojan horse, helping to undermine the established principles of society in just the same way as the beliefs of the *philosophes* (synthesised in the *Encyclopédie*) which aimed to popularise rational knowledge and a critical approach, gradually formed into a revolutionary creed which fatally weakened the *ancien régime* 'which had already begun to collapse under the impact of impending bankruptcy and the measures adopted to avert it'.[1]

Along with the simpler fashions of the 1780s, most notably those for men inspired by English country clothing, went a general relaxation of manners and appearance, which, as has been seen, worried some French critics who discerned therein the roots of a potentially destabilised society. Others, with the virtue of hindsight, looked back to the years before the Revolution as a time of social and political stagnation, of cynicism, of mockery and the overriding pursuit of pleasure. The comte de Ségur claimed that 'la coquetterie, la galanterie des Femmes, le libertinage des Hommes, sont les fruits d'une longue paix, du désoeuvrement, du luxe, de la richesse . . .'[2] Mary Wollstonecraft in her rambling dissertation on French society and the corruption of courts, *An Historical and Moral View of the Origin and Progress of the French Revolution* (1794), blamed 'the idle caprices of an effeminate Court', while at the same time noting the paradox that it was the abandonment of etiquette that had undermined society; the French Queen 'wished to throw aside the cumbersome brocade of ceremony without having discernment enough to perceive that it was necessary to lend mock dignity to a court where there was not sufficient virtue or native beauty to give interest or respectability to simplicity'.[3]

Visiting France in the summer of 1788, John Villiers found that 'the whole kingdom seems ripe for a Revolution; every rank is dissatisfied – they despise their king; they detest their queen'. Fear and reverence were no longer enough to prevent the voicing of discontent and the people 'now begin to conceive a relish for liberty'; politics was the main topic of conversation.[4] Over the next few years society and culture were transformed; dress, as a crucial form of visual communication, played a major part in this process – an index of the dramatic events of the times. So startling was this new sense of the urgency of change (quite removed from the familiarity and traditions of the *ancien régime*) that many people realised that the break with the past was final; a new concept of modernity evolved, which costume did much to promote. Looking back in the early nineteenth century to the years before the French Revolution, many writers recalled an age which seemed distant and remote; some regretted the lost significance of clothes in the same way that novelists during the 1920s celebrated that decade's modernity and yet looked back with some nostalgia to the vanished Europe of before the First World War.

In 1788 political and financial considerations impelled the king to summon the Estates General (which had not met since 1614); the formal opening ceremonies took place in May 1789 at Versailles. The ladies of the court ordered *grandes toilettes* from the fashionable *modistes* and at the opening session on 5 May, the Queen wore a gown of violet over a skirt of silver tissue. A taste of trouble to come was provided by the furore over the official costumes to be worn by the three Estates. The First Estate, the clergy, wore the appropriate clerical dress which ranged from the scarlet vestments of the cardinals to the humble black *soutane* of the parish *curés*. The Second Estate (the aristocracy) wore the black silk *habit à la française*, trimmed with gold braid, a lace cravat, and a plumed hat *à la Henri IV*. The Third Estate (who represented the vast majority of the people from the upper bourgeoisie to the peasants) was ordered to wear plain suits of black cloth, black stockings, a plain muslin cravat and the short black cloak worn by lawyers and the professional nobility, the *noblesse de robe*. Mary Wollstonecraft commented that '. . . the nobility were gaudily caparisoned for the show, whilst the commons were stupidly commanded to wear the black mantle that distinguishes the lawyers'.[5] This hierarchy of dress caused great offence to the Third Estate, not so much because of the sobriety of their ordained costume (this, after all, was a fashionable trend in men's attire), but because they resented the invoking of such an archaic sumptuary law, no longer relevant to the changing times. The deputies of the Third Estate wanted to wear their own clothes (as did members of the British House of Commons) and not a court-imposed costume that emphasised their lowly place in the political hierarchy.

One of the most vociferous of the protestors against these costume regulations was the comte de Mirabeau, who had joined the Third Estate and is represented, symbolically, in his costume (the only man so dressed) in the right foreground of David's *Oath of The Tennis Court* (pl. 85). One of the most striking images of the Revolution, the drawing records the stirring events of 20 June when the Third Estate, having defied the King by seceding from what they regarded as a meaningless charade, declared themselves to be a National Assembly. The scene depicts the oath sworn by the deputies to the new constitution; their arms are raised in echo of David's

85 J.-L. David, *Le Serment du Jeu de Paume*, 1791. Pen and bistre wash. Versailles. (Photo: © Réunion des musées nationaux)

Oath of the Horatii of 1784 (Paris, Louvre). On the table stands Jean-Sylvain Bailly, elected President of the National Assembly, reading the oath; like Mirabeau, he also wears the black cloth suit of the Third Estate. Most of the deputies, however (apart from those in clerical dress) wear the English-influenced styles which, as has been seen, were equated with progress and democracy; they included the coat sloping away at the sides, the waistcoat cut short across the waist and the collared redingote, which was more tailored to the body than its English original. David has emphasised the musculature of the body under the tightness of the coat; his working method was to draw the figures heroically nude and then lightly clothe them.[6] David's unfinished work, exhibited in 1791, contains elements of truth and fiction, as great propaganda does. He was probably present on this great occasion, noting in his sketchbook, '. . . beaucoup de gens font leurs serment avec les chapeaux qu'ils levent en l'air j'en ai vu le faire avec leurs chapeaux au bout de leurs cannes'.[7] He was also concerned to depict the clothing of the deputies as accurately as possible, which seems, in the main to have been fashionable costume and not the official dress of the Third Estate, which was, at best, only spasmodically worn from the beginning and which was abolished in October 1789.

By 1791 the political situation had evolved so rapidly that David's picture proved impossible to finish even though he had brought it up to date by depicting Robespierre in a prominent position (clutching his breast and standing near to Mirabeau) and including a symbolic *sans-culotte* on the left.[8] David knew the power of visual images, the symbolic importance of clothing which was to play such an important role over the next few years. Most of the deputies in the *Tennis Court* wear their own hair; only some older men, and perhaps those with aristocratic sympathies, appear in wigs. The *Journal de la mode et du goût* (15 November 1790) remarked that it was now the fashion for men, in line with the vogue for simpler styles in dress, to have their hair 'coupés et frisés comme ceux d'une tête antique'; a particularly popular hairstyle was named *à la Titus* in imitation of the actor François-Joseph Talma's appearance in the role of the Roman Emperor in Voltaire's play *Brutus* in May 1791.

The *Journal de la mode et du goût* (1790–93) records the different ways in which clothing reflected a constantly shifting political situation and the nervous tensions in society. For example, the first issue of the magazine, in February 1790, illustrates 'un homme vêtu d'un habit noir à la Révolution', a black cloth coat with a red waistcoat. Bearing in mind that black cloth had been ordered for the Third Estate, black could be interpreted as a democratic colour. But

black *silk* was the fabric worn by the nobility in their official costume, and thus might indicate aristocratic sympathies. Black was also mourning wear, and the *Journal* (15 April 1790) noted that some 'aristocrates décidés' had chosen to wear mourning dress as an expression of sorrow at the decline of the monarchy. At the beginning it seems to have been a light-hearted game – witty speculation on political identity through clothing – but during the Terror costume for men and women was guided more by a fearful instinct for self-preservation, with the adoption of plain, simple styles, than motivated by the concerns of fashion.

It was a period of confused sartorial signals. A few devoted Republicans such as Robespierre, retained *ancien-régime* styles of dress – powdered wig, silk coat and breeches. In Louis-Léopold Boilly's portrait of Robespierre (*c*.1791; pl. 86) the deputy from Arras, founder of the Jacobin Club and virtual ruler of France by the spring of 1793, wears an elegant striped silk coat over his buff-coloured *gilet* (waistcoat) and knee-breeches; even his accessories, the diamond knee-buckles and the snuff-box which he holds, echo the pre-Revolutionary past. Georges Duval, a Republican himself, remembered in his *Souvenirs de la Terreur* that 'Robespierre était poudré, frisé, parfumé, et cent fois plus muscadin qu'aucun de nous';[9] a *muscadin* was a mid-eighteenth century word for a scented fop.

As a contrast, Duval recalled the slovenly appearance of the revolutionary journalist Jean-Paul Marat

86 L.-L. Boilly, *Maximilien de Robespierre, c*.1791. Oil on canvas. Musée des Beaux-Arts, Lille.

in his threadbare coat, tricolour cockade and stockings, plush breeches, red *gilet* and unbuttoned shirt collar; his shoes were tied with string. Duval recorded a conversation between Danton and Marat, the former declaring that patriotism did not prevent the wearing of a clean shirt and a cravat.[10]

Most men chose the middle way between Robespierre's finical elegance and the unkempt appearance of Marat; they wore, as in the Oath of the Tennis Court, plain coats and redingotes. The *Journal de la mode et du goût* in February 1792 stated that it had virtually stopped describing men's dress as it had changed so little; 'les habits, pour la plupart, sont bruns ou noirs, les redingotes du plus mauvais goût; les gilets presque tous rouges'.[11] No doubt most men of the upper and middle classes were reasonably presentable in dress and appearance, but there was a general perception, particularly among foreign observers that they erred on the side of neglect in dress; this was probably due to the fact that only a few years ago, as Arthur Young stated, the French had been noted for their obsession with fashion, and seemed to have now gone to the other extreme. Helen Maria Williams, a supporter of the Revolution, thought a Frenchman was 'at pains to shew that he has wasted as few moments as it was possible at his toilette, and that his mind is bent on higher cares than the embellishment of his person';[12] Dr John Moore in the summer of 1792 found 'a great affectation of that plainness in dress and simplicity of expression which are supposed to belong to Republicans'.[13] Male portraits of the early 1790s often reveal a mixture of simplicity and a kind of dishevellment in dress, indicative of the breaking up of the old certainties. François-Xavier Fabre's portrait of Laurent-Nicolas de Joubert (*c.*1790; pl. 87) shows the sitter in his shirt-sleeves and double-breasted satin *gilet*; a striped scarf is knotted round his neck over the open shirt, and has one corner thrust through a waistcoat buttonhole. Only a short while earlier, such an upper-class or professional sitter would not have appeared in his portrait in shirt-sleeves, which were only acceptable for the images of craftsmen, or artists in the open air – like More's self-portrait of 1783 (pl. 53); it was now fashionable for men to be painted in their working clothes.

By the early 1790s some young men were beginning to replace their knee-breeches with pantaloons, tight versions of the working-class trousers. Not only were they more comfortable than breeches (which dress reformers declared to be unhealthy as they hindered the circulation at the knee) but they were more aesthetically pleasing, emphasising the unfettered line of the legs, like a statue of antiquity. Most of all, such garments paid tribute to their wearer's political views, in support of the *sans-culottes*, who by the late summer of 1792 were a potent political force.

The first Terror took place in September 1792, when a large number of prisoners suspected of counter-revolutionary views were massacred by the *sans-culottes* of the Paris *sections* (local administrative assemblies). It is to this that Walpole refers in a letter to Lady Ossory in October 1792: 'The cannibals triumph, and unless they devour one another, behold a republic of twenty millions of assassins . . . Even that wretch Philip l'Egalité will triumph, and be proud of the trousers he wears, that he may be *sans-culottes*.'[14]

Philippe-Egalité, *ci-devant* duc d'Orléans, member of the Jacobin Club and deputy to the new assembly, the National Convention of 1792, had underlined his political correctness by adopting *sans-culotte* dress, which Madame Tussaud remembered as: 'a short jacket, pantaloons and a round hat, with a handkerchief worn sailor-fashion loose round the neck, with the ends long and hanging down . . . the hair cut short without powder *à la Titus*, and shoes tied with string.'[15] Unfortunately, this studied display of sympathy with the working classes did nothing to prevent the Duke's execution a year later, in the autumn of 1793.

During the euphoria of the early months of the Revolution, most of the fashion magazines reflected the general enthusiasm for the new spirit in politics. And, as fashion feeds on novelty, there was an extra welcome for the infusion of new themes in dress inspired by such political events as the Tennis Court Oath, and the storming of the Bastille on 14 July 1789. There were textiles and accessories (buckles, jewellery, head-dresses, fans, etc.) that commemorated these events. Most of all, it was the tricolour which caught the imagination of the people. Supposedly designed by the marquis de Lafayette as a sign of unity between Paris (the city's colours were red and blue), and the monarchy (white was the Bourbon colour), it was worn by men and women in the form of a hat cockade and as a design motif in dress. For men it appeared in coats, *gilets* and stockings; some of these garments still exist.[16] Talleyrand, bishop and deputy (he had elected to sit with the Third Estate) officiated at the Fête de la Fédération to celebrate the first anniversary of the fall of the Bastille wearing a cope of red, white and blue. It was an early example of what the journalist Prudhomme described as 'l'effet puissant du langage des signes', which was to have an even greater impact on dress in the following years.

For women the tricolour motif appeared in striped ribbons and dresses. The *Journal de la mode et du goût* for 5 March 1790, noted that large numbers of women 'se montrent patriotes, en adoptant les couleurs de la Nation'; the accompanying illustration showed a woman in a gauze bonnet decorated with a tricolour cockade and ribbons, and a Circassian gown 'rayée des trois couleurs de la Nation'. The duchesse de Gontaut recalled the appearance of Madame de Genlis (now citizeness Brûlart) at a ball in Paris, 'her hair without powder, though it was still the fashion to wear it; she wore a most extraordinary costume, composed of the three revolutionary colours', as she danced to the strains of the savage Jacobin song, 'Ça Ira'.[17] It's not clear what kind of dress she was wearing, whether the fashionable tricolour stripes, or the kind of muslin embroidered with tricolour bouquets advertised in the *Journal de la mode et du goût* for 15 April 1790.

Other ways of incorporating the tricolour theme in women's dress included such tailored outfits as redingotes and riding habits, the latter had recently become popular in France among supporters of the Revolution and thus attired they were often referred to as Amazons of Liberty. Redingotes and riding habits, being derived from masculine styles, helped to promote the image of women as soldiers in the revolutionary cause; 'nous sommes devenues tous soldats' declared the *Magasin des modes nouvelles* in September 1789. Coats and riding habits were often of blue, edged with red braid; they were worn, respectively, with white linen skirts and white waistcoats. They were clearly inspired by the uniform of the National Guard, which consisted of a blue coat with white revers, red collar and cuffs and white waistcoat and breeches.

In terms of everyday dress, jacket and skirt styles were both practical and tactful, for they recalled the clothing of the working woman, however remotely.

Made of printed cottons they, too, could be of red, white and blue; made of silk they were often of sombre colours, such as the *pierrot* jacket of 'feuille-morte' satin *à la démocrate* that the *Journal de la mode et du goût* advertised in February 1792. Two versions of the short stylish *pierrot* with its characteristic back frill, can be seen in Boilly's *The Dead Mouse*, *c.*1793 (pl. 88) and in François-André Vincent's *Mademoiselle Duplant* (1793; pl. 89). Boilly's sentimentalised scene shows a woman in satin *pierrot* and skirt; as an instinctive fashion-plate artist, he lays stress on the fashionable silhouette by exaggerating the length of the satin skirt. Vincent's Mademoiselle Duplant wears a particularly stylish ensemble, consisting of a striped jacket and skirt, a starched muslin *fichu* (as is also worn in the previous plate) and a yellow shawl wound around the waist and tied at the front. The jewellery is of the simplest kind (anything else would have been politically unsound), consisting of plain gold hoops in the ears and gold links which fasten the high-collared shirt.

Another popular *déshabillé* was a sleeveless bodice worn peasant-style over the chemise gown, as can be seen in a portrait by the émigré artist Henri-Pierre Danloux, of Mademoiselle Rosalie Duthé (1792; pl. 90). Danloux met the singer, actress and courtesan (she numbered among her lovers the King's brother, the comte d'Artois) in London in 1792. It seems that she chose the rather theatrical pose herself, holding an allegorical scene with the figure of Hope looking out to sea at a departing ship, an allusion to her wish to

88   L.-L. Boilly, *The Dead Mouse*, *c.*1793. Oil on canvas. The Wallace Collection, London.

89 (facing page)   F.-A. Vincent, *Mademoiselle Duplant*, 1793. Oil on canvas. Gulbenkian Foundation, Lisbon.

return to France, an impossibility in the circumstances. In spite of her political beliefs, Mademoiselle Duthé wears the fashions which had been promoted by the French Revolution: the simple white dress, the muslin scarf knotted carelessly round her neck and the plain white silk scarf tied in a bow in her hair. The vast headdresses of the 1780s had given way to smaller hats – the fashion magazines refer to bonnets *à la paysanne*, *à la citoyenne*, *à l'Americaine* – to scarves knotted in the form of the working-woman's headwear and to bandeaux *à l'antique*.

By the summer of 1791 the political situation had deteriorated and many had fled abroad, including the King's brothers, the comte de Provence and the comte d'Artois. Increasingly, the very notion of fashion was under attack as an aristocratic and bourgeois concept. That autumn the American Gouverneur Morris noted that most of the fashionable *modistes* had left Paris, among them Rose Bertin, who took with her 'quinze caisses contenant tout ce qui peut servir à parer la femme, des étoffes, des soieries, des velours, des dentelles, des plumes, des rubans . . .'[18] Such luxury fabrics would have been out of place in a France that was rapidly moving towards a republic. The fashion magazines, which had initially welcomed the Revolution, now deplored the decline in fashion which it was felt political events had brought about. There was little scope in the repetition of the same simple styles, the chemise gowns, the jackets and skirts; the *Journal de la mode et du goût* (5 February 1792) stated that it was rare to see a woman in the formal robe (i.e. an open gown with a separate skirt) even at her marriage. A few months before, the *Journal* had commented on the prevailing taste for white; 'Ce costume sied également aux jolies femmes et à celles qui ne le sont pas, aux vieilles comme aux jeunes; tout consiste dans le choix des rubans, des nuances et des formes que la mode établit.'[19]

White was both flattering and apolitical, or rather it could be claimed either as the Bourbon colour or as a classical, republican colour; but it suited the simple *toilettes* that political expedience required. David's portrait of *Louise de Pastoret* (*c*.1792; pl. 91) shows a sitter wearing what is possibly the same kind of dress as Mademoiselle Duthé, but painted in a far more sensitive way, the artist alert to the mood of austerity which permeates this painting. Sitting in front of a stark, unfinished background, Madame de Pastoret wears a white dress with an overbodice (possibly sleeveless), blue sash at the waist and a white kerchief negligently arranged; her hair, in need of setting in curls, falls in loose waves on to her shoulders. David is always sensitive to the implications of dress in his portraits. He can paint costume and accessories with the loving absorption of Ingres, but some of his most moving images, like that of Madame de Pastoret,

91   J.-L. David, *Louise de Pastoret*, *c*.1792. Oil on canvas. The Art Institute of Chicago. The Clyde M. Carr and Major Acquisitions Funds, 1967, 228. Photograph copyright 1993. All rights reserved.

reflect in their economy of detail and bare essentials, the political and social tensions of the period.

It has been pointed out that most artists in France supported the Revolution; they were, on the whole, middle-class and progressive in their attitudes. Some did leave France in the sense of failing to return from abroad, but only a few were actually classed as *émigrés*, the most famous being Vigée-Lebrun who left in the autumn of 1789.[20] Artists enjoyed relative immunity during the revolutionary period, some, like David, taking an active part in politics and involved in state propaganda. Portrait artists, when their aristocratic patrons had vanished, turned to a wider range of sitters, painting them in their simple, everyday costume; at the Salon of 1793:

Les modèles posent dans leurs vêtements quotidiens. Les femmes sont représentées en 'chemise', avec un simple fichu voilant la poitrine. Les perruques ne sont plus à la mode; on porte les cheveux dénoués. Seul un ruban orne la tête. On porte aussi les cocardes républicaines.[21]

Portraits continued to be popular, even though some critics regarded them as a bourgeois concept; in a time of volatile politics with people unsure what the future might hold, a portrait was a personal memento, a permanent record. Modest simplicity in dress was *de rigueur* especially during the years of the Terror (1793–4), as Gérard's *Madame Lecerf* (1794; pl. 93)

90   H.-P. Danloux *Mademoiselle Rosalie Duthé*, 1792. Oil on canvas. Staatliche Kunsthalle, Karlsruhe.

shows. The artist's cousin wears the simplest style of chemise dress with a plain drawstring neckline; the fabric is either cotton or taffeta (the simplest of all silk weaves) and brown in colour. The *Journal de la mode et du goût* (15 January 1792) urged the wearing of such 'moderate' colours, in preference to black, red, white and blue, which the editor felt had become too politicised.

It was impossible, however, to remove ideology from dress. Even though the Republican authorities decreed the liberty of sartorial expression – 'chacun est libre de porter tel vêtement ou tel ajustement de son sexe qui lui convient'[22] – it would have been rash, especially during the Terror, to hint at *ancien-régime* luxury in dress. So Madame Lecerf's shawl and fichu

are of plain, matte white, and only the silk ribbon in her modest muslin cap provides a small touch of feminine frivolity. In her cap she has placed a tricolour cockade; these were made compulsory for women from September 1793 (and for men from July 1792) and their use lasted into the Directory period.

There is also a cockade, somewhat half-heartedly added, in David's portrait of Emilie Sériziat (1795; pl. 92); it is pinned to the green silk ribbon of the straw hat which she wears over a lace-trimmed cap. Like Madame Lecerf, Madame Sériziat wears a chemise gown, but a more stylish one, fitted in to the waist, and with a drawstring neckline, the strings of which pass over the shoulders, fastening at the back; David is very exact in these details. It is an ensemble both modest and elegant, suitable for all occasions in a period when nearly all distinctions of dress had disappeared. Mesdames Lecerf and Sériziat wear the kind of dress that most middle-class women (and those of the upper classes who had elected to stay in France) would have worn during the Terror and in the uneasy months after the downfall of Robespierre in July 1794.

Information on women's costume is limited after the fashion magazines fell silent in the spring of 1793; they did not re-emerge until 1797 when it seemed that the political situation had become stabilised. What information exists comes from (unillustrated) fashion supplements in such papers as the *Journal de Paris*, and the famous (although undated) gouaches attributed to Pierre-Etienne Lesueur (see pl. 94)

Une femme s'etoit placée à la sortie de la Ville, et distribuoit des cocardes, des chansons, des bouquets, des rubans, et de l'eau de vie aux Volontaires qui partoient pour la Vendée.

Jeune fille vêtue à la Grecque.

Jeune fille en bouffant, et fichu montant.

Premiere maniere de relever la Robe.

Autre maniere de relever la robe, portant le petit casin.

Citoyenne en Schal.

which record everyday life during the revolutionary years. Lesueur was a member of the Société Populaire et Républicaine des Arts, which had been set up in the autumn of 1793 to discuss the place of the arts in a republic; he may have taken part in their deliberations in April of the following year on the proposal to establish a national costume, and he certainly submitted designs for such clothing for both men and women, although the latter were not seriously considered as candidates for Republican dress (see Chapter 3 for a discussion of the various types of national costume proposed by a number of artists).

Plate 82 shows a selection of women's costume from the mid-1790s. On the far left is a working woman dressed in a striped jacket and white skirt, handing out tricolour ribbons and cockades to the volunteers setting off to quell the Royalist uprising in the Vendée in 1793. Next to her is a girl dressed *à la grecque* in a short-sleeved embroidered tunic, a loose tube of white muslin not unlike the early chemise gowns of the 1780s, but girdled under the bust with a belt containing a cameo. The next three women demonstrate various types of the more structured chemise gowns and the figure on the right wears a rare open gown over a white skirt. In a period when there is little choice in dress, accessories such as shawls and scarves played an important role, providing variety and the opportunity for graceful drapery *à l'antique*.

How such costumes relate to the advertisements for the fashions, ready-made, available by post in the *Journal de Paris* is hard to say. A Madame Teillard had, in 1790, placed an advertisement in this paper offering a range of ready-made costumes including chemises, levites, and 'economical' robes (which, according to the *Journal de la mode et du goût*, took only half the fabric of ordinary dresses). Three years later, the same dressmaker (this word must now be used, for the *ancien-régime* distinctions between *couturière* and *modiste* had vanished), advertised in the *Journal de Paris* a wide range of dresses, including a front-buttoning 'habillement à la républicaine' which had a Roman belt fastened at the side. A later supplement in the same paper (of 31 October 1794) presented a further range of costume influenced by the antique, such as a Greek chemise worn with a Juno belt (might this be what Lesueur depicts?), a robe and skirt *à la romaine* and a round robe *à la Diane*.

It was with a profound release of pent-up emotion that people celebrated the fall of Robespierre; it took the form of a passion for dancing and for the wildest extravagance in dress in reaction against the Jacobin Republic of Virtue. Louis-Sébastien Mercier in his sequel to the *Tableau de Paris*, the *Nouveau Paris* (1798) described the cathartic *bals à la victime* held in Paris in the winter of 1794, when women wearing the skimpiest of white dresses, added to them red

94 P.-E. Lesueur (attr.), female costumes, mid-1790s. Gouache. Musée Carnavalet, Paris.

La Belle Espagnole, —ou— la Doublure de Madame Tallien.

Fig. 87.

ribbons in imitation, it was said, of the cut made by the guillotine's blade. Women danced, he claimed, with a kind of religious ecstasy wearing muslin shifts *à l'antique* over flesh-coloured underwear of knitted silk; their hair was arranged like that of classical busts, and they wore sandals on their feet. This, said Mercier, was known as dressing *à la sauvage*, and he wondered if the sexual abandon seen in these *bals à la victime* might have been inspired by Holbein's print, the *Dance of Death*: 'Dans ce lieu enchanté, cent déesses parfumees d'essences, couronnées de roses, flottent dans des robes athéniennes . . . Là les femmes sont nymphes, sultanes, sauvages. Toutes les femmes sont en blanc, et le blanc sied à toutes les femmes. Leur gorge est nue, leurs bras sont nuds'.[23]

Mercier is *the* chronicler of the excesses in fashion which are associated with the raffish society of the Directory, and particularly with such famous *demimondaines* as Thérèse Tallien. The playwright Antoine-Vincent Arnault described her as Egeria, the goddess of fountains, and Laure Junot, later duchesse d'Abrantès remembered her elegance in robes of India muslin draped in antique style and her glossy black hair *à la Titus*. Plate 97 may be a portrait of Madame Tallien by a pupil of David, of about 1794–5. She wears the simplest of muslin shifts, knotted on the shoulders and bound round the waist with a blue silk sash, which echoes the ribbons in her hair, arranged in

classical style. The yellow wool shawl with a Grecian ring design emphasises the graceful curve of her bare arm; Directory beauties placed as much importance on the elegant management of these shawls as the *ancien régime* placed on the perfect deployment of the fan.

The overwhelming impression created by such a dress was of the sexual freedom that many critics found to be the *leitmotif* of high society in the Directory. English caricaturists in particular poked fun at the extremes in classical dress adopted by such *élégantes* as Madame Tallien: Gillray in *La Belle Espagnole, ou la Doublure de Madame Tallien* (1796; pl. 95) depicted her or a lookalike, in a sleeveless décolletée gown of printed muslin, slit to the thigh. It seems likely that Gillray used as inspiration a fashion plate from Heideloff's *Gallery of Fashion* published in February of that year, 'New Dress in the Roman Style' (pl. 96). The dress, more modest than Gillray's version, is a dress of puce-coloured satin with white cambric sleeves and a 'Roman mantle of scarlet kerseymere' (a fine wool).

Gillray has (erroneously) given his 'Madame Tallien' somewhat negroid features in reference, perhaps, to the prominence of Creole ladies in Directory society, the most important being Josephine Beauharnais who married the young General Bonaparte in 1796. Mesdames Tallien, Bonaparte and Récamier formed a trio of the most fashionable ladies

whose *toilettes* were occasionally thought to be immodest, but always in the best of taste. These leaders of fashionable society were the models for the deceptively simple and stylish outfits seen in the plates of the *Journal des dames et des modes*, which began in 1797 with the aim of recording immediate fashion, publishing plates, every few days, by such artists as Carle Vernet and Philibert-Louis Debucourt. The editor claimed that the fashions were sketched from life at the places for fashionable promenades in Paris, such as the Tuileries and the Champs-Elysées, but most of all the gardens of Tivoli and Frascati which had opened in the grounds of mansions formerly owned by the aristocracy. These gardens offered elegant walks and waterways, decorative temples and gilded and mirrored apartments where people ate and danced to the new waltz, which shocked English visitors because the dancers held each other closely. The *Lady's Magazine* recorded with a mixture of horror and fascination the extremes of fashion to be seen at Tivoli and Frascati; the issue for May 1798 claimed that French manners had not changed in spite of the Revolution – 'they are still a dancing nation' – and that the costume of the women had become indecent in their propensity to dress *à la sauvage* and *à la grecque*. Even the editor of the *Journal des dames et des modes* had to emphasise that the dresses which he illustrated were not taken from 'filles publiques' but from the group of about sixty to eighty *élégantes* who set the fashions. If these costumes appeared indecent to his provincial readers, it was just that they had not yet become accustomed to them, in contrast to the Parisians who were quite *blasé* about

the amount of nudity to be seen in the capital.[24] Some art critics felt that the semi-nudity of much fashionable dress had contributed to the vogue for indecency in portraiture. Instancing a portrait of Madame Récamier (Versailles) by Eulalie Morin, in which the sitter's dress almost falls off her shoulder, and Girodet's *Mademoiselle Lange as Danaë* (Minneapolis Institute of Arts), where the sitter is naked except for an elegant peacock-feathered head-dress which might have come straight from the *Journal des dames et des modes*, a visitor to the Salon of 1799 claimed: 'Le costume actuel a donné lieu à plusieurs personnes du sexe de se faire peindre nues et par conséquent d'une manière très indécente...' For this tendency he blamed the authorities' toleration of lax morals and manners.[25]

Not only did women sometimes appear semi-nude in dresses revealing the bosom and the arms, but the shape of the figure was also outlined by the popular clinging and semi-transparent muslin gowns. In Boilly's *'Point de Convention'* (*c*.1798; pl. 98) the woman is dressed *à la sauvage*, with a sleeveless transparent gown (over the briefest of shifts) revealing her bare legs and sandalled feet. Fanny Burney remarked when visiting Paris in 1802, apropos of women's dress: 'THREE petticoats? No one wears more than one! STAYS? every body has left off even corsets! – Shift sleeves? not a soul now wears even a chemise'. At the age of fifty, she chose to ignore the fashions which were intended for youth, and aimed to 'come forth as a Gothic anglaise, who had never heard of, or never heeded, the reigning metamorphoses'.[26] Later, Fanny Burney admitted that the very immodest clinging draperies were not as common as popular prejudice suggested, but it was this kind of dress that was only slightly exaggerated in the fashion plates and in the work of such artists as Boilly and Vernet, who christened such fashion victims *merveilleuses*.

The male counterparts to the *merveilleuses* were the *incroyables*, descendants of the *muscadins* and macaronis in their obsession with extreme forms of fashion, which now took on the exaggerated masculine styles influenced by English costume, which had first appeared in the 1780s. In Boilly's painting, the *incroyable* offering money to the *merveilleuse* wears a tight-fitting coat with huge lapels, two waistcoats (this was a vogue begun in the 1780s) and skin-tight breeches of the sort that critics condemned as immodest. His powdered hair, cut short on top and at the sides to give a fashionable dishevelled look, and his vast green cravat that almost hides his chin, indicate that he is a sympathiser of the exiled monarchy – powder was linked to the wigs of the *ancien régime*, and green was the colour associated with the comte d'Artois, brother to the comte de Provence who in 1795 had proclaimed himself Louis XVIII.

98   L.-L. Boilly, *'Point de Convention'*, *c*.1798. Oil on canvas. Private Collection.

As part of the Thermidorean reaction provoked by the demise of Robespierre, a number of young men chose to wear costume that ran counter to the prevailing Jacobin orthodoxy of unkempt attire and support for the *sans-culottes*. There were battles in the streets between the *muscadins* or *jeunesse dorée* (the name *incroyable* was a slightly later appellation) and the Jacobins; the former attacked the *bonnet rouge*, the red collar and the cockade of their opponents, and the latter attempted to remove the green collars and cravats of their enemies, and even forcibly to cut their hair short, *à la Titus*. With the establishment of the Directory late in 1795, a bourgeois republic with a franchise based on property, the Jacobins were marginalised and middle-class values began to prevail. The characteristics of the dress of the *jeunesse dorée* were tight-fitting coats with huge collars and revers, calf-length breeches or long pantaloons, a cravat of ferocious stiffness which made it difficult to move the head and hair cut unevenly, sometimes with long side-locks called *oreilles de chien*; the *bicorne* hat, said Mercier, stuck out like a dormer window. This is the kind of costume that Carle Vernet depicts in his famous drawings of the *incroyables* of 1797–8 (pl. 99); the term was one of amazement rather than a precise sartorial type, for there were a number of variations on this theme. The *incroyable* here conforms precisely to Mercier's famous description in *Le Nouveau Paris* (1798), paraphrased above.[27] What Mercier and others found strange, was the mixture of styles producing a kind of hybrid: the perfume, powder and finicking attention to detail of the fop, allied to the affectation of English dress with its high-collared coats, emphasis on fine starched linen and neckwear, and boots.

Most Frenchmen, however, avoided the more exaggerated aspects of fashion in preference for a style that was understated yet elegant, a more refined version of the costume of an English country gentleman. This is what Pierre Sériziat wears in his portrait by David of 1795 (pl. 102). Seated in the countryside on his dark green riding cloak with its gold-braided collar, he wears a black high-collared coat, chamois-leather breeches and top boots, double-breasted *gilet* and crisp white linen. French manufacturers were increasingly following the English lead and producing a greater range of woollen cloths which the new styles of tailoring demanded; Monsieur Sériziat's riding mantle is likely to be a coarser, more practical wool, but his coat may be a fine face-cloth (one with a smooth surface) or a similar lightweight woollen fabric emphasising the lines of the body.

Apart from fashionable pursuits, the image which most men wished to project was that of sober reliability; the beginnings of industrialisation and the events of the French Revolution, had influenced men to appear as though dressed for work – of a profes-

99 C. Vernet, *'Incroyable'*, *c.*1797–8. Pen, brown ink and brown wash. Hazlitt, Gooden & Fox, London.

sional or intellectual kind. It is the kind of sober restraint that is reflected in portraits of the time, both in France and England; national differences were revealed more in the nuances of dress than in the basically similar garments which comprised the male wardrobe. The palette is a limited one, dark colours throwing white linen into relief. One of the best examples of this sobriety of costume is Raeburn's *David Anderson* (1790; pl. 100). The black cloth double-breasted coat is cut away at the front so that the bottom of the white waistcoat can be seen above the grey breeches; he holds a wide-awake hat, and the only jewellery which convention allows (gold seals), can be seen at his waist.

This is the kind of costume that was to be adopted all over western Europe and North America by the end of the eighteenth century, and with hindsight the inevitability of its adoption, given the economical and political circumstances of the times, is clear. However, the embroidered silk suit had been for so long a part of very formal costume that it refused to disappear altogether, even though it was far removed from everyday dress. This sartorial confusion can be seen in

element of etiquette. At first there were some odd juxtapositions of costume, as contemporaries noted, for many government ministers and other visitors to the First Consul's receptions were unused to formal dress; the result, according to A.C. Thibaudeau in his *Mémoires sur le Consulat* was often 'une vraie mascarade'. Some men turned up in formal dress, the *habit habillé*, others in frock coats; 'quelques-uns avaient les cheveux poudrés, le plus grand nombre était sans poudre; il n'y manquait que les perruques . . .' Although in theory there were no rules about hair, the First Consul let it be known that powder and a black silk bag [*bourse*] would please him; consequently men with short hair when they attended one of his audiences had to powder it and attach the bag to the back of their coat collar.[28]

Napoleon decreed that on formal occasions the high-collared *habit habillé* or *habit à la française*, with its curved fronts and fine embroidery, should be worn by those who were not entitled to civil uniform; the coat was worn with a white *gilet*, white knee-breeches and white silk stockings. Many men, used to less restricting dress, found this costume most uncomfortable; the artist Pierre-Paul Prud'hon, for example, who had to wear the *habit habillé* when visiting the imperial court (he was tutor to the Empress Marie-Louise), was 'comiquement affublé d'un costume de cour, l'epée au côté, le claque sous le bras, gêné plus qu'on ne

100 (above) H. Raeburn, *David Anderson*, 1790. Oil on canvas. National Gallery of Art, Washington. Widener Collection.

101 Anon., caricature from *Charis*, 1803. Engraving. By courtesy of the Board of Trustees of the Victoria and Albert Museum, London.

102 (facing page) J.-L. David, *Monsieur Sériziat*, 1795. Oil on canvas. Louvre, Paris. (Photo: © Réunion des musées nationaux)

the satirical frontispiece to the 1803 issue of *Charis* (pl. 101), a German magazine published in Leipzig, 'für das Neueste in Kunst, Geschmack und Mode'. The Janus-like figure is half dressed in a pantaloon suit with high-collared coat, a large cravat and boots; the other half, in powdered wig, sports the style of the *ancien régime*, the embroidered silk coat and waistcoat, knee-breeches and *chapeau-bras*.

Paradoxically, the old style is the newest, as the figure looks forward to 1803 dressed in the kind of costume that continued to be worn at most European courts and which was to be given a further boost under the Napoleonic Empire.

In 1800, Napoleon, now First Consul, moved into the former royal palace of the Tuileries and gradually a court in embryo was formed, with its concomitant

103 J.-A.-D. Ingres, *Hippolyte-François Devillers*, 1811. Oil on canvas. Foundation E. G. Bührle Collection.

peut dire'.[29] And Marshal Ney commented 'If the Emperor wishes to encourage velvet-wearing and embroidery, I am very willing to buy dress coats; but as to wearing them, that is another matter'.[30]

The *habit habillé* was heavy (with interlining and profuse embroidery) and too ostentatious for most men; it had lost the elegance of the *habit à la française* under Louis XVI and it was quite out of step with the general tendencies in male fashion. For this reason, it is hardly ever depicted in portraits, although there are a number of men painted in the not dissimilar civil uniforms which were established under the Empire. One such is Ingres's *Hippolyte-François Devillers* (1811; pl. 103), dressed in his costume as Director of Probate and Estates, black coat with silver embroidery, cream *gilet* with silver embroidery and white *culotte*. However skilful Ingres's touch in the depiction of such details of dress as the heavy three-dimensional embroidery, the delicate French needle-lace of the shirt frill and ruffles and the diamond-studded sword hilt, the costume looks as if it wears the sitter and not the reverse. The head, unadorned by a wig, and with thinning, receding hair, seems remote from the over-decorated costume, the ostrich-plumed *chapeau-bras* and the sword.

It was difficult for men not used to war to cope with a sword; the formal bicorne hat, or *claque*, also presented problems on formal occasions. With the declaration of the Empire in the spring of 1804, the *Journal de Paris* stated that young men were beginning to take lessons in etiquette from 'maîtres de tenue, qui leur apprendront a se présenter avec grace, a saluer avec profondeur, a tenir leur claque sans gêne, a porter l'habit brodé avec aisance & l'epée avec dignité'.[31] Later that year the *Journal* remarked that some pre-Revolutionary fashions were returning, such as embroidered waistcoats, coats lined with silk and swords – all of which looked rather odd when worn with the modern, classically inspired hairstyle: 'l'on voit souvent ce costume français surmonté d'une tête romaine'.[32]

Unless one attended court frequently – either in France or England – there was no need to wear the formal embroidered suit; such garments could either be hired or bought second hand if required. Thomas Pougher Russell, from a prominent Birmingham family and a French citizen since 1809, attended the wedding of Napoleon and Marie-Louise in 1810; even though he was a distant spectator in a gallery seat in the Louvre, he had to wear court dress. This he decided to have made, rather than hiring, 'as I may probably have other occasions for using it' – he also wore it to one of the balls celebrating the marriage; but he had to hire a sword and borrow a lace frill and ruffles. His suit still exists in Birmingham; it consists of a dark mulberry-coloured wool coat with cut-steel buttons, an embroidered ivory silk waistcoat, black satin breeches and a black bicorne hat.[33] It must have been a modest costume when set beside the French embroidered *habits habillés* and glittering civil uniforms.

Some years later, in 1818, Henry Angelo visited Paris with the hope of seeing Louis XVIII at the Tuileries, but initially he was refused admission, 'my braided frock coat, lined with silk not being considered a proper habillement'. He went off to a *fripier* (a second-hand clothes dealer) and bought a 'suitable dress' which turned out far too tight, and in which he felt encased as in a suit of armour.[34] Angelo does not describe this 'suitable dress', so overcome was he by a sense of grievance that his frock-coat was not thought presentable even for a mere bystander in the presence of the King. In England men had to wear court dress at levees and Drawing Rooms held by royalty; the costume consisted of a silk coat and knee-breeches, embroidered waistcoat and the hair or wig dressed and powdered (see pl. 129). But even in England, where no revolution had intervened to promote Republican styles of dress, the prevailing trend was towards simplicity, and it is rare to find a portrait of an English sitter in the kind of court dress that Beechey paints in his portrait of Sir John Reade (1811; pl. 104). More at ease in this costume than Ingres's Devillers is in his, there is a greater sense of unity about the ensemble, from the powdered wig, the green velvet suit and the restrained embroidery of the silk waistcoat, to the gestures of the hands. The portrait by Ingres, incomparably the better of the two, depicts the costume in such a way that it brings out the shiftiness and unease of the sitter.

The French had established a complicated hierarchy of civil uniform to give dignity, discipline and structure to a new society, but the style and decoration went against the tenor of the times. This is not to say that men were generally averse to a codified system of clothing which might be brightly coloured and highly decorated – after all, military uniforms played a major part in the appearance of men in the late eighteenth and early nineteenth centuries, and peacock officers in uniform were a staple of the novels of the period. But a sense of individualism and personal choice in clothing was thought important in an age of burgeoning democracy, even if the result might be, in England particularly, one of sober uniformity. The artist John Hoppner, in Paris with Farington during the Peace of Amiens in 1802, compared the 'picturesque' appearance of Frenchmen whose desire to 'please their own fancies is more their object than to imitate', with Englishmen who aim at an 'appearance of substantial prosperity, which brings them nearer to an equality'.[35]

The Prince of Wales, the future George IV, was to be seen in Hyde Park, 'dressed as plain as the most humble individual in the kingdom'.[36] Affecting bright colours and lavish trimmings in his salad days (and retaining an abiding love for uniforms), by the end of the eighteenth century the Prince in his everyday costume which was noted for an elegance of fit, could rightly be called the First Gentleman in Europe. Robert Dighton's equestrian portrait of the Prince of Wales (1804; pl. 105), shows him in a double-breasted high-collared coat known as a 'Jean de Bry', tight pantaloons and hessian boots; his hair is curled in the fashionable Titus cut and he wears a round hat with a curved brim. Here the costume is worn for riding, but it was an equally fashionable morning walking-dress, as can be seen from the same artist's *Beau Brummell* (1805; pl. 106). The fashion magazine *Le Beau Monde* (1808) is quite explicit on the all-important details of the Prince's taste in dress, cited as a model for others to follow. His

> morning dress is either a chestnut brown or bottle green cloth coat with a fancy stripe waistcoat, and light stone-colour musquito pantaloons. The coat is made short in the waist, and the skirts without pockets or flaps with a silk or covered button of the same colour; the cape or collar is made to sit close around the neck with a becoming fall in front, which shows a small portion only of the waistcoat. The lower part of the lapel is not cut in the usual vulgar manner but forms an elegant slope . . .[37]

The Prince of Wales, like a later monarch, Edward

VII, was very knowledgeable about fashion. His estranged wife, Princess Caroline of Brunswick, commented sarcastically that 'he understands how a shoe should be made, or a coat cut . . . and would make an excellent tailor, or shoemaker, or hairdresser, but nothing else'.[38] The Prince's two main tailors were Schweitzer and Davidson of Cork Street, and John Weston of Old Bond Street. The Royal Archives, which list the Prince of Wales's expenditure on clothes (which was enormous), indicate, from the beginning of the nineteenth century, that the most popular colours for coats and greatcoats were sombre – dark blues and greens, grey, brown and olive; these colours were more flattering to the fuller figure, but the styles were tight-fitting and the records also show

104 W. Beechey, *Sir John Reade*, 1811. Oil on canvas. Art Gallery of Ontario, Toronto.

gentleman; he helped to create a look which relied on exquisite tailoring and the careful selection of accessories for its effect. Harriette Wilson's *Memoirs* record how Brummell's word on dress was law; men 'made it a rule to copy the cut of [his] coat, the shape of his hat, or the tie of his neckcloth' – even the Prince of Wales was reputed to watch him dressing. Typical *obiter dicta* included: 'No perfumes, Brummell used to say, but very fine linen, and plenty of it, and country-washing', and, 'If John Bull turns round to look at you, you are not well dressed, but either too stiff, too tight, or too fashionable'.[39]

Brummell's conception of what a gentleman should wear was based on neatness, cleanliness, harmony and lack of affectation. His views on dress followed those of Lord Chesterfield in the mid-eighteenth century, that an Englishman should choose the happy medium between an excessive reliance on the latest fashions and being quite indifferent to them. In Brummell's *Male and Female Costume*, a survey of dress, part-historical, part-contemporary, which he composed during his exile, he noted that 'there is quite as much vanity and coxcombry in slovenliness as there is in its most extravagant opposite', and he attacked 'the minor poet who goes into company with a dirty neckcloth and straggling locks', just as much as the 'dandy who scorns to have an id–e–a beyond the set of his clothes'.[40] Brummell's refined sobriety of dress

105 (above) R. Dighton, *George, Prince of Wales*, 1804. Pen and watercolour. The Royal Collection, © 1994 Her Majesty Queen Elizabeth II.

106 R. Dighton, *George Bryan Brummell*, 1800. Pencil and watercolour. Sale, Christie's, London, 21 March 1989, lot 79.

a constant letting-out of garments to accommodate the Prince's expanding girth. Dighton's image of the Prince is fairly flattering, or at least a tribute to the skills of his tailors, whose subterfuges to restrain the royal belly (clever interlining of the coats, the use of 'belts' or corsets) are also revealed in the accounts; other caricaturists were less complimentary, presenting the Prince as a philandering, obese glutton, the 'Prince of Whales'.

The Prince must occasionally have cast an envious eye over the slim figure of his sartorial mentor, George 'Beau' Brummell, who had resigned his commission in the army to devote himself to a 'life of pleasure'. This mainly consisted of a club-man's masculine way of life, revolving around St James's, to which he brought wit and superb good taste, particularly in dress. He it was who turned the art of masculine attire into the supreme expression of being a

was quite the reverse to that of the dandy (which he is sometimes erroneously called) whose costume relies for effect on exaggeration. Captain Jesse recalled:

> His morning dress was similar to that of every other gentleman – Hessians and pantaloons, or top-boots and buskins, with a blue coat, and a light or buff-coloured waistcoat; of course, fitting to admiration, on the best figure in England. His dress of an evening was a blue coat and white waistcoat, black pantaloons which buttoned tight to the ankle, striped silk stockings, and opera hat; in fact he was always carefully dressed, but never the slave of fashion.[41]

Harriette Wilson, visiting Brummell in Calais (he had fled there as a bankrupt in 1816) described his talent as 'that of having well-fashioned the character of a gentleman',[42] a theme taken up by Virginia Woolf in an essay on Beau Brummell, where she tries to pin down his 'curious combination of wit, of taste, of insolence, of independence'. Her pursuit of his character (as distinct from the idea which we all have about Beau Brummell) failed then as it would now, and the novelist resorts to describing his lasting influence on the male image, 'cool, refined and debonair'. 'His clothes seemed to melt into each other with the perfection of their cut and the quiet harmony of their colour'.[43] It is unfortunate that he was never painted by Lawrence, or indeed any artist of note. It is a paradox that Beau Brummell has become entwined in any discussion about dandyism, for his understated elegance in dress is inimical to the excesses of the dandy in England, whose direct line of descent is from the Restoration fop and the eighteenth-century macaroni. Max Beerbohm (*Dandies and Dandies*, 1896) admired Brummell as the 'Father of Modern Costume', his clothing 'so quiet, so reasonable, and . . . so beautiful; free from folly or affectation, yet susceptible to exquisite ordering; plastic, austere, economical'.[44] It is dress that is both democratic and élitist; democratic in the sense of the practical origin and modest simplicity of the styles of costume, élitist with regard to the expense of high-quality tailoring and accessories, and the privileged existence that the clothing celebrates.

Brummell's 'philosophy of clothes' (to use Carlyle's phrase) is less akin to that of the English dandies of the 1820s, with their padded coats and peg-top trousers, than to the French dandy of the mid-nineteenth century, whose severe black and white costume was a protest against bourgeois vulgarity and the self-indulgent sartorial statements of the Bohemian. As defined by Baudelaire, such a dandy was 'the man who is rich and idle, and who, even if blasé, has no other occupation than the perpetual pursuit of happiness . . . whose solitary profession is elegance'; even so,

such dandyism does not just consist in 'an immoderate taste for the toilet and material elegance', for such things are only the 'symbols of his aristocratic superiority of mind'.[45]

Baudelaire's famous discussion of the dandy in his essay *The Painter of Modern Life* (1859) is a celebration of the modernity of dress, a refusal to claim (as many critics did) that the past had produced superior styles in costume. The sober clothing of the man of fashion (reaching its apogee in the French dandy) placed him firmly in the context of the present; it alluded to professional status, the importance of work and to political equality in its uniformity of colour. Dark colours and sombre clothing also hinted at Renaissance portraits and poetry with their complex visual and literary allusions; black in particular, with its context of mourning, emphasised the man of sorrows, the intellectual, the writer. Byron, for example, liked to

107 A.-L. de Roussy Girodet-Trioson, *François René, Vicomte de Chateaubriand*, 1807. Oil on canvas. Musée d'Histoire de la ville de Saint-Malo.

wear black; it made him look slimmer, made his skin appear whiter and added the air of romantic melancholy appropriate for a fashionable poet with a scandalous private life. Chateaubriand, in his portrait by Girodet of 1807 (pl. 107) has also chosen to be portrayed in black. Exhibited at the Salon of 1810 under the title '*Un Homme méditant sur les ruines de Rome*', the author poses, artfully windswept, in black coat and greatcoat, black cravat at his neck. Madame de Rémusat remembered Chateaubriand as being 'most careful and affected in his dress', and here a sombre palette has been used for dramatic effect to create an image self-consciously contrived; the eighteenth-century gesture of placing the hand between the buttons of the waistcoat has been retained, not so much to demonstrate the elegance of the movements of the hands, nor the luxury of lace ruffles (which no longer existed in everyday dress), but as a Romantic expression of feeling, hand on heart. The author's pose, clothing and hairstyle is meant to suggest intellectual ferment, although when Napoleon viewed the portrait it reminded him of 'a conspirator who has just come down the chimney'.

Chateaubriand's appearance of slight dishevelment is not only created by the disorder of his hair, but also by the fact that his coat looks rather too big for him, not sitting particularly well on the shoulders, with sleeves full at the top and extending over his hand. These are features that can be seen in most contemporary male portraits, even that of Brummell himself, and which reflect a preference for ease and comfort in dress over artistic demands for a more sculpted torso. On the other hand, very tight-fitting breeches or pantaloons could cruelly reveal any imperfection in men's lower limbs.

By the end of the eighteenth century, English tailors who had had a long experience of fine cloth (as distinct from silk) to hone their skills, were acknowledged as fashion leaders. This supremacy was the culmination of a process of political and social events which had moved men towards a new 'democratic' self-image, manifested in a preference for modest simplicity of style and fabric. In 1796 *The Taylor's Complete Guide, or A Comprehensive Analysis of Beauty and Elegance in Dress* was published by a 'Society of Adepts in the Profession'. Once and for all it established the credo of the fashionable tailor whose aim, paradoxically, was not so much to be fashionable as to be timeless and classical in his clothes; 'it is but of little consequence to a complete Taylor what the Fashions are; his business is to fit the body, that no constriction or unnatural compression may be felt in any part'.[46] A good tailor, then as now, was able through his art, to hide a multitude of sins in the shapes and misshapes of his clients, and to bring out their best points. In Pierce Egan's travelogue, *Life in London*, written in 1820, the stylish man-about-town Corinthian Tom, takes his country friend Jerry Hawthorne to the fashionable tailor Dicky Primefit of Regent Street, whose aim, we are told, was:

> The art sublime, ineffable,
> Of making middling men look well.[47]

By this time, Regent Street, instigated by the Prince Regent in 1813, rivalled Oxford Street in the elegance of its fashion shops, but the area of Bond Street and around St James's specialised in menswear. From the late eighteenth century we begin to learn for the first time some of the names of fashionable tailors and suppliers of accessories, not just through trade cards and invoices, but through contemporary letters, diaries and novels, all of which reflect the new importance given to the details of men's clothes. In T.S. Surr's satirical novel, *A Winter in London* (1806), the hero Edward Montagu, a foundling, is amazed at the complicated business of being equipped as a man of fashion:

> When he stopped at a tailor's in Bond Street, expecting to be measured for a suit of clothes, what was his surprise to learn that Mr. Larolle made only coats; and that they had a dozen doors further to drive before they reached 'the first hand in the world at waistcoats, braces and inexpressibles'. The same 'artist' who excelled at fitting a dress shoe, would have been intolerable as the manufacturer of a pair of boots; and though Mr. Flint the hatter, assured them that for round walking hats and hunting hats, there was not a superior shop in London; yet he would confess that for an opera hat Mr. Breach did certainly 'cut all the trade'.[48]

For most of the eighteenth century, especially at the higher levels of society, customers bought their own fabrics which they took to the tailor; since the cost of the clothes consisted mainly in the fabrics, the profit margins for tailors were low, and some began to turn their attention to offering ready-to-wear goods as well as bespoke.[49] A reduction in the costs of such fabrics as wool and cotton, a result of the mass production of the new technology, led during the nineteenth century to an increased demand for ready-made clothing. At the top of society, however, men continued to have their clothes made for them and the art of the tailor became even more important in an age when cut and construction had prevailed over luxury of fabric and trimming. By the early nineteenth century the tailor's word was law and the customer was able, with his advice, to select fabrics on the premises. Changes in fashion – often merely modifications of existing styles or slight nuances of detail or colour – were arrived at by a process of consultation between tailor and fashionable customer.

It is not clear, for example, whether it was Brummell or the tailor John Meyer of Conduit Street who invented the strap worn under the instep and attached to the hem of the trouser to prevent it wrinkling.

In Pierce Egan's comic account of life in Regency London, the tailor Dicky Primefit was 'principally distinguished for the cut of his coats', for these were the most important items in the masculine wardrobe and the true tests of tailoring skills. From the *Taylor's Complete Guide* we note that the 'principal part of the Tailor's business is the measuring, cutting and making a coat', and it continues: 'It matters not whether narrow or broad Backs are the Rage of Fashion, stand-up or turn-down Collars, short or long Waists, or whatever turn the cut of the Skirts may take, the ultimate end is to cut and fit well . . .'[50]

Firmly woven woollen cloth best demonstrated a perfect cut when the coat was fastened; the back of the garment was usually only thinly interlined, so that a sculptural, muscular effect could be obtained, at least on a man with a good figure, a fashion-plate ideal (see pl. 109). In addition, there was often judicious padding at the front of the coat to emphasise the pectoral muscles and to give the impression of a more slender waist. The waist also appeared slimmer due to the somewhat top-heavy proportions of the coat, with its very high collar and the bulk of the gathered-in sleeve at the shoulder. The effect could sometimes be one of aggressive masculinity with a slightly comic appearance, as in Rowlandson's *Elderly Buck Walking with a Lady* (c.1800; pl. 108). The artist has segmented the squat figure of the man by emphasising the constituent parts of his costume – the wide *bicorne* hat, the almost square coat and the rectangles created by the turned-down tops of the boots. The man's too-tight coat (it has to be left unbuttoned) and his awkward gait present a caricature image which is the reverse coin of the fashion-plate archetype such as Horace Vernet's *Incroyable* (c.1810; pl. 109) where the cut of his coat with its well set-in sleeves, flattering back seams and crisp vertical pleats is essential to the stylish appearance, together with elegant gestures and deportment.

Coats could either be single-breasted or double-breasted, the latter the more popular style, as contemporary portraiture indicates. They could be cut square across the waistline, or – as in the morning coat – with a sloped front; in both cases, the fabric at the sides and at the back was severely curtailed. Older and more conservative men, however, as is often the case, preferred the fuller, more comfortable and less revealing styles of their younger days – as with women's dress, the new fashions promoted the cult of youth and required a slim figure. Lawrence's *Sir Robert Wigram* (1816; pl. 110) is a portrait of an elderly man, successful in business and a former Member of Parlia-

108 T. Rowlandson, *An Elderly Buck Walking with a Woman*, c.1800. Pen, red ink and watercolour. Yale Center for British Art, New Haven, CT. Paul Mellon Collection.

109 H. Vernet '*Incroyable*', c.1810. Watercolour. Hazlitt, Gooden & Fox, London.

ment; sitting in a slightly awkward pose and with rather old-fashioned clothes, but confident of his achievements, he is reminiscent of Hogarth's *Captain Coram* (1740; London, Coram Foundation). But

silk stockinette which, claimed the *Taylor's Complete Guide*, had to be lined for decency, either with swanskin (fine flannel) or cotton. Leather breeches were worn for sporting occasions and as an informal morning walking costume. Doeskin and chamois leather in particular were soft and malleable enough to cut well, even if on occasion they incurred the wrath of a perfectionist such as Beau Brummell; seeing Lord Frederick Bentinck one day he attacked his 'bad knees, my good fellow, bad knees . . . and his parting words on leaving were to "be sure to burn those leather breeches of yours".'[52] A dress reformer such as Walter Vaughan in his *Essay Philosophical and Medical concerning Modern Clothing* (1792) was not alone in attacking the 'compression of tight leathern Breeches' which could cause numbness, but he was forced to admit that they 'are extremely handsome and very fit to expose a muscular Thigh . . .'[53]

As the coat was cut away so radically at the front and sides, a new importance was placed on men's legs; the tall, slim man with broad shoulders and a kind of indolent elegance of pose was the *ne plus ultra* of masculine style by the second decade of the nineteenth century. It can best be seen Vernet's *Incroyables* and Ingres's drawings of English and French sitters made during his stay in Rome from 1806 to 1820. Horace Vernet, grandson of Moreau le Jeune and son of Carle Vernet who, in the late 1790s, had produced the original series of *Incroyables et Merveilleuses*, was commissioned by the editor of the *Journal des dames et des modes* to produce a new set of images of contemporary fashions; they were engraved between 1810 and 1818. Plate 111 is one such *Incroyable, c.*1811; his stylish arrogance and perfect tailoring acknowledge the supremacy of English modes. The dress-coat is cut away at the front and with abbreviated tails at the back to reveal the full splendour of his legs tightly encased in knit pantaloons. Pantaloons were remotely descended from the tights worn by Pantaleone in the *commedia dell'arte*, but the more immediate derivation lay in the garments which were part of Hungarian hussar uniform. Such hussar costume basically consisted of a dolman (or jacket) fastened with braided loops (frogging), a fur-lined and braided sleeved mantle (or pelisse), tight pantaloons often braided on the upper thigh and boots. Since the middle of the eighteenth century it had been a popular masquerade costume and an influence on men's fashionable clothing. It was a costume which particularly attracted the Prince of Wales. As a child he had appeared with his brother Prince Frederick in an entertainment devised by their governess in 1769 'in rich Hussar Habits of white sattin embroidered with gold & trimm'd with sable';[54] as an adult his accounts from the 1780s are full of orders for frogged coats, fur pelisses and hussar boots.[55] Hussar costume with its romantic martial air

whereas Captain Coram is shown in his practical greatcoat, a happy acceptance of his humble origins and hard physical work, Wigram appears in the black suit of a prosperous merchant or professional man. The suit consists of a double-breasted coat cut capaciously in an old-fashioned style, waistcoat and black satin knee-breeches worn with silk stockings and black leather pumps. The powder from his hair falls on the collar and shoulder of his coat, a study in contrasts between the light and the dark; a tax on hair powder in 1795 gave the final death-blow to a fashion that had for many years been on the wane, and which by the early nineteenth century was only retained by a small percentage of men, mainly for professional and occupational reasons.[51]

The knee-breeches, also, indicate a man of elderly years and traditional habits, for by this time they had been replaced, even at court, by trousers, or what *Le Beau Monde* (1808) called 'stocking-breeches and stockings all in one piece . . . [a] longitudinal pantaloon'. Knee-breeches were sometimes retained in the masculine wardrobe for summer wear, made of such light materials as nankeen (a washable cotton fabric, closely woven and usually buff in colour) and knitted

must have had particular appeal for a prince who was not allowed to lead his troops himself, but who was fascinated by rich and exotic clothing. He was painted a number of times in hussar costume, including a portrait by Reynolds (1785) (present whereabouts unknown) in masquerade dress and one by Beechey (1798) (Royal Academy of Arts, London) in the braided uniform of the 10th Light Dragoons; under his aegis, this regiment, of which he was appointed Colonel Commandant in 1793, adopted various elements of hussar dress, and in 1805 the name itself – part of that trend towards the appearance of hussar regiments in the early nineteenth-century British Army.

Hussar regiments wore some of the most dashing uniforms during the Napoleonic period and it was inevitable that some of this glamour rubbed off on to civilian clothing. Contemporary portraits show men in stylish frogged coats, such as David's *Comte de Turenne* of 1816 (Copenhagen, Carlsberg Glyptothek) and a number of drawings by Ingres, for example *Sir John Hay and his Sister Mary* (London, British Museum) and *Mr and Mrs Woodhead and Henry Comber* (Cambridge, Fitzwilliam Museum) also of 1816. The characteristic applied braid of hussar pantaloons was not transferred into fashionable pantaloons which were plain and, for daytime wear, light in colour. In

an ideal world they might have reminded the spectator of noble antique nudity, but more often they courted censure as they tended to outline and emphasise the male genital area; no wonder polite society referred to them as inexpressibles. A Persian ambassador to England found such garments 'immodest and unflattering to the figure . . . [they] look just like underdrawers – could they be designed to appeal to the ladies?'[56] Ingres's *Lord Grantham* (1816; pl. 112) wears pantaloons which, although tight, do not produce the effect of nakedness seen in Vernet's *Incroyable*; what they *do* show is the reality of the horizontal wrinkling of the fabric when pushed into the fashionable boots which fitted closely at the calf – here the boots are hessians, short riding boots curved to a point in front and trimmed with a decorative tassel.

Once the long-established tyranny of the knee-breeches was in decline, men's netherwear could include a wide range of bifurcated garments. From the late 1790s, for example, the Prince of Wales's clothing accounts list pantaloons of nankeen, stockinette and kerseymere; there were 'lilac striped callico Pantaloons' (1798), fine doeskin pantaloons (1801) and 'Brown Silk Pantaloons with feet' (1802) – in other words, tights – which clearly wore out quite quickly, as there are a number of references to such items

needing 'new Legs' or being re-footed. At the same time the Prince was ordering trousers in a variety of fabrics, including kerseymere, flannel, fine cotton and calico. Trousers were distinguished from pantaloons by being looser in fit and humbler in origin, being descended from working-class garments; wide trousers were also worn by sailors, and it was perhaps no accident that they appear to have been first worn by fashionable men at Brighton in the early years of the nineteenth century. As with pantaloons, light colours and fabrics were preferred, *Le Beau Monde* of 1808 laying down the law thus: 'some few striped trowsers we have seen worn, but they are considered as only adapted for dirty weather, or for wearing at the watering places'.[57] In short, the more practical aspects of trousers, such as the patterned fabrics (see the striped trousers of pl. 109) which might indicate their functional origin, were in England dispensed with in favour of the impractical, light colours that required constant laundering. Trousers could vary in width from the modest proportions of the evening style which was often worn with an instep strap to preserve an unbroken, unwrinkled line, to the very wide 'cossack' trousers named in honour of a visit made by Tsar Alexander I of Russia to England in 1814. These cossacks were cut very full (they were almost as wide as the original sailor's slops, or trousers) and gathered into a waistband; when worn with stays by fashionable dandies, the result was almost feminine as the pleated fabric of the trousers flared over the hips. Abhorring what Brummell would have called such a 'mountebank appearance', *The Ton* (1819) declared: 'The gross error of the shallow-pated Dandies in wearing these loose trowsers is most ridiculous. The first introduction of them was to imitate the Cossacks. Now that the war is over, it was expected that these street Danglers would have been put on the civil list'.[58]

By the 1820s men's trousers had assumed the sober, modest form which appears in the portrait of an unknown man of 1820 by Pierre Duval-Lecamus (pl. 113), and which they were to retain until the end of the century. Formal everyday costume has now become the dark (usually black) cut-away coat and trousers, worn with a short, light-coloured waistcoat and black top hat. Against the creeping sobriety of men's clothing, only the whiteness of the linen stands out, the starched linen shirt collar and neckcloth or cravat acting as a stiffened support for the head. In France as in England, hair powder had been virtually abandoned in everyday life by the beginning of the nineteenth century, and what makes these men look so modern is their hair, cut short and arranged with natural simplicity in a variety of styles ultimately derived from the 'classical' cut of the 1790s, but, increasingly, with the addition of side-burns. Hair was

sometimes oiled (with bear grease, or macassar oil from the nut of the Ceylon oak) to make it darker and a more dramatic foil to the pallor of the complexion. As masculine dress grew darker and less obviously swayed by the vagaries of fashion, the head and neck area were more than ever open to first impressions, to the indication of character; the becoming negligence of the hairstyle and the subtle choice of cravat (*à la Byron* – unstarched and tied in a floppy bow; *à la Napoleon* – untied, but crossed over at the front; and many other types) framed the face and helped to express the personality. The Romantic hero, as Stendhal knew, did not need exotic clothing; he required well-tailored dark clothing, a slim and youthful figure and a face expressive of emotion and sensitivity. The traits of the ideal modern man are listed thus:

1. Un esprit extrêmement vif.
2. Beaucoup de graces dans les traits.
3. L'oeil étincelant.
4. Beaucoup de gaieté.
5. Un fonds de sensibilité.
6. Une taille svelte, et sur-tout l'air agile de jeunesse.

Furthermore, such a man 'faut être homme charmant dans une soirée, et le lendemain gagner une bataille, ou savoir mourir'.[59]

In the dullness of the post-Napoleonic world, which Stendhal so much deplored, these last aims would be hard to achieve even for one of his heroes possessing the six features listed above. The nuances of men's dress and general appearance might reveal an ardent and poetical soul, but how could it express any sense of drama? The answer lay with the greatcoat, a capacious and swashbuckling garment which had, so to speak, expanded from the late eighteenth-century redingote. The redingote was a garment sanctified to the memory of Napoleon; the Emperor's famous coats (usually grey) of fine woollen cloth from Louviers were simply styled (he preferred ease to fashion) with a high collar and double-breasted fastening. A more fashionable style by the beginning of the nineteenth century was the caped greatcoat, a loose coat with an extra cape or shoulder mantle, such as Ingres outlines in his *Studies of a 'Carrick'* (pl. 114); further studies of this garment exist in the Musée Ingres at Montauban.[60] These drawings might be related to the artist's *Self-portrait* of 1804 at Chantilly, or they may reflect Ingres's general fascination with the dramatic possibilities of the fall of drapery at the shoulder – such coats appear in a number of portraits.

The fashionable Carrick greatcoat, as it appears draped over the back of the chair in the portrait by Duval-Lecamus, had four overlapping capes. The same style is worn by Augustin Jordan in his portrait by Ingres of 1817 (pl. 115). It is a vast garment, ample

113 P. Duval-Lecamus, *Portrait of a Man*, 1820. Oil on canvas. Hazlitt, Gooden & Fox, London.

of fabric and reaching to his ankles; with its turned-back front lining and bulky sleeves there is a faint echo of the massive sleeved mantles seen in early sixteenth-century German dress. Ingres makes a point of contrasting the heavy solidity of Jordan's costume with the delicacy of the dress of the child, Adrienne, with her floral headdress and cotton frock trimmed with a fringe and broderie anglaise.

For an artist whose forte lay in the exact depiction of the details of dress, it is curious that sometimes these emerge better in Ingres's drawings than in his paintings. In his portrait of Joseph-Antoine de Nogent (1815: Cambridge, MA, Fogg Art Museum), for example, the sitter stands awkwardly full-length (rare for a small portrait), overwhelmed by a voluminous collared greatcoat; the costume studies for this painting, at the Musée Ingres, look more attractive than the finished garment, possibly because they are less detailed and less clumsily draped over the body. It is unfortunate for Ingres that the portrait of Monsieur de Nogent now hangs next to David's fine portrait of

Emmanuel Joseph, Abbé Sieyès (1817; pl. 116). The Abbé, deputy in the National Assembly (he figures prominently in David's *Oath of the Tennis Court*, seated to the right of President Bailly), constitutional expert (he helped to plot the *coup d'état* of 18 Brumaire and create the Consulate) and Napoleonic count, was exiled, along with David, at the Restoration. His glossy black double-breasted coat, lined with satin, worn with a white waistcoat and black trousers, is modestly, conventionally fashionable for a man of his age, although the tousled hair *à la Titus* (perhaps a wig) makes him look younger. The bulky coat does not dominate his appearance, but gives *gravitas* to an elder statesman, to a man whom David clearly found sympathetic both as a person and as a politician.

★　　★　　★

As men's dress moved towards uniform sobriety at the end of the eighteenth century, so women's dress also seemed to be infected by a similar desire for modest

115 J.-A.-D. Ingres, *Augustin Jordan and his Daughter*, 1817. Graphite on white wove paper. Courtesy of the Fogg Art Museum, Harvard University Art Museums. Bequest of Grenville L. Winthrop.

116 J.-L. David, *Emmanuel-Joseph, Abbé Sieyès*, 1817. Oil on canvas. Courtesy of the Fogg Art Museum, Harvard University Art Museums. Bequest of Grenville L. Winthrop.

simplicity in style and a passion for white. English reactions to the French Revolution influenced the way in which dress developed during the 1790s. To begin with there was considerable enthusiasm in some upper and middle-class women towards the events of 1789, and a kind of patriotic pride that many Frenchwomen had adopted informal English styles in dress; but this initial reaction turned into more muted support, and then – with the deepening tragedy of the downfall of the monarchy and the advent of the Terror – ancient antipathies to French manners and dress re-emerged. Accounts of the maenad revels of the *tricoteuses*, of the female radicals who adopted men's dress and the *bonnet rouge*, and of the semi-naked women who danced with pagan abandon at the *bals à la victime* were widely circulated, and a correlation was made between the so-called licentious styles in French dress and the anarchy of successive political systems.

From 1793 Britain and France were at war, and to some extent communication of respective fashions was interrupted. The two countries developed along different lines, although the basic shapes of fashion remained the same. The French pursued a pure, classical style, while the English sought refuge in the comfort of the dress of the more recent past; French dress evidences a love of simplicity of line, whereas English costume is a sometimes cluttered synthesis of the prevailing Neoclassical styles with the addition of Romantic ornament.

In the mid-1790s, however, the prevailing theme in English dress was quiet simplicity; it is the most sober period in the history of dress of the whole eighteenth century. Dresses in the predominant white muslin were softly draped in the style of the chemise gown, or in the popular wrapping-gown. The subjects of both Raeburn's *Jacobina Copland* (*c.*1794; pl. 117) and Samuel de Wilde's *Portrait of a Woman* (1795; pl. 119) wear wrapping-gowns of white muslin with no adornment whatsoever. The dresses are kept in place by a sash at the waist, but for extra decency the two women wear *chemisettes* or underbodices of fine muslin; in the de Wilde drawing it is attached to a ruff at the neck. In both portraits the hair is long, curled and lightly powdered, but Mrs Copland has wound a white muslin scarf round her head, perhaps in imitation of the radical chic styles, *à la paysanne* or *à la citoyenne*, which had percolated through to the English fashion magazines.

These simple dresses with their slightly rising waistlines are reflected in the most famous of all English fashion magazines, Heideloff's *Gallery of Fashion* which appeared from 1794 to 1802. The *Gallery* claimed to be a record 'of all the most fashionable and elegant Dresses in vogue', rather than a blueprint for the future; it aimed to show the taste and restraint to be seen in English costume, rather than the wild exaggerations of French dress (for example the stark simplicity *à l'antique* of a Madame Tallien, as in plate 97). The result was often a compromise between the

'elegant simplicity' of ancient Greek dress, which the *Gallery* admired, and the English attraction towards such features as Vandyke trimming, Tudor ruffs and various kinds of applied decoration. Even when a nod is made in the direction of the antique, it is never purely classical. A *robe à la grecque* (August 1799) is made of gauze and trimmed with Vandyke lace, and a 'New Dress in the Roman Style' for February 1796 (pl. 96) turns out to be of puce coloured satin, worn with a scarlet mantle embroidered in gold. Even a simple afternoon dress, as illustrated in plate 118, is trimmed with embroidery and lace, the hair being arranged, so the *Gallery* informs us, '*en colimaçon*' (like a snail) and decorated with ribbon bandeaux. These are the kind of fashion details which would be glossed over by such artists as Raeburn, who preferred to concentrate on the slightly hazy effect created by the layers of plain white muslin in the dress, which echoed the pale, powdered, loose curls of the hair.

All kinds of cotton, and especially muslin, were *de*

rigueur for fashionable dress; in an age when distinctions between formal and informal dress were increasingly blurred, fine muslin was acceptable on all occasions. In England raw cotton imports quintupled between 1780 and 1800, the price falling steeply once the plantation system was established in the American south. Cotton was easily adaptable to the new machinery and to the factory system, and there were eager markets for the resulting fabrics both at home and abroad. Fashion magazines promoted a wide range of cotton fabrics in their descriptions of dress and in the accompanying plates; one publication, *Ackermann's Repository of Arts, Literature, Commerce, Manufactures, Fashions and Politics* (1809–28) actually included fabric samples as patriotic advertisements for the new technology. In France during the 1790s there was a massive shift from wool and linen to cotton, which increased during the Empire and under the Restoration, as a result of mass production.[61]

With the trend towards simpler styles in dress and cheaper fabrics, women increased the size of their wardrobes; in addition to clothes made by a dressmaker (the more complicated styles), a woman with moderate sewing ability (or her maid) could make herself plain, everyday clothes and caps. The amount of fabric needed for a dress decreased as the 1790s progressed. When the eponymous heroine of Fanny Burney's novel *Camilla* (1796) was shown some fine lawn, she declared that it was 'enough for three whole dresses; why, it's a whole piece; and I dare say I can get a handkerchief and an apron out of it into the bargain'.[62]

A piece was thirty yards, so each dress would have taken just under ten yards; a few years later Jane Austen informs us that an average cotton gown would require only about seven yards. By that time, even in England, dresses were becoming more exiguous, with short sleeves and fabric clinging to the body. This trend was taken up by the caricaturists, and Rowlandson, for example (see pl. 108), satirises the young belle aping the extremes of French dress *à la grecque*.

As well as clothing made by the dressmaker, or made at home, there was an increased range of ready-to-wear garments available in London and the main provincial cities. Throughout the eighteenth century a considerable range of ready-made goods could be bought. These were mainly items for the less well-off – caps, cloaks, aprons, quilted skirts, jackets – made usually of the cheaper fabrics such as wool and linen mixtures and the humbler types of woollen cloth, but by the end of the century there were also such fashionable garments as women's greatcoats and Brunswick gowns (long-sleeved sack-backed walking costume). In addition, with the growing emphasis on cottons at this period, specialist linen shops appeared

117 H. Raeburn, *Jacobina Copland, c.*1794. Oil on canvas. National Gallery of Canada, Ottawa.

118 (facing page left) N.W. von Heideloff, 'Afternoon Dress' *Gallery of Fashion*, 1796. Aquatint engraving. Yale Center for British Art, New Haven, CT. Paul Mellon Collection.

and muslin 'warehouses' (the contemporary name for emporia where ready-made goods were stocked) which offered made-up muslin dresses and muslins to buy by the yard or piece.

As might be expected of the country that was the first to move towards industrialisation, England led Europe in terms of the amount and quality of retail establishments. By the end of the 1820s, although there were still some fashionable shops in the City of London, the Strand and Covent Garden (one of Jane Austen's favourite shops was in Henrietta Street, Covent Garden), the widest range of goods was to be seen in Regent Street and Oxford Street, the latter, according to an 1817 guide, possessing the greatest number of fashion shops in one street in the whole of Europe.[63] It can be argued that in England, 'the first of the world's consumer societies had unmistakably emerged by 1800'.[64]

However, in terms of fashion, this society was still dependent on the prevailing French styles, even in times of war; the fashion impulse emanating from Paris could not be ignored, particularly once a reasonably firm government had been established and such publications as the *Journal des dames et des modes* began to appear. Furthermore, although England was in Napoleon's words, 'a nation of shopkeepers', it did not have any celebrated dress designers, as was the

case in France. A French title for an English fashion magazine was thought to give that publication extra cachet, so, for example, there were such journals as the *Miroir de la Mode*, *Le Beau Monde* and *La Belle Assemblée*, all of which described, in the words of another magazine, the 'Actually Prevailing Female Fashions of London and Paris'. What helped to make

119 (above) S. de Wilde, *Portrait of a Woman*, 1795. Pencil and watercolour. Yale Center for British Art, New Haven, CT. Paul Mellon Collection.

111

121 Illustration of a Roman matron, from A. Lens, *Costume des Peuples de l'Antiquité*, 1776. Engraving. British Library, London.

open-sided) can be seen in David's portrait of Henriette Delacroix, Madame de Verninac (1799; pl. 120), whose pose is clearly inspired by an engraving of a Roman matron in André Lens's *Costume des peuples de l'antiquité* (1776; pl. 121). Madame de Verninac, with her heavy archaic beauty must have been David's ideal woman, so close was she to his classical ideal. How real is her dress? It certainly relates to the sleeveless tunics buttoned on the shoulder seen in David's *Oath of the Horatii* and in his *Brutus* (Paris, Louvre), and one art historian has indicated his view that the artist renounced current fashions in favour of long white tunics which permitted him to concentrate 'l'attention sur des éléments caractéristiques de la personne, le visage, et les mains. Il peut ainsi concilier son souci de l'individuel et son désir de style'.[66] Whatever the answer, David has certainly intended to make the portrait a contemporary image, linking the white cotton shift so much in tune with Directoire style, with a fashionable fringed shawl embroidered after an antique pattern in a lotus and palmette design.

David's portrait of Madame de Verninac might depict an ideal dress or a real one, but in the latter case – in spite of the comments made by critics of women's costume – it would have been worn with an under-bodice veiling the nipples and providing some support for the bust. Many portraits which show sitters in what appear to be garments of negligent simplicity, such as David's *Madame Récamier* of 1800 (pl. 122), on closer observation represent dresses which have a firm bodice structure and well set-in sleeves. Juliette Récamier was famous for her beauty and the perfect taste of her salon; John Carr noted that she was 'one of David's most enthusiastic admirers, and has carried the rage for Grecian undress to an extremity'. Her bedroom, he continued, was one of the sights of Paris, the bed 'upon which this charming statue reposes' having 'on each side . . . altars on which are placed Herculaneum vases of flowers, and a large antique lamp of gold'.[67]

David poses his sitter on a replica of an antique *chaise-longue* which he had had made, together with other 'antique' furniture, for use in his studio;[68] perhaps Madame Récamier wished to look like a wall painting from Herculaneum, to match the decor of her bedroom. Whatever the genesis of the painting, she disliked the portrait, found it too frigid and did not like being portrayed with bare feet. It remained unfinished as David refused to alter it, a beautiful if slightly intimidating icon of Neoclassical art. Understandably, maybe, the sitter preferred Gérard's later portrait of 1805 (pl. 125) where the costume and pose are infinitely more coquettish; for, in David's portrait the costume is quite severe, with its reinforced bodice supporting the bust and cut modestly high in the front

French fashions irresistible – apart from the long-established conviction held by many Englishwomen that they were innately superior to the home product – was the strong sense of unity in design. By the end of the 1790s, the overwhelming classical influence was to be seen in art, in furnishing and in dress. John Carr, an English visitor to France during the Peace of Amiens, visited a restaurant in the Tuileries Gardens 'admirably painted after the taste of Herculaneum', where he saw 'some beautiful women present, dressed after the antique, a fashion successfully introduced by David'; he noted how the classical statuary in the Louvre had inspired women 'with new ideas of personal decoration'.[65]

It would not have been altogether surprising if David had helped to create a type of fashionable dress for women; his knowledge of classical costume was great and his interest in contemporary dress was profound. Public viewing of his history paintings encouraged open debate on the clothing depicted therein, and when visitors looked at the dress worn by Hersilia, the central figure in *The Intervention of the Sabine Women* (1799; Paris, Louvre), it was remarked how close it was to current fashion *à la grecque*. In the preparatory drawing for the figure of Hersilia, the costume was an open-sided Greek *peplos* with an over-fold, but in the final picture it became a sleeveless shift girdled under the bust and open down one side. A similar costume (although not, presumably,

120 J.-L. David, *Henriette Delacroix, Madame de Verninac*, 1799. Oil on canvas. Louvre, Paris. (Photo: © Réunion des musées nationaux)

and at the back. As distinct from the original chemise with its simple T-shape, or the sleeveless cotton shift worn by Madame de Verninac, the dress worn by Madame Récamier is of quite a complex cut, with a separate bodice and skirt sewn together at the waist. Late eighteenth-century dressmakers usually left some surplus fabric at the top of the skirt at the back, hanging down inside after the skirt had been pleated on to the bodice; this allowed for later alterations, but also gave a fashionable fullness and slight bounce which can be seen in a number of portraits, including that of Juliette Récamier. The fullness of the pleated folds of muslin at the back of the dress is even more clearly emphasised in a portrait of Lady Pamela Fitzgerald and her daughter (pl. 123) attributed to an artist identified only as 'Mallary', about whom nothing is known. The sitter was the illegitimate daughter of Madame de Genlis and Philippe Egalité; she was the wife of the revolutionary Irish politician Lord Edward Fitzgerald, who was killed in 1798. If the portrait is to be dated *c*.1800, it is curious that she does not wear mourning for her husband; however, she was known for the occasional eccentricity of her dress (sometimes affecting 'the dress of a Peasant'[69]), which is not altogether surprising given her parentage. In this portrait the gathered white muslin dress is worn over an underbodice and there might be a small

pad of fabric at the back which helps to create the flowing lines of the rear drapery. The affection between mother and daughter is emphasised by the identical fabric of their dresses; both frocks appear to have a drawstring neckline, which was a simple but effective way of varying the pleats of the fine muslin.

By the end of the 1790s the waist was very high, sometimes right under the bust, as in Ingres's drawing of a woman, possibly Gerard's mistress Barbara Bansi (*c*.1800; pl. 124). Sitting on a parapet overlooking a southern landscape, she is dressed suitably *à l'antique* in a high-waisted round gown of cotton, with short sleeves of dimity (a cotton with a small raised pattern, often of spots). This kind of dress would have a drawstring neck so that the pleats could be arranged becomingly over the bosom, and a drawstring under the bust at the top of the skirt which would form a kind of bibbed front, separate from the bodice. The variety of dress fastenings at this period is immense, with drawstrings, tapes, buttons, and so on; they cannot be easily 'read' in portraits and require a knowledge of how the garments are made – luckily, a considerable number of these dresses survive.

Barbara Bansi's hair is bound round her head in Grecian style, with a plait acting as a bandeau, and the front and side locks carefully curled like cedilla accents; Madame Récamier's front hair in the David portrait is styled in a similar fashion. Both women look as though they have dressed their hair with the fashionable 'huile antique' which was popular in France. John Carr noted in 1802: 'The French ladies every morning anoint their heads with the antique oil; their sidelocks are formed with small circles . . . and the hair behind is rolled into a rose, by which they produce a perfect copy of the ancient bust'.[70] Antique statuary, both male and female, inspired women's hairstyles and the wigs which every *élégante* had on her dressing table. From 1798 some fashionable Frenchwomen began to wear their hair cropped *à la Titus* (in England this style appears slightly later, being mentioned for the first time in 1800 in Heideloff's *Gallery of Fashion*). The *Journal de Paris* (1802) commented: 'plus de la moitié des femmes élégantes ont actuellement les cheveux ou une perruque à la Titus', and a few days later: 'Les coëffeurs ne peuvent assez promptement fournir toutes les perruques à la Titus qui leur sont demandées'.[71] In his *Nouveau Paris* (1798) Mercier observed the rage for wigs among Parisian ladies, claiming that they metamorphosed women into a 'gallery of pictures'; his complaint was not against the style of such wigs, but the expense of time and money which women devoted to such frivolities.

Given the views of many artists on the superiority of classical over contemporary dress, it is not surprising to find that they tended to approve of hairstyles which looked more natural and revealed the shape of the head. Henry Angelo, in his *Reminiscences*, recalled with distaste women's hairdressing in the 1780s, 'the frizzed toupé and large drop sausage-curls on the neck, hiding that beauty which extends from the ear to the shoulder'. He continued: 'The portraits of Sir Thomas Lawrence, Sir William Beechy, and Shee, when speaking of the present coiffure, compared with those of Sir Joshua Reynolds &c must convince any one, though of little judgement, of the *vrai modèle* of beauty'.[72]

The *vrai modèle*, according to Angelo was the 'Grecian style', which brings us back to Barbara Bansi sitting on the parapet with its antique relief. Not only would her dress have been thought to be Grecian in style, but her accessories also. On her feet she wears *cothurnes*, a kind of buskin worn by actors in the classical Greek theatre and described in the *Journal des dames et des modes* (1798) as 'des sandales attachées avec des rubans qui s'entrelacent autour de la jambe'. At about the same time the *Journal* carried articles on how to drape the fine shawls of wool or cashmere which were the indispensable complement to the classical white gowns. Such shawls were both warm (essential in a chilly northern European climate) and elegant; they could, in the words of *La Belle Assemblée*

(1808), be arranged on the figure 'like the drapery of our Grecian statues'.

Fine woollen shawls had been brought back from India to England from the 1760s; originally a masculine garment in Indo-Persian societies, in Europe they were adopted by fashionable women as the perfect accessory for the simpler styles of dress of the late eighteenth century. The *Journal de la mode et du goût* for 5 June 1790, described (and illustrated) a cashmere shawl as a 'toilette à l'anglaise', part of the prevailing Anglomania, and it was rapidly adopted by Frenchwomen. The finest shawls of cashmere (the wool of the Kashmir goat) draped wonderfully well, as Barbara Bansi's indicates, and they had immense seductive appeal, which Gérard demonstrates in his portrait of Madame Récamier (pl. 125).

123 'Mallary', *Lady Pamela Fitzgerald and her Daughter*, *c*.1800. Oil on canvas. National Gallery of Ireland, Dublin.

124 (facing page) J.-A.-D. Ingres, *Barbara Bansi*(?), *c*.1800. Pencil. Cabinet des Dessins, Louvre, Paris. (Photo: © Réunion des musées nationaux)

125 (F.-P.-S Gérard, *Madame Récamier*, 1805. Oil on canvas. Musée Carnavalet, Paris.

This portrait reveals more of the sitter's charms than in her earlier image by David. She is, in fact, painted in the flimsiest of muslin shifts (which deliberately gives the impression of underwear) but her bosom is supported either by an under-bodice, or by a lightweight 'divorce' corset which was designed to separate the breasts and push them forward. Madame Récamier was famous for her shawl dance which she performed at her soirées, and which showed off the splendours of her breast and naked arms. 'With a long scarf in her hand she went through all the poses, wherein the light tissue becomes in turn a girdle, a veil and a drapery. Nothing could be more graceful, more decorous, or more picturesque than this succession of harmonious attitudes, worthy to be perpetuated by the pencil of an artist.'[73]

Madame Récamier's 'attitudes' were possibly inspired by those of Emma Hamilton, although they appear to have been less 'artistic' and more obviously sexual; this, at any rate, is the impression which Gérard conveys. However, the antique-inspired dress and shawl gave the performance a certain *ton*, and possibly inspired the appearance in *Corinne* (1807), a romantic novel by Madame de Staël, of the eponymous Greek lyrical poetess 'qui se montre sur un char antique, en costume de Sibylle, avec un châle de l'Inde roulé en turban autour de la tête'.[74] The author herself was painted by Vigée-Lebrun (c.1808; Geneva, Musée d'Art et d'Histoire) as Corinne, holding a lyre and dressed in a sleeveless shift embroidered round the neck, and with a similarly embroidered mantle wrapped around the lower half of her body. It is a somewhat unfortunate image, for the simpering expression and the classical tunic are better suited to a young girl than to a woman of her mature years.

The French Revolution, claimed Madame de Genlis, had removed many of the distinctions in dress between formal and informal, between old and young. In pursuit of the currently fashionable youthful image, older women had to be careful not to adopt styles which were more suited to the *jeune fille*, but to still appear *à la mode*. White was thought flattering to all ages, from maid to matron. *La Belle Assemblée* (1808) admired 'the chaste, neat and simple elegance of the white robe', and in Jane Austen's *Mansfield Park* (1814) we are told, 'a woman can never be too fine when she is all in white'. It was advisable, however, for the older woman to wear fuller gowns with sleeves, and to cover the decolletage with a fichu or *chemisette*. The popular round robe could be covered with a tunic top, or an over-gown, often of transparent material. Girodet's *Angélique-Adélaïde de Meliand, Marquise de la Grange* (1809; pl. 126) shows the sitter in a white dress, and an over-gown of muslin caught under the bust with a cord of plaited yellow silk. This over-gown has a

flattering, softly ruffled collar which helps to frame her face, as does the fashionable hat of yellow felt trimmed with ribbon and ostrich plumes; the only jewellery is a fine bracelet of gold chain with a small diamond. Altogether it is a costume both fashionable and unostentatious, suitable to the gravity of the occasion – the marquise holds a letter referring to the battle of Wagram (a French victory over the Austrians) in which one of her sons was wounded.

Wearing one gown over another, of similar or contrasting colours and fabrics, varied the wardrobe and provided scope for personal taste. The *Empress Josephine* was painted by Gros in 1809 (pl. 127), in a dress of cream-coloured cashmere, with a deep woven border based on a design of stylized flowers and palmettes, which she wears over a short sleeved dress of muslin or silk gauze. Over her shoulder and round her waist is draped a long red cashmere shawl with a black border print, and over her head a transparent 'Roman' veil of gauze edged with gold, held in place with a long antique pin similar to that which Madame Récamier wears in her hair in Gérard's portrait.

Josephine was particularly fond of shawls; Madame de Rémusat said that she had so many of these that 'she sometimes had them made into gowns, or bedquilts, or cushions for her dog'.[75] In a list of her clothes made in 1809, there are so many shawls that they are listed by colour – red, amarante (a purplish colour), yellow and white are the most popular – and then mixed colours (woven or embroidered designs, and 'schals rayés de plusieurs couleurs').[76] An inventory of effects made after her death in 1814 includes a large number of shawls and 'sept robes de cachemire de différentes couleurs et qualités . . .'[77] Many of these shawls were supplied to her by the couturier Louis-Hyppolite Leroy who was as assiduous in his self-promotion and flair for design as Rose Bertin under Marie-Antoinette. First heard of as an employee of a *magasin de nouveautés* (the new name for mercers), and then of a well-known *couturière* Madame Raimbault, he seems to have been introduced to the future Empress Josephine towards the end of the Directory. By the time of the coronation, in December 1804, he was well enough established in high society to provide the costumes for Emperor, Empress and the new court. His skill was not in the art of design, but in interpreting designs from an impressive stable of artists, including Philibert-Louis Debucourt, Jean-Baptiste Isabey and a theatre designer called Auguste Garnerey who was particularly fond of costume and accessories *à la style troubadour*.

Leroy's registers in the Bibliothèque Nationale in Paris list orders from the Empress, such as gowns of cashmere, muslin and Chambéry gauze (Canterbury muslin). In the *Compte general des dépenses faites pour les atours de Sa Majesté . . . pendant l'année 1809*, there are

126   A.-L. de Roussy Girodet-Trioson, *Angélique-Adélaïde de Meliand, marquise de la Grange*, 1809. Oil on canvas. Matthiesen, London.

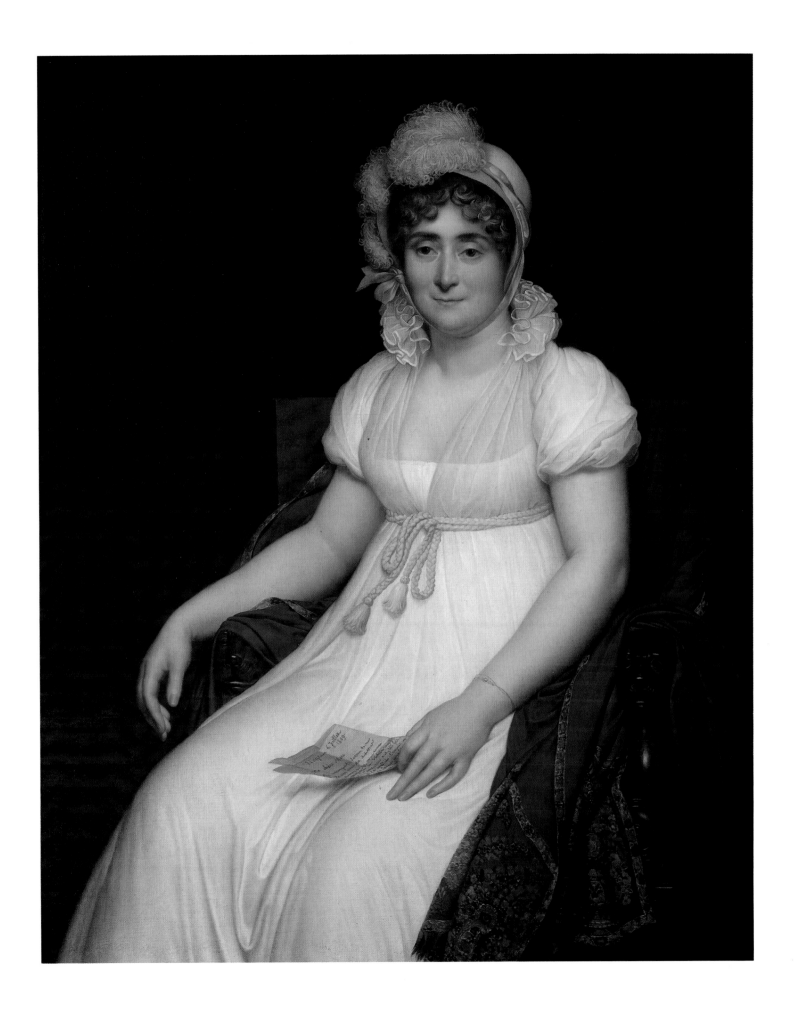

Leroy robes of crepe and tulle (net), various *robes de bal* and court dresses. These last-named are referred to, in the old style, as *grands habits*, so, for example, we find 'un grand habit velours bleu impérial et la robe en tulle brodé or et pierres', and again, 'un grand habit complet tout brodé en plain dessin plumes de paon . . .', the design embroidered in gold, silver and rubies.[78] It was not surprising that although Josephine had 600,000 francs per annum for clothes and personal expenses, she usually spent far more; the 1809 inventory, for example, shows that she spent 920,816 francs in that year.

By far the most popular fabric in this 1809 inventory is cotton, some two hundred gowns in various styles but mainly round gowns, or tunics of embroidered muslin to be worn over satin dresses. Josephine's daughter Hortense recalled how the First Consul hated the ladies of his court wearing English muslin, and when he questioned his wife or stepdaughter they would reply that their dresses were made of Saint-Quentin linen; however, their smiles would give them away, resulting in gowns torn by an enraged Napoleon – 'Ce désastre des toilettes se répéta plusieurs fois, et il fallut en venir au satin et au velours'.[79] The establishment of an imperial court provided further encouragement towards the wearing of such luxury fabrics as satin, velvet and lace.

The Leroy registers give some idea of how sumptuous dress could be at the court. The two clients with the largest number of orders during the last years of the Empire, were Caroline Murat, Queen of Naples, and Catherine of Württemberg, Queen of Westphalia. Caroline Murat had a particular love of luxury fabrics, ordering, for example, in 1812 a white cashmere hunting costume embroidered in silver and a *grand habit* of rose-coloured tulle lined with rose satin. In the same year Queen Catherine ordered, among other items, two court dresses, one of blonde (silk lace) lined with satin and the other of lilac tulle lined with satin; robes of embroidered tulle; robes 'Bingalines' (Bengal muslin) and redingotes of cashmere.[80]

Like any famous couturier, Leroy was able to come to terms with the shifting political fortunes of the times. In 1810 he provided the trousseau[81] for the new French empress, Marie-Louise, whose 'marked absence of elegance' (in the words of the duchesse d'Abrantès) ensured that even his stylish toilettes did not have the same impact as they had had on Josephine. Napoleon's valet Constant stated that Marie-Louise had little idea how to dress and underspent her annual allowance of 500,000 francs. It was unfortunate that she was so tall (she loomed over Napoleon) for the high-waisted style of dress made her look even taller, particularly when worn with the long court train. However, even after the downfall of

Napoleon, Marie-Louise (now Archduchess of Parma) continued to order clothes from Leroy, as did many of the Bonaparte ladies. The couturier was also quite happy to provide outfits for the ladies of the Allied generals and politicians, such as the Duchess of Wellington, who in 1814 ordered a court dress of silver-spangled tulle and a number of hats.[82]

Leroy was able to provide every kind of dress and accessory that could be required. When Napoleon decided – in imitation of the *ancien-régime* custom for hunting liveries – that each member of his family should have an *habit de chasse* for their individual courts, Leroy supplied them. Madame de Rémusat remembered:

> The costume of the Empress was amaranth velvet, embroidered with gold, with a toque also embroidered in gold, and a plume of white feathers. All the Ladies-in-Waiting wore amaranth. Queen Hortense chose blue and silver; Madame Murat, pink and silver; Princess Borghese, lilac and silver. The dress was a sort of tunic, a short redingote in velvet, worn over a gown of embroidered white satin; velvet boots to match the dress, and a toque with a white plume.[83]

Like the great Charles Frederick Worth, couturier to the court of the Second Empire, Leroy's skills extended to the execution of fancy dress, both for the carnival (which had been restored by Napoleon in 1801), and for the elaborate *bals masqués* which celebrated great occasions of state, such as the birth of the heir, the King of Rome, in 1811.

In his pre-eminent status and the diversity of his talents, it has aptly been said that Leroy was to fashion what David was to art. It was Leroy who supplied the coronation and court costumes that David depicted in the *Coronation of Napoleon* (1807–5; pl. 162). It is Leroy's celebrated outfits that are worn in the official portraits of the royal Bonaparte ladies wearing the *robes de cour* based on the costume worn by the Empress Josephine at the coronation (discussed in detail in Chapter 3).

One example of this court dress must suffice: in Gérard's *Marie-Julie Bonaparte, Queen of Spain, with her Daughters Zenaïde and Charlotte* (1808–9; pl. 128), Marie-Julie wears a dress of white satin embroidered in gold, with long (detachable) sleeves; her court train fastened under the bust is of red velvet embroidered in gold. It is a costume that is both regal and in the spirit of contemporary dress, with its high waist and delicate embroidery. Aided by Talleyrand, Josephine was determined to introduce a stylish court, the model for others to follow. Some aspects of *ancien-régime* etiquette were re-introduced, such as formal presentations, the royal arm-chairs (only the imperial couple were allowed these chairs) and the old court

127 A.-J. Gros. *Empress Josephine*, 1809. Oil on canvas. Musée Masséna, Nice.

cheveux à la Titus, et des robes dessinant les formes'.[84] However, there was no real likelihood of court fashions reverting to Bourbon styles, as Napoleon wished for his own distinctive imprint on a new kind of court. As he admired the high-waisted, short-sleeved dresses which Josephine wore with such grace, he was keen that court dress should relate to contemporary styles, but be made of luxurious French fabrics. The resulting costume consisted of a white dress, embroidered, with short sleeves (to which long sleeves could be added for very formal occasions) and a court train of coloured silk, usually velvet, also embroidered.

Embroidery played a key role in formal dress during the Empire; it replaced the ribbons, frills and furbelows which had characterised court dress during Bourbon rule. Costume now provided flat painterly surfaces on which the embroiderer could display his or her skills in design, incorporating not just the Napoleonic bee, but a range of classical and exotic motifs, as well the ever-popular flowers. For court-wear dresses and trains could be embroidered in real gold and precious stones; less expensive embroidery might include spangles, coloured silks and foil, and bugle (glass) beads.

The Napoleonic court (and the satellite courts linked to it) had come into being through military conquest; at its heart it was a military and administrative machine, a court for men rather than for women. Apart from the royal princesses, the wives of courtiers and the ladies in attendance on the Empress, there were not that many women at court. Full court dress with a train was only worn on such occasions as presentation to the Emperor and Empress, New Year's Day, formal court balls and functions held in the *grands appartements* at the Tuileries; it appeared alongside men's court uniform and the *habit habillé*. But, whereas the men could find hardly any other occasion to wear the *habit à la française*, the women, discarding their trains, could wear the elegant high-waisted dress as formal fashion.

At the Restoration the *robe de cour* was retained in its Empire style, but with the addition of lace lappets (streamers) in the hair; the delicate spiky lace collar called a *chérusque* (which can be seen in plates 128 and 141) was abandoned in favour of a broad, heavy lace collar. Some women, like the comtesse de Boigne disapproved of these additions which were felt to be too fussy for the graceful Neoclassical lines of Empire court dress:

'To the imperial costume all the paraphernalia of the former style of dress was added, and this was singularly incongruous. To our Grecian style of hairdressing, for instance, these ridiculous lappets were added, and the elegant chérusque, which

128   F.-P.-S. Gérard, *Marie-Julie Bonaparte, Queen of Spain, with her Daughters Zenaïde and Charlotte*, 1808–9. Oil on canvas. National Gallery of Ireland, Dublin.

ritual of ceremonial dressing for the day was revived for the Empress. Emigrés were encouraged to return and were asked to recall details of court life under Louis XVI, as was Madame Campan, who had been First Woman of the Bedchamber to Marie-Antoinette and who now kept a school for young girls.

There was considerable debate as to the form which court dress was to take, some women worrying that hoops and powder might be revived. 'Elles voyaient juste', said one contemporary, 'car de vieilles matrones de la cour de Louis XV soutenaient que l'on n'avait point bon air avec les modes grecques et romaines, et que la corruption des moeurs datait des completed a garb copied from Van Dyck, was replaced by a heavy mantilla, and a kind of pleated plastron . . .'[85]

In fact, according to the comtesse, the new First Lady (Madame) at the French court, Louis XVIII's niece, the duchesse d'Angoulême, had wanted to restore hoops in court dress, in the style of the *ancien régime*, but this was overruled as being, in the words of the duchesse d'Abrantès, akin to 'the barbarism of the middle ages'. One can sympathise with this comment, if we compare the stylish court costume of the First Empire, with the overblown dress worn at the English court, as in plate 129, *Court Dress*, 1807, from *Le Beau Monde*. Here, the woman's dress has the three-dimensional trimmings and large hoop of the eighteenth century, which looks absurd with the high waist of contemporary fashion. In 1810 Louis Simond watched Englishwomen attending the King's Birthday: 'The ladies who go to court on the birth-day are dressed in the fashion of fifty years ago, as more suitable, I suppose, to the age of their majesties'. When these ladies sat in their sedan chairs, he continued, 'their immense hoops are folded like wings, pointed forward on each side'. He concluded that their appearance 'does not ill resemble a foetus of a hippopotamus in its brandy bottle'.[86] To a Persian observer at about the same time, English ladies in court dress 'seemed to be standing in full-blown tents . . . [with] Phoenix-like feathers in their hair.'[87] In the light of such comments (and because Englishwomen themselves on the whole found this dress archaically cumbersome) it is hardly suprising that there are no portraits depicting female court dress in England in this period.

Towards the middle of the first decade of the nineteenth century, however, a gradual trend in the direction of fuller, more decorated costume can be seen, even in France. The Neoclassical look of extreme simplicity began to disappear; dress no longer clung to the figure as it had at the turn of the century. On the eve of the coronation, late in 1804, the *Journal de Paris* regretted the decline in women's dress which had been inspired by 'la pureté des dessins de David . . . l'élégance des formes antiques'; fashionable women, it was claimed, no longer wore just a simple robe, but a *collerette*, a redingote and sometimes a cashmere shawl as well.[88]

The *collerette*, a ruff of lace or cotton, was a popular historical revival, one of the first intimations of the romantic *style troubadour* which affected dress in France, particularly from the second decade of the nineteenth century. The *Journal de Paris* throughout 1804 noted the popularity of these ruffs which looked pretty, but which made it as difficult for a fashionable woman to move her head, as it was for a man to

move his wearing a stiffened cravat. These *collerettes* were called *à la reine Mathilde*, after the wife of William the Conqueror, in imitation of the ruff worn by a popular actress in a current theatrical production; there was a further allusion to Queen Matilda with the display of the Bayeux Tapestry (which she was, erroneously, supposed to have worked with her ladies) in Paris from October 1803 to January 1804, while Napoleon prepared for an invasion of England. These *collerettes* continued to be widely worn until the

129 Anon., 'Court Dress', from *Le Beau Monde*, 1807. Coloured engraving. Private Collection.

compromise costumes of transparent cottons, gauzes and nets over silk under-dresses. Gauzy, floating fabrics softened the silhouette and added subtleties of colour; Zenaïde and Charlotte Bonaparte, for example (pl. 128) wear frocks of pink silk under gossamer dresses of white muslin.

Satin was particularly popular as winter formal wear during the second decade of the nineteenth century. Sometimes it could be mixed with muslin, as in David's *Comtesse Daru* (1810; New York, Frick Collection) where the white satin dress has short puffed sleeves slashed to reveal a white muslin under-sleeve. Her rosy, homely face with its unflattering bathing-cap-like headdress of white flowers, is painted with the same dispassionate quality that David brings to all his portraits, including those of his wife and daughters. The artist's portrait of his wife, *Marguérite-Charlotte David* (1813; pl. 131), is the reverse of the obsequious image which a society painter might depict. Is it possible to sense something of their troubled early marriage in her wary expression and his calculated portrayal of her plain features made even more so by the corkscrew curls of her hairstyle and the over-elaborate *toque* with its ostrich plumes? There is a slightly odd conjunction of the middle-aged head with the girlish body which is emphasised by the simple satin dress with its short puffed sleeves. Madame David's beautiful arms however, draw our attention by the way the artist paints the supple cashmere shawl, an area of vibrant colour as a contrast to the pallor of the dress and headwear.

end of the period; they looked as attractive with dresses of white cotton (see pl. 130) as with the gowns of satin and velvet that returned to favour in the decade 1810–20. Vernet's *Merveilleuse* of *c*.1812 wears a *collerette* of starched muslin with her dress of white cotton which is trimmed with broderie anglaise at hem and cuffs. The dress, although white, is no longer imitative of classical styles; the bodice, now back-fastening, is pleated on to a skirt which is increasingly wider at the hem. This new emphasis on the fullness of the skirt (aided by the introduction of gores, wedge-shaped inserts which added width) was further stressed by decoration at the hem such as multiple flounces and pleating (see pl. 138), lace, embroidery and padded trimmings such as rouleaux. Sleeves became more complex and while the short puffed sleeve was often retained, the arm was sometimes covered in a transparent over-sleeve of silk gauze, called an *aerophane*, quite modest in style as worn in the Vernet fashion drawing, but much larger and more prominent towards 1820, as can be seen in Constable's *Mrs James Andrew* (pl. 133).

In France the establishment of an imperial court helped to revive the silk industry which had suffered badly during the Revolution and the succeeding years of political instability. Even under the Consulate, when fine muslins had been all the rage, but when the wearing of silk was gradually being made a political priority by Napoleon, women of fashion adopted

124

The plain shawls (*schals unis*) of the late eighteenth-century, with their simple border designs, had by the establishment of the Empire, given way to larger, wider rectangular styles with elaborate oriental motifs, such as the popular pine-cone and the 'Paisley' pattern still familiar today; a good example is the shawl seen in Girodet's *Marquise de la Grange* (pl. 126). By the early nineteenth century imitation cashmere shawls were being produced in Norwich, Paisley and Edinburgh, either of cotton or silk mixed with wool, or very fine wool. In France the couturier Leroy commissioned designs from Isabey and Vernet for home-woven shawls with European designs of bouquets and garlands; some of these shawls, produced by the textile firm of Ternaux in 1811–12, were presented to the Empress Marie-Louise. Nothing, however, could match the real cashmere shawls for lightness and warmth and this preference is clearly marked in contemporary portraiture, particularly in France where an element of conspicuous expenditure played an important part in Empire society.

There were, however, other fashionable alternatives to the large wide woollen or cashmere shawls. These included narrow stoles of lace, net or gauze; of fur or swansdown lined with satin; of striped silk, known as Circassian scarves (see pl. 137); and of plaid – part of the French fascination with things Scottish – an example of which can be seen as worn by Vernet's *Merveilleuse*. Cashmere shawls, however, provided the best possibilities for graceful drapery and were widely worn even on formal occasions. In 1814, after the first defeat of Napoleon, one English visitor to the Opéra in Paris found the French ladies too 'undressed' in their 'high flower-pot bonnets and shawls'; in the following year, at the same venue, another Briton noted the Parisiennes in 'high-crowned plume-covered bonnets and shawls; the latter a most favourite article of their dress, and the most acceptable present from their admirers'.[89]

Elegantly arranged though these shawls appear in portraits, to a British eye they created in reality a muffled look, which reminded one observer of 'matrons taking care of a cold and sore throat'.[90] The English fashion magazine, *La Belle Assemblée* (1806) thought that shawls were more likely 'to conceal and vulgarize, than to display the contours of an elegant form';[91] it may be for this reason that they are less likely to appear in British portraiture. Also, it has to be said that the loose draperies which a shawl created were more in tune with the more classically harmonious and unified styles of French dress than with the exaggerated quasi-historical costume which the English had evolved. When, in 1814 and in 1815, English and Frenchwomen met for the first time after many years of warfare, they surveyed each other's costume with surprise and not a little hostility. The

English visitors were amazed at the towering feathered hats and the high-waisted dresses of the Parisian *élégantes* who took 'little mincing Chinese steps' beneath their wide flounced skirts.[92] In return, the French deplored the dress of Englishwomen with their tight-waisted bodices, fierce corsetry and small, poky headwear. The French view of English dress is seen in Vernet's caricature 'Costumes anglais', from the journal *Le Bon Genre* (1814; pl. 132); the artist has drawn attention to the rigidly boned stays which emphasise the bust and waist, the fussy details of the bodice and sleeves and the unbecoming head-dresses. James Simpson, in his *Paris after Waterloo*, recalled meeting a Frenchwoman in the Tivoli Gardens who 'screamed with mirth when she described the English long waist and little shell of a bonnet'.[93] The return to the natural waistline in English dress (though vastly exaggerated by critics and caricaturists) encouraged a revival of tightly laced and more heavily boned stays, 'deformity once more drawing the steeled boddice upon the bruised ribs', in the words of the *Mirror of the Graces*, 1811. The editor of this fashion and etiquette compendium regretted the abandonment of 'the easy shape and flowing drapery' in dress, in favour of tight-fitting costume supported by corsets that pushed up the bosom, to make 'a sort of fleshy shelf, disgusting to the beholders, and certainly incommodious to the bearer'.[94] This is one of the aspects of English dress which Vernet has emphasised, even in the dress of the most fashionable woman in his satire, leaning on the arm of her beau dressed in his frogged pelisse coat. This woman's rigid bodice further emphasises the breasts by its decorative trimming, but

132 H. Vernet, 'Costumes anglais', from *Le Bon Genre*, 1814. Engraving. Private Collection.

along with the English waist, she has included such elements of French dress as the ribboned hem and sleeves *à la mameluke* (that is arranged in puffs of material), a style named after the Battle of the Nile in 1798.

Although the fashion magazines, both French and English, describe a bewildering variety of headwear – turbans, caps, bonnets and hats – the French preference seems to have been for straw hats (as in the illustration of Vernet's *Merveilleuse*) or for *toques* of varying fabrics (see Girodet's *Marquise de la Grange* and David's portrait of his wife), all decorated with soft and becoming ostrich plumes. By comparison, Englishwomen had no sense of loyalty to a particular style, embracing a vast array of headwear, including the unappealing (at least to French eyes) poke bonnet; this originated in the late 1790s, and has been chosen as a typically English style by Vernet for his 'Costumes anglais' – it is second from the left in plate 132. Just looking at one year of an English fashion magazine gives some indication of the jostling and varied fashion influences at work within the realm of headwear. *La Belle Assemblée* for 1808, for example, offers in February, pearl-trimmed Mary Queen of Scots coifs, fringed gold or silver Chinese turbans and muslin (Chambéry) turbans; in March the editors suggested an 'Anne Boleyn cap of black lace, tamboured in shaded green silk or chenille'; in April there were Minerva bonnets and Grecian 'mobs' (caps), followed by a number of other 'antique' styles over the next few months, such as bandeaux, diadems and coronets; and, finally, in December we read about Spanish hats of 'satin, frosted velvet, and gold or silver tissue', which, doubtless could be worn with the costume recommended for September, 'a plain Spanish robe of white or pea-green sarsnet, with . . . [a] hinged ruff à-la-Cléopatre'.

The next two portraits of English sitters, painted towards the end of the period, show two of the styles mentioned by *La Belle Assemblée*, the mob cap, as worn by Constable's *Mrs James Andrew* (1818; pl. 133), and the turban, as seen in Beechey's *Lady Catherine Manners* (pl. 134), exhibited at the Royal Academy in 1820. Mrs Andrew wears a dress of white silk gauze over greeny-white satin, the bodice trimmed with horizontal bands of piping and a large satin bow at the high waist; *aerophanes* of silk gauze cover the arms and make the skin beneath appear whiter, the shimmering movement of the fabric reflected in the loose handling of the paint. There is no idealisation in the way the artist paints the strong, plain face, which (like that of Madame David) seems slightly at war with the artificial curls of the hair and the elaborate head-dress; Mrs Andrew's cap is of muslin, trimmed with net and tying with long silk tassels at the side. The dress, with its layered horizontal look created by the frilled net collar of the *chemisette* and the piped satin bodice decoration, is a style more suited to the slimmer figure which the fashion magazines assiduously promoted, claiming that 'excessive repletion' not only led to unattractive weight gain, but to 'disorders of the complexion'. Furthermore, said the *Mirror of the Graces* (1811) there was an increased movement towards greater demarcation in dress among women of different ages; young women looked best in pastel colours, whereas the 'lady of majestic deportment' was better advised to choose 'the fuller shades of yellow, purple, crimson, scarlet, black and grey'. Old, neglected notions of the suitability of dress for different ages, classes and occasions, were on the verge of being revived and were to turn into the full-blown panoply of Victorian sartorial etiquette.

133   J. Constable, *Mrs James Andrew*, 1818. Oil on canvas. Tate Gallery, London.

lace both French and English.[95] The catalogue of the clothes of Queen Caroline of Brunswick, who died a few weeks after the coronation of George IV in the summer of 1821, contains dress accessories, spencers (short jackets) and dress trimmings of various kinds of lace. The royal wardrobe (which was sold at auction in February 1822, fetching £972 17s 3d) included dresses of net and gauze trimmed with lace, in the dramatic colours which she favoured, so alien to English notions of restraint and quiet luxury.[96]

It was Beau Brummell's theory, perhaps developed during his exile in France, that in women's costume, there should be 'one predominating colour to which the dress should be subordinate'; to clothe the top half of the body in one colour and the bottom half in another, he declared, was far too theatrical and inharmonious.[97] This was a reference to the various forms of short jackets, some sleeved, some sleeveless, which had been in fashion from the 1790s; these included the spencer, which derived from the *pierrot* (see pl. 88), and the *canezou*. Both spencer and *canezou* (differences in style are slight) could be made of a wide range of fabrics and trimmed according to the prevailing taste; by the second decade of the nineteenth century they were usually coloured, in contrast to the white of the dress. As these jackets were tight to the body, they appeared as a kind of bodice to the skirt of the dress beneath; this ensemble, then, forms a bridge between the gown made in one piece and the totally separate bodice and skirt style which came into being by the end of the period.

It is rare to find these short jackets making an appearance in portraiture; perhaps because they were too informal, but also because they broke up the line of the dress with its flowing drapery. Artists encouraged their sitters to drape scarves around themselves instead, or to wear long-sleeved garments like the *douillette*, a kind of indoors redingote. The distinction between these two garments is not very clear. The *Journal de Paris* (1804) states firmly: 'une douillette sert dans l'appartement, et on sort avec une redingote',[98] but the fashion magazines list both types of coat as being made of a wide range of fabrics from wool and velvet to cotton. The Empress Josephine's redingotes, as listed in the 1809 and 1814 inventories, are made of fabrics as diverse as casimir (fine woollen cloth), satin, vicuna, knitted silk and muslin; some are lined with fur for outdoors and others, like the *redingotes Lévantines*, may be indoor wrapping gowns. Such indoor gowns were a stylish and more practical alternative to the shawl, particularly for older women, as Marie-Laetitia Bonaparte, 'Madame Mère' in Gérard's portrait of 1803, (pl. 135). Napoleon's mother, by then in her fifties sits close to a sculpted bust of her son, with a view of the Tuileries, where he resided as First Consul, in the background. The image of this

As we approach 1820, it once again becomes easier to distinguish types of dress, from the formal to the informal. The hierarchy is not as complicated as it had been in the eighteenth century and was to become by the middle of the nineteenth century, but clearer than it had been during the Revolutionary and immediately post-Revolutionary period, which affected dress all over Europe. It is clear, for example, that while Mrs Andrews is wearing day dress, Lady Catherine is in evening costume, a high-waisted satin dress with a wide, low neckline edged with lace; the short, puffed sleeves are looped up with braid in imitation of Renaissance slashed sleeves and the mixture of the historical with the exotic (in the form of the jewelled and plumed turban) is particularly English. Alongside, and gradually replacing the muslin dresses and *demi-robes*, were tunics, scarves, veils and mantles of lace, tulle, blonde and net. Lace had been revived for court dress in France, and although it was never to regain the importance it had during the eighteenth-century, it had remained in favour for wedding dresses and trousseaux, accessories and layettes. The inventory of the Empress Josephine's effects in 1814 included dresses and redingotes of lace as well as fichus, *mantelets*, *chemisettes*, ruffs, jabots, veils and aprons of

Another coat-like garment which may relate to the redingote is the pelisse. Originally, in the eighteenth century this was a fur-lined cloak with slits for the arm; Mrs Siddons, in Gainsborough's portrait (pl. 78) wears such a garment, edged with fox fur. By the early nineteenth century the pelisse had become a fairly close-fitting sleeved coat, sometimes lined with fur; in Leroy's registers, for example, Queen Caroline of Naples is listed as ordering a blue velvet pelisse lined with grey fox in 1814.[99] How far this type of pelisse is similar to the *witzchoura*, a fur-lined coat of Polish origin, which is mentioned from about 1808, is not clear; possibly the *witzchoura* was less fitted and sometimes appears with a hood. It was a popular garment with Josephine, and her 1814 inventory lists 'videchouras' of white satin lined with sable, poppy velvet lined with chinchilla and *nacarat* (orange-red) velvet lined with golden fox.[100]

By this time, the pelisse had also become a kind of indoor dress, the *pelisse-robe*, front-fastening all the way from neck to hem and made of a variety of fabrics, including wool, silk and cotton. The duchesse d'Abrantès remembered one of the outfits worn by the ever-stylish former Empress after her divorce, during her last years: 'a robe of fine soft India muslin, delicately wrought with small stars... made in the form of a pelisse', worn over a turquoise silk slip and fastened with turquoise silk bows all the way down the front.[101] Queen Caroline of Brunswick, at her death, had a number of pelisses, for both outdoor and indoor wear; these included, for example, a pelisse of white velvet lined with fur and 'superbly embroidered in gold, with bullion tassels', and an 'elegant purple lutestring Pelisse, lined white silk, and beautiful Vandyke trimming'.[102]

The graceful lines of the pelisse with its high waist, cross-over bodice and long tight sleeves extending well over the wrist, can be seen in Ingres's drawing of Caroline Murat (*c*.1814; pl. 136). This study probably relates to a recently discovered full-length portrait of the Queen of Naples[103] wearing a totally black ensemble – velvet dress, lace ruff and mantle, and hat trimmed with ostrich feathers; the costume would appear to be mourning for the Empress Josephine and was completed after Ingres returned to Rome from Naples. Queen Caroline was noted for her stylish toilettes, Queen Hortense recalling: 'nulle autre ne posséda comme elle l'art d'attirer et de charmer par une grâce qui avait quelque chose de la noblesse asiatique et séduisante des odalisques'.[104] This trait would undoubtedly appeal to Ingres, who in the drawing illustrated here, has given the Queen a kind of stylized oriental immobility of pose and features, emphasising the tall, plumed *toque*, from under which a few curls of hair escape, and the pendant three-drop (girandole) earring.[105]

135 F.-P.-S. Gérard, *Marie-Laetitia Bonaparte, Madame Mère*, 1803. Oil on canvas. National Gallery of Scotland, Edinburgh.

mother to a dynasty is one of dignified splendour, her head dressed in the curls, diadem (of gold, pearls and a cameo) and veil of a noble Roman matron. Her dress is of white silk embroidered in gold, over which is worn a green velvet over-gown, probably a *douillette*; a red cashmere shawl is draped over the arm of her chair.

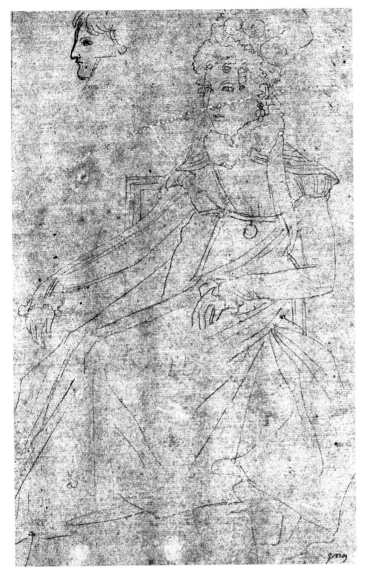

The pelisse is *the* fashionable day dress of the 1820s, and has begun to appear in portraits by that time. Painted in 1820 (dated the following year), David's portrait of the Bonaparte sisters (pl. 137) shows Charlotte on the left in a blue silk pelisse trimmed with satin ribbon; the frilled silk ruff and the ruched upper sleeve are 'Renaissance' features influenced by *le style troubadour* (see Chapter 3). Zenaïde wears a more formal costume of black velvet, trimmed with embroidered net; her sleeves, with their puffed satin inserts, also reflect the historical theme. The two daughters of Joseph Bonaparte (seen as young girls with their mother, the Queen of Spain, in pl. 128) retain elements of their former grandeur in the heavy Empire sofa of red velvet embroidered with golden bees and in their jewelled fillets – Charlotte's of pink topazes and tiny pearls set in gold and Zenaïde's of coral cameos in gold.

In a sense, this dress with its opulence and luxury fabrics, looks forward to the bourgeois society of the

1820s and 1830s so vividly illuminated by Stendhal and Balzac. More characteristic of the period are two final images which summarise the grace and elegance of costume in France and England towards 1820. Plate 138 is Géricault's portrait of Laure Bro (*c*.1818), his landlady and the wife of a noted Bonapartist who had taken part in many military campaigns. Géricault painted relatively few portraits, mainly those of his friends, and this image of Laure Bro is a labour of love in every sense of the word, a sympathetic yet honest depiction of character, with a painter's eye for textures, contrasts and place. Seated in an almost bare room, Laure Bro wears a dress of white muslin, bound under the bust with a blue silk girdle, the colour echoed in her satin shoes with their ribbon lacing. This is not a portrait of an *élégante*, although the dress derives from the kind of fashionable styles illustrated in Vernet's *Merveilleuses*, such as plate 130 (incidentally, Géricault was a friend of Vernet whose studio, close by, was a meeting place for artists,

136 (above left) J.-A.-D. Ingres, Study for *Caroline Murat*, *c*.1814. Pencil. Musée Ingres, Montauban.

137 J.-L. David, *Charlotte and Zenaïde Bonaparte*, 1820–1. Oil on canvas. Collection of the J. Paul Getty Museum, Malibu, California.

138 J.-L.-A.-T. Géricault, *Laure Bro*, *c.*1818. Oil on canvas. Sale, Sotheby's Monaco, 3 December 1989, lot 510.

writers and liberal politicians). Madame Bro's costume is simple and unadorned, the bare neckline emphasising the beauty of her shoulders and her long neck, in the same way that the severity of the hairstyle stresses the bone structure of the face. The artist has used the classic gesture of crossing the arms over the belly, reinforcing the elegant display of the arms and hands by painting one white silk glove on (pl. 138a); these gloves are as beautifully painted, and as moving, as those curiously over-large kid mittens lined with white satin that are worn in Ingres's *Mademoiselle Rivière* (Louvre). The *tour de force* of Géricault's portrait, however, must be the painting of the Italian straw bonnet, with its gauzy muslin veil draped over it. We are to assume that the sitter has just come in,

taken off her hat and draped her shawl over her chair; slightly warily, she waits for the artist to begin his work. Some art historians have seen this portrait as dating from after Géricault's departure for England in

138a Géricault, *Laure Bro* (detail of pl. 138).

1820. The style of the dress would not support this argument, but the poetic quality of the portrait and the lyrical landscape (of rural Paris, looking towards Montmartre) indicate a familiarity with English art.

The last image in this chapter demonstrates the English affinity between costume and landscape which characterises the period of this book. It is Turner's *England: Richmond Hill on the Prince Regent's Birthday* (*c*.1819), of which plate 139 is a detail. The curve of the river and the rounded foliage of the trees echo the costume and accessories. The general style of dress in this most romantic of periods consists of high-waisted dresses with full, softly rounded sleeves and small neat hairstyles with plumed hats *à la Renaissance*. Turner is adept at catching the salient details of dress, even in a landscape painting where the figures are quite small. He has noticed how the waistline had become very high as we approach 1820; this has the result, as in the woman third from the right, of pushing up the bust into tightly corsetted globes. The short-bodiced gowns are cut quite full at the back and the artist has caught the graceful folds of drapery of the seated figures in the centre. The dresses flare out gradually towards the hem and additional slight movement is created by shawls and summer pelisses. In the right-

hand group, for example, the central figure wears a pelisse over a gown and she gestures to the woman next to her who wears a yellow dress with a loose white mantle.

Certain aspects of costume and appearance have often fascinated artists. Fuseli, for example, seems to have been obsessed with the elaborate hairstyles of the late eighteenth and early nineteenth centuries, which he exaggerated in his art. Turner was attracted to the way in which the long, swan-like necks of high fashion were emphasised by the swept-up hairstyles, small neat *toques* and the necklines of the gowns cut quite low and straight across at the back. This type of neckline and hairstyle was influenced by mid-seventeenth century Dutch fashions; the high-waisted gowns of satin or velvet, with their rounded, softly pleated sleeves were inspired by early sixteenth-century costume. It is a period when revivals of this kind are cleverly incorporated into contemporary fashion, such artistic references being particularly pleasing to an artist such as Turner (and to Ingres also) who was well versed in history. This kind of gentle romanticism in dress blends past and present, in modest fulfilment of an enduring strain in English art.

139 J. M. W. Turner, *Richmond Hill on the Prince Regent's Birthday* (detail), *c*.1819. Oil on canvas. Tate Gallery, London.

131

3

The Stuff of Heroes: Historical Themes in Dress and Art in France

Nous parlerons de l'habillement des François, parceque l'habillement
chez un peuple est mis au rang des choses publiques,
soit par rapport a lui-même, soit par rapport aux autres peuples . . .
Les habits des nations illustres deviennent bientôt communs dans l'univers;
parceque l'on se porte naturellement à imiter ceux qu'on admire,
ceux qu'on aime. C'est ainsi que les habits des Grecs & des Romains
ont tour-a-tour dominé parmi les nations.
(J.F. Sobry, *Discours sur les principaux usages de la nation françoise*, 1786)

Our grandfathers as they appear in their portraits,
with their coats all embroidered in the fashion of Louis XV's time,
seem plainly ridiculous; but our remoter ancestors, with their doublet-and-hose,
and the armour which it was customary to wear in the days of François I
are invested with a splendid aura of romantic mystery,
as they gaze severely down upon us from their vast portraits.
(Stendhal, *Life of Rossini*, 1824)*

140   David, *Paris and Helen* (detail of pl. 148).

In the previous chapter there were many references to dress *à l'antique*, particularly with regard to women. A love of antiquity in art and literature was not, of course, an innovation of the eighteenth century, but dates from at least the Renaissance. From the early sixteenth century in France men of learning and taste (including royalty) collected antiquities and commissioned copies of classical works of art; the literature and history of ancient Greece and Rome were widely read and disseminated through a wide range of literary, visual and applied art forms. But it does seem that during the eighteenth century a general admiration of classical antiquity turned into a desire to put into practice some of the tenets expressed by the political philosophers of the ancient world, to create an ideal state based on virtue. This, after all, lies at the heart of Rousseau's political theories, that 'Popular Will' can best be expressed through virtuous citizens. As Louis Bertrand points out in *La Fin du classicisme et le retour à l'antique*, Rousseau was not particularly versed in the classics, but, 'à cause de son goût pour la nature et pour une simplicité un peu fastueuse dans les moeurs et dans le costume, il devait se sentir attiré vers les anciens et chercher chez eux des modèles'. In *Emile*, for example, the hero prefers the books of the ancients to those of his own time, and Rousseau himself had a particular taste for Plutarch, which, as he reveals in the *Confessions*, helped to form 'cet esprit libre et républicain' which influenced his whole life.[1] Roman history, and especially the period of the Roman Republic, was admired as a source of antique virtue. *Philosophes* such as Montesquieu in *De l'Esprit des lois* (1748) conjured up visions of the citizen of ancient Rome 'tout entier dans l'amour des lois et de la patrie', fired with enthusiasm by civic pageantry and stirring spectacle.[2] The view of most *philosophes* was that, while ancient Greece might charm the senses, Rome and Sparta would reach out to the soul, to encourage the sense of virtue so essential to a republic.[3] Not that there was any real desire that France should become a republic, a form of political system thought to be more appropriate to small countries and city states; it was, however, a convenient stick with which to attack the ills of contemporary society. Such beliefs, however, were the fertile soil in which revolutionary thought flourished at the end of the eighteenth century.

The most popular themes in French history painting, particularly from the last quarter of the century, were taken from ancient Rome.

The heart of French historicism was the return to an austere early Republican Rome. In almost every year after 1777, Roman themes figured twice as often as Greek ones. Mostly, they show characters in a moral dilemma – Regulus, Brutus, Torquatus, Virginius, Cornelia, Scipio, Marius, Cato, Agrippina or Belisarius – choosing the noblest course of action or suffering nobly.[4]

Of Greek authors, Homer was a popular source; in his *Réflexions sur quelques causes de l'état présent de la peinture en France* (1747), La Font de Saint-Yenne recommended the Iliad and Odyssey as material for artists. Of the Greek revival period, Plutarch's *Lives* provided inspiration for both writers and artists.

Practical encouragement for history painters wishing to depict the glory that was Greece and the grandeur that was Rome, came in the form of illustrated publications relating to the art and artefacts that were being discovered and 'uncovered' throughout the century. The first systematic excavation of Herculaneum took place in 1738, to be followed ten years later by Pompeii (which was not identified as such until 1763). The comte de Caylus described the wall paintings of Herculaneum in a publication of 1751, and followed this with his comprehensive *Recueil d'antiquités égyptiennes, étrusques, grecques, romaines et gauloises* (1752–67), a study of antique art from the original objects brought forth by the new discipline of archaeology. It was the German writer and archaeologist Johann Joachim Winckelmann, however, who enthused a whole generation of writers and artists with his lively yet erudite publications on antique art, an essay on the imitation of Greek painting and sculpture (1755) and the famous *Geschichte der Kunst des Altertums* (1764) which two years later was translated into French as the *Histoire de l'art chez les anciens*.

Winckelmann's belief that Greek art was superior to that of Rome was reflected at this point in the eighteenth century in both fine and applied art, in painting, architecture, interior design, and – if Baron Grimm is to be believed, in his often quoted comments made in 1763 – in dress as well:

Depuis quelques années, on a recherché les ornements et les formes antiques; le goût y a gagné considérablement, et la mode en est devenue si générale que tout se fait aujourd'hui à la grecque. La décoration intérieure et extérieure des bâtiments, les meubles, les étoffes, les bijoux de toute espéce, tout est à Paris à la grecque; nos petits-maîtres se croiraient déshonorés de porter une boîte qui ne fût pas à la grecque.[5]

Baron Grimm was, perhaps, using a little poetic license to amuse his foreign readers; it is hard to discover a particular taste for Greek influence on dress and textiles in the mid-eighteenth century, although there might have been temporary whims for such accessories as 'boites à la grecque' to be carried by fashionable fops (*petits-maîtres*). Interior design and

141 David, *Coronation of Napoleon* (detail of pl. 162).

century shift of the sort that some twenty years later would become the fashionable chemise gown.

Vien was in Rome during the 1740s when the excavations of Herculaneum had opened new vistas on antique art. He, like other interested artists, would have been made aware of the use of colour in wall paintings, although the discovery of the more highly regarded classical statuary helped to foster an erroneous notion of white clothing and drapery, which affected history painting and costume. The situation is further complicated by the fact that, when copying Greek works of art the Romans often misunderstood the clothing, which is hardly surprising, for it was far more complex and sophisticated than the dress of ancient Rome. Inevitably, misconceptions about classical dress appeared in costume books and in the works of writers on antique art; eighteenth-century artists, finding it difficult to get back to accurate original sources, even if they thought the task worth considering, often opted for more generalised draperies.

These had the effect of giving a classical air to compositions that were basically Rococo in concept, such as Carle van Loo's *Offering to Cupid* (1761; pl. 142). In a pastoral setting worthy of Boucher, a young Greek maiden makes her offering aided by her female attendant; a young man, possibly her lover, is also about to offer his garland of flowers to Cupid. Van Loo has made quite a serious study of the clothes, even if they are arranged in a way to suit mid-eighteenth-century tastes, with the emphasis on full-ness at the hips created by over-tunics and fairly voluminous draperies; there is, perhaps deliberately, no sense of any particular fabric for the clothing. The young man wears a short tunic and a mantle fastening on one shoulder, a *chlamys*; the attendant has a long tunic, *chiton*, which fastens, correctly, on top of the arms with a series of brooches or pins. The dress of the main protagonist appears to have been interpreted by the artist as one tunic over another; although two gowns could be worn in this way, it is more likely that van Loo is misconstruing the popularity of a large over-fold to the *chiton* which would then be girdled under the bust. The same misapprehension seems to occur in Vien's *The Virtuous Athenian Girl*, engraved in 1763 (pl. 143), where the artist has depicted a sleeveless tunic, a simple rectangle of fabric fastened with a brooch on the shoulder and worn over a slit skirt or under-tunic, a style particularly favoured by Spartan women who were known as the 'hip-showing ones'. Vien may also have had something similar in mind for the dress worn by his *Young Corinthian Girl*, engraved in 1765 (pl. 144), a short-sleeved tunic girdled round the waist and open down the side from above the knee. In both cases the costume only serves to emphasise the stocky, asexual

furniture[6] can be more readily seen as influenced by Greek taste, and perhaps Grimm, like art critics of the time, was indulging in some wishful thinking, in the hope that women, in particular, would abandon their Rococo frills for the kind of restrained simplicity to be seen in Vien's classical paintings. Joseph-Marie Vien's paintings of the early 1760s were, to contemporary eyes, imbued with antique learning (Lenoir called him 'Le nouvel Homère') and exact as to details of dress and furnishings; to modern eyes they are over-refined, anaemic and not particularly convincing as classically-inspired art. The *Cupid-seller* (Château de Fontainebleau) was one of the paintings 'dans le goût et le costume antique' that Vien exhibited at the 1763 Salon; Diderot admired 'une élégance dans les attitudes, dans les corps, dans les physionomies, dans les vêtements . . .'.[7] To modern eyes, perhaps, it is precisely this 'elegance', an over-polished 'Rococo classicism' that fits uneasily with the Hellenistic frieze effect for which the artist aimed.[8] Nor are the costumes particularly successful, only the main, seated, figure wears an approximation to a classical tunic, which, nonetheless, looks rather like an eighteenth-

143 (far left) J.-M. Vien (after), *The Virtuous Athenian Girl*, 1763.

144 J.-M. Vien (after), *The Young Corinthian Girl*, 1765.

figures, producing – together with the details of the antique furnishings – a chilly and pedantic image of the classical past. The best history painting, as David's work was to prove, lay in invention as well as in academic research.

Invention, too, although of a far less scholarly kind, lay behind the popular mythological portrait of the eighteenth century, where more attention was paid to sex appeal than to verisimilitude in dress. Nattier's portraits of ladies clad in white shifts and asymmetrical draperies, wearing knotted fur-skins, diamond hair crescents and garlands of flowers, were very much in vogue, especially at the French court from the 1730s. It was a fashion linked to the theatre; Madame de Pompadour's private Théâtre des Petits Cabinets (inaugurated in 1747) performed operas and plays with popular mythological themes, for example Rameau's *Les Surprises de l'amour* (1748) with the marquise as Venus, in a blue and white costume embroidered with silver.[9]

In a more serious vein, it was Vien's ambition to portray sitters in the new classical style which he had made popular. His portrait of the marquise de Migieu (1764; pl. 145) is such an attempt, with the antique furniture, the basket of flowers and the profile bust of the sitter's father. The marquise herself has her hair fashionably dressed in contemporary style, with pearls and a *pompon* of blue flowers. The blue dress, al-

though an invention of the artist, is in fact based on high fashion with its square neckline and elbow-length sleeves which Vien has trimmed with pearls; the shift, decorated with lace at neck and sleeves, is the actual garment which the sitter would have worn.

Vien also painted the royal favourite Madame du Barry in 1771 (Versailles, Chamber of Commerce) *à l'antique*, as a Muse in a Neoclassical shift. Rather more revealing was Drouais's portrait of the marquise, exhibited at the Salon that year, in which she was dressed as a Muse, in 'light and transparent drapery'; the consequent outcry caused the painting to be removed and its appearance altered.[10] Just a few years later, high fashion was to catch up with portraiture, and white muslin chemise gowns became the rage, a trend led by Marie-Antoinette, as has been seen. The Queen's preference for light, floating fabrics and the grace of her deportment often caused her to be compared to the beauties of mythology. Seeing her in 1775 Walpole waxed lyrical: 'Hebes and Floras and Helens and Graces, are streetwalkers to her. She is a statue of beauty, when standing or sitting; grace itself when she moves'.[11] Madame Campan, First Woman of the Bedchamber to Marie-Antoinette, recalled that when the Queen was 'clothed in a light dress of gauze or taffety, she was compared to the Venus di Medicis and the Atalanta of the Marly gardens'.[12] In the later 1770s, the artist Jean-Frédéric Schall painted the

Queen as a Vestal Virgin in a high-waisted white gown, a white mantle and a veil over her uncompromisingly fashionable coiffure.[13] Perhaps this dress, or something similar was the inspiration for the 'chemises à la Vestale de mousseline blanche' which the *Cabinet des modes* noted in 1787.[14]

In the following year, inspired by the descriptions of ancient Greek life in the Abbé Barthélemy's popular *Voyage du jeune Anacharsis en Grèce* (1788), Vigée-Lebrun held her famous Greek party, to which all her guests were bidden to come appropriately dressed. Her husband came as the Greek lyric poet Pindar, with a crown of laurels on his head. Women guests were offered draperies from her studio, no doubt in the hope of avoiding the motley collection of 'antique' outfits which might have otherwise appeared; the aim was for the *mise-en-scène* to appear like a Poussin painting. The artist herself appeared in a white tunic which she claimed was her everyday costume, to which she added a veil and a chaplet of flowers. Perhaps the dress was similar to the loose white shift which she wears in the self-portrait with her daughter of 1789 (Paris, Louvre); her right arm is bare, suitably antique, and a red shawl is tied as a sash round her waist. From Vigée-Lebrun's self-portraits we know that she liked the simplicity of the chemise dress, and from a miniature of her by François Dumont of 1793 (pl. 146) it would seem that she liked to paint in a costume inspired by the antique over-tunic style seen in van Loo's *Offering to Cupid*.

Dumont is, however, painting a real dress, which consists of a yellow silk tunic with sleeves and hem embroidered with green leaves, a white skirt and a sleeveless painting robe; a striped scarf is tied, as a bandeau, in the hair.

By this time it can sometimes be difficult to distinguish fashion from fantasy in dress, so popular were classical styles as part of contemporary costume. Not surprisingly, given the vogue for semi-transparent muslins in high fashion, the full, loose dress of the golden age of ancient Greek civilisation (i.e. the voluminous yet clinging fine linen *chiton*) was preferred to the heavy immobility of archaic costume. The seductive charms of muslin which revealed the figure have been noted in the dress of fashionable portraits, as discussed in the previous chapter. Miette de Villars in his *Mémoires de David* recalled that the *merveilleuses* of the Directory imitated the elegant nudity of such famed beauties as Venus, Diana, Flora and Aspasia (courtesan and mistress of Pericles), 'mais pas une n'eût voulu consentir à adopter le vêtement sévère de Lucrèce ou de Cornélie'.[15]

It is maybe one of the beauties of Corinth whom the sitter imitates in Louis Gauffier's *Portrait of a Lady in a Landscape* (1794; pl. 147), although the setting is Italian, the waterfalls of Tivoli and the Villa Maecenas in the background. In a spotted muslin gown, gold laced sandals and a shawl draped over the head in antique style, she inscribes a message on the tree, a conceit seen fairly frequently in portraiture and de-

rived from Ariosto's *Orlando Furioso*. The scroll (sometimes a Sybilline attribute) is meant here to indicate learning and truth, as is the Greek lyre, the attribute of Apollo.

From the middle of the eighteenth century, the impulse towards the classical seemed unstoppable and writers began to consider the subject of the costume of antiquity, at first as an appendage to art,[16] but by the 1770s as a subject in its own right. It was unfortunate that during this decade the first history of fashion in France was published, Guillaume-François-Roger Molé's *Histoire des modes françaises* (1773) for the book was ignored in favour of the histories of classical dress which also appeared, such as Michel-François Dandré Bardon's *Costume des anciens peuples* (1772) and André Lens's *Le Costume des peuples de l'antiquité* (1776). Molé had hoped that his work would be of use in the theatre and to artists, and would serve to promote contemporary costume which had so often been attacked by critics and philosophers. His introduction attacked the absurdity of antique dress being worn by modern Frenchmen:

A quoi sert, sur-tout dans les monumens publics, de donner à nos Princes des habits Grecs ou Romains?

Je respecte infiniment l'antiquité; mais nos Princes sont Français, & c'est les rendre en quelque sorte étrangers à leur nation que de ne les pas représenter avec les ornemens de leur siècle & de leur pays.[17]

The tenor of the times was against him; anything to do with current fashion was not deemed worthy of serious consideration. In a similar way, the Rococo in art had been unable to fulfil the new ideological and intellectual demands of the times, and became side-tracked into a semi-erotic and moralising channel, to re-emerge in the early nineteenth century as a facet of *le style troubadour*. Both dress and art were increasingly influenced by a powerful movement towards antiquity, which grew as knowledge about the past, mainly acquired from archeological discoveries, became more widespread.

An early costume book, such as the *Costume des anciens peuples* by Dandré Bardon, might be written more out of aesthetic interest than for a readership with antiquarian knowledge. Dedicated to the marquis de Marigny, who had helped to popularise *le goût grecque*, the book is little more than a collection of plates, some of which have been taken from contemporary paintings of classical subjects, such as Carle van

Loo's *Sacrifice of Iphigenia*, 1757 (Potsdam, Sans-Souci); the compiler stated that his aim was to 'présente les objets plutôt pour entrer dans les vues des artistes, que pour servir d'époque à l'histoire'.[18]

In contrast to this rather 'free' interpretation of classical dress, Lens's *Costume des peuples de l'antiquité* (see pl. 121) is a comprehensive work which concentrates on Roman costume, not just that worn by civilians and the military, but the clothing worn at religious and secular ceremonies. There is, for example, detailed information on Roman triumphal pageantry, from the decoration of the triumph cars to the houses and temples 'ornés de festons & de guirlandes', while 'dans la joie publique les Citoyens s'habilloient de toges blanches . . .'[19] This is the kind of detail that an artist such as David would require for the production of the great state festivals of the 1790s, and it seems likely that he either owned or was familiar with Lens's book.[20]

Well-acquainted with the publications of Winckelmann and Caylus, Lens took issue with the latter regarding the depiction of costume in classical art. Caylus believed that the Greeks did not always show real dress in their art, but merely draperies, a view taken up by Diderot in his review of the Salon of 1767: 'Les Grecs si uniment vêtus ne pouvaient meme souffrir leurs vêtemens dans les arts. Ce n'était pourtant qu'une ou deux pièces d'étoffes négligemment jettées sur le corps.'[21] This fallacy, that the ancient Greeks wore little more than 'artistic' draperies in vase paintings and statuary, became so firmly entrenched in the minds of critics and artists (and sometimes art historians) that it has proved quite difficult to dislodge; as Greek art was considered to be the crowning achievement of European civilisation it was difficult to contemplate the commonplace fact of real clothes on legendary heroes and heroines. It was Lens's belief, and quite correct, that the Greeks in their 'poetic' mode did wear less clothing than they would have ordinarily worn, but that it was real and not imaginary costume.

This is a lesson that David takes to heart, for the clothes in his history paintings are clothes and not just pieces of cloth. The mantle worn by Paris in *Paris and Helen* (1788; pl. 148) is a Greek open-sided *chlamys*, which fastens on the shoulder. He wears his customary Phrygian cap (indicating his origins in Asia Minor) with its slightly pointed crown and ear-flaps pinned up at the sides; it is a rather chic affair, possibly theatrical, or at least a studio prop, of dusky pink felt with gold embroidery. Helen's body, invisibly corsetted, is glimpsed through her fine muslin shift embroidered with gold at neck and hem; her lower half is draped in a pink mantle embroidered in a lotus and palmette design. While in Rome David might have seen the marble statue known as the *Farnese Flora*

(now in the Museo Nazionale, Naples, and thought to be a Roman copy of a fourth-century BC Greek Aphrodite); Helen's dress, creased in clinging, vertical folds, falls off her shoulder in the same way as in the Flora.

This painting with its erotic subject − Helen, the faithless wife of Menelaus, seducing Paris − and sumptuous treatment of flesh and fabrics, was meant for the comte d'Artois. One art historian has seen the painting as a reference to the supposed love-affair between the comte and Marie-Antoinette, which was the subject of scurrilous pamphlets at the time; she cites in favour of an anti-monarchical element in the painting, the liberty cap on Paris's head and what she assumes is a tiny fleur-de-lis embroidery on Helen's dress.[22] This argument has been refuted, I think satisfactorily, by the identification of the 'fleur-de-lis' as a minute three-leaf sprig, far too small in any case to be a convincing piece of anti-court propaganda.[23] Furthermore, the cap that Paris wears is the Phrygian cap, not the red *bonnet rouge* which derives from the *pileus* worn by Roman slaves released from bondage;[24] David, with his detailed knowledge of classical costume, could easily distinguish one from the other.

David's genius was to combine scholarship in details of the dress and furnishings, with 'invention', meaning not the depiction of imaginary costume (for, as seen, the artist relied on seeing the actual garments in his studio), but a wholly new way of viewing clothing in the context of character and situation. It was not pedantic antiquarianism, but the use of accurately observed costume which maximises the impact of the painting; in the case of *Paris and Helen*, and *Telemachus and Eucharis* (pl. 149), the clothing helps to produce an erotic charge which is never seen in the work of his teacher, Vien.

The artist's use of the gesture of costume, the way, for example, Helen's *chiton* falls down her arm, the way her tasselled mantle trails on the ground or the way Telemachus's gold-embroidered fillet lies on his shoulder, is related to his sense of theatre. David began to draw stage costume from the late 1770s, with a particular interest in the design of classical roles.[25] By this time, under the impact of Neoclassicism, theatre costume was beginning to rid itself of the plumes, stiffened gilded corselets and embroidered silks which were *de rigueur* until that time. Until the advent of the great actor Talma in the late 1780s, reform in theatre dress was half-hearted. Talma recalled that one of his predecessors, Henri-Louis Lekain, had tried to make some improvements to antique dress as worn on the stage, but 'the simplicity of it was lost in a profusion of ridiculous embroidery . . . Would he have dared to risk naked arms, the antique sandals, hair without powder, long draperies and woollen stuffs? . . . Such a toilet would

have been regarded as filthy and abominable and certainly most indecent'.[26] Talma was making a reference
here to his appearance in the minor role of Proclus in
Voltaire's *Brutus*, performed in November 1790; his
costume of short tunic and toga was designed by
David and caused a sensation when compared to the
traditional costume worn by the other actors. It was
clear that he wore no breeches under his tunic, and
when a horrified actress, Mademoiselle Vestris, re-
proached him for indecency, he replied – no doubt
coached by David – that the Romans never wore
such garments. It was during this performance that as
the last lines of the play were spoken, the cast assumed
a living tableau of David's painting *Brutus*, exhibited
at the Salon of 1789, just a few weeks after the fall of

the Bastille; the subject of the painting – the legendary Roman hero who had destroyed a decadent monarchy only to be forced to condemn his own sons to
death for trying to overthrow the Roman Republic –
appealed to the political sympathies of both artist and
actor.

So, too, did the idea of purging the artifice of the
theatre with reform in dress inspired by art. Diderot
in his *Discours de la poésie dramatique* (1758) had called
for stage design to be influenced by intellectual visual
models like the paintings of Poussin; addressing himself to actors, he suggested that they visit art galleries
if they wished to learn how to dress correctly. By the
end of the 1780s, David's paintings were clearly the
models to follow in terms of classical costume, and as

148   J.-L. David, *Paris and
Helen*, 1788. Oil on canvas.
Louvre, Paris. (Photo: ©
Réunion des musées
nationaux)

such referred to in the most important book on stage dress, J.C. Le Vacher de Charnois's *Recherches sur les costumes et sur les théâtres de toutes les nations* (1790). This lavishly illustrated book (as well as plates depicting all the major theatrical roles, it includes diagrams of various kinds of classical garments) emphasised the increasing importance of accurate costume for both designer and artist.

For a host of political and cultural reasons everything classical became the rage. The actress Louise Fusil recalled in her *Souvenirs* that the year 1791 'nous transforma en Spartiates et en Romains; tout nous rappelait les temps antiques, les tableaux de David, les meubles, des appartements, les costumes de Talma . . .'[27] Like David's studio, Talma's house contained copies of classical antiquities and garments such as togas and tunics;[28] their mutual enthusiasm for the classical past was such that visiting the theatre for a Talma performance must have been like stepping into a history painting by David, while even the artist's earlier works, such as the *Oath of the Horatii* (exhibited at the Salon of 1785) have a theatrical quality, the male costumes in particular looking as though designed for Talma. The women in this painting play supporting and minor roles (as they were to do as wives and mothers during the Revolution) and their costume is given far less attention. Actresses were less fired with enthusiasm for meticulous accuracy in their stage costumes; perhaps for them classical dress was not the pleasing novelty it was for their male co-performers, as it was fairly close to fashionable clothing. Even so, contemporaries felt that the prevailing popularity of stage plays costumed *à l'antique* helped to further classical styles in dress. A.L. Millin's *Dictionnaire des beaux-arts* (1806) under the heading 'Antique' discusses the importance of David and his school, distinguished for 'la fidelle observation des costumes', and continues apropos of the theatre: 'les dames grecques et romaines parurent pour la première fois vêtues et coiffées à l'antique; et c'est de là que le goût des habits et des coiffures à l'antique s'est répandu dans la société'.[29]

From the middle of the 1790s, the artistic booty collected by French armies all over Europe, but particularly from Italy, began to arrive in Paris; stored in the Louvre (first known as the Musée de la République, and from 1803 the Musée Napoléon) and constantly added to, the classical art and antiquities especially proved an invaluable source of inspiration to painters and to anyone interested in antique costume. More books were published on the history of the clothing of classical antiquity, including the deeply researched three-volume work by J. Malliot, 'Ancien Directeur de l'Académie des Arts de Toulouse', entitled *Recherches sur les costumes, les moeurs, les usages religieux, civils et militaires des anciens peuples* (1804). Like its predecessors, the book aimed to be the definitive source-book for artists – 'les artistes désiraient un livre classique sur le costume et les moeurs des anciens peuples'. Most of all, in a climate where French arms triumphed and an empire was declared in the spring of 1804, artists needed information on the dress, the customs and ceremonies of ancient Rome, not so much the Rome of Brutus but that of Caesar and Augustus; this Malliot provided in exhaustive detail with an impressive range of source-material.

For the author, Greece was less important; the arts of civilised living – 'quelque chose qui annonce la douceur et l'urbanité' – in which the ancient Greeks excelled, were out of tune with the martial ethos of early nineteenth-century France. 'Les Grecs étaient magnanimes, subtils, et faisaient grand cas de leur liberté; mais ils étaient inconstants, légers, perfides, parjures . . .'[30] It is this sense of the insidious subtlety and luxury of the Greek civilisations of antiquity that David conveys in such paintings as *Paris and Helen*, in contrast to the austerity and heroic virtue to be seen in the *Horatii*, and the *Brutus*. In a diminished form, perhaps, this softness and eroticism can also be seen in one of David's last mythological paintings, *The Parting of Telemachus and Eucharis* (1818; pl. 149), which, like most of the artist's output in exile, has often been seen as indicative of a decline in quality. From the second decade of the nineteenth century, classicism was on the wane. With a firmly established monarchical system in France came a return to luxury, ousting classical austerity; in art, in dress and in the theatre, the taste was for the contemporary or for the medieval and Renaissance past. David, certainly, in *Telemachus and Eucharis* seems to have lost interest in the background historical details which add so much to the earlier mythological paintings; it is no longer easy to distinguish one texture from another in his depiction of fabrics. Again, compared to the virile lover with his muscled body in *Paris and Helen*, Telemachus is painted as a slightly delinquent youth with a somewhat epicene face and physique; it is difficult to consider him as the warrior son of Odysseus. The image of Eucharis, however, is one of the most beautiful in David's oeuvre; the sad innocence of a beautiful girl is in marked contrast to the worldliness of the designing woman in *Paris and Helen*. Eucharis wears a red sleeveless *chiton* embroidered in gold and held with jewelled clasps on the shoulder and down the sides; round her waist is a sash of green embroidered in a gold bee-like motif. The hair is arranged with a bunch of curls forming a kind of pony-tail, a young girl's informal adaptation of the elaborate styles of high fashion *c*.1818, but one which fits in too with antique hair-dressing; a gold-braid ribbon bandeau adds a further classical touch.

*   *   *

Classicism was also employed as an element of propaganda in art, dress and customs, which were to play their part in the regeneration of French society during the French Revolution.

History painters had been urged to produce works which, in the words of the author of *Le Costume des peuples de l'antiquité*, should be imbued with 'la simplicité & la noblesse des formes Grecques ou Romains'; their aim should be to represent 'les faits mémorables de l'antiquité'. Such deeds, as further critics elaborated and exhibited paintings indicate, were to celebrate such themes as civic virtue, great acts of heroism, the nobility of true rulers and leaders towards their people, the suffering of men and women under tyranny and so on. French history could also supply models of this kind, a trend that had been officially encouraged under Louis XVI, but during the French Revolution only classical subjects were approved. To the author of an *Essai sur les moyens d'encourager la peinture, la sculpture, l'architecture et la gravure* (L'An III, 1794–5) French artists in their search for 'l'image des héros', looked outside their own country; '. . . c'est à Sparte, c'est à Athènes, c'est à Rome, c'est chez les peuples Orientaux qu'ils ont placé le lieu de la scène et choisi leurs personnages'.[31] Furthermore, when compared to the dress of antiquity, French costume, according to this author, offered nothing to the artistic imagination.

One way in which the classical past could be invoked was through state pageantry, based on the Roman triumphal procession and civic entertainments. This was not a new idea in France, for during the Middle Ages and early modern period the tradition of the *joyeuse entrée* – the royal or princely triumphal entry into a city, to celebrate a victory or a state occasion such as a royal marriage – was firmly established. A typical formula for such events might include the greeting of the royal person by allegorical figures representing the city and acclaiming the virtues of the honoured visitor, tableaux vivants at the city gates and in the streets on the same themes, the procession and presentation of civic dignitaries, formal

dinners, speeches and theatrical entertainments. By the eighteenth century the full-scale *joyeuse entrée* had dwindled to an elaborate, official welcome of the princely personage,[32] but the concept still remained. More lavish entertainments were the court *fêtes* organised by the department of the Menus-Plaisirs, which had been founded under Louis XIV; teams of artists and designers working in two large workshops in Paris and Versailles provided the artistic and theatrical effects for royal celebrations of victories, treaties, births and marriages. A system was thus already in place – combining the visual arts with music and the theatre – which could be used for didactic purposes in the state pageants of the revolutionary period.

Furthermore, there was the democratic tradition of the carnival with its opportunities for political commentary. Until it was forbidden in 1791 – 'il est expressément défendu à tout citoyen de se déguiser, travestir ou masquer[33] – the carnival often incorporated processions with topical interest. In 1783, for example, there was a statue of Liberty on a chariot during the carnival in Paris, 'treize cariatides soutenaient l'idole figurant les treize cantons d'Amérique récemment émancipés'.[34] At Perpignan in 1790 the National Guard took part in the carnival and a tableau was acted out in which an aristocrat opposed to the Revolution, was overcome by an alliance of King and citizens.[35] The journal *Révolutions de Paris* declared in 1790, apropos of a national *fête* to be held at Notre-Dame: 'Il faut des fêtes patriotiques à un peuple libre. Un grand concours de citoyens dans un même lieu, des solemnités réligieuses, de l'appareil, de la musique, des danses, des repas, des chansons civiques . . .' Such festivals, the editor averred, would move the spirit and rekindle love of one's country.[36]

It was the classical past and, in particular, the Roman Republic which provided the main inspiration for French revolutionary pageantry; 'le beau idéal antique est un peu républicain' claimed Stendhal.[37] It was obvious that David, with his expertise in classical art and costume and with his fiercely Republican views, would be chosen to mastermind such ceremonies. How much he actually did himself is not clear, and he may just have been responsible for sketching out the general plan; no designs exist except for the mysterious *Triumph of the People* (pl. 150). His knowledge of allegory and classical symbolism would be essential, and his hundreds of drawings done in Rome would provide ideas for costume, triumphal arches, effigies and so on; finally, his interest in the theatre helped with the dramatic effects and the overall design.

David's first pageant was for the ceremonial procession that took the remains of Voltaire to the Panthéon (formerly Ste-Geneviève) on 11 July 1791. The funeral chariot, designed like a Roman triumphal car, contained an effigy of Voltaire, a broken lyre by his side, made by Madame Tussaud's; it soon discoloured in the pouring rain. The chariot was drawn by twelve white horses led by attendants in Roman costume copied from David's sketches of the bas-reliefs on Trajan's Column in Rome; it was surrounded by men of letters, artists and actors impersonating the famous characters in Voltaire's plays, all dressed *à l'antique* by David, their togas bedraggled in the unceasing bad weather.[38]

As the French Revolution progressed and a republic came into being, the *fêtes* became more complex, the symbolism more arcane, the expenditure greater; as the new regime under Robespierre instituted the rule of Terror, the pageants provided a kind of theatrical catharsis in which the emotions of the people could be channelled to serve as propaganda for the State. No other art form could reach so wide an audience, and the festivals could be enjoyed as dramatic entertainment even if the more recondite allusions were not wholly understood. For the convinced Republican (and it was tactful to appear so after the abolition of the monarchy in September 1792) some endurance was needed, for the *fêtes* lasted for hours, as the processions moved through the streets from one station to another. David's Fête de la Réunion for 10 August 1793, lasted for sixteen hours. It began with a fountain of regeneration set up in the Place de la Bastille; this took the form of a statue of Nature, her breasts spouting pure water which was ceremonially tasted by the President of the National Convention, members of the government and representatives of the provinces. Then there was a march to the Champ de Mars, with various stopping places en route. This procession included deputies from the Convention each carrying 'un bouquet forme d'épi de blé & de différens fruits', officials in their distinctive costume, such as the judge in his black gown and the mayor in his tricolour sash, working people in their occupational dress, and so on. A triumphal car contained old people carried by their children – 'exemple touchant de la piété filiale, & de vénération pour la vieillesse . . .'; another contained an urn decorated with garlands and containing the ashes of those heroes who had died for their country. On a car representing a hearse lay emblems of the deposed monarchy and the arrogant baubles of the nobility – 'orgueilleux hochets de l'ignorante noblesse'. The procession made its way through the Place de la Révolution where a statue of Liberty had been erected, to which people made offerings of 'rubans, tricolors, bonnets de la liberté . . .'; at the Place des Invalides there was a huge figure of the French people annihilating the monster of federalism. The final destination was the Champ de Mars where an 'autel de la Patrie' was set up and a religious service held.[39]

This *fête* celebrated the attack on the Tuileries palace on 10 August 1792, which led to the downfall of the monarchy. Like so many of the pageants, it inspired a theatrical version, *La Réunion du dix-Août, ou l'inauguration de la République*, which was performed at the Opéra in April 1794. The drawing by David (pl. 150)[40] may be related to the festival or to the theatrical production; the theme is the defeat of the monarch (in crown and ermine-trimmed robe) by the citizens of the new French Republic. The French people appear in the form of Hercules with his club, seated on a chariot accompanied by Equality and Liberty with their attributes; this triumphal car rolls over the symbols of despotism and superstition. Its progress is hailed by such past martyrs of liberty as Brutus (in accurate tunic and toga), Cornelia, mother

of the Gracchi (in tunic and *palla*, or mantle) and William Tell (in generalised sixteenth-century Swiss-German costume).

The last major *fête* designed by David was the festival of the Supreme Being, held on 8 June 1794, in honour of this new state religion decreed by Robespierre. After a ceremony which took place in the front of the Tuileries, when statues of Atheism, Discord and Egotism were destroyed, there was a procession to a 'mountain' erected in the Champ de Mars on which sat representatives from all age groups from the *sections* of Paris, the women and girls dressed in white with tricolour sashes and flowers in their hair. Robespierre, elected President of the National Convention on 4 June, was determined to make the maximum impact with this festival which celebrated his republic of virtue ('la vertu est l'essence de la république'), and the climax of the day's events was a march up the 'mountain' when people consecrated themselves to the Supreme Being. All the deputies of the Convention wore their red and blue costumes designed by David; the artist, who took an active part in revolutionary politics, also wore his costume as 'représentant du peuple' and, according to Delécluze, he waved his hat decorated with a tricolour panache, to set the cortège in motion.[41] In contrast to the uniformity of the deputies' clothing, Robespierre appeared in an elegant outfit which reminded George Duval of a courtier at Versailles; along with his 'habit d'un bleu tendre avec collet et parements de même étoffe . . . il portait un elegant gilet de bazin blanc à vastes revers, et une culotte de nankin des Indes; un jabot superbe ondulait sur sa poitrine; sa jambe était pressé par un bas de soie blanc; ses pieds étaient chaussés de l'escarpin; il n'y manquait que le talon rouge . . .'[42] (red-heeled shoes had been worn by royalty and aristocracy).

Robespierre's ideas about the need for government and society to be imbued with virtue and purity derived from Rousseau. In such a state, women were to be wives and mothers, guardians of the republican flame; the active role which the feminists had hoped for never materialised.[43] Only occasionally did working-class women in particular become a political force, when roused to action in times of severe economic crisis, in order to find food, lodging and clothing, the essentials of existence; then they were a ferocious element, feared by men.

Many middle-class women, in a century that placed high esteem on the cultivation of classical knowledge, were aware of the lessons which the past could teach to the present. Madame Roland, while acknowledging that 'Rousseau pointed out to me the domestic happiness to which I could aspire', also stated: 'Plutarch had prepared me to become a republican; he roused that strength and stateliness of character which constitute one; he inspired me with a real enthusiasm in favour of public virtues and liberty'.[44] It was Plutarch's *Lives* which, in September 1789, inspired a deputation of the wives and daughters of artists to the National Assembly in order to offer their jewellery to the nation. Plutarch referred to Roman ladies who had offered their jewellery so that a sacrifice, in the form of a golden cup, could be offered to Apollo. It proved a popular subject for artists[45] and it inspired a pamphlet by one of the deputation to the Assembly, Madame Moitte, entitled *L'Ame des Romaines dans les dames françaises*, in which she urged all her female readers to leave off 'nos amusements folâtres et nos précieuses parures'.[46]

The dress which these women wore on their visit to the National Assembly is perhaps the first instance of what was to become a kind of classical uniform worn at state festivals; it consisted of a white dress with a tricolour sash and cockade in the hair. As one historian has remarked: '. . . on les rencontre partout, devant les autels de la Patrie, aux fêtes de la Loi, aux Jacobins, jeunes filles vêtues de blanc et couronnées de roses, femmes mariées portant des robes blanches voilées de crêpe et des ceintures tricolores . . .'[47] The role of women at state festivals was both decorative and symbolic. Louis-Antoine de Saint-Just 'proclamait dans un discours que le seul rôle public de la femme etait de se faire l'ornement des fêtes nationales',[48] and the author of a pamphlet *De la Condition des femmes dans les républiques* (1799) stated that 'les femmes sont les Prêtresses de cette Divinité'[49] (i.e. *la Patrie*). Some of them were literally priestesses, even goddesses during the short-lived religion of the Supreme Being, 1793–4. Dressed in white, with the blue mantle of the Virgin Mary (whether this was a deliberate choice, or an unconscious act, is not clear) and a *bonnet rouge*, all of which made a pleasing tricolour image, the Goddess of Reason, often impersonated by an actress, was installed in churches which were converted to Temples of Reason. In November 1793 Duval saw the actress Mademoiselle Maillard, 'l'une des plus belles femmes de l'époque', placed in office as Goddess of Reason in Notre-Dame. Preceded by her priestesses (the corps de ballet from the Opéra) all dressed in white with tricolour sashes and artificial flowers in their hair, and followed by members of the *commune*, of the revolutionary committees, of the Jacobin Club, and others, the Goddess arrived 'le bonnet phrygien en tête, le cothurne aux pieds, revêtue d'une tunique blanche et d'une chlamyde de bleu flottante . . .', and was seated in the sanctuary of the Virgin Mary.[50] The female figure, in the shape of a woman dressed in the white tunic of antiquity, personified Liberty in the national pageants (see pl. 150) and also the State. A decree of 21 September 1792 (the day the monarchy was abolished) declared that the seal of the State was to be the figure of France 'sous les traits d'une femme vêtue à l'antique, debout, tenant de la main droite une pique surmontée du bonnet phrygien ou bonnet de la liberté, la gauche appuyé sur un faisceau d'armes . . .'[51]

The potent symbols of the Revolution – the antique costume, the fasces (fraternity) and, above all, the *bonnet rouge* – are here incorporated into the personification of the State. It might be worth noting here that the Phrygian cap and the *bonnet rouge* are often conflated, as in the decree quoted above. According to A.-E. Gibelin, in his work *De l'Origine et de la forme du bonnet de la liberté* (1796) this was because artists often used both forms indiscriminately in their painting, not aware that only the semi-oval *bonnet rouge* (without side flaps) was to be equated with liberty, as it derived from the cap given to Roman slaves when they became free. Perhaps with the virtue of hindsight, Gibelin proposes the theory that those countries disposed to an aristocratic political system chose to wear hats with a large brim, whereas those with republican inclinations preferred a soft bonnet.[52] In March 1792 the editor of *Révolutions de Paris*, ridiculing the three-cornered hat as undemocratic, made the prophetic comment that the time would soon come when aristocrats and others ill-disposed to a republic, would see the *bonnet rouge* as 'un objet de terreur'.[53]

Not all working-class men during the height of the Revolution wore the *bonnet rouge*; some wore a battered hat which had once been fashionable, like the *bicorne* worn in *Simon Chenard as a Sans-culotte*, Boilly's painting of the actor taking part in the Fête of the Liberty of Savoy at Chambéry on 14 October 1792 (pl. 151). His costume, designed by the Jacobin artist Sergent-Marceau (Antoine-François Sergent), who helped David with some of the festivals, comprises a black slouched hat decorated with a tricolour cockade, a brown *carmagnole* (a short jacket), greyish-black trousers, a striped double-breasted *gilet*, a blue cotton scarf and fabric shoes to protect feet unused to wooden sabots; the pipe is an authentic *sans-culotte* touch.

The *Révolutions de Paris* first noted the appearance of the *sans-culottes* in 1790, and over the next few years they became an important element in the political situation, their ferocious behaviour and deliberately cultivated uncouthness often being an embarrassment to their Jacobin allies. Their costume, as Duval pointed out in his *Souvenirs de la Terreur*, was not just the shabby torn clothing remotely derived from everyday fashion, which most working men wore, but incorporated elements such as the knotted scarf, the loose trousers, the sabots and the *carmagnole*, all defiant statements of class. The *carmagnole*[54] was associated with the inhabitants of Marseilles who had

146

Loi'. His assistants, virtuous citizens of various ages, wore either tunics *à l'antique* or 'l'habillement de Sans-culotte'; they were all festooned with tricolour ribbons, sashes and feathers. The young celebrants, *les elèves*, were to be dressed in white tunics and also decorated with the tricolour.[55] It is difficult not to agree with Carlyle's comment that 'fantasy with her mystic wonderland plays into the small prose domain of sense'.[56]

However unpalatable the notion of collective *sensibilité* and mass exultation in fancy dress, linked to virtue, the revolutionary festivals both national and local had produced a language of signs, and demonstrated the importance of symbolism. The arts, including costume, had become politicised, and in a climate of moral certainty, regulations as to what constituted republican forms were initiated. The concept of freedom is only relative, and in dress it has never truly existed; we are all subject to rules and customs, written and unwritten. How much more was this the case during the French Revolution when a new society had to be constructed almost from scratch and when every element of existence had to be re-assessed and scrutinised in the harsh light of a republic. This included costume, both official dress and the clothing of the individual, which were both exclusively male concerns.

As has been seen, one of the first acts of the new National Assembly in 1789 was to abolish the court-imposed costume decreed for the Estates. In the first flush of enthusiasm of the abolition of feudal rights and the Declaration of the Rights of Man, which established the principle of equality for all, some men wished to get rid of all clothing that denoted rank, such as uniform. In the autumn of 1790 the National Assembly, according to the *Révolutions de Paris*, even discussed the abolition of the uniform of the National Guard set up only the previous year, as it was felt such costumes placed barriers between people and pandered to vanity. Ecclesiastical dress was also considered for abolition, after the nationalisation of Church property, the suppression of religious orders, and the Civil Constitution of the Clergy (1790), which demanded an oath of loyalty to the constitution. There was no evidence, declared the *Révolutions de Paris* early in 1791, that Christ had asked his disciples to wear distinctive clothing; 'devant Dieu et la patrie, tous les citoyens sont frères'.[57]

All citizens may have been brothers, but they were soon to be distinguished from each other by the new hierarchy of dress that the authorities contemplated. Over the next few years a system of official costume was set up which came to be more elaborate and wider-ranging than anything under the *ancien régime*, reaching its apotheosis with the Empire, together with the most showy military uniforms that the world has

originally come from Carmagnola, near Turin, and who brought the garment with them to Paris, along with the song that was written for their troops and which became the national anthem.

During the years of the Terror, 1793–4, the *sans-culottes* had a high political profile and as the visible embodiment of the working man they played their part in the state festivals and in the secular ceremonies that replaced religious services. In 1793 the year was divided into ten months (each named after an aspect of the climate or the seasons); each month consisted of three *décades* of ten days each, the tenth day being a holiday devoted to the celebration of republican virtues. No one is quite sure what precise form such ceremonies took, or, indeed, how often they were performed; they appear to have been a curious mixture of religious and civic entertainments, with appropriate readings and hymns, the costume of the participants mingling the classical with the republican and working-class. Typical of the instructions given is a surviving *Programme d'une cérémonie en l'honneur de l'égalité, de la liberté et de la raison, propre à être exécutée tous les Décadis dans toutes les Communes de la République* (1793). The ceremonies were led by an elderly man known as Le Sage, wearing a long white tunic, a red jacket belted at the waist and a short blue mantle covering his shoulders; on his head was a tricolour bonnet and on his chest the inscription 'La

seen. Furthermore, the idea of a national costume for the French citizen was also under consideration, although the editor of the *Révolutions de Paris* in 1790 put his finger on the main problem with this notion, namely that not everyone would be able or willing to afford it: 'L'uniforme nationale auroit peut-être moins d'inconvéniens si tous les individus de la République, pauvres comme riches, avoient la faculté de s'en revêtir; mais puisque la dixième partie des habitans de l'empire peut à peine se le procurer, citoyens, renoncez-y tout-a-fait'.[58] Carlyle made the further point in his *Sartor Resartus* that even if a particular style of dress was enforced, there would be those who would circumvent the spirit of the law by wearing luxurious fabrics. Citing the case of the famous suit of leather worn by the Quaker George Fox, he comments: 'Would not the rich man purchase a waterproof suit of Russia Leather; and the high-born Belle step forth in red or azure morocco, lined with shamoy; the black cowhide being left to the Drudges and Gibeonites of the world; and so all the old Distinctions be re-established.'[59]

But in late eighteenth-century France the concept of a national costume based on reason had taken hold of the imagination of writers and artists. In Louis-Sébastien Mercier's futurist vision *L'An 2440: rêve s'il en fut jamais* (1770), suppressed as an anti-government satire, the author describes a transformed Paris, with elegant squares and straight streets, the Bastille destroyed and the Supreme Being worshipped in the Temples of God. The theatre and the arts were inspired by grandeur and virtue, and Reason was the guiding star of government; a Rousseauist philosophy is clearly at work here. Everyone is 'dressed in a simple modest manner', with no gold or luxury, and – unusually for Utopian dreamers – Mercier is fairly precise about the details of dress, particularly for men; women are largely ignored. The hair is no longer a 'plaistered pyramid of scented pomatum' with stiff curls, but arranged in a more natural style; the costume consists of a loose gown over 'a sort of vest', with a sash around the waist: tights and buskins complete the picture.[60]

A quarter of a century later, Moreau le Jeune's *Costume of a French Republican* (pl. 152) is a similar amalgam of figure-hugging antique 'nudity' with elements from theatrical dress. It is an elegant outfit based on fashionable dress, with its short, lapelled 'vest', tight pantaloons, hussar boots and round hat, here trimmed with a feather. The theatrical part of the costume is the short gown with wide revers and sleeve slashes in Renaissance style. Moreau's interest in fashion extended to his work as a theatre designer, and he would have been familiar with this type of coat which, like other elements of sixteenth-century costume, was a shorthand for the dress of the past

both in art and on the stage. This drawing might have been intended for a revolutionary journal called *Le Républicain français* which was discussed in 1793[61] or it could have been one of the designs submitted to the Société Populaire et Républicaine des Arts in the following year, when the subject of a national costume was debated among the member artists.

Although opinions were canvassed on dress from both the general public[62] and from artists, it was the views of the latter that counted, as their ideas could be visualised and they had, over a number of years, paid a great deal of attention to costume in their art. Serious consideration was given only to men's costume, because of the limited rôle for women in the events of the Revolution, who, being disenfranchised,[63] had no political contribution to make. During the discussions of the Société Populaire et Républicaine des Arts in the spring of 1794, the subject of women's dress was briefly mentioned,[64] but it was not really in contention when compared to the importance of establishing a national costume for men. But what form should such a costume take? It had to be pleasing aesthetically, and most artists thought this was synonymous with antique dress; it had to conform to Rousseauist notions of hygiene and

Costume du françois Republiquain

152 J.-M. Moreau, *Costume of a French Republican*, c.1793–4. Pen and ink and watercolour over pencil. Hazlitt, Gooden & Fox, London.

ease of movement; it had to incorporate republican ideals of simplicity without any distinctions of class.

The artists' discussions on dress were published in *Aux Armes et aux Arts*, the journal of the Société Républicaines des Arts, in April 1794. Isabey argued for a costume based on military uniform but in antique style. Jean-Joseph Espercieux thought that there should be two types of national costume, one for civilians and the other for men who wished to defend their country, but both should be chosen from either classical or Arab dress. Sergent-Marceau spoke up for a toga-like garment, probably akin to the costume depicted in a watercolour he had exhibited at the Salon of 1793 (untraced) and which, according to the *livret*, 'est de forme demi-circulaire & se jette sur les bras ou les épaules'; it was to be worn from the age of twenty-one like the *toga virilis* of ancient Rome.[65]

These deliberations resulted in a pamphlet entitled *Considérations sur les avantages de changer le costume français*, which called for clothing inspired by the idea of equality, '...un costume national dicté par la raison et approuvé par le bon goût'.[66] It was almost a foregone conclusion that David – 'un génie sublime qui produira le meilleur costume' – would be requested to produce designs for 'republican' clothes 'au caractère de la Révolution'.[67]

David's interest in antique dress and his commitment to the Revolution made him the ideal choice for such an official commission. For some years he had been sketching ideas for a national costume, and in the summer of 1792 Dr John Moore refers to drawings made by the artist 'in which full as much attention is paid to picturesque effect as to conveniency'. The costume that David proposed, according to Moore 'resembles the old Spanish dress, consisting of a jacket with tight trowsers, a coat without sleeves above the jacket, a short cloak which may either hang loose from the left shoulder or be drawn over both; a belt to which two pistols and a sword may be attached, a round hat and a feather...' Moore noted that 'part of this costume is already adopted by men' (probably a reference to the 'tight trowsers' or pantaloons), but that he had 'only seen one person in public equipped with the whole', dressed in blue jacket and pantaloons, with a white coat which had a scarlet collar; this tricolour figure was well armed and martial in bearing, although 'on enquiring, I find he is a miniature painter'.[68]

Moore's account of a 'Spanish' element in David's designs probably refers to a short doublet-like jacket, the coat with slashed sleeves (like the Moreau drawing) and the cloak over one shoulder. It does not sound particularly classical in style, although another contemporary comment in 1792 describes the coat as being tight-fitting 'comme la tunique romaine'.[69] This would appear somewhat closer to David's famous cos-

153a J.-L. David, *People's Deputy*, 1794. Pen and watercolour. Musée Carnavalet, Paris.

153b J.-L. David, *French Citizen*, 1794. Pen and watercolour. Musée Carnavalet, Paris.

149

tume designs of 1794 (pls 153a and 153b) which mix the antique with the historical. The designs, of which eight survive – two civilian, five official and one military[70] – are based on the classical idea that men of action and active citizens wear short knee-length tunics, while the dignity of legal office demanded a long gown and voluminous mantle. The costume of the citizen (pl. 153b) consists of a tunic-like coat with an embroidered 'antique' design, pantaloons, a mantle decorated with tasselled fastenings, not unlike an Arab *burnous*,[71] and a *toque* with cockade and heron feather; a tricolour sash is wound round the waist. The deputies (pl. 153a) also wore short tunics, sashes and *toques*, but boots like Roman buskins instead of shoes and a cloak based on the open-sided classical mantle, appropriately inscribed with the tenets of the French Revolution. The open shirt collars give freedom from constraint and indicate the man of action. The historical and theatrical element is to be found in the *toque* and in the wrapped-over tunic, which derive from the sixteenth century. The short tunic-coat in particular was a sixteenth-century garment associated on the stage with such monarchs as Francis I and the popular Henry IV; it was worn, for example, by Talma in one of his famous roles, as the king in M.-J. Chénier's anti-monarchical play *Charles IX* performed in 1789 and 1790.[72]

Talma was one of the few people (mainly the artist's friends and pupils) who actually wore David's costume, in spite of running the risk of public ridicule and even of being taken for a foreign spy. Such a costume was too out of step with contemporary fashion to be wholly acceptable to the average person. It was acceptable within a picture frame or in the theatre or even as official costume, but not as street fashion. In any case, only a few weeks after the appearance of David's designs, the Jacobin regime which had ordered them was overthrown, David was imprisoned and the idea of a national costume for citizens abandoned.

David's attitude to the wearing of dress outside the mainstream of fashion seems somewhat ambivalent. He himself was a man of rather old-fashioned elegance in costume. As Delécluze noted:

Si l'on excepte la petite cocarde tricolore qu'il portait à son chapeau rond, tout le reste de son costume, ainsi que sa manière d'être, l'auraient plutôt fait prendre pour un ancien gentilhomme en habit du matin, que pour l'un des membres les plus ardents du comité de sûreté générale.[73]

He does not seem, himself, to have worn the citizen's costume which he was so keen for others to wear and, as for the costume of the representative of the people, it is not clear if he wore his own rather flamboyant design (as, for example at the Fête of the Supreme

Being) or the dark blue suit with red collar and revers and tricolour sash which most deputies had worn since 1792. His own preference was for costume to be fairly well fitted to the body, in the eighteenth-century manner, and not for the billowing draperies that some of his students wore in imitation of antiquity. It is a slight paradox that the figure most resembling the artist in costume (apart from the wig and the sword) appears as the posturing *ancien-régime* artist in Pierre-Nolasque's Bergeret's lithograph of *David's Studio* (*c*.1800; pl. 155). David and his pupils, adopting poses from *The Sabines*, and dressed for the most part in tight-fitting pantaloons, with shirt sleeves rolled up, confront a defiant painter of the Rococo school.

The word 'Rococo' was first used in David's studio by the artist Maurice Quaï in the later 1790s to mean, in the words of a French dictionary in 1842, 'tout ce qui est vieux, et hors de mode dans les arts, la littérature, le costume, les manières, etc.'.[74] Quaï led the sect called *les primitifs* in David's studio, who wished to return to sources such as Homer and Ossian to inspire art and dress. He himself wore a long ankle-length tunic and a huge mantle in imitation of what he imagined was Homeric costume, 'cet admirable costume grec primitif dont la disposition est si majestueuse et si élégante'.[75] Quaï and his disciples grew rather distant from David, not considering their master primitive enough, and regarding anything other than archaic art as decadent. Ossian was admired because it was seen as both Celtic and primitive, an unassailable combination; the few references to dress in James MacPherson's supposed 'translations' of ancient Gaelic poems, gave more licence to artists, who were not constrained by facts in their depiction of costume, which is usually a free mixture of the classical with elements of 'barbaric' nudity.[76]

Others of David's *atelier* wore dress inspired by ancient Greek costume of the classical period, the fifth century BC, and some chose Roman clothing, seeing the toga and the *pallium* as the most dignified garments of antiquity. David's studio provided all the source-material for those of his pupils with an interest in the classical past; over the years his research into the art and customs of antiquity, both for his paintings and for the state festivals, had resulted in a fine collection of books, art objects and copies of classical works. After David's release from prison late in 1795, his energies were devoted to his work, notably to history painting; he was no longer involved with such national *fêtes* as continued, a pale shadow of what they had been, under the new Directory.[77] His studio became the centre of his world, an antique kingdom which impressed his pupils and foreign visitors who made the cultural pilgrimage to Paris in the early nineteenth century. Among them was John Carr who commented:

154   J. Chinard, *Self-portrait*, *c*.1800. Terracotta. Musée Girodet, Montargis. (Photo: Conway Library, Courtauld Institute of Art)

150

I could not help fancying myself a contemporary of the most tasteful times of ancient Greece. Tunics and robes were carelessly but gracefully thrown over the antique chairs which were surrounded by elegant statues and ancient libraries, so disposed as to perfect the classical illusion.[78]

Surprisingly, there are not many self-portraits of artists dressed *à l'antique*. Some of David's pupils appear to be clothed in this way in their self-portraits, but on closer examination they usually wear cloaks or gowns wrapped around themselves in imitation of classical drapery. The few self-portraits that exist where artists depict themselves in real classical costume include *Abel de Pujol* (1806; Valenciennes, Musée des Beaux-Arts) and *Joseph Chinard* (c.1800; pl. 154), where both sitters have chosen the Roman *pallium*, a wide rectangular mantle which derived from

the Greek *himation*, a garment associated with the philosopher and thinker. (The toga symbolised rank, and was, in ancient Rome, an Establishment garment.) The *pallium* was usually worn over a tunic, but Chinard seems to be wearing an open shirt and hose with classical laced buskins. The sculptor has correctly interpreted the characteristic gesture of those wearing the *pallium*, of the right arm being supported by the wrapped-around mantle and the hand grasping the folds of material over the breast.

The austerity of this costume which emphasised the intellect and ignored worldly success may have appealed to artists and to dress reformers, but it was only one strand of the complicated tapestry of official dress that evolved during the 1790s. In the 1780s J.-F. Sobry in his *Discours sur les principaux usages de la nation françoise* had argued for the adoption of a long tunic or *simarre* for official costume, to be worn with sandals as

155 P.-N. Bergeret, *The Studio of David*, c.1800. Lithograph. Kupferstichkabinett, Staatliche Museen zu Berlin.

a healthier alternative to shoes.[79] The firmly established correlation between the heroic deeds of classical antiquity and the stirring events of the French Revolution ensured that even after the downfall of the Jacobin regime a preference for the forms of antique republican dress was manifest in discussions about official costume. The rationale behind the official dress of the Directory, averred Delécluze, was to efface 'tout souvenir du costume révolutionnaire, si hideux et si désordonné' and to ordain 'un costume qui se rapprochait autant que possible de la forme antique, afin de satisfaire et de flatter même le goût qui régnait alors.'[80] Thus, the costume of the legislative body comprising the Council of Five Hundred and the Council of the Ancients, was a long white tunic with a full open-sided mantle. It was a style that particularly appealed to the curator of the new Musée des Monuments Français, Alexandre Lenoir, who thought such costume was a logical addition to women's classically inspired dress:

> Pendant le cours de la révolution, des peintres habiles ont essayés a changer le costume français. On vit alors les hommes du gouvernement adopter unanimement un costume plus raisonné et mieux composé que celui que nous portons encore; mais cet habit fut abandonné dès son invention . . .[81]

The deputies soon found their antique clothes cumbersome, and two years after the foundation of the Directory, a decree of 29 brumaire, An VI (19 November 1797), established a compromise costume consisting of a blue coat, pantaloons, tricolour sash and feathered *toque* (quite close in style to David's drawing in pl. 153a), but with the addition of a scarlet woollen mantle embroidered round the edge with an antique design; a number of these so-called 'togas' still survive in museum collections.[82] The effect must have been quite theatrical when all the deputies were in session in their red mantles; such a 'great quantity of red clothing', declared the *Moniteur* for 21 February 1798, 'fatigues the eyes extremely; yet it must be admitted that this costume has in it something beautiful, imposing and truly senatorial'.[83]

The wearing of official costume by members of the government had been discussed since the spring of 1792 and was hastened by the rapid course of events which led to the establishment of a republic later that year. A first step was made with the dress of the deputies, but most of the energies of the regime under Robespierre seemed to have been directed towards the costume of state propaganda in the form of the *fêtes nationales*. Not until the very end of the Terror did the attention of the authorities turn towards a wider application of official dress, resulting in David's designs for such costume in 1794. Although out of favour for his uncompromising ultra-republicanism, David was surely the inspiration for the official costumes of the Directory, although according to the Abbé Grégoire the designs were a team effort produced by a number of distinguished artists including Moreau le Jeune, Regnault and Vincent.

Grégoire, the son of a tailor and one of the first deputies to move from the First Estate to the Third (he appears in a prominent position in the group of clerics in the centre foreground of David's *Tennis Court Oath*) seems to have had a particular interest in costume as a visual code. 'Le langage des signes a une éloquence qui lui est propre: les costumes distinctifs font partie de cet idiôme; ils réveillent des idées et des sentimens analogues à leur objet'.[84] In September 1795 Grégoire produced a *Rapport et projet de décret présentés au nom du Comité d'Instruction Publique sur les costumes des législateurs et des autres fonctionnaires publics* in which he states the thesis behind the wearing of such costume, that it gives dignity to the *office* rather than to the wearer; he (the wearer of official dress) thus indicates that he is accountable to the State. There follows a list of offices and their costumes, with some general comments about the need, for example, for long and dignified robes for legislators and the judiciary. In the same year the Committee of Public Instruction (which had been established early in 1794 to inform people about the role of the arts in a republican state) commissioned a set of designs from Jacques Grasset de Saint-Sauveur for the new official costume. As seen, such designs incorporated ideas of classical antiquity, but without Jacobin austerity; they also had to signal a modest return to luxury without implying monarchical leanings. The costume of the Directorate symbolised what Jacques Grasset de Saint-Sauveur called 'la richesse d'une nation opulente';[85] it was more Renaissance than classical, as can be seen in plate 156, *A Member of the Directorate in his 'grand costume'*. On formal occasions the five Directors wore a blue *habit-manteau* embroidered in gold, white tunic and white pantaloons; a red silk cloak and a round hat ornamented with a tricolour panache completed the outfit. The ordinary costume was similar in style, but with a red *habit-manteau*; altogether, the designs have a refinement and elegance which might indicate an attribution to Moreau le Jeune. In the flesh, however, they often produced what the duchesse d'Abrantès described as 'burlesque pomp', and although a few kind souls said the costume reminded them of the time of Francis I, many more commentators found them absurdly theatrical. Like the other official costumes of the Directory, they were a gift to the English caricaturists; in 1798 Gillray produced a series of twelve plates, *French Habits*, which poked fun at this kind of dress, and where the figures were given the faces of the Whig opposition. In 1799 the *coup d'état* of 18 brumaire (9 November) ended the Directory,

Membre du Directoire Executif
dans son grand Costume.

156 J. Grasset de Saint-Sauveur, *A Member of the Directorate in his 'grand costume'*, 1795. Coloured engraving. By courtesy of the Board of Trustees of the Victoria and Albert Museum, London.

Philippe, son of Philippe-Egalité. Bergeret noted how the newly returned deputies in 1830 spent some time debating their costume: '... L'on n'avait que l'embarras du choix depuis la carmagnole jusqu'au manteau à la Henri IV, ou bien la prétendue toge du Conseil des Anciens, ou l'habit des représentants du peuple. Mais tous ces costumes ramenaient avec eux des souvenirs pénibles, irritants ou révolutionnaires ...'[88] He recalled how his master David had tried to create 'un costume français et national' during the French Revolution, which – he writes with the virtue of hindsight – was doomed to fail as it was too French; he follows this rather startling comment with a jaundiced discussion as to why the French are too influenced by English dress, an argument that harks back to the 1780s; *plus ça change* ... David retained his interest in 'costume français et national' by designing an official dress for the Consuls (Château de Versailles). The watercolour, which must date to 1799, shows a white tunic-coat with gold embroidery in classical style, blue pantaloons, red boots embroidered in gold and a round hat of red velvet trimmed with feathers. Round the neck is a large gold collar (a chain of office) with linked gold plaques and the head of the Republic on a blue enamel medallion. David had clearly lost none of his fondness for tricolour imagery, which might have been thought a bit inappropriate as the new regime tried to distance itself from the recent past. The costume also has a kind of Ruritanian excess about it and it was rejected by Napoleon, although some elements were retained; the pantaloons with hussar embroidery of David's design appear in the final choice of uniform (see pl. 158), and the linked gold collar possibly inspired the chain of the Légion d'Honneur.

Carle Vernet's design for the costume of the Consuls (pl. 157) is more in tune with the movement away from classical decoration towards a costume relating more to contemporary fashion. This watercolour (a preparatory drawing for an engraved series which seems never to have been published) illustrates a blue double-breasted coat (*habit dégagé*) with pantaloons; there is a modest amount of silver embroidery; the double-breasted red waistcoat is embroidered in gold and the costume is completed with black half-boots and a black hat with a tricolour cockade. It is a stylish outfit but more akin to the dress of the humble legislators than to the grander costume that Napoleon envisaged for himself and his fellow-Consuls. Delécluze noted that only a few days after seeing David's design Napoleon ordered his ministers and top functionaries into the formal *habit à la française*,[89] which is what he himself was to adopt in 1802, after being made Consul for Life, and in which Ingres painted him in 1804[90] (Liège, Musée des Beaux-Arts).

which was replaced by a Consulate; of the three Consuls it was clear from the start that Napoleon was *primus inter pares*, a position confirmed when he was elected First Consul early in 1800. Under the Consulate, and even more under the Empire, the legislative bodies became less important; the Council of State was the only significant group.

Napoleon was quick to realise the importance of costume as a force for dignity and discipline in his new government, and before the end of 1799 he began to issue a series of decrees on official uniform. As well as the costume for the legislators (a Tribunate, suppressed in 1807, and a Legislative Council) which was a blue embroidered *habit* – they lost their antique togas – there was more elaborate official dress for the Council of State and for the Senate.[86] English visitors to Paris during the Peace of Amiens often commented on the French passion for putting more and more officials into uniform; it was a matter of importance, noted John Scott, 'what uniform a senator shall wear who discusses their constitutional characters ...'[87]

This comment was made in 1814 and the discussions were still going on as late as 1830 after the revolution that removed Charles X, the last Bourbon king, and replaced him with the citizen-king Louis-

Consuls.

nᵒ 13.

quelque chose qui sent le militaire, il n'y a pas de mal à cela'.[91]

Napoleon's choice of dress was always carefully calculated, and the military touch reminded people of the source of his power. 'Not everyone has the right to dress simply' was one of his maxims, and whether dressed in his ordinary blue consular costume or his military uniform, the effect was that of deliberate simplicity. Joseph Farington, in Paris in 1802, was only one of many visitors who noted the First Consul, 'dressed in Blue, much more plain than His Officers, which gave him additional consequence, for the power & splendour of his situation was marked by the Contrast, as commanding all that brilliant display'.[92]

Napoleon's inventories reveal a number of formal suits – 'habits de soie brodés' – but his own inclination was for military costume, even during the Empire, chosen so that he would stand out among the glittering court uniforms and *habits habillés*. His everyday choice was that of the Colonel of the Chasseurs à Cheval de la Garde, which was green faced with red; he was buried in this uniform. For Sundays and special occasions he wore the blue coat faced with white of Colonel of the Grenadiers à Pied de la Garde. This is what David paints in his portrait *The Emperor Napoleon in his Study* (1812; Washington, National Gallery of Art); as well as the uniform coat (decorated with the insignia of the Légion d'Honneur), Napoleon wears the knee-breeches of white kerseymere which he wore – never trousers, according to his valet Constant – during the Empire.

In the spring of 1802 a splendid procession took place from the Tuileries palace to Notre-Dame, for a religious service to celebrate the Concordat with the Papacy. It was an occasion of splendid pomp and ceremony led by Napoleon in his gold-embroidered scarlet consular suit, with the famous Pitt diamond in the pommel of his sword – it can be seen in the Gros portrait. A few months later, Napoleon was Consul for Life and began to turn his attention towards imperial power.

One of the most powerful weapons of a monarch was patronage and this could operate through the medium of a knightly, chivalric order; as early as 1802 Napoleon turned his mind towards the establishment of such an order, but one that was to be based on merit and not on birth. The Légion d'Honneur[93] was finally inaugurated in the summer of 1804, a few months after Napoleon had assumed the hereditary title of Emperor. The first distributions of the order took place at the Invalides on 14 July, and two days later at Boulogne in a stage-managed gesture of defiance preparatory to the proposed invasion of England. The collar of the order incorporated the image of eagles, which in June of 1804 had been adopted as

For the moment, however, Napoleon thought it appropriate for the Consuls' costume to consist of the *habit dégagé* (blue for everyday, red for formal occasions) and white pantaloons. Gros's portrait of *Bonaparte as First Consul* (*c*.1801–2; pl. 158) shows the formal red velvet cut-away coat embroidered in gold with a honeysuckle motif (note how it fastens in the 'feminine' way, right over left), pantaloons embroidered in gold *à la hussar* and hessian boots. This costume was comfortable (above all Napoleon liked ease in dress) and flattering to a slim figure. As the virtual ruler of France, right from the beginning of the Consulate, he could dispense with the *ancien-régime* accessories of lace cravat and ruffles which the other two Consuls wore, in favour of the black military cravat seen in the Gros portrait. At the celebrations for the 14 July (the only national *fête* retained in France by the time of the Consulate) in 1802, Thibaudeau commented on the appearance of the First Consul in his

> habit habillé de soie rouge brodé à Lyon, sans manchettes et avec une cravatte noire. Cet accoutrement parut assez bizarre; on ne lui en fit pas moins compliment sur son bon goût, excepté pour la cravate. Il répondit en riant, 'Il y a toujours

an emblem of Empire; the eagle was also linked to the Roman army and to Charlemagne, a symbolism that Napoleon eagerly embraced. Reading such costume histories as Malliot's *Recherches sur les costumes, les moeurs, les usages réligieux, civils et militaires des anciens peuples* . . . (1804) on the military origin of the title 'emperor' would support Napoleon's *de facto* claim to such power: 'Le nom d'empereur, imperator, ne fut dans les commencements qu'un titre honorable décerné par les troupes à un general qui avait donné des preuves de son courage et de sa capacité . . .' Such an honour would come with rich trappings, 'L'or, l'argent, les pierreries, la broderie, les étoffes les plus précieuses . . .'[94]

The Carolingian empire claimed direct descent from that of Rome, and Napoleon turned to Charlemagne for the creation of an imperial nobility and as the inspiration behind his coronation, which took place in December 1804. In his search to be the new Charlemagne, Napoleon commissioned research into Carolingian costume and regalia. The emperor, following the custom of medieval kings, chose a personal emblem to decorate his official costume, possessions and furnishings. Lenoir discovered that when the grave of Childeric (the founder of the Merovingian dynasty who died in 481) in Tournai was opened in the mid-seventeenth century[95] it was found to contain hundreds of gold insects, variously identified as bees or cicadas, the latter being an ancient Chinese symbol of immortality; such items might have decorated the king's clothes or his horse harness. As a result, Napoleon decided on the bee; it was a symbol of the hard work that the emperor undertook on behalf of his people, and it was an attractive object which could be incorporated into a wide range of the applied arts, including textiles.

During much of 1804 protracted discussions took place over the form of the coronation; how far was it to follow the ritual for French kings laid down in the twelfth century, how far – given that Christianity had only recently been restored officially in France – should the religious element be emphasised? Not only was the coronation of Napoleon to be considered, but also that of his wife; the authorities had to go back as far as 1610 for a precedent, the last crowned queen of France being Marie de' Medici. The line between the creation of a new dynasty and the traditions of the old regime, especially with regard to something as ancient as a coronation, had to be carefully drawn.

Like Charlemagne, Napoleon too wanted the Pope's presence at his coronation, and at the end of November 1804 the rather unwilling pontiff was brought to Paris. Originally the coronation was to have taken place in the Champ de Mars, scene of some of the great events of the French Revolution, including the pageants organised by David (there was

no question of the ceremony taking place at Rheims like those of all previous French monarchs) but Napoleon finally chose Notre-Dame. The cathedral had suffered during the Revolution and repairs were necessary; the opportunity was taken to add some appropriate touches, such as statues of Clovis and Charlemagne, in honour of the occasion. David was employed to design the interior as if in a theatre, with

158 A.-J. Gros, *Bonaparte as First Consul*, c.1801–2. Oil on canvas. Musée de la Légion d'Honneur, Paris.

tiers of seats covered with velvet on either side of the nave; the church was carpeted and the walls decorated with gold-fringed hangings, as can be seen in Jean-Baptiste Isabey's drawing of the coronation (pl. 159). David was responsible for the overall design, and working with him was Isabey who (with the help of Jean-Baptiste Regnault) planned the costumes. The whole enterprise took on the nature of a vast theatrical pageant and had to be planned with military precision. David made models of the interior of Notre-Dame, in which were placed wooden dolls dressed in paper costumes; rehearsals with these dolls took place on a large table in the Emperor's study. Isabey's drawing shows the culmination of the coronation ceremony when the Emperor crowned himself; this is sketched lightly in the background, before the altar, Napoleon standing next to the seated Pope with Josephine kneeling a few paces in front. The artist has given prominence here to both the graceful lines of the women's court dress, based on contemporary fashion, and the 'Renaissance'-inspired attire of the dignitaries of the Empire.

Napoleon had firm ideas on what his coronation costume should be, and after some discussion a clever compromise was reached between the traditional (in the style of ancient royalty) and the classical (the modern Caesar). It is clear, for example, on looking at a state portrait of a Bourbon king, that the mantle that he wears has been the inspiration behind Napoleon's own, although there are differences in cut and arrangement on the body. Louis-Michel van Loo's portrait of Louis XV (*c.*1761; pl. 160) is typical of the genre; it is dominated by the huge blue velvet mantle embroidered with fleurs-de-lis and lined throughout with ermine. Diderot, commenting on this 'grand habit de cérémonie', rather dismissively continued: 'cette espèce de vêtement lui donne moins la majesté d'un roi, que la dignité d'un président au parlement'.[96] This would have been regarded by most people as a somewhat splenetic statement, for Louis XV, whatever his other faults, was generally held to be royal in his demeanour, a characteristic not given to his successor. (What would Diderot have made of Napoleon's coronation costume?) It is worth noting also that the costume worn under the coronation mantle of Louis XV is the silver tissue doublet and trunk hose of the Order of the Saint-Esprit based on late sixteenth-century dress; it was one of the styles that helped to inspire Isabey's designs for the costume of great officials of the Empire.

It is fortunate that the inventories for the coronation costume survive, giving some indication of the luxury and vast expense of this occasion. For the actual ceremony in Notre-Dame the Emperor wore a white satin tunic embroidered in gold and fringed at the ankles.[97] Originally, to complement this classical tunic, Roman sandals were envisaged, but the Emperor decided that shoes would be more dignified; as a compromise the gold embroidery was based on a strap design, imitating laces. The imperial mantle was of purple (*pourpre*, i.e. purplish-red) velvet, lined with Russian ermine decorated with tufts of black astrakhan; the fur alone cost 18,220 francs and made the garment so heavy that Napoleon almost fell over with the weight. The embroidery on the mantle, a design of gold Ns, bees, olive, laurel and oak leaves, was provided by the firm of Picot and cost 15,000 francs. The silks were supplied by the most fashionable Paris mercer Levacher, who had earlier provided Napoleon with a red silk Consular suit, courtesy of the city of Lyons, in the hope (to be fulfilled) that the silk industry would be resuscitated under the aegis of what was already in 1802 a court in embryo.

The imperial jeweller Biennais supplied the Emperor's diadem of gold laurel leaves, an inspired design which emphasised the classical imagery and enabled Napoleon's face to be clearly seen. The regalia was also created by Biennais; it comprised the sceptre, based on that of the fourteenth-century king, Charles V, and the Hand of Justice and sword which were supposed to be Charlemagne's. These can be seen in Ingres's famous portrait of Napoleon in coronation costume (1806; pl. 161)[98] which astounded contemporary opinion with its sense of the 'primitive' and the Gothic. Art historians have speculated on what sources Ingres might have used for such an arresting image; these include the figure of God in the van Eycks' *Ghent Altarpiece* (the main panels of which were in Paris as part of the art booty from the Netherlands), an engraved Roman gem of Jupiter (which might have inspired the signs of the zodiac), and an engraving from an ivory diptych of a Byzantine emperor.[99] Did Ingres (or Napoleon for that matter) perhaps also know of the famous mosaic in San Vitale, Ravenna (*c*.547), depicting the Emperor of Byzantium and his court? Both priest-king and potentate, Justinian wears the open-sided imperial purple mantle or *paludamentum*, descended from the antique *chlamys* and the forerunner of nearly all state mantles in western Europe, including Napoleon's coronation

costume. Justinian, like Napoleon, was a brilliant soldier and administrator; he also knew the value of good visual propaganda.

In order to achieve his dramatic vision of Napoleon, Ingres had to take some liberties with the truth; this artistic freedom was the result of not being granted a sitting by the Emperor, but he must have had access to the costume and the regalia. To create the effect of an almost disembodied head, Ingres heightened the ruff of Alençon lace and omitted altogether the matching lace cravat which would have broken into the curves created by the ermine cape and the collar of the Légion d'Honneur. In addition, he changed the embroidery design both on the white satin tunic and on the velvet mantle.

Ingres's master David, for all his skills as a portraitist

160 L.-M. Vanloo, *Louis XV*, *c*.1761. Oil on canvas. Wallace Collection, London.

161   J.-A.-D. Ingres,
*Napoleon on the Imperial
Throne*, 1806. Oil on canvas.
Musée de l'Armée, Paris.

and his interest in official costume, never painted such a potent image of Napoleon in coronation robes.[100] Ingres succeeded, perhaps because he made the Emperor a deity, and this was not David's way in his art, although in life he was prone to hero-worship, first Robespierre and then Napoleon. David, however, as the greatest artist of his day, with his skill in dealing with such a large cast of players, and with his proven ability at visual propaganda, was the only real choice to paint the *Coronation of Napoleon* (1805–7; pl. 162) which he described as 'le plus important de mes ouvrages'. Appointed Premier Peintre de l'Empereur a few days after the coronation, early in 1805 David began the Herculean task of working up scores of drawings of poses and costumes and asking for the clothes worn by the participants to be sent to him in the huge studio which was necessary for the completion of such a large painting. Portrait sessions were requested with as many sitters as possible; stand-ins included his two daughters and his friend the actor Talma.

Two sketchbooks in the Fogg Art Museum, Cambridge, Massachusetts,[101] show David's working methods. As with the *Oath of The Tennis Court*, the artist drew many of the figures naked or semi-nude with the clothes lightly outlined on the body; there were then further studies with more detail given to the costume. Sometimes these details are quite explicit, with, for example, precise patterns for embroidery, particularly on the court dresses of the princesses. The drawings are often inscribed with reminders to check on such particulars as to how hats were worn and there are notes on costume, often minute details; one folio shows Hortense de Beauharnais holding the hand of her son Napoléon-Charles, and David has written 'il y a de l'or autour de la fraise'[102] – this was the lace collar *à la Médicis*, the best example of which is to be seen in the portrait of Josephine in the *Coronation* (pl. 163). In his studio David experimented with different ways of arranging cloaks and trains, but there were so many people to be included that some of the minor figures look rather cramped, their clothes tighter to the body than the artist had envisaged in some of his drawings.

It took some time for David to decide how Napoleon should be depicted and at what moment during the ceremony. One of the artist's early sketches showed the Emperor with his left hand on

162   J.-L. David, *Coronation of Napoleon*, 1805–7. Oil on canvas. Louvre, Paris. (Photo: © Réunion des musées nationaux)

kept. As Napoleon admired the graceful lines of the Neoclassical high fashion, this was decided on, with some added historical touches such as the puffed upper sleeves with embroidery and jewelled bands in imitation of Renaissance slashing (where the top fabric is cut away to reveal another beneath – a style popular from the late fifteenth to the mid-seventeenth century), and also the raised collar (*chérusque/fraise*) in silk lace embroidered with gold.[103]

Josephine's dress was designed by Isabey and made up by Leroy. It was of white silk brocaded in silver and embroidered with golden bees and a design, with a fringe at the hem, like that on the Emperor's tunic. It is thus described in Percier and Fontaine's *Livre du Sacre* (1807): 'robe à manches longues de brocart d'argent semée d'abeilles d'or, brodée sur les tailles; le bas de la robe brodé et garni de franges et crépines d'or; le corsage et le bord des manches enrichis de diamants.' Isabey's drawing in the *Livre du Sacre* illustrating this dress shows the coronation mantle looped up on Josephine's left shoulder, whereas in the original decree of 29 messidor, An XII (18 July 1804), it was intended to hang from both shoulders. It was actually worn, as David shows, with straps over the shoulders to hold it up, as it was so heavy (it weighed eighty pounds) being made of velvet embroidered and lined with ermine like that of the Emperor; it was only ever worn once again, by Napoleon's second wife Marie-Louise, at her marriage in 1810.

In the grandeur and conception of the *Coronation* David was clearly influenced by the great Marie de' Medici cycle by Rubens, which also provided inspiration for some details of the sumptuous costume. Isabey also seems to have been prompted by the popular taste for the more slender and graceful styles of the late medieval period; the high waist, the sleeves reaching to the knuckles of the fingers and the elegant line of the long neck recall – as does the prayerful pose – a late Gothic, Burgundian princess as depicted by Hugo van der Goes or Hans Memling. Kneeling, and in profile, her face which was made up by Isabey, looks closer to that of a young woman in her twenties than to her real age of forty-one; the refinement of her features is complemented by the delicate Neoclassical design of her glittering diamond comb and tiara and the simple diamond drops in her ears. One of her chief beauties, averred the duchesse d'Abrantès, 'was not merely her fine figure, but the elegant turn of her neck, and the way in which she carried her head'. Just after the moment during the ceremony that is captured by David, the Emperor crowned Josephine, taking great trouble, according to the duchesse, in placing the crown correctly, 'as if to promise her she should wear it gracefully and lightly'.

Josephine's train, in David's painting, is held up by two of her ladies, Madame de la Rochefoucauld and

163   David, detail of the Empress Josephine from *Coronation of Napoleon* (pl. 162).

164   J.-A-D. Ingres, *Napoleon in the 'petit habillement' of the Coronation, c.*1804 Pencil. Musée Ingres, Montauban.

his sword hilt crowning himself; another showed the act of self-coronation with a sword clutched to the breast. This was thought to be both awkward and undiplomatic in the presence of the Pope, and it was suggested (possibly by Napoleon's sister Pauline) that David should show the Emperor in the act of crowing Josephine; this was the moment chosen.

Considerable thought went into the design of the Empress's coronation costume, which mingled the historical with contemporary fashion. It was out of the question to return to the *grand habit* of the *ancien régime* with its fiercely boned bodice and hooped skirt, although one regal garment, the formal train, was

160

her Mistress of the Robes, Madame de Lavalette. In reality, this task was performed by the five imperial princesses – Napoleon's three sisters Elisa, Pauline and Caroline, his brother Joseph's wife Marie-Julie and Josephine's daughter Hortense. But the Emperor's sisters made so much fuss about this 'menial' task that they prevailed upon David to show them quite removed from the immediate vicinity of the Empress. They stand to the left, a sparkling jewelled group in their coronation costume which consisted of an embroidered white silk dress and a court train of coloured silk held in place by a decorative girdle at the high waist-line. This kind of dress, as already noted, was to become court dress, not just in France, but throughout the Empire.

David's slight economy with the truth in depicting Josephine's train-bearers, was not the only less-than-honest image in the *Coronation*. Although Napoleon's mother Madame Mère had refused to attend the coronation, David places her in a central position in a royal box; this would not have been done without the Emperor's agreement. The Pope, his right hand half raised in somewhat unwilling benediction, does not wear his papal tiara, which is held by one of his two (there should have been five) train-bearers. Napoleon's valet Constant recalled the fuss over the depiction of Cardinal Caprara, in attendance on the Pope (although he was not actually at the ceremony); when the Cardinal complained about being painted without a wig (he even protested to Talleyrand), David refused any amendment, loftily declaring, 'Never will I degrade my brush by painting a wig'.[104]

The coronation was not just the apotheosis of Napoleonic splendour, but the inspiration for the costume of court officials and dignitaries of the Empire. Viewing David's painting, the Emperor made the surprising remark to the artist: 'C'est très bien, vous m'avez deviné, vous m'avez fait chevalier français'.[105] To modern eyes, Napoleon's coronation costume looks more classical than anything else, but the long tunic and mantle relate to those worn by French kings since the early Middle Ages; was this what the Emperor had in mind, or was it a reference to the nobility of the pose? The comment is more apt if we turn from the *grand costume* worn during the actual ceremony, to the *petit costume* which was worn on the morning of the coronation for the journey to Notre-Dame and for the festivities afterwards. Constant is best suited to describe this costume, which is illustrated by Ingres, *Napoleon in the 'petit habillement' of the Coronation* (pl. 164). It consisted of

gold embroidered silk stockings with the Imperial crown worked in the corner; white velvet shoes, laced and embroidered with gold; white velvet breeches embroidered with gold at the seams, with

diamond buttons and garter-buckles; the vest also of white velvet embroidered with gold and diamond buttons; the coat of crimson velvet faced with white velvet and which before and behind was one glittering mass of gold embroidery. The short cloak was crimson, lined with white satin; it hung over the left shoulder, and was fastened across the right breast with a double clasp of diamonds.[106]

With this costume, designed by Isabey and inspired by styles of the later sixteenth century, the Emperor wore a black velvet hat with white feathers *à la Henri IV*, decorated with diamonds. Madame de Rémusat, one of Josephine's closest ladies-in-waiting, thought the Emperor looked impressive in this 'superb dress'; others, such as the comtesse de Boigne, considered that he was too short and plump to carry off such a swashbuckling costume.

Napoleon felt the costume suited him – as a 'chevalier français' perhaps – and he wore it for very formal occasions, such as his marriage to Marie-Louise, the marriages of his siblings and grand state banquets. He had three *petits costumes* during his reign, one for the coronation, one ordered in 1806 and one in 1810 for his second marriage; the mantle for the last one survives, a lustrous garnet velvet with heavy three-dimensional gold embroidery by Picot.[107] In addition, Napoleon had a green velvet *petit habillement* (part of which survives) as King of Italy; his coronation took place in Milan in 1805.[108]

The costume of the great dignitaries of the Empire and of the royal household was based on Napoleon's *petit costume*. It consisted of a knee-length tunic-coat and a short cloak of velvet (taffeta in summer), both embroidered, *culotte* and waistcoat, white sash, lace cravat and a feathered hat; rank was distinguished by colour and by the type and amount of embroidery. Apart from Napoleon, the grandest costume was that of the Imperial princes in white embroidered in gold. All the departments which made up the Emperor's official household had a different colour, the most important being the red and silver of the office of the Grand Maréchal du Palais, in charge of all the royal palaces. General Duroc, duc de Frioul, held this position until his death in 1813 and was painted by Gros (one of a series of portraits of senior court officials) wearing his official uniform (Château de Versailles). The lavishly embroidered red velvet costume of his successor Marshal Bertrand has survived and gives some idea of the splendour of these court uniforms which Isabey and David created and depicted.[109]

Such styles in costume appealed to Napoleon, for they embodied popular notions of romantic chivalry, recalling in a vague way the time of the Chevalier Bayard 'sans peur et sans reproche', and – later in the sixteenth century, Henry IV, whose martial valour, amorous exploits and freedom from bigotry were equally appreciated. It was in the late sixteenth century, in 1578, that the Order of the Saint-Esprit was founded, the everyday costume (doublet and trunk hose of silver tissue, short cloak and feathered hat) remaining much the same for some two hundred years (see pl. 160). It was this unbroken link with the past that appealed to a new dynasty; aesthetic considerations made the period attractive to artists and fashion designers such as Isabey and Garnerey. Somewhat ironically, on the eve of the French Revolution the costume of the Saint-Esprit was 'modernised' into an *habit à la française* of black velvet, but retaining the short cloak (black lined with green, and embroidered in gold) and a black velvet Henry IV hat with white feathers.[110]

★   ★   ★

Although Neoclassicism was the dominant artistic style during the period covered by this book and an important influence on fashion, it was not the only one. *Le style troubadour* became very popular in both art and dress, 'ce moyen âge qui n'est pas le moyen âge' in the words of Théophile Gautier, the inventor of the term (a perjorative one),[111] but it is worth noting that the eighteenth century too was interested in the medieval and Renaissance past.

Paintings of *fêtes galantes* by such artists as Watteau, Lancret and Pater achieve a sense of the elegaic through their use of 'historic' dress, sometimes the costume of the *commedia dell'arte* which was based on sixteenth-century modes and which blends perfectly with contemporary fashion to create an ambience of mystery and fantasy. As the court declined in power during the second half of the eighteenth century, it retreated even more to the pursuit of such entertainments as the rural masquerade held in gardens landscaped in the English manner. The very irregularity of Nature, it was thought, was more akin to the 'Gothic' (a term used very loosely to encompass any period from the Dark Ages to the late medieval) than to the icy perfection of classical art. English gardens, English architecture (fake ruins and Gothick houses in the style of Strawberry Hill) and the plays of Shakespeare (adapted by Jean-François Ducis for the French stage) began to inspire a few patrons, artists and designers in the late eighteenth century.

The historian Norbert Elias found that Rousseau had struck a chord in aristocratic hearts with his notion of Nature as a refuge from 'oppressive political restraints'. Country life was often linked with an idealised past 'which took on the character of a dream image. Country life became a symbol of lost innocence, of spontaneous simplicity . . . an opposite image to urban court life with its greater constraints, its more complex hierarchical pressures . . .'[112]

It was the fashions of the sixteenth and early seventeenth centuries that had most appeal throughout the period, although from the early nineteenth century the dress of the Middle Ages began to attract interest. In the eighteenth century the term 'Spanish dress' was widely used in France for what in England was more often called Vandyke costume. It was a style that incorporated elements of late sixteenth-century and early seventeenth-century fashions, such as lace ruffs or collars, ribbon trimmings and rosettes. For women the dress usually comprised a tight bodice and a skirt with fullness over the hips (it was close to the eighteenth-century aesthetic in costume); for men it was doublet and knee-breeches, the latter being cut like the eighteenth-century *culotte*. It was a type of costume that attracted Rococo artists; they liked its asymmetry and the three-dimensional effects created by such details as ruffs, ribbon lacing and slashed sleeves. It is often interpreted in a light-hearted spirit, theatrically Arcadian, as in Drouais's group portrait of the *Marquis de Sources and his Family* (1756; pl. 166), exhibited at the Salon of 1759 as 'un concert champêtre'; the figures look as if they personify 'Music' in a pastoral tableau vivant. The silk taffeta costume, copiously trimmed with ribbon, looks real; it relates to surviving theatre dress which is often made of bright colours and profusely decorated for maximum dramatic effect.

Why the interest in Spain? It was a country somewhat isolated from the rest of western Europe and regarded as rather backward in political and economic terms; there was a sense of Spain as exotic, a land of mystery where distinctive styles of dress deriving from the seventeenth century were still worn, an unbroken link with the past. When Madame Geoffrin, 'ennuyé de ne voir que des Alexandres, des Césars, des Scipions . . .', asked artists to 'chercher dans les habillemens Européens quelque sujet qui pût faire effet',[113] the result was a number of paintings with sitters dressed *à l'espagnole*. First off the mark was Carle van Loo with *La Conversation espagnole* (for the Salon of 1755) and *La Lecture espagnole* (for the Salon of 1761); both paintings are now in the Hermitage, St Petersburg. The artist's nephew Louis-Michel van Loo was also inspired to produce, for the Salon of 1769, two paintings depicting Spanish or Vandyke dress, *A Spanish Woman Playing the Guitar* (untraced) and a companion piece *A German Woman Playing the Harp* (pl. 165). Although the harp is mid-eighteenth century, the costume demonstrates a serious attempt to return to the seventeenth century, albeit more inspired by the Netherlands than by Spain. The men's costume with its softly layered linen ruff, silk doublet, hose and short cloak, is clearly derived from Flemish dress of the 1620s, possibly with Rubens in mind; fashions in the Southern Netherlands (under Spanish Government), not suprisingly, were influenced by Spanish styles. The costume of the harpist dates from later in the seventeenth-century; the low, bare neckline, long pointed bodice, full rustling silk skirt and the hair adorned with pearls, all recall portraits by an artist such as Vermeer. It is a style of dress akin to the fashions of the late 1760s, giving the harpist a modish appearance and setting her apart from the purely historical masculine characters.

In terms of the fashionable female image, 'Spanish' dress was protean in its application. It could demonstrate (through knowledge of the past) the learning and education of the sitter; it could also create an Arcadian mood, often slightly frivolous. It provided, as a popular masquerade costume, a rare opportunity for a woman to appear *en travesti*, as a Spanish page like Chérubin in Beaumarchais's *Marriage of Figaro*; a half-length portrait by Drouais, possibly of Madame du Barry (1765; New York, Metropolitan Museum of Art) shows the sitter playing the guitar, her hair curled like a masculine wig and dressed in a satin doublet with lace ruff and cuffs.

Beaumarchais's popular plays, *The Barber of Seville* (1775) and *The Marriage of Figaro* (1784) encouraged a fashion for Spanish dress during the 1780s, which was linked with the vogue for the pastoral. Black and red were colours associated with Spanish dress, and became popular in the 1780s, in England as well as in France; George Selwyn, English wit and friend of Horace Walpole, described women as looking like

165   L.-M. Vanloo, *A German Woman Playing the Harp*, 1769. Oil on canvas. Private Collection, France, formerly with Colnaghi, London.

163

chimneys on fire with their black velvet gowns and red petticoats. Labille-Guiard painted *Madame Louise-Elisabeth de France, Infante d'Espagne* in 1789 (Château de Versailles). The sitter wears a fashionable French version of Spanish costume, a black dress with puffed, slashed upper-sleeves lined with red and a matching hat trimmed with red and white feathers.

As a fashionable court artist, Vigée-Lebrun also painted this type of costume. The Wallace Collection in London possesses a ravishing portrait of Madame Adélaïde Perrégaux (1789) dressed in black velvet trimmed with red and a kind of Rembrandtesque cap on her head, a soft velvet 'beret' decorated with red feathers. *Marie de Gramont, Duchesse de Caderousse* (1784; pl. 167), shows an equally stylish but more pastoral version of black and red Spanish dress, with the sleeves tied in at the shoulder with ribbon bows, a large muslin veil and a straw hat; Vigée-Lebrun recalls in her memoirs that she persuaded the duchess to leave off her powder and that she (the artist) arranged the hair in an informal 'irregular' style to suit the mood of the portrait. It is clearly inspired by Rubens's '*Chapeau de Paille*' (London, National Gallery) which Vigée-Lebrun had admired on a visit to the Low Countries in 1782, and which is itself a depiction of the kind of Arcadian costume popular in the Netherlands in the early seventeenth century. As noted in the Introduction, the Rubens portrait also inspired – although less closely with regard to the details of costume – Vigée-Lebrun's *Self-portrait in a Straw Hat* (pl. 17).

Moving from the depiction of real dress into the realm of fancy dress, are Fragonard's famous *portraits de fantasie*, painted during the late 1760s and 1770s; the dates, and even the identities of some of the sitters, are in doubt. The costume makes no pretence at exact historical detail, but is a lyrical and imaginative interpretation of the past, working out Diderot's idea that the identity of a sitter was less important, particularly to posterity, than the ideas and the poetry which a good portrait should contain.[114] Diderot's own portrait in this series (pl. 168), painted a few years after van Loo's image of him (*c*.1767; pl. 19), emphasises his intellectual qualities as thinker and philosopher, with the choice of a generalised historic costume; both portraits show Diderot at work, but van Loo's use of contemporary fashion, however informal, was thought (by Diderot, at any rate) to create too lightweight an image. While Diderot had complained about the absence of his wig in the van Loo portrait, such an item of costume would have been inappropriate and an unwelcome intrusion into Fragonard's concept of the sitter as in direct line of descent from the philosophers of the past. Fragonard depicts him in a yellow doublet with lace-trimmed collar and cuffs and a loose mantle lined with red; a golden chain, in

Renaissance style, hangs over his shoulders. The colour range – warm, glowing yellows and reds predominating – is much the same in the other *portraits de fantaisie* and the costume is fairly similar in style, showing familiarity with Spanish art (which Fragonard would have seen in Naples), with Rubens and van Dyck. The portrait of his patron, the Abbé de Saint-Non (Barcelona, Museum of Modern Art) shows a swashbuckling hero dressed in red and brown with thigh-high boots, plumed hat and sword; it recalls a number of Baroque equestrian portraits, with perhaps a sense, too, of Don Quixote – Cervantes's novel being very popular in France.[115]

Fragonard, an artist quite uninterested in the dry

166 (facing page) F.-H. Drouais, *Marquis de Sources and his Family*, 1756. Oil on canvas. Versailles. (Photo: © Réunion des musées nationaux)

academicism of his contemporary Vien, seems nonetheless to have been receptive to a wide range of visual and artistic sources which provided romantic links with the past; these included the carnival, the *commedia dell'arte*, the *fêtes galantes* of such artists as Watteau, and Rubens's Medici cycle which he studied and copied in the palais de Luxembourg in 1767. The influence of Rubens can clearly be seen in Fragonard's portrait of *A Woman with a Dog* (pl. 169) which probably dates from the early 1770s. The loose handling of the paint and the deliberate vagueness or 'impression' of the costume make the details hard to discern, but the soft opulence of 'baroque' dress is cleverly conveyed. The starched ruff merges into a flattened collar at the front of the neckline; at the centre of the bodice is pinned a jewelled pendant, with a string of pearls looping over the shoulder, a feature seen often in Rubens's portraits and those of his fellow Flemish artists. The rich horizontality of early seventeenth-century fashion is brought out here, emphasised by the hanging cloak lined with ermine; only the high-piled hair and the liveliness of the features (although the face has a Rubens-like plumpness) indicate the eighteenth century.

The genius of Fragonard (like that in Gainsborough's portraits of women in historical fancy dress) is to turn history into poetry. If this is true in the portraits, it is even more so with regard to the rapturous, dream-like pastoral paintings, Mozartian in their lightness of touch and intensity of feeling – *Così fan tutte* comes particularly to mind. *The Progress of Love*, begun in the early 1770s and finished in 1777, was commissioned by Madame du Barry, but she eventually refused the four panels; it is not clear if this was due to the waning popularity of this kind of late Rococo art or difficulties with the artist. The paintings are now in the Frick Collection, New York (see pl. 170). More lively than the sleepy hedonistic pastorals of Boucher, Fragonard's paintings are more thoughtful, even slightly melancholy. What Fragonard did learn from Boucher, however, was a sense of theatre, of gesture; the lover and his beloved are frozen in dramatic pose, as if playing to an invisible audience. The costume is painted in quite a different way from the *portraits de fantaisie*, being more detailed and finished, closer to real theatrical costume or to that worn at aristocratic *fêtes galantes*. The man wears fanciful 'Spanish' costume, doublet and hose, a black cloak lined with red (under his right hand) and a ruff. The young woman is fashionably dressed in the style of the early 1770s with a low square neckline and full skirt; the touches of 'historic' costume – the ruff, the blue shoe rosettes and ribbons at the waist of her dress – are also *à la mode*. The borderline between the real and the make-believe is kept intentionally blurred.

The influence of 'Spanish' dress would not have

169   J.-H. Fragonard, *Woman with Dog*, *c.*1772–3. Oil on canvas. The Metropolitan Museum of Art, New York. Fletcher Fund 1937.

been as modestly popular as it was (far less important than Vandyke dress in England), if it had not been for the cult of Henry IV throughout the eighteenth century and until the 1820s. It has already been noted earlier in this chapter how much Henry IV was admired as an enlightened monarch, the father of his people. Voltaire's epic *Henriade* (1724) went through many editions and scenes from the life of Henry IV proved popular with artists throughout the eighteenth century,[116] particularly under Louis XVI who was hailed as a new Henry IV on his accession in 1774.[117] Voltaire's great poem, popular plays and histories of the first Bourbon king of France and, above all, Rubens's Marie de' Medici paintings, inspired art and fashion *à la Henri IV*. Marie-Antoinette, who loved masquerades and dances, decided on her accession to the throne to introduce a 'historical' ball dress. The comte de Ségur noted how the younger members of the court led by the comte d'Artois, discussed 'the dresses, customs, and entertainments of the courts of Francis I, Henry II, Henry III, and Henry IV', settling on the last-named as the theme for royal balls during the winter season of 1774–5. François Métra, editor of the *Correspondance secrète, politique et littéraire*, remarked in January 1775 that 'cet habillement est deja établi pour les bals . . . tous les hommes étoient en canons, manteaux, écharpes, noeuds de rubans aux jarretières & aux souliers, chapeaux à plumes & à plumes immenses; les femmes en collets montés & robes plissées . . .'[118] The costume was becoming to young men, according to Ségur, but 'quite the reverse to

167 (page 165)   E.-L. Vigée-Lebrun, *Marie de Gramont, duchesse de Caderousse*, 1784. Oil on canvas. The Nelson-Atkins Museum, Kansas City, Missouri (Purchase: Nelson Trust through exchange of the Bequest of Helen F. Spencer and the generosity of Mrs George C. Reuland through the W. J. Brace Charitable Trust, Mrs Herbert O'Peet, Mary Barton Stripp Kemper and Rufus Crosby Kemper Jr in memory of Mary Jane Barton Stripp and Enid Jackson Kemper and Mrs Rex L Diveley).

168 (facing page)   J.-H. Fragonard, *Denis Diderot*, *c.*1769. Oil on canvas. Louvre, Paris. (Photo: © Réunion des musées nationaux)

men of a mature age, and of a short and corpulent stature'.[119] The short rounded trunk hose (to which the *canons* were a tube-like extension) seemed to cut off the leg above the knee and proved an unpopular choice for men used to the more graceful line of the *culotte*. For women the new dress for court balls proved more popular, at least for a time. The large whaleboned farthingale of late sixteenth-century fashion could be equated with the court hoop of the late eighteenth; the be-ribboned and feathered hats in vogue during the 1770s could – at a pinch – resemble the plumed *chapeau à la Henri IV*. Plate 171, a drawing by Claude-Louis Desrais of a design for the royal ball dress, shows the way in which such historical elements as the raised open collar and the slashed, puffed sleeves could be incorporated into the formal open robe of the court of Marie-Antoinette.

Although the Henry IV dress was supposedly only worn during the mid-1770s, after which, in the words of Ségur, 'the old court dress triumphed over our chivalrous costumes', it seems to have continued in high esteem with the Queen. In 1782 she appeared at a court ball, dressed as Gabrielle d'Estrées, mistress of Henry IV, in white and silver gauze, with the great Regent diamond in her black hat decorated with white feathers. *Portrait of a Woman* (1779; pl. 172) by Louis-Roland Trinquesse has been described as being of Marie-Antoinette, although the features are

172 L.-R. Trinquesse, *Portrait of a Woman*, 1779. Oil on canvas. Sale, Christie's, Monaco, 3 April 1987, lot 76A.

not very close to those of the Queen. But on the table to the left is a bust of Henry IV, and the dress of the sitter is a fashionable version of the popular historical dress. It is made of white satin with slashed sleeves over gauze undersleeves, trimmed with pearls; the hat is the characteristic Henry IV type of black beaver with white ostrich plumes, which had entered the fashionable female wardrobe during the 1770s. Another style from the late sixteenth and early seventeenth centuries which became part of fashionable dress was the slightly raised 'Medici' collar, either of lace, or – as in the Trinquesse portrait – of pleated muslin. During the 1780s Marie-Antoinette ordered from Madame Eloffe (one of her *modistes* and *couturières lingères*) a number of these collars or 'chérusques en fraise' which were usually pleated or embroidered. The dress in the Trinquesse portrait has the slight fussiness of detail that indicates a real costume with 'historical' features. In *The Reader* (c.1786; pl. 173) by Marguerite Gérard and Fragonard, the costume has the perfect quality of a historical fashion plate, that is fashion ostensibly influenced by the past but idealised and conforming to the current fashionable aesthetic. From the 1780s Dutch seventeenth-century art was an important influence on some artists in France; the precision of interiors and furnishings, as well as research into the costume, foreshadows the meticulous attention to detail of the *style troubadour* artists of the early nineteenth century. Obviously aware of the work of such artists as Vermeer, de Hooch and Terborch, Gérard has taken trouble with

170 (facing page) J.-H. Fragonard, *The Meeting*. Oil on canvas. Copyright, The Frick Collection, New York.

171 C.-L. Desrais, design for a ball dress. Pen and wash. Kunstbibliothek, Berlin.

169

of the standing woman – something indefinable, perhaps the gestures, the subtleties of underpinnings which help to create particular ways of standing or sitting and the general sense of contemporary fashion which permeates what is meant to be a historical piece serve to produce that dreaded form of art, the 'costume painting', which was to flourish in the nineteenth century, initiated to some extent by the artists of *le style troubadour*.

This form of art, a style also called 'anecdotique' or 'chevaleresque', as François Pupil points out in the definitive work on the subject, *Le Style troubadour, ou la nostalgie du bon vieux temps* (1985), often told a story, usually from the Middle Ages but also from the Renaissance (the period ranged from the twelfth century to the sixteenth century); they told of the romanticised exploits of real heroes from Saint Louis to Bayard, or the imagined lives of lordly knights and their ladies. Even when Neoclassical art appeared to reign supreme, the cult of national heroes in French history was at the same time given official encouragement. Artists were urged, as in La Font de Saint-Yenne's *Sentiments sur quelques ouvrages de peinture* (1753), to tackle subjects like St Louis, Charles VII, Bayard and Francis I.[120] Rigoley de Juvigny, in his work *De la Décadence des lettres et des moeurs . . .* (1787) sighed for the days of chivalry which, he claimed, 'élevoit l'âme, l'embrasoit de l'amour de la gloire . . . faisoit des Héros . . .'[121]

Reminders of past French glories also helped to console the nation for defeats inflicted on their armies in Europe and in the colonies; 'la gloire de Bayard et des anciens chevaliers consola des défaites de Rosbach, de Québec, et de Pondichéry'.[122] Paintings that recalled French triumphs during the Hundred Years War against England were admired, as well as scenes that depicted the nobility of soul of such heroes as Bayard. Usually, as René Lanson remarks in his *Le Goût du moyen age en France au XVIIIe siècle*, the costume was all jumbled up: 'nulle différence ne fut établie entre les époques; Bayard et les barons du XIe siècle se ressemblèrent par leur costume et leurs sentiments'.[123] In Jean-Simon Barthélemy's *Entry into Paris of the French Army, 1346* (exh. 1787; pl. 174) (recording the retaking of the capital from the English) the armour is reasonably accurate, but the rest of the costume of slashed doublet and hose, as worn by the welcoming citizens of Paris, derives from sixteenth-century dress. A far less consistent mixture of clothing occurs in Girodet's drawing of *The Generosity of Bayard* (pl. 175) a few years later. The artist, while giving Bayard an early sixteenth-century beard and armour, contrives to make him look more the antique hero than the Renaissance warrior; the 'tunic' has a classical design on it and the armour fits the arms and legs like a second skin, imitating nudity. The pages

173 M. Gérard and J.-H. Fragonard, *The Reader*, c.1786. Oil on canvas. Fitzwilliam Museum, Cambridge.

the background and with the costume, particularly the tactile qualities of the satin, velvet and fur. The seated woman wears a dress of cream satin under one of the short-sleeved, fur-lined velvet jackets seen only in Dutch art of the mid-seventeenth century; such an attractive garment would fit in well with the vogue, during the 1780s, for short, flared jackets. The large, feathered hats also popular in the 1780s provided another link with the popular conception of seventeenth-century headwear. The standing woman is dressed in a costume of white satin, the long pointed bodice-front and the skirt closely pleated over the hips, being carefully copied from Dutch seventeenth-century genre painting; the long sleeves, however, are from the eighteenth century, as are the embroidered fichu and the posy of fresh flowers. In spite of the attention paid to the details of the clothing – even down to depicting the skirt seams of the seated figure and the horizontal creases formed by the tight bodice

170

are dressed in generalised versions of sixteenth-century costume and the young women (the girl from the village whose virtue had been respected by Bayard in his 'generosity', with her attendant) wear dress that, not very successfully, blends contemporary fashion with some features of Renaissance dress, such as the ruff and the slashed, puffed sleeves.

Progress towards accuracy in the costume of history paintings, which dress historians often like to believe is – or should be – the Holy Grail of artists, was limited by the availability of sources, particularly for the medieval period. This was partly remedied by the publication of Dom Bernard de Montfaucon's *Monumens de la monarchie françoise* (1729–33) in five volumes, describing and illustrating the visual remains of the monarchy from the Middle Ages; the aim was to include 'tout ce qui, dans l'ancienne France, concernait la royauté, l'Eglise, l'ameublement, la mode, la guerre, les fêtes, les funérailles, et les tombeaux'. Royalty was shown 'dans toutes les actes de leur vie, fêtes, chasses, batailles, lits de justice et cérémonies réligieuses, de sorte que le lecteur connaît les habits, les armes et même les différentes genres de peinture et de sculpture de chaque siècle'.[124]

Although the quality of research was often uneven and the illustrations were fairly basic (ensuring its lack of general appeal) it was to prove a popular source-book with artists interested in the medieval history of

France; the anecdotal approach and the cult of personality (giving faces and costumes to famous people who previously were little more than names) made Montfaucon crucial to the development of *le style troubadour*. One of his assistants was Jean-Baptiste de La Curne de Sainte-Palaye whose publications – *Mémoires sur l'ancienne chevalerie* (1753) and *Histoire littéraire des troubadours* (1774) – helped to introduce the Middle Ages to a wider public. With a clever mixture of fact and fiction, La Curne de Sainte-Palaye brought the period to life, skilfully 'editing' medieval manuscripts to bring out the drama of feudal times, the tournaments, the royal banquets and entertainments. He helped to create the popular types of the knight and his lady, inspired by love and honour, which proved such a popular feature of troubadour art. In addition, from the 1770s onwards, were published volumes of medieval poetry, *chansons de geste*, the stories of the Knights of King Arthur. Plays such as Dorment de Belloy's *Siège de Calais* (1765) and *Gaston et Bayard* (1771) and Louis-Sébastien Mercier's *Mort de Louis XI* (1783) also reflected this new trend, although it has to be said that, as with the painting of similar themes, the costume on the stage was a mixture of the contemporary with late sixteenth-century dress; eighteenth-century styles were inimical to medieval clothing.

Although there was a general feeling among the revolutionaries of the late eighteenth century that the Middle Ages had been an unprogressive and backward period, there was a sense – even during the iconoclasm of the Terror – that France's medieval heritage should be saved, particularly after the suppression of

171

the religious orders in 1790, when their treasures came on the market and many valuable works of art were threatened with destruction. After the nationalisation of Church property, the authorities set up a commission to save religious treasures; in 1791 the Couvent des Petits-Augustins became a repository for all kinds of church furnishings, including tombs and stained glass, and in 1793 it was re-named the Musée des Monuments Français and opened to the public a couple of years later.

The museum became a major source of inspiration to artists working in the *style troubadour*, evoking the past as a series of romantic episodes with a somewhat idiosyncratic juxtaposition of objects, some real, some manufactured; the centre-piece of the garden, for example, was the tomb of Héloïse and Abelard, which had been constructed by the curator, Alexandre Lenoir, to help create 'la douce mélancholie qui parle à l'âme sensible'. Lenoir's aim seems to have been to create a sense of theatre. Like a modern tourist re-creation of the past, the visitor's attention was gripped at the beginning and he was led on a mainly chronological survey through history, in a kind of romantic Gothic gloom; 'en arrivant à la salle d'introduction, on apperçoit les Valois se cacher dans des chapelles obscures . . .'[125] Objects from the Middle Ages and later periods were often mingled for dramatic effect; 'un visage léonardesque rehausse un costume médiéval, un lustre hollandais illumine une voûte gothique; une beauté rubénienne joue du clavecin dans un décor Renaissance'.[126] It was no wonder that the Musée des Monuments Français became such a magnet for artists, and indeed for foreign visitors to Paris. Farington's diary records a visit in 1802 to this 'Assemblage of Monuments from Abbies & Churches', where 'an Artist will find much curious matter for study, as the Costume of Dress for near 1000 years past may be studied in this place'.[127] In fact Lenoir's published catalogue (1800–6) stressed the value of the museum as a source of costume information, the entries for each century being prefaced with a dissertation on the dress of the time. Together with Montfaucon, the Musée des Monuments Français became an indispensable fund of information on medieval dress for the authors and artists producing costume history books, which in the early nineteenth century began to concentrate on the Middle Ages.

The 1802 Concordat had re-established Christianity, and later that year Chateaubriand published *La Génie du christianisme* in which he argued the case for religion on primarily aesthetic grounds; the Middle Ages, he thought, was the peak of Christian civilisation. Returning *émigrés* brought with them knowledge of foreign literary and artistic cultures, particularly those of the Middle Ages and the Renaissance which they associated with monarchy.

French military successes under Napoleon and his generals could just as well evoke episodes in medieval warfare and chivalrous exploits as events from classical antiquity. The Napoleonic regime – as symbolised in the luxury and inspiration behind the coronation – identified more with the medieval and Renaissance past than with the austerity of republican Rome. 'The court of the new Charlemagne', remarked Lady Morgan, '. . . assumed a character of gothic grandeur, wholly destructive to that tone of republican simplicity which Brutus Bonaparte had once contributed to establish.'[128]

Napoleon's artistic patronage reinforced the link between his dynasty and the safely remote early medieval past. He undertook the restoration of Saint-Denis, the burial-place of the French monarchy, which had been badly damaged during the Revolution, and in 1811 commissioned a series of paintings depicting French kings from Merovingian times to the thirteenth century; among them was a work in the sacristy by Charles Meynier, *Charlemagne Consecrating the Church of Saint-Denis* (1812; *in situ*), for which Montfaucon was the source.[129] The Emperor also instructed Gros to decorate the dome of the Panthéon with figures of Clovis, Charlemagne, St Louis and Napoleon himself, all surrounding St. Geneviève, the patron saint of Paris.[130]

From being almost a term of abuse in the mid-eighteenth century (or at least, appreciated only by a select few), by the time of the Empire the word 'Gothic' had become a term of approbation. David's famous prophetic comment in 1808 is worth quoting: 'Dans dix ans, l'étude de l'antique sera delaissée. Tous ces dieux, ces héros seront remplacés par des chevaliers, des troubadours chantant sous les fenêtres de leurs dames, au pied d'un antique donjon'.[131] According to Delécluze, from the earliest years of the nineteenth century some of David's pupils had begun to abandon a study of antique art in the Louvre, preferring to visit the Musée des Monuments Français in pursuit of historical French subjects for their paintings; among these artists were Pierre Révoil and François Fleury Richard, both of whom were typical of 'troubadour artists' in their attention to historical detail. Révoil's scene of a tournament painted in 1812 (Lyon, Musée des Beaux-Arts) depicts the great fourteenth-century hero Bertrand du Guesclin (the theme was taken from La Curne de Saint-Palaye's *Mémoires sur l'ancienne chevalerie*); the costume is mainly medieval (albeit with a few touches of 'Vandykerie'), but of the fifteenth rather than the fourteenth century. Fleury Richard's *Valentina of Milan Mourning the Death of her Husband,* exhibited at the Salon of 1802, relied on research at the Musée des Monuments Français. The painting, once owned by the Empress Josephine (and now only known through preliminary studies, a copy and an engraving), showed the weeping widow of the duc d'Orléans in fairly accurate early fifteenth-century dress. The costume of the seated figure is copied from the recumbent tomb effigy in Lenoir's museum (see pl. 177), and consists of a gown belted at the waist, with long tight sleeves to the wrist, over which is the royal *seurcot ouvert*, an open-sided surcote edged with ermine. Fleury Richard took immense trouble with the costume; he went to the Print Room in the Bibliothèque Nationale to look at the sources which Montfaucon had used, noting the details of clothing and colour, as well as making frequent visits to the Petits-Augustins.[132]

The close-fitting costume worn by Valentina of Milan (who died shortly after her husband, thus appealing to the sentimentality that is such a crucial element of *le style troubadour*) was very much in tune with early nineteenth-century styles in dress, the lines of which emphasised the figure. Jean-Antoine Laurent's *Héloïse in the Cloister* of 1812 (pl. 176) shows the famous lover of Abelard (the ashes of both were taken to Paris in 1800 and later buried at Père Lachaise) about to abandon her secular finery in preparation for taking the veil. Instead of the correct twelfth-century costume, the artist has chosen a form-fitting dress under a semi-transparent open surcote;

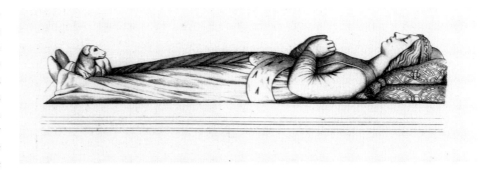

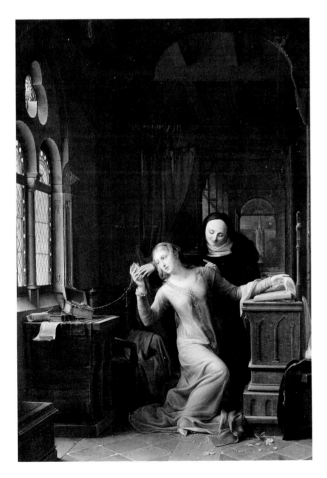

the effect is more fashionable than medieval, although Laurent has clearly studied the costume of the Middle Ages both in the Musée des Monuments Français and the costume books which used material from Lenoir's museum. Such costume-history books included the popular *Recueil des costumes français . . . depuis Clovis jusqu'à Napoléon I*, which came out in monthly parts from 1809–13.

The *Recueil des costumes français*, with text by L. Rathier and illustrations by M.-M.-F. Beaunier, was dedicated to the Empress Josephine who was particularly interested in *le style troubadour* and whose collections of art contained works by Bergeret and Fleury Richard. The inventory of her possessions on her death in 1814 included such works by Fleury Richard as the *Valentina of Milan* discussed above, and two works described as 'Les Adieux de Charles VII à Agnès Sorel' and 'Henry IV étant allé voir la belle Gabrielle'; in addition, Josephine seems to have collected such historical curiosities as the hair of Agnes Sorèl and part of Henry IV's moustache which was taken when the royal tombs at Saint-Denis were opened up during the Revolution.[133]

In spite of the fact that the slim lines of late medieval costume were appreciated in troubadour art and that some items of historic revival dress were given such names as 'gothic' (collars and ruffs for example), the styles of the Middle Ages did not really affect high fashion. The coronation had sanctified the taste that already existed in art and in the theatre for Renaissance costume, and it was the richness and luxury of the dress of the sixteenth and early seventeenth centuries that continued to inspire fashion. Two works of art at the Wallace Collection in London show the Josephine's fondness for the raised 'Medici' collar which she had made part of court dress. An ivory miniature by Louis-François Aubry of about 1805 shows the Empress Josephine in blue velvet decorated with pearls, and with a large open standing collar of embroidered silk; at about the same time Pierre-Paul Prud'hon's unfinished portrait of the *Empress Josephine* (pl. 178) merely sketches out a low-cut dress and a spiky *chérusque* of muslin or blonde.

One of the features of dress seen from the Middle

177 M.-M.-F. Beaunier, sepulchral statue of Valentine de Milan in the Musée des Monuments Français, from the *Recueil des Costumes Français . . . depuis Clovis jusqu'à Napoleon 1*, (1809–13)

176 J.-A. Laurent, *Héloïse in the Cloister*, 1812. Oil on canvas. Napoleon Museum, Arenenberg.

Francis I in 1546 (1812; Paris, Louvre), which is remarkable for the accurate detail of the costume. Gros drew on the work of such artists as Titian and Primaticcio, of the Clouets and the French sculptor Jean Goujon; some of his preparatory studies also indicate his familiarity with the work of German, Swiss and Netherlandish artists.[134]

The popularity of Henry IV continued unabated into the nineteenth century. As a symbol of reconciliation, he was the subject chosen for Gérard's painting, *Henry IV Entering Paris* (Château de Versailles), which was exhibited at the first Salon of the Restoration in 1817. The scene represents Henry's entry into Paris in 1594; as a recent convert to Catholicism, he hoped to unite a divided country; the painting is more allegorical than truthful in that it depicts all the parties to the conflict, some of whom were not present on that occasion. Again, as with the Gros painting of Charles V and Francis I, serious research was undertaken by Gérard; he used Montfaucon and other costume books, other possible sources being illustrations to Voltaire's *Henriade* and Rubens's sketches of the proposed but never carried-out cycle of the life of Henry IV.[135] Slightly earlier, Ingres was working on his *Henry IV Playing with his Children* (1814–17; Paris,

Ages to the nineteenth century was the use of ermine, a fur which was reserved for the aristocracy and – even more – for royalty. In 1813 Queen Hortense commissioned Fleury Richard to paint her portrait (Lyons, Musée des Beaux-Arts) in a dress of amaranth velvet with a hem of ermine; this band of fur, a style of the late fifteenth-century, is one of the rare examples of medieval costume seen in real fashion and a reminder of the royal status of the sitter. Even more potent is the ermine-trimmed pelisse worn by the duchesse d'Anglouême with a feathered hat decorated with fleurs-de-lis, in the detail (pl. 179) of Gros's *The Embarkation of the Duchess d'Angoulême at Pauillac*, which was exhibited at the Salon in 1819. The dramatic scene shows the daughter of Louis XVI rallying Bordeaux to the Royalist cause after Napoleon's exile to Elba; the ermine and fleurs-de-lis of the costume signal royalty, while the ostrich plumes and slashed sleeves recall the period of the Duchess's forebears in the sixteenth century.

Of all the sixteenth-century French monarchs, Francis I and Henry IV were the most popular; *rois chevaliers*, successful warriors and patrons of the arts (particularly Francis I), both kings were also famed for their *galanterie*. Their exploits in love and war, their qualities as statesmen and their humanity were favourite topics for many artists including those not usually considered as painters in the troubadour style. Gros, for example, one of the artists involved in the decoration of Saint-Denis, produced a work showing the *Emperor Charles V Being Received at Saint-Denis by*

174

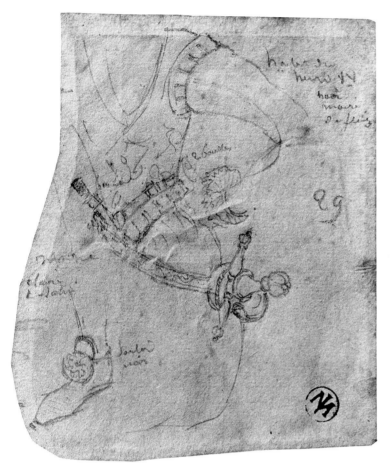

Petit Palais) for which plate 181 is a study. It shows the more intimate side of the King, being interrupted *en famille* by the Spanish ambassador who stands in the doorway in his stiffened trunk hose, padded doublet and short cloak, the chain of the Order of the Golden Fleece around his neck. Henry is formally dressed in matching doublet and breeches, with ruff and the Order of the Saint-Esprit dangling from the ribbon round his neck; his son, the future Louis XIII, holds aloft his father's feathered hat. The Queen's costume can barely be seen, but Ingres has sketched in the soft bulk of early seventeenth-century dress, and outlined the 'Medici' collar which opens like a fan behind her head; more detailed drawings of Marie de' Medici's costume and that of the royal children are held in the Musée Ingres at Montauban. There are also some studies for the costume of Henry IV which Ingres made over a number of years.[136] Plate 180 is a drawing (after a portrait by Frans Pourbus the younger in the Louvre) of Henry IV's costume. Ingres has picked up the contrast between the tight torso of the doublet and the oval bulk of the padded breeches; he has sketched the tabbed shoulder wing (under which the sleeve would probably be laced) and such details as the silk rosette on the shoe.

Few other artists have been as assiduous in their research into historical dress and so prolific with re-gard to their resulting drawings as Ingres. Some of these drawings, the bulk of which are housed in the Musée Ingres, relate to the artist's history paintings; others – as in Rubens's famous Costume Book in the British Museum – seem to have been made out of interest in the subject, for education and possible future use in his studio. Unlike the Costume Book, however, it has not proved possible to identify most of the sources for Ingres's drawings; he was less interested in the genealogical and antiquarian aspects of costume than was Rubens and more attracted to the artistic qualities of historic dress. This is why, perhaps, Ingres uses costume in a more poetic way and at the same time achieves greater depth than other *troubadour* artists. Some of Ingres's drawings are taken from Montfaucon and presumably from other published costume sources; others, such as plates 182 and 183, have not been identified, although there are colour notes and sometimes descriptions of the dress. Plate 182 is a sheet of watercolour drawings of fifteenth- and early sixteenth-century costume, most of which can be identified as Italian dress. Plate 183, on the other hand, is a drawing of two *chaperons*, which is a more northern European form of headwear, widely worn in France and the Netherlands during the four-teenth and fifteenth centuries; it was a rolled hood which, as Ingres's drawing indicates, could be worn

180 (above left) J.-A.D. Ingres, costume study for Henry IV, c.1814–17. Pencil. Musée Ingres, Montauban.

181 (above right) J.-A.-D. Ingres, study for *Henry IV Playing with his Children*, c.1814–17. Pen and ink. Musée Ingres, Montauban.

175

either carried over the shoulder and held by its long streamer, or liripipe, or worn twisted round in a variety of ways, on the head as a hat (by the fifteenth century it was no longer worn *per se* as a hood – i.e. as a covering for head and shoulders with an aperture for the face).

Since hardly any of Ingres's historical drawings are dated, it is no easy task to link them to the paintings, but it is tempting when looking at *Paolo and Francesca* (1819; pl. 184) to think that the artist might have used these two sheets of costume studies, one for the costume of Paolo and the other for the *chaperon* worn by Lanciotto as he appears from behind the arras. The story, taken from Dante, shows Francesca (married against her will to Lanciotto Malatesta, lord of Rimini) in love with her husband's younger brother Paolo; the lovers, while reading the story of Sir Lancelot, were surprised by the jealous husband who killed them. Ingres produced a number of paintings on this subject, of which only the Angers version is dated.[137] The costume is a mixture of the fifteenth and

very early sixteenth centuries, which nonetheless blend together into a harmonious whole. Perhaps Ingres deliberately chose to dress Lanciotto in the dark pleated gown (*houppelande*) and the black *chaperon* (both of which look closer to northern European mid-fifteenth century costume than to that of Italy), as a contrast to the bright colours of the young lovers. Paolo wears a short green doublet embroidered in gold and with slashed sleeves showing the shirt beneath, red hose, yellow shoes, a small red cap (*beretta*) and a tabard-like over-garment known as a *giornea*; this kind of costume can be seen in Mantegna's frescoes of the early 1470s for the Camera degli Sposi, in the Palazzo Ducale, Mantua.

Francesca is shown in the costume of the turn of the sixteenth century (with the high bust of the early nineteenth century); it consists of a red gown, cut straight across at the neckline and slashed with white on the sleeves. Her hair is centrally parted, plaited at the sides and falls over her left arm; it frames a face which has the averted eyes and slightly sly look of a

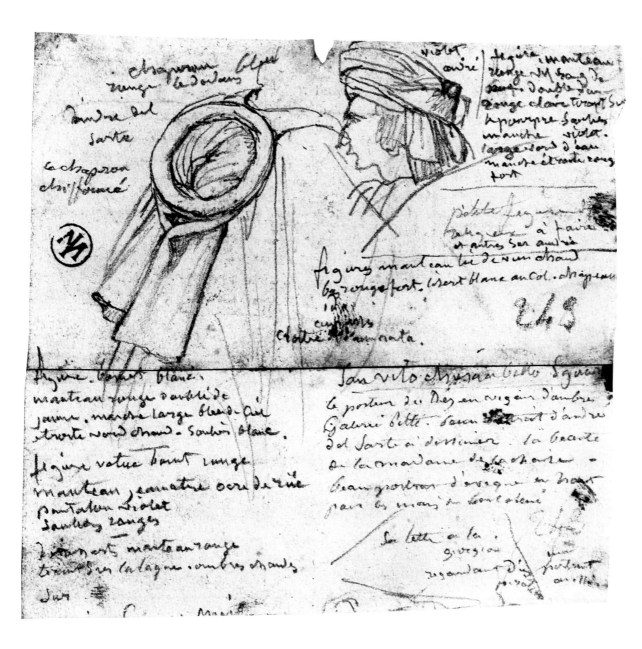

183 J.-A.-D. Ingres, costume drawing of two chaperons, with notes on dress. Pencil. Musée Ingres, Montauban.

Madonna by Raphael. The red and white dress of Francesca is reminiscent of the fashionable ensemble worn by Madame de Senonnes in her portrait by Ingres which was finished in 1816 (pl. 186); it is a very fashionable costume, clearly influenced by the vogue for the Renaissance. Ingres was working on the portrait of the vicomtesse de Senonnes at the same time that he was contemplating the early versions of *Paolo and Francesca*; a link between the two may be the costume study (pl. 185) for the pose of Francesca, where the model wears a plain high-waisted gown with back fullness. The same fullness of the pleated fabric at the back of the gown can be seen in the portrait of Madame de Senonnes, although the placing of the figure is slightly different.

Marie Marcoz, bourgeoise, divorcée and mistress of the vicomte before she married him in 1815 (his family regarded this as a *mésalliance*), had the lush,

opulent beauty which brought out the best in Ingres, and which her dress and accessories emphasise in this sumptuous portrait. A number of drawings at Montauban indicate that the artist had her seductive charms very much in mind; one shows her full length in the pose of David's *Madame Récamier*, another shows her semi-naked, a lightly suggested corset (of the fashionable divorce type) separating her breasts.[138] The costume and accessories gave Ingres the chance to demonstrate his virtuoso skills in painting textiles and jewellery. Madame de Senonnes wears a dress of red velvet with white satin puffs on the sleeves in imitation of Renaissance slashes; a fringed satin sash ties under the bust. The silk *chemisette* with attached blonde ruff emphasises the whiteness of the shoulders and bosom as she leans slightly forward, sitting on a yellow sofa over which is draped a fine cashmere shawl with a paisley pattern. Posing his subject in

front of a mirror so that back views could be seen was a device favoured by Ingres and probably taken from Dutch seventeenth-century art; it can also be seen, for obvious reasons, in fashion plates. Here Ingres shows us the back view of the hair (styled *à la Madonna*) with its jewelled comb, the cobweb silk of the tiered ruff and the elegant slope of the shoulders. The artist's appreciation of the qualities of jewellery, both its craftsmanship and its relation to the body and to the dress, is fully brought out here, perhaps for the first time in his portraits; it was a talent he developed to a fine art in such later portraits as *Madame Moitessier* (London, National Gallery), where the dress of printed floral silk competes on equal terms with the opulent mid-nineteenth-century jewellery, to create almost an *embarras de richesse*. Madame de Senonnes's jewellery is equally colourful and varied – diamonds, rubies, peridots, acquamarines and fine gold chains – but it is in a lighter Renaissance revival style, which complements the dress. The *tout ensemble* anticipates Baudelaire's comment, reviewing the Salon of 1846, 'M. Ingres *adores* colour, like a fashionable milliner . . .' (italics added); the poet's own famous phrase, 'luxe, calme et volupté', seems also well-chosen with regard to the artist's accomplished portrait of Madame de Senonnes.

Ingres's love-affair with colour can also be seen in his *Raphael and La Fornarina* (1814; pl. 187).[139] According to legend, the artist fell in love with a humble beauty who became his model for the *Madonna della Sedia* (Florence, Pitti Palace), seen in the background

of Ingres's painting; on the easel is an unfinished portrait of *La Fornarina* (Rome, Galleria Borghese). The painting is dominated by the great sweep of Raphael's vast black cloak lined with red, which only reveals soft red shoes, part of his striped doublet sleeve and the shirt-sleeve underneath with a tiny ruffle at the wrist. La Fornarina's costume is a carefully observed study of female fashion in the second decade of the sixteenth century, which in Italy was characterised by softly rounded shapes – particularly the huge sleeves which were often padded and slashed to reveal a contrasting fabric beneath. It is a costume that emphasises (not distorts, as in northern Europe) the curves of the female body; no doubt this partly explains Ingres's love for such a style, as well as his admiration for Raphael. Thus he emphasises the curve of the neck and the almost boneless shoulders which appear hardly able to support the large, squashy

186 (above) J.-A.-D. Ingres, *Marie Marcoz, vicomtesse de Senonnes*, 1816. Oil on canvas. Musée des Beaux-Arts, Nantes.

185 J.-A.-D. Ingres, study for figure of Francesca. Pencil. Musée Ingres, Montauban.

184 (facing page) J.-A.-D. Ingres, *Paolo and Francesca*, 1819. Oil on canvas. Musée des Beaux-Arts, Angers.

187 J.-A.-D. Ingres, *Raphael and La Fornarina*, 1814. Oil on canvas. Courtesy of the Fogg Art Museum, Harvard University Art Museums. Bequest of Grenville L. Winthrop.

sleeves of the dress. The dress itself is made of green velvet lined with red; gold braid decorates the hem and edges the slashes on the sleeves. Green was not a popular colour for dress in the eighteenth and early nineteenth centuries, but it was one of the favourite Renaissance colours (associated with lovers); Ingres's skill in painting the depth of velvet – both the colour and the soft pile of the fabric – cannot be equalled. Completing the rounded look of La Fornarina's costume is her turban-like headdress of striped silk edged with a fringe; this was known as a *scuffia* and was a fashion unique to early sixteenth-century Italy. Ingres clearly found it an attractive head-dress, for it appears worn by his *Grande Odalisque* of 1814 (Paris, Louvre), with a similar gold band and jewelled ornament to those in La Fornarina's hair. With the Renaissance-inspired costume of the early nineteenth century, came the popular Madonna hairstyle as worn by Madame de Senonnes (and Géricault's *Laure Bro*, pl. 138), and also soft fabric turbans *à la Raphael*. How much Ingres's paintings helped to popularise such 'historic' elements in high fashion must remain conjectural; what is clear is that both in his portraits and in the history paintings he could capture the self-absorption which is essential to the true painter of fashion, but at the same time by his technical mastery, intelligent composition and sense of history raise his subjects to paintings of importance. Above all, Ingres knew how essential to his work – and to that of any serious artist – was a knowledge of and sympathy with costume. To him, as to Delécluze, costume was 'un objet sérieux d'études', crucially linked to politics and manners. Delécluze can have the last word here: 'Puisque ces habitudes extérieures ont tant de puissance sur le commun des hommes, quel empire ne doivent-elles pas exercer sur les yeux et l'imagination d'un artiste . . . ?'[140]

4

Remembrance of Things Past: Image and Reality in Fancy Dress in England

Every person, luckily for me, looked handsomer in their fancied
dresses than their real ones, consequently were contented
with themselves and satisfied with my summons;
Vandykes, Hussars, Croats, Pandours, Spaniards, ancient Frenchmen,
Indians from the Lake Huron and River Senegal, Turks, Armenians, Moors,
and some ideal personages made up a very handsome appearance of your sex.
The gentlemen (excepting some few who chose to come as sailors)
had taken more pains with their dress than the ladies,
and succeeded better. There were so many shepherdesses
that their crooks formed a little thicket;
the Rubens' wives, the Mary of Medicis, the Isabella of Spain, Jane Seymour,
les Filles de Patmos, the Mrs Fords out of the Merry Wives of Windsor,
however, shone conspicuous and picturesque amongst them . . .
(Elizabeth Countess of Moira to her brother Francis,
about her masked ball, 1768;
Historical Monuments Commission, Hastings MSS., III, p. 150)

I conceive that the past is as real and substantial a part of our being,
that it is as much a *bona fide* undeniable consideration
in the estimate of human life, as the future can possibly be . . .
The past . . . has received the stamp of truth,
and left an image of itself behind.
(William Hazlitt, *Table Talk*, 1821–2)

The different ways in which the historic past is represented in dress and then in art are, on the whole, differences of reality rather than ideology, of masquerade costume rather than state uniform or dress reform, although, with regard to the latter, artists such as Reynolds attempted to create a 'timeless' form of clothing based on classical draperies. The historic past in England is mainly about English history, notably of the sixteenth and early seventeenth centuries; there is a sub-text of the Neoclassical throughout the period and there is some interest in the medieval or Gothic from the late eighteenth century onwards, but in terms of dress, the English Renaissance triumphs over all, culminating in the 'Elizabethan' extravaganza of the coronation of George IV in 1821. It is a sense of history most aware of the national past, not too far removed to be inaccessibly remote and close enough to provide tangible evidence of its culture in the form of art and literature; there are close links with the theatre and with antiquarian study.

Many people, and not just those in the upper classes of society, discovered the romance of the historical past at masquerades; there the costume of famous and infamous characters in English history – however inaccurate they might appear now – brought the past to life as though from a play by Shakespeare or a painting by Holbein or van Dyck. 'I must tell you how fine the masquerade of last night was', gossips Horace Walpole to a correspondent in 1742:

> There were five hundred persons, in the greatest variety of handsome and rich dresses I ever saw . . . There were dozens of ugly Queens of Scots . . . the Princess of Wales was one, covered with diamonds . . . The finest and most charming masks were their Graces of Richmond, like Harry the Eighth and Jane Seymour, excessively rich and both so handsome . . . There were quantities of pretty Vandykes and all kinds of old pictures walked out of their frames.[1]

The popularity of Vandyke dress cannot just be explained as an artistic convention, but must also relate to the vogue for the masquerade throughout the eighteenth century; it was the masquerade that acted as a kind of catalyst in the production of fancy-dress portraits. It was in order to help masqueraders, artists and theatre designers that in 1757 Thomas Jefferys published his important work, the title of which is worth quoting in full as a summary of the predominant artistic influences on historic dress in life and art in the period: *A Collection of the Dresses of Different Nations both Ancient and Modern, and more particularly Old English Dresses after the designs of Holbein, Vandyke, Hollar and others*. A further two volumes were published in 1772, giving a total of 480 plates of costume;

the majority of the illustrations are of historical dress, as the title implies, but there are also oriental costumes (quite a large section), dress from around the world and some examples of popular stage costume.

Although Jefferys's book was meant to be a popular work, he does include 'an Account of the Authorities from which the Figures are taken', and also a brief history of dress, one of the first attempts to define a chronology of the subject. Before Jefferys's *Collection of the Dresses*, there were a few works which dealt, albeit somewhat elliptically, with the history of dress, but these were not easy of access. The most famous must be Randle Holme's *Academy of Armoury*, published in Chester in 1688; it is a kind of lexical encyclopaedia, illustrating the vocabulary associated with heraldry, of all the 'Artificial things, such as are Wrought or Invented by the Wit, Art or Endeavours of Man . . .' Illustrated with tiny postage-stamp-size plates, this vast work is a mine of information (though difficult to mine) on the history and origins of a wide range of dress. This published work is only the tip of the iceberg as far as Randle Holme is concerned, for the British Museum contains many manuscript volumes detailing his research (mainly heraldry and genealogy), including a history of dress from the time of the Roman occupation of England, a period of 'barbarous rudeness', to the 'civility' of the late seventeenth century when the author was writing. This particular manuscript (Harley MS 2014) as an illustrated source for the history of dress, was consulted by a number of antiquarians and dress historians both in the period under discussion and later.[2]

Antiquarian research had been pursued in England from the late Middle Ages, but was placed on a firm footing with the inauguration of the Society of Antiquaries in London in 1717; during the eighteenth century it became a fashionable pastime. At the centre of the antiquarian circle was Horace Walpole, whose correspondence reveals a wide range of historical interests and whose fertile imagination threw up countless projects. Inspired by his purchase in 1758 of some forty volumes of the manuscripts of George Vertue (which he used as the basis for the *Anecdotes of Painting*, published from 1762 to 1780), Walpole toyed with the notion of writing a history of 'dresses and customs from old pictures, something in the manner of Montfaucon's antiquities of France'.[3] Some years later Walpole proposed to publish a work on Gothic architecture, to which the Revd Michael Tyson, a noted antiquary, was to write a 'history of fashions and dresses'.[4] Neither of these suggestions seems to have come to fruition, although Walpole continued to collect material, both visual, documentary and in the form of surviving items, which might prove useful in similar endeavours. Many of his correspondents – with whom he exchanged antiquarian

188 Cosway, *Charles, 4th Earl of Harrington, with his Dog, Peter* (see pl. 243).

gifts, advice and views – were learned clerics not overburdened with pastoral duties, but indefatigable in their zeal for recording the evidence of the past. Volumes of their unpublished labours – scrapbooks of engravings of coins, seals, brasses, drawings and water-colours of tombs, stained glass and Gothic architecture, all carefully annotated – lie in the Manuscript Room of the British Museum.[5] Walpole himself was a magpie collector with a dilettante enthusiasm for such curiosities as Cardinal Wolsey's hat, a pair of embroidered gloves which had belonged to James I, various suits of armour, the spurs worn at the Battle of the Boyne by William III, and so on.[6] The gloves were worn at a 'festino' for some French visitors which Walpole held at Strawberry Hill in 1769: 'At the gates I received them dressed in the cravat of Gibbins' carving and a pair of gloves embroidered up to the elbows that had belonged to James I. The French servants stared, and firmly believed this was the dress of English country gentlemen'.[7]

Walpole also possessed, he tells us, a trunk of masquerade costumes, for such entertainments were 'one of my ancient passions formerly', he noted in a letter to Horace Mann in 1770. The costumes are not specified, but might very well have included the popular Vandyke dress which we know Walpole admired; on his visits to country houses he often jotted down the details of the clothing in portraits by van Dyck. It is in this style of dress that he was depicted by John Giles Eccardt, in 1754 (pl. 189); he wears a Vandyke suit, the collar and cuffs edged with bobbin

189 J. G. Eccardt, *Horace Walpole*, 1754. Oil on canvas. National Portrait Gallery, London.

lace and a black cloak lined with blue silk draped over his shoulder. The use of such costume underlined the intellectual interests of the sitter and it was not uncommon to be painted in this way; the great Scottish antiquarian David Steuart Erskine, 11th Earl of Buchan, was painted by Reynolds in Vandyke costume in 1764 (the half-length portrait is in the National Gallery, Cape Town). Walpole's interests are manifested in the costume he wears (the pose, too, is taken from van Dyck), the copy of *Aedes Walpolianae* (1747) and the glimpse of Strawberry Hill in the background.

Walpole was elected a Fellow of the Society of Antiquaries in 1753, although he does not seem to have been an assiduous member, lacking clubbability and finding, one suspects, more entertainment (even humour) in the study of antiquities than was proper. It was a point of view which the antiquarian Francis Grose understood; this Falstaffian character, who did much to popularise the study of antiquities, writes in the *Antiquarian Repertory* (1775): 'It has long been the fashion to laugh at the study of antiquities, and to consider it as the idle amusement of a few humdrum plodding fellows . . . heaping up illegible Manuscripts, mutilated Statues, obliterated Coins, and broken Pipkins . . .' However, he continues in a more serious vein, 'without a competent fund of Antiquarian Learning, no one will ever make a respectable figure, either as a Divine, a Lawyer, Statesman, Soldier, or even a private Gentleman . . .' Furthermore, a knowledge of the costume of the past was of use at masquerades, for the theatre and for artists. Without such information, one might see on the stage, for example, Shakespeare's Mark Anthony in a 'tye wig', and the 'beautiful Cleopatra' in 'ample hoop and chased watch'; in art, with a depiction of, say, the Battle of Hastings, the artist might be guilty of showing William the Conqueror 'in the character of a French Mareschal, his huge peruke and drapery waving in the wind . . .'[8]

Publications such as *Archaeologia* (the journal of the Society of Antiquaries) and compilations such as the *Antiquarian Repertory* which was described as a 'Miscellaneous Assemblage of Topography, History, Biography, Customs and Manners . . . to Illustrate and Preserve several Valuable Remains of Old Times',[9] contain much useful information for the historian of dress in the form of transcribed wardrobe accounts and sumptuary ordinances, but there is no real sense of historical context or of a discussion of costume *per se*.

The first really comprehensive study of the history of dress in England was undertaken by Joseph Strutt; his two major works are the *Complete View of the Manners, Customs, Arms, Habits &c of the Inhabitants of England* (1774–6) and the *Complete View of the Dress*

and *Habits of the People of England* (1796–9). One of the first pupils at the Royal Academy (he gained a gold medal in 1770 for history painting[10]), he soon realised that a more lucrative career lay in commercial engraving which he combined with antiquarian research to produce books appealing to the educated layman as well as the specialist. In his first work, *The Regal and Ecclesiastical Antiquities of England* (1773), he had already noted how artists were 'extremely deficient in their delineations of the early history', with regard to dress, a state of affairs that his subsequent research did much to remedy. His illustrated notebooks in the British Museum and his costume drawings in the Society of Antiquaries (pl. 190) indicate the extent of his studies into the history of dress, his familiarity in particular with most of the major collections of manuscript material available to students. The

selection of his drawings in plate 190 ranges from the fourteenth century to the seventeenth, the top right-hand illustration being taken from Randle Holme.

In his published works, Strutt's brief was not just to write a history of fashion, but to cover – albeit sometimes erratically – the history of such aspects as official, ceremonial, military, clerical, court and theatre costume. All sources were grist to his mill – such historical records as livery regulations, inventories and wills, contemporary poetry, plays, diaries and memoirs, and a wide range of visual material from illuminated manuscripts to caricatures. He looked at such works as Montfaucon's *Monumens de la monarchie française* (he was described by Walpole as the 'English Montfaucon'), but his stated aim was to write about the people of England and not limit his research to royalty. Inevitably, given the sometimes uneven

190 J. Strutt, costume drawings. Pen and ink and pencil. Society of Antiquaries, London.

nature of his sources – scarcer in the early periods, with unsure dates – Strutt was more at ease with the Middle Ages and the Renaissance than with the pre-medieval era. As a pioneer in the field, he was aware of his limitations, admitting to some confusion and ignorance over the names of garments, especially in 'remote periods'; this is understandable, as the nomenclature of dress changes over the centuries. In any work that copies visual sources, there are bound to be errors in the interpretation of the originals, particularly with regard to the details of dress in the earlier periods, when hardly any costume survives for comparison. Strutt was aware of the importance of being as accurate as possible within these limitations, noting that his illustrations 'are faithfully copied from the originals, without an additional fold being made to the draperies, or the least deviation from the form of the garments.'[11]

One of the obvious sources for a study of costume in England, particularly from the Middle Ages, is effigeal sculpture, which survives in large quantities in churches. As interest in Gothic architecture grew during the second half of the eighteenth century, so too did a fascination with funerary monuments, partly fuelled by a growing Romantic attachment to the idea of death (which inspired a pleasant melancholy) and partly by antiquarian and genealogical enthusiasm for such tangible links with our ancestors. From the later eighteenth century a number of works were published on tomb sculpture, such as Richard Gough's *Sepulchral Monuments in Great Britain* (1786) and – with a more detailed commitment to costume – Charles Alfred Stothard's *Monumental Effigies of Great Britain*, produced in serial form from 1811 and completed in 1832 after the author's death. This important work aimed to 'elucidate History and Biography' by the representation of images from the Norman Conquest

to the reign of Henry VIII, and to 'explain the costume adopted at different periods in England' by means of clear and detailed engravings. Stothard made a serious attempt to discuss 'the various dresses which present themselves to us on our Monumental Effigies, [which] were not at all introduced by any inventive or whimsical fancies in the sculptor'; such tomb figures, he maintained, were the only existing portraits in many cases, of 'our Kings, our Princes, and the Heroes of ages famed for chivalry and arms'.[12]

Stothard was the son of a well-known book illustrator who specialised in historical, particularly medieval subject-matter. It was not surprising that Stothard *fils* should himself become interested in the Middle Ages; like Strutt, he occasionally dabbled in history painting, producing in 1810 'a spirited picture, representing the murder of Richard the Second in Pontefract Castle, in which the characteristic dresses of the time were strictly adhered to'.[13] But his main interest was in drawing the medieval past, whether it was from tomb sculpture, stained glass, illuminated manuscripts or such works of textile art as the Bayeux Tapestry. In 1816 Stothard was appointed Historical Draughtsman to the Society of Antiquaries, who commissioned him to make a complete set of drawings from the Bayeux Tapestry; his research proved to his own satisfaction that the Tapestry was 'coeval with the period succeeding the Conquest', and his findings were published in 1821, the year of his death.[14] Stothard's sympathy with medieval art can also be seen in his drawings from illustrated manuscripts, such as the *Romance of Alexander* (1338–44); plate 191 is his drawing from folio 58, a group of young people. He has captured the charm and playfulness of this *bas-de-page* scene, rendering the simple lines of the costume with accuracy and perception.

The neat shape of the women's heads in this drawing and their close-fitting dress, would appeal to the fashion aesthetic of the early nineteenth century, but in England – as in France – there is no real evidence that medieval styles inspired contemporary costume. This is somewhat curious considering how much the Gothic style influenced other visual arts, and literature as well. Architecture, furniture and garden follies were designed in Gothic style, albeit in a sometimes capricious and tongue-in-cheek way. Literature, too, found medieval themes to be a selling point. The controversies over James MacPherson's supposed 'translations' of the Gaelic poet Ossian, and Thomas Chatterton's fabricated poems which he claimed as the work of a fifteenth-century monk, tended to absorb antiquarians rather than the general public, but they helped to place medieval poetry in the spotlight. At about the same time, the Revd Thomas Percy published his *Reliques of Ancient English Poetry* (1765), which contributed to the rediscovery of the chivalry

191 C. A. Stothard, drawing taken from the Romance of Alexander. Bodleian Library, Oxford. Douce 264. Pen and ink and coloured wash. Witt Collection, Courtauld Institute of Art.

and romance of the Middle Ages. Gothic novels, tales of mystery and imagination, were popular, from Walpole's *Castle of Otranto* (1764) and Ann Radcliffe's *Mysteries of Udolpho* (1794), to the witty parodies of the genre by Thomas Love Peacock, at the end of the period.

As an influence on fashion, the medieval remained a closed book. It was not just that there was hardly any actual surviving costume from the Middle Ages (not much, after all, exists from the sixteenth and early seventeenth centuries), but the visual material, such as tomb sculpture and illuminated manuscripts, was largely unfamiliar, the concern of a relatively small group of antiquarians and artists. Most important of all is the fact that medieval costume had not been synthesised into theatre dress or history painting even when circumstances were appropriate for its appearance. As with masquerades, it was the costume of the sixteenth century and that of van Dyck, that was the guiding spirit on the stage and in history painting, when the 'olden times' were called for.

In spite of the careful research of Strutt and Stothard with regard to medieval dress, and even the novels of Sir Walter Scott which were based on considerable antiquarian study, the Middle Ages was largely conceived in popular costume books as a kind of free-for-all of all periods, where accuracy was at a low premium. Highly coloured works such as Charles Hamilton Smith's *Selections of the Ancient Costume of Great Britain and Ireland* (1814) place inaccurately dressed people in imaginary dramatic landscapes or contrived architectural settings in an attempt to improve on the past, 'to restore the mutilations, correct the drawing of the figures, and to vary and animate the attitudes'.[15] The following year Hamilton Smith was responsible for the illustrations to Samuel Rush Meyrick's *Costume of the Original Inhabitants of the British Islands*, where the plates (of the early 'Roman-Britons' to the sixth century) depict dress which is totally fanciful, a mixture of classical drapery with touches of the late medieval and Vandyke.[16]

Such works are typical of the kind of popular and often trivialised costume history of the Middle Ages which were produced during the nineteenth century and which were the source for endless Victorian tableaux vivants and *bals masqués*. The serious study of medieval dress and its representation in art, as in the work of the Pre-Raphaelite painters, lies beyond the scope of this book.

In any period, the past can perhaps be more easily conjured up through historical personalities; this was as true in the eighteenth century as it is in the present day, when novels, plays and films with historical themes, or even visits to Madame Tussaud's are all enjoyed. In the eighteenth century the past was regained for a large number of people through surviving relics associated with famous people, or the dress of their time, or their images on the stage or in art, or at such popular entertainments as fairs or waxworks. In London, collections of historical costume could be seen at the British Museum from its inception in 1753 and during the 1770s and 1780s at Sir Ashton Lever's house in Leicester Fields, where Fanny Burney saw 'the dress worn in Charles Irst's time', and Sophie von la Roche 'enjoyed seeing dresses belonging to kings and queens, lords and ladies, three hundred years or more, offering a splendid selection of models for masked fancy dress'. On another visit, to the Tower of London, Sophie saw the sword used to behead Anne Boleyn and the stuffed horse ridden by Queen Elizabeth at Tilbury.[17] The *Companion to every Place of Curiosity and Entertainment in and about London and Westminster* for 1767, noted that at Salmon's Royal Waxworks near Temple Bar the public could see such tableaux as Henry VIII introducing Anne Boleyn to court, the meeting of Mary Queen of Scots with Queen Elizabeth I, and Charles I blessing his children the day before his execution. Many of these scenes were based on sentimental imagination rather than fact, but this was a matter of indifference to an audience out for a romantic thrill. Nor would the costume have been particularly accurate, but it was at least based on the images of such famous historical figures easily recognisable from their portraits. Only Anne Boleyn might have presented a problem as a slightly less well-known figure; if we are to be guided by Hogarth's famous engraving of *c.*1729, whereas Henry VIII would be shown in the bulky costume familiar from the Holbein portraits, Anne Boleyn might have appeared in a dress vaguely based on the well-known painting by Rubens of Helena Fourment (see p. 193).

For there was no real consensus as to how famous historical figures were to be depicted on the stage or in art, except for a very few characters – like Henry VIII – a folk hero, larger-than-life and instantly identified through his girth and composite Holbein costume. In Valentine Green's 1792 engraving (after Johann Gerhard Huck) of the *Marriage of King Henry the VIII with Ann Bullen, 1533* (pl. 192), the King's skirted Holbeinesque jerkin can be seen, albeit worn over eighteenth-century knee-breeches; the artist has also tried to indicate the bulk of Renaissance costume with the ermine-lined robe of state, and the fullness of the slashed sleeves. But here, Henry's costume, as that of his courtiers, is an uneasy mixture of the styles of the later sixteenth and early seventeenth centuries – invented 'collar-ruffs', tunics over knee-breeches, Vandyke rosettes on the shoes and so on. Apart from the pearl-trimmed headdress which Anne Boleyn wears, there are no recognisable features of sixteenth-century costume in the dress of the Queen and her

192 V. Green after J. G. Huck, *Marriage of King Henry VIII with Ann Bullen, 1533*, 1792. Engraving. Royal Society of Arts, London. (Photo: Courtauld Institute of Art)

194 (facing page bottom) J. Downman, *Edward IV on a Visit to the Duchess of Bedford is Enamoured of Lady Elizabeth Grey*, 1797. Oil on canvas. Sale, Christie's, London, 11 March 1960, lot 129.

attendant, the soft folds of the muslin gowns and veils being more akin to the styles of the early 1790s.

Although scenes from early Tudor history were popular as tableaux vivants, in the theatre and in history painting, the costume of the period was neither really appreciated nor understood. Edward Dayes in his *Essays on Painting* (1805) thought that 'Holbein had not taste enough to change the grotesque fashions of the court of Henry the Eighth . . .'; he noted some improvement in costume under Elizabeth I, but reserved his unqualified approval for the reign of Charles I, 'an epoch of taste'.[18]

As history painting was closely linked with representations of the past in the theatre, it was inevitable that art would reflect the confusion of costume styles seen on the stage. For much of the eighteenth century, particularly during the first half, stage costume was a mixture of contemporary fashion with the traditional elements of the Baroque theatre – the sweeping trains and asymmetrical decoration of women's costume, and for men the large peruke, the stiffened 'Roman' tunic (see the actor James Quin on his pedestal in Hogarth's *Analysis of Beauty*, pl. 21), and the plumed helmet. Such costumes were interchangeable for a variety of roles, although there were certain outfits identified with such characters as Henry VIII, Falstaff (a kind of Punch costume with Vandyke trimmings) and Richard III, the part in which Garrick made his debut in 1741. Hogarth's famous portrait of the actor painted a few years later (Liverpool, Walker Art Gallery) shows him as Richard III in a puff-sleeved, fur-lined gown (à la Holbein), over doublet, trunk hose and ruff; in short, the costume of the

sixteenth century rather than that of the time of the last Plantagenet king. It must remain a matter for conjecture how much this costume was an innovation of Garrick's, but it remained the definitive Richard III costume into the following century; the Museum of London has Edmund Kean's dress for this role and it looks very like that worn in the Hogarth painting of Garrick.

The costume of Richard III is one of the plates on stage dress that Thomas Jefferys published in his *Collection of the Dresses* where credit was given to Garrick for his reforms in the theatre; 'the Dresses are no longer the heterogeneous and absurd Mixtures of foreign and antient Modes which formerly debased our Tragedies, by representing a Roman general in full-bottomed peruke, and the Sovereign of an Eastern Empire in Trunk Hose.'[19]

Garrick's reforms, such as they were, were motivated as much by vanity as by a quest for historical accuracy; being fairly small in stature, he disliked the traditional 'tragedy' stage costume – especially the towering feathers – which he thought produced an ill-proportioned image. But from the second half of the eighteenth century, a period when theatres were enlarged and a greater distance placed between the actors and the audience, more emphasis was placed on spectacle and more attention given to costume; this coincided with an interest in antiquarian research and an enthusiasm for history painting. From the 1760s newspapers increasingly refer to the popularity of 'old English habits' as a kind of uniform stage costume for plays with historical themes.[20] Although it is not quite clear what this type of costume was, it is likely to have been a hybrid Tudor-cum-Vandyke dress, which would suit very well the perennially popular history plays of Shakespeare, as well as comedies by Ben Jonson. It also appears to have been a popular costume for masquerades, being chosen by both George II and the Duke of Cumberland at Ranelagh in 1749, according to Walpole; some years later, the *Town and Country Magazine* reported that it was worn by Oliver Goldsmith at the Pantheon. On the same occasion the Duke of Gloucester also appeared in 'the old English habit' but with a 'star on the cloak'[21] – this would have been the Garter star and the costume itself might very well have looked like the Vandyke doublet and knee-breeches which the Duke of Somerset wears in his statue by Rysbrack (see pl. 214). Whatever this 'old English' costume was, although it was 'historical', it was not authentic; it was only towards the mid-nineteenth century that real attempts were made to produce accurate and consistent historical dress on the stage.[22]

The theatre played an important part in eighteenth- and early nineteenth-century culture, both in dress and in art. It has already been seen how fashionable actresses like Frances Abington were fêted as leaders of fashion; this was the case also with Garrick, whose letters indicate that he gave advice to members of the nobility on what they should wear for grand occasions such as the royal birthdays. Such well-known actors appearing on the stage in fashionable forms of 'historic' dress, such as the 'old English habit', accustomed the audience to this kind of historical reference; off the stage, also, at masquerades (Garrick was very fond of this form of entertainment) actors helped to popularise the past. History painters, too, could find inspiration in the theatre, particularly from the 'after-pieces', dramatisations of popular events, performed after the main play and sometimes linked to it. Such events, might include triumphs in war, the death of heroes such as Nelson, and coronations; a few days after the coronation of George II in 1727, Drury Lane theatre showed an extended scene from Shakespeare's *Henry VIII* which showed Anne Boleyn being crowned at Westminster.

Patriotic pride in the glories of English history and in great works of literature inspired the work of a number of artists, which to some extent was coloured by their familiarity with the conventions of stage costume. Both Valentine Green's 1791 engraving (after Huck), *Lady Elizabeth Grey at the Feet of Edward the Fourth, Soliciting the Restoration of her late Husband's forfeited Lands, 1465* (pl. 193) and John Downman's *Edward IV on a Visit to the Duchess of Bedford is Enamoured of Lady Elizabeth Grey* (1797; pl. 194), show the dramatic gestures of a theatre performance. In Downman's painting the actress Eliza Farren inspired the appearance of Lady Grey, wearing the black silk dress of a conventional stage heroine, albeit in late eighteenth-century style; the jewellery (rosary and cross) and the Vandyked lace collar and cuffs, are shorthand indicators of the historic past. Downman used his own children as models for Lady Grey's offspring, with no real attempt at historical accuracy in their dress at all, except for lace collars and a slashed upper sleeve. Edward IV's costume with its tinsel trimming, has the slightly absurd look of theatrical dress out of context, the knee-length 'shorts' acting as a 'modesty piece' over the tight hose which would have been part of late fifteenth-century clothing. In the Valentine Green illustration, the slashing of fabric on the dress of nearly all the characters, is a somewhat desperate way of signalling times past; so fanciful is the costume and yet so vague that only by reading the rubric can it be understood that the scene dates from the time of Edward IV. As there was no real agreement as to how medieval dress should look, it seems in art (as it probably would to us on the stage of the time) to have a quality of unreality, as painters and designers fell back on the established conventions of sixteenth- and early seventeenth-century dress.

Elizabeth Woodville (her more familiar name, although it was her maiden name) made a secret marriage to Edward IV in 1464. It was this character that Walpole's niece Maria Waldegrave appropriately assumed at a masquerade in 1770, for she had secretly married George III's brother, the Duke of Gloucester in 1766, a union not publicly acknowledged until 1772. Walpole tells us that her costume was 'grey and pearls with a black veil'.[23] The Duke of Gloucester

193 (top) V. Green after J. G. Huck, *Lady Elizabeth Grey at the Feet of Edward the Fourth. Soliciting the Restoration of her late Husband's forfeited Lands, 1465*, 1791. Engraving. (Photo: Courtauld Institute of Art)

attended the same event dressed as Edward IV, so the marriage appears to have been a fairly open secret.

Valentine Green's Edward IV scene, and that of the marriage of Henry VIII with Ann Boleyn, were from a series of twelve plates which the engraver commissioned between 1786 and 1792, entitled *Acta historica reginarum anglia*; it was history presented as romantic episodes in the lives of queens of England, as dramatic tableaux vivants. Scenes included the death of Lady Jane Grey; Mary Queen of Scots about to be executed (pl. 197); the birth of Edward, first Prince of Wales to Queen Eleanor; Queen Matilda asking Queen Maud for the release of her husband King Stephen; and Queen Elizabeth at Tilbury. No matter if the scene was medieval or later, the costume shows the same mixture of Renaissance and Vandyke features for the men, and for the women it tends to be contemporary fashion with the addition of veils, ruffs, pearls and draperies; only the image of Mary Queen of Scots is distinct, the headdress, ruff, jewellery and black dress taken from the famous portrait of the Queen attributed to Pierre Oudry (there are a number of versions, the most famous the full-length in the Scottish National Portrait Gallery, Edinburgh).

As such engravings proliferated, either sold in their own right or as illustrations to English history books, the 'romance' of the past was discovered. The aim of history, at this popular level, was, in the words of David Lowenthal, '... to make the past present, to bring the distant near ... to call up our ancestors before us with all their peculiarities of language, manner and garb ... to rummage in their old-fashioned wardrobes.'[24] The past became more and more expressed in terms of the visual, whether it was romanticised episodes from history or scenes from such great literature of the past as Shakespeare and Milton. Valentine Green's *Acta historica reginarum anglia* was a modest venture, but there were other far more ambitious schemes, such as Bowyer's *Historic Gallery*, launched in 1792, where over one hundred paintings of English history were commissioned and later engraved; the project proved a financial loss for Bowyer, in the same way that Alderman Boydell's gallery of paintings based on scenes from Shakespeare (opened in 1789) also came to grief.

One of the problems with regard to Boydell's Shakespeare Gallery was that the paintings did not match the genius of the literature. This was also true with Milton; Fuseli's paintings from the great poet's work (exhibited in 1799 and 1800) failed to impress the public,[25] not so much due to lack of poetic imagination (the artist claimed, in fact, that the English didn't care for 'poetical painting') but, one suspects, that the scenes did not depict the 'realities' (in other words the details) which Fuseli so deplored in history painting. In one of Fuseli's lectures, entitled 'Historic Invention Administers to Truth', it was his thesis that too much detail, especially in dress, was to be avoided, as it destroyed 'grandeur' and made the artist 'a mere copyist'.[26] This argument led, as it does in his painting of the blind Milton dictating to his daughters (1793; Chicago, Art Institute), to the poet being depicted in indeterminate, 'timeless' dress, whereas his daughters are shown — being far less important in the scheme of things — in typically Fuseli-like stylised versions of fashionable dress. A similar feeling can be seen in Romney's painting on the same theme and of the same year (pl. 195), intended as a frontispiece to William Hayley's life of Milton. Romney paints the 'great Bard', as he calls him, in a black gown which completely covers his body, thus obviating the tedious detail of seventeenth-century dress, although the artist — in a nice, intimate touch — has given him the appropriate informal footwear of the period, square-toed mules. The two daughters are depicted, perhaps as an indication of Puritan simplicity, in plain, almost working-class dress of the late eighteenth century; in their short-sleeved shifts, coloured skirts and stays (on the left), they could have stepped out of a rustic scene by Opie or Morland. With this painting of quiet industry and contemplation by Romney the details of dress are almost irrelevant; it is a long way removed from the world of the theatre and the masquerade.

195   G. Romney *Milton Dictating to his Daughters*, 1793. Oil on canvas. Private Collection.

Milton, perceived by some artists as a proto-Romantic hero misunderstood by the Establishment[27] did not capture the public imagination either in art or – unsurprisingly – as a possible character for a masquerade. It was character rather than aesthetics which motivated such choices; it was 'a crowd of Henrys the Eighth [and] Wolseys', which Walpole noted at a masquerade in 1770, the Duke of Cumberland being one of the former. These were costumes for fun, and not for immortality on the canvas; the only portrait of someone as Henry VIII is Reynolds's charming affectionate parody of the famous Holbein image, his *Master Crewe* of 1776 (private collection).

For women, the romantic heroines of the sixteenth century were more popular in art. Elizabeth Montagu chose the costume of Anne Boleyn for her portrait by Christian Friedrich Zincke in 1740; what the costume was like is unrecorded, but no doubt it included a headdress based on the French hood decorated with pearls which Anne Boleyn wears in the familiar, anonymous image seen in the National Portrait Gallery in London, and elsewhere;[28] one of the rare portraits in which this type of head-dress appears is Thomas Bardwell's *Anne, Countess of Strafford* of 1752 (Duke of Buccleuch). On the whole, however, early Tudor costume with its stiffness and angularity appealed neither to women nor to artists; later in the sixteenth century with the appearance of the ruff and the flattering Marie Stuart cap, these features could be incorporated into eighteenth-century portraits, as in Francis Cotes's *Lady Ann Astley* (*c*.1760; pl. 196). It is possible that the sitter may be painted as Mary Queen of Scots; this was a popular masquerade costume with a distinctive iconography – either the Queen in white mourning, which went hand in hand with the concept of the tragic virgin heroine (Walpole tells us that white satin and muslin were *de rigueur* for the part), or the Queen in black velvet from the portrait of 1578 attributed to Oudry, painted during her captivity in England.[29] It is the Oudry portrait that provided the inspiration for the image of the Queen in Valentine Green's 1790 engraving, *The Death of Mary Queen of Scots, 1587* (pl. 197). While all the other figures (except for Mary's ladies whose dress follows the Reynoldsian dictum of something modern mixed with the general air of the antique), wear Vandyke costume (the right-hand group looking like the Gunpowder Plot conspirators from the famous anonymous engraving of 1605 in the National Portrait Gallery), the Queen's appearance is more or less recognisably late sixteenth century. The lace-edged heart-shaped cap became Mary's sartorial signature and a fashionable form of headwear in the middle of the eighteenth century. In history painting it served to identify her, even when the rest of the costume might be more contemporary than historical, as in Gavin Hamilton's

196 F. Cotes, *Lady Ann Astley*, *c*.1760 (?). Pastel. Sale, Phillips, London, 24 November 1980, lot 132.

The Abdication: Mary Queen of Scots Resigning her Crown (Glasgow, Hunterian Art Gallery) which was commissioned by James Boswell in 1765; the Queen wears a flowered silk dress in eighteenth-century style and on her head a Marie Stuart cap, topped with a tiny black silk hat.

Hamilton studied in Rome with the Scottish artist

197 V. Green after J. G. Huck, *The Death of Mary Queen of Scots, 1587*, 1790. Engraving. Royal Society of Arts, London. (Photo: Courtauld Institute of Art)

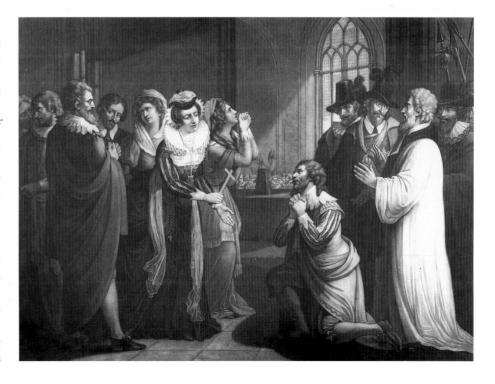

David Allan, who also chose Mary Queen of Scots as a theme for a cycle of paintings of which four are extant, from 1790–91. Within the context of the late eighteenth century the costume is reasonably accurate, especially for the men; Mary's dress incorporates the usual clichés of the sixteenth-century originals, the characteristic cap and the large raised ruff. Allan did a considerable amount of research into costume, writing to his patron, the Earl of Buchan, 'I have with some difficulty found out many of the old Scottish dresses. I shall aim at character and costume'.[30] The Earl of Buchan, one of the leading antiquarians in Scotland, employed Allan to find and copy historic portraits for his Temple of Caledonian Fame, a portrait-gallery of famous Scots, living and dead. This proved a useful source of information for Allan's own history painting; he also studied works of costume history such as Strutt's *Complete View of the Manners, Customs, Arms, Habits . . .* , the figure of Henry Prince of Wales in his *Costume Sketches: 'Dresses of 1500'* (pl. 198), is taken from that source. These sketches are from a series of drawings (Edinburgh, Scottish National Portrait Gallery) by Allan for his projected series on the life of Mary Queen of Scots and for other subjects of the sixteenth and early seventeenth centuries, such as Henry IV of France;[31] the Mary Stuart cycle was possibly inspired by Rubens's Marie de' Medici sequence.

Without the tragic resonance of Mary Queen of Scots, but with an equally strong image, was Elizabeth I, particularly late in life when her portraits show an icon-like figure – a high, curled wig and vast hooped dress all hung about with bushels of jewels. Jefferys's *Collection of the Dresses* includes a plate entitled *The Habit of Queen Elizabeth in 1559*, but the costume derives from the famous Ditchley Portrait of the early 1590s (now London, National Portrait Gallery) and the characteristic tilted farthingale of the end of the sixteenth century has become the fashionable hooped skirt of Jefferys's time. The extraordinary artifice of late Elizabethan costume had to be modified for eighteenth-century consumption into a softer, less rigid and more comfortable and flattering style, which nonetheless retained such characteristic features as the high open ruff or collar. At a masquerade at the Pantheon in 1772, Lady Margaret Fordyce, in the words of the *Town and Country Magazine*, 'in the dress of Queen Elizabeth, appeared infinitely more charming than any idea we can form of the fair Queen Bess'. Unfortunately, there is no description of her dress on this occasion, but in a half-length portrait by Gainsborough of a few years later (formerly Dalmeny; sold Sotheby's, London, 10 April 1991, lot 86), Lady Fordyce wears a Vandyke collar and a feathered, pearl-trimmed hat, perhaps the kind of 'high crown hat' that, according to the *Public Advertiser* was worn by 'a lady of the time of Queen Elizabeth' at a masquerade in 1774.[32]

Historical enthusiasm for the late sixteenth century also infected fashionable costume during the 1770s. Walpole, in his correspondence with Lady Ossory, describes the dresses worn at a famous ball given in

March 1773 by the French ambassador to London. It probably helped also to popularise the taste for styles *à la Henri IV*, which were possibly adopted by the new French queen for the *bals parés* at court the following year. At the French ambassador's entertainment there were to be two sets of quadrilles, performed by dancers dressed in Elizabethan costume and that of Henry IV: 'Being antiquarians or historians, one set is to appear like the court of Henri Quatre', and the other set 'are to dance the brawls in ruffs and fardingales'. The first set, according to Walpole, the 'Henri quatres and quatresses, . . . [were] all in white, the men with black hats and white feathers flapping behind', and the Elizabethan set danced in 'blue satin with blond, and collets montés à la reine Elizabeth'.[33] The 'Henri quatresses' may very well have worn something like the costume depicted in Reynolds's stunning *Charlotte Walpole, Countess of Dysart* (1775; pl. 199). This is an open robe of white silk trimmed with gold braid and worn over a layered petticoat or skirt decorated with gold tassels; the sleeves have bands of braided gold silk in imitation of a Renaissance slashed sleeve, complementing the raised Medici collar. The whole ensemble is a tribute to the artist's skill in rendering the details of a real fancy dress and to his theories of the Grand Style, the dignity of the conception and the references to Rubens and van Dyck in the pose. Reynolds's theories on the preference for the general over the particular in the Grand Style, which he expounds in his *Fourth Discourse* of 1771, prompted Gainsborough's comment: '. . . the Grand Style must consist in plainness and simplicity, and . . . silks and satins, pearls and trifling ornaments would be as hurtful to simplicity as flourishes in a Psalm tune'.[34] Reynolds's portraits in the Grand Style usually do concentrate on 'plainness and simplicity' at the expense of 'something of the modern' which present-day viewers might prefer, but with Lady Dysart the artist has made a triumphant marriage between theory and reality.

The dancers described by Walpole dressed in Elizabethan style with their blue satin trimmed with blonde (silk lace) and 'collets montés', bring to mind Gainsborough's portrait of the Hon. Frances Duncombe of *c*.1777 (pl. 200): this fairytale image mingles the dress of the past (the spiky lace collar, the gown with slashed sleeves and pearl trimmings and the feathered satin hat) with the style of contemporary fashion (the looped-up gown *à la polonaise*). The direct inspiration for Frances Duncombe's costume comes from the popular portrait by Rubens of the early 1630s of his second wife, Helena Fourment. Now in the Gulbenkian Collection, Lisbon, for much of the eighteenth century it hung at Houghton Hall, Norfolk, and was attributed by Walpole to van Dyck[35] and as such engraved by McArdell (pl.

201), although correctly assigned to Rubens by Jefferys in his *Collection of the Dresses* (1757) as *Habit of Rubens Wife in 1620*, 'a second Helen for Beauty . . . [she] afforded him great Assistance in the Figures of Women which he painted'.[36] The main features of this costume are a dress of black silk with a bunched-up overskirt, open sleeves with additional

199 J. Reynolds, *Charlotte Walpole, Countess of Dysart*, 1775. Oil on canvas. By courtesy of the Board of Trustees of the Victoria and Albert Museum, London.

200 T. Gainsborough, *Hon. Frances Duncombe, c.*1777. Oil on canvas. Copyright, The Frick Collection, New York.

gauzy oversleeves tied with ribbon, a slightly raised collar, an asymmetrical jewelled chain looping over the shoulders from a central brooch, a hat fastened up to one side with ostrich feathers and a fan made of the same feathers.

No costume was more popular for masquerades from the 1730s to the 1770s than this 'Rubens-wife' dress.[37] One example must suffice, Hudson's full-length portrait *Mary Panton, Duchess of Ancaster*, of 1757 (pl. 205), with the rotunda at Ranelagh Gardens in the background. The Arcadian feeling of the original has been rather lost in this somewhat prosaic rendition, but the Duchess (or her dressmaker) has ensured that some of the features of the Rubens costume have been incorporated: the feathered hat, the transparent silk oversleeves tied with ribbon, the jewelled chain and the amplitude of the skirt, which is emphasised here by the wide hooped petticoat of the mid-eighteenth century.

The Rubens portrait proved a fruitful source of inspiration for artists from the beginning of the eighteenth century. George Vertue noted under the year 1732 that John Vanderbank had painted a portrait of his wife 'in a habit somewhat like a picture of Rubens' wife', and that he had begun the vogue for dressing his female sitters in this costume.[38] From the late 1720s, there are drawings by Vanderbank and others depicting this type of costume in outline, with the feathered hat, the wide, descending lace collar and the full rounded sleeves often pushed up above the wrist. The popularity of the image was augmented by the drapery painter Joseph van Aken who (until his death in 1749) worked for a number of prominent artists such as Hudson and Ramsay and produced a number of variations on the dress and the pose of the original portrait.[39] The portrait also appears in such teaching manuals and pattern books as *The Artist's Vade Mecum*, 1762 (pl. 203). The ability to paint sitters in this fashion became an indispensable requirement for the fashionable artist.

From the 1770s, features of this costume entered the fashionable female wardrobe, especially the wide-brimmed hat (called the 'Rubens hat' by the *Fashionable Magazine* in 1786) and the bunched-up skirts of the robe *à la polonaise*. In the hands of a genius such as Gainsborough, the historical features of the Rubens costume are depicted with the misty romanticism that characterises many of his portraits during this decade, perhaps as a riposte to the certainties of Reynolds's Grand Style. While *Frances Duncombe* is one of the most ravishing examples of this genre, another is a portrait of about the same time, the *Hon. Mrs Graham* (Edinburgh, National Gallery of Scotland), who is dressed in a white gown edged with pearls over a skirt of ruched pink silk. It is not surprising that both these portraits with their mysterious dreamy quality and the

artist's imaginative use of dress to invoke the past, should have inspired Millais's famous painting *Clarissa: A Recollection of Gainsborough* (1887).[40] A fainter echo of the Rubens portrait can be seen in Gainsborough's portrait of his daughter, Mary, in 1777 (pl. 204) where the details of the dress and hair almost merge into the background. Only the tilt of the feathered hat recalls Rubens, and the slightly stiffened 'baroque' collar has become a soft muslin frill edging the bodice neckline. The black silk necklace is worth a brief mention, a revival of a Jacobean style that drew attention to the whiteness of the skin, it features in dress from the 1750s as a simpler alternative to the lace ruff which is also part of high fashion, as worn by the Duchess of Ancaster (pl. 205).

Rubens's fondness for painting his family (including both his wives), meant that there were other portraits for artists to copy. At a masquerade given in 1755 at Somerset House by the Russian ambassador to celebrate the birth of the future Tsar Paul I, Walpole noted the appearance of Lady Betty Spencer as Rubens's wife, but 'not the common one with the hat';[41] it's impossible to know which one he meant. Walpole himself possessed, at Strawberry Hill, a group portrait by Eccardt, described as '*Charles Churchill and Lady Maria Walpole his wife, with their eldest son Charles*, taken from the picture at Blenheim, of Rubens, his wife and child'[42] (pl. 206). The painting by Rubens which dates from *c.*1632–4, is now in the Metropolitan Museum of Art, New York; it has been fairly faithfully copied by Eccardt, although he has obviously altered the faces and reduced the Junoesque proportions of Helena Fourment for the figure of Maria Walpole. She stands, bare-headed, in a black satin dress, the layered white collar slightly raised, and she holds an ostrich-feather fan; Colonel Churchill wears a black Vandyke suit and the small boy in his kilted-up frock wears the 'pudding' or stuffed fabric headdress which young children wore to protect their heads – a custom that died out by the later eighteenth century.

Another popular painting by Rubens was his self-portrait of 1609 with his first wife Isabella Brant; sometimes known as '*The Honeysuckle Bower*', it shows the couple in the Spanish-influenced costume of the southern Netherlands. Now in the Alte Pinakothek, Munich, in the eighteenth century it was on show at the Elector Palatine's gallery in Düsseldorf, where Allan Ramsay saw it in 1757, on his way home from Italy; he recorded it in a shaky drawing, the pose fairly correct, but the costume perhaps recalled from memory, for Isabella's dress is envisaged as having an open raised collar and soft wide sleeves rather than, the rigid face-framing Spanish ruff and tight sleeves of the original. Many years later Richard Cosway etched a *Self-portrait with his Wife Maria* (1784; pl. 207), in-

201 J. McArdell after Rubens, *Helen Fourment*. Mezzotint. Hon. Christopher Lennox-Boyd.

202 (far right) T. Jeffreys, '*Habit of Rubens Wife*', from *A Collection of the Dresses of Different Nations*, 1757. Engraving. British Library, London.

Habit of Rubens Wife, in 1620.

203 Anon., illustration from *The Artist's Vade Mecum*, 1762. Engraving. Yale Center for British Art, New Haven, CT. Paul Mellon Collection.

204 (far right) T. Gainsborough, *The Artist's Daughter Mary*, 1777. Oil on canvas. Tate Gallery, London.

205   T. Hudson, *Mary Panton, Duchess of Ancaster*, 1757. Oil on canvas. Grimsthorpe and Drummond Castle Trust.

Lebrun, she also painted herself after his '*Chapeau de Paille*'), is shown here in the plumed hat and oversleeve tied with ribbon of the Gulbenkian portrait.

The pose of Rubens and his wife in the '*Honeysuckle Bower*' was also possibly the inspiration behind Reynolds's double portrait of *Sir Watkin Williams Wynn and Lady Henrietta Somerset* (*c*.1769; pl. 208). Dressed for the masquerade, with masks in their

hands, they both wear Vandyke costume of the kind sometimes called Spanish (or Italian) for its use of trimmings such as ribbons, braid and bows. A man of diverse cultural achievements (including the study of antiquities), Sir Watkin was also interested in private theatricals, which took place at Wynnstay from the early 1770s, after his marriage to Lady Henrietta; the couple could very well be depicted in the kind of theatrical Vandyke costume which is listed in the Wynnstay theatre wardrobe.[43]

A certain amount of confusion existed then, as now, over the nomenclature of these types of historic dress. Even with the specific costume of the Gulbenkian Rubens, there could still be uncertainty over the attribution, as has been seen, with Walpole opting for van Dyck. The merging of the costume of

spired by the '*Honeysuckle Bower*'. Known for his interest in fashion (both contemporary and historical), the artist depicts himself in a figured doublet and breeches, a cloak over his right arm and a Rubens hat with a feather. Maria Cosway, also an artist of some repute and equally interested in Rubens (like Vigée-

Rubens and van Dyck in the eighteenth century was not surprising given the closeness of both Flemish artists and the fact that, for example, the Gulbenkian portrait, was painted in the decade during which van Dyck worked in England. Vertue refers to 'the habits of the Time of Vandyke and Rubens' as though they were to be considered together.[44]

Portraits by van Dyck, however, were more readily accessible for artists and their clients than were paintings by Rubens. In 1749 Elizabeth Montagu based a masquerade costume on a van Dyck portrait of Henrietta Maria; it was made of white satin, with lace kerchief and ruffles and her hair was 'curled after the Vandyke portrait' (which she does not identify). The ensemble was so impressive that the artist William Hoare was commissioned to paint her portrait (now lost).[45] Such bluestocking ladies were happy to be painted in a costume that was both attractive (white silk and pearls flattered the complexion) and indicated educated tastes and a knowledge of history. Moreover, as Hazlitt explained, the English preferred the gentility of van Dyck to what he called the 'excessive elasticity' of Rubens. Englishwomen as painted by van Dyck, had 'a cool refreshing air about them, a look of simplicity and modesty . . . and a certain air of fashionable elegance, characteristic of the age in which he flourished'.[46] An air of fashionable elegance is clearly to be seen in Ramsay's *Lady Mary Coke*, 1762 (pl. 209), and the artist has also caught the intellectual pretensions of this somewhat eccentric woman as she stands holding a seventeenth-century theorbo (which she had borrowed from a friend and proved reluctant to return), in a pose taken from van Dyck's *Beatrice de Cusance* in the Royal Collection. Lady Mary's costume with its flat collar and white satin bodice and skirt, looks realistic and is copied with understanding from van Dyck's portraits of Henrietta Maria; there is even a serious attempt to reproduce the more natural waist level of the 1630s, by means of a wide ribbon over the long pointed bodice of the early 1760s.

It was with the same aesthetic sympathies that the *Lady's Magazine* in 1759 advocated a return to 'the short waist of our great-grandmothers', illustrating the advice with an engraving from Wenceslas Hollar's *Ornatus muliebris anglicanus* of 1640,[47] one of the earliest series of English fashion plates. Hollar's exquisite and detailed fashion engravings were able to supply more information on Vandyke fashions than the sometimes more generalised costume depicted by van Dyck himself. They thus proved useful as ideas for fancy dress, and if one recalls the title of Jefferys's costume book, the 'old English Dresses' are described as after 'the designs of Holbein, Vandyke, Hollar, and others'. Mrs Montagu noted in 1742 that two of her friends, including Mrs Pendarves (later Mrs Delany)

were preparing for a masquerade to be given by the Duchess of Norfolk, and 'they are to be dressed after Hollar's Prints'.[48]

At about the same time, according to Elizabeth Montagu, Mrs Pendarves was engaged in copying van Dyck's *Lady Dorothy Sidney, Countess of Sunderland*,

209 A. Ramsay, *Lady Mary Coke*, 1762. Oil on canvas. In a private Scottish collection.

immortalised as the poet Waller's beautiful Sacharissa. The best-known portrait (Petworth House, W. Sussex), shows the sitter with flowers in her hair and a romantic fanciful costume of which the predominant feature is vast sleeves turned over to show a deep orange-red silk lining; a gold embroidered silk scarf floats over her arm.[49] This kind of pastoral mood, which van Dyck had introduced from the Netherlands[50] (and which ultimately derived from Italy), gave portraits a more relaxed, and 'timeless' quality. According to William Sanderson's *Graphice* (1658), van Dyck was the first painter in England who 'e're put Ladies dresse into a careless Romance'. His clientele, thus garbed, wear loose, low-cut gowns, often with floating gauzy scarves, tied-in sleeves and jewels as dress fastenings. The style was taken up from the middle years of the seventeenth century by Sir Peter Lely, with a heightened awareness of the seductive possibilities of Arcadian *déshabillé*, which well suited the hedonistic Restoration court.

The great popularity of the pleasure gardens of London, especially Vauxhall and Ranelagh, encouraged the vogue for rustic masquerade costumes – shepherdesses, milkmaids, haymakers – which tied in with the artistic preference for costume that, if not exactly 'timeless', had stood the test of time. A type of dress thus evolved that employed the familiar mixture of the fashionable with elements of the historical; artists, suggested Gérard de Lairesse in the 1738 translation of his *The Art of Painting*, should blend 'the Fashion with what is Painter-like; as the great Lely did'.[51] Fashionable mid-eighteenth-century artists such as Hudson were quick to jump on the artistic bandwagon, producing portraits of this hybrid kind, such as the image of Elizabeth Pole in his painting of Sir John Pole and his wife, 1755 (pl. 210). Sir John's silver-braided suit is real costume; that of his wife copies the shapes and colours of contemporary fashion (the full-skirted dress with its tight bodice is made of the lustrous salmon-pink satin which was very much *à la mode* at the time), but it is the invention of the artist. Using the basic fashion shape, Hudson builds up the pastoral mood with a (real) straw hat, a basket of flowers and a selection of 'historic' features taken from van Dyck and Lely (possibly via the drawings of van Aken who made costume studies after these artists and Kneller too).[52] Such elements include the short scallopped sleeve laced in at the shoulder, over the chemise, with pearl laces; the bodice of the dress trimmed with pearls; and the gold-embroidered silk gauze scarf which is fastened at her bosom and floats over her left shoulder. Although this is not a real dress, something along these lines would be worn for such a part as that of a pastoral nymph at a masquerade, for no real ingenuity with regard to dress was required other than touches of the prettily rural.

Fanny Burney described such fancy dress as 'hackneyed' and in Samuel Richardson's novel *Sir Charles Grandison* (1754) the heroine Harriet Byron has her unease about attending the masquerade confirmed by the costume ordained for her, as an 'Arcadian princess' in a dress of blue satin, 'the skirts edged with silver fringe . . . all set off with bugles and spangles which make a mightly glitter. I am to be allowed a kind of scarf, of white Persian silk, which, gathered at the top, is to be fastened to my shoulders, and fly loose behind me'. As with the portrait of Lady Pole, the fashionable mid-eighteenth-century width of skirt was to be suggested without an obvious hoop, for 'they wore no hoops in Arcadia'.[53]

Eighteenth-century notions of aesthetics and propriety could not countenance the loosely draped gowns worn over no underwear other than a transparent shift which are to be seen in portraits by Lely; Walpole commented, erroneously, that although 'Vandyck's habits are those of the times', Lely's were invented, 'a sort of fantastic night-gowns, fastened with a single pin'.[54] It was not so much the type of dress which was objected to (which was, after all, a form of *négligé* which the eighteenth-century lady had in her wardrobe, just as her Restoration ancestress did), but the fact that such excessive informality featured in the public arena of the portrait; such a costume, being very loose and revealing, could easily become indecent. It is therefore quite surprising to come across a portrait of a sitter painted in the middle of the eighteenth century wearing such a dress. In Hayman's *Benjamin Hoadly and his Wife* (c.1747; pl. 212), the costume is an almost exact copy of that worn in a portrait by Lely, possibly of the Duchess of Portsmouth, mistress to Charles II.[55] Originally painted in the late 1740s, Dr Hoadly, with his old-fashioned short periwig, formal suit and laced waistcoat, makes an odd contrast to his wife in her Lelyesque gown; no doubt the proprieties were assuaged by the mask in her hand, an allusion to her husband's profession as a playwright. Paradoxically, the lady's attempts at an historical – even 'timeless' – dress, proved unsuccessful and some time during the 1770s her hairstyle was altered to bring it up to date, in a fashion much further removed from Lely's time than the loose curls of the late 1740s.[56]

Artists such as Hudson and Hayman used van Dyck, Lely and Kneller in a fairly indiscriminating and unsophisticated way when compared to Reynolds and Gainsborough, whose touch is more subtle. According to Northcote, Reynolds disliked Lely and Kneller, particularly the latter, who he thought was mainly responsible for what Walpole called the 'low ebb' of the arts in the early eighteenth century, through his lack of imagination with regard to pose and dress. However, Reynolds did use Kneller occasionally as a

dress and the hair and floating, gauzy scarves. The skilful artist (or his drapery painter) could use such features to give a romantic, 'historical' gloss to a costume that was still recognisably high fashion, and could thus be appreciated as of the time and yet timeless. In the hands of a master such as Gainsborough, it becomes almost irrelevant which bits of the costume are real and which fantasy. His portrait of his daughters, Margaret and Mary (c.1774; pl. 211), is a good example of this merging processs, fanciful historical details of dress superimposed on the fashionable outline. Margaret (on the left) has a costume with a theatrical feel to it (possibly studio items), consisting of a white gown and blue skirt trimmed with silver; pearls and a silvery scarf decorate her neckline. Mary's gown of dusky pink has short scallopped sleeves in the Lely style, a bodice front that suggests the 1670s design of sloping sides with a triangular underbodice, forming a point at the centre of the neckline, and – for good measure – a fringed sash in oriental style. The sisters are cleverly united by means of a gold embroidered gauze scarf which Mary holds in her left hand and drapes over Margaret's shoulders. With a slightly different arrangement of accessories – a turban as well as a fringed sash, or a cameo and sandals – this type of easy-fitting dress could, with equal ease, create the semblance of an 'oriental' or a 'classical' portrait. At times, the dividing line between these categories can be blurred, and they become more a convenience for dress historians, perhaps, than an indication that artists were always aware of such categorisation.

211 (above) T. Gainsborough, *The Artist's Daughters Margaret and Mary*, c.1774. Oil on canvas. Private Collection.

212 F. Hayman, *Benjamin Hoadly and his Wife*, c.1747. Oil on canvas. Wellcome Institute Library, London.

source for the design of some full-length portraits, for example *Elizabeth Gunning, Duchess of Hamilton and Argyll* (pl. 27) where the influence of Kneller's *Mary Compton, Countess of Dorset* (Hampton Court) can be seen. In Reynolds's work also, as in the portraits by a number of other artists, the influence of Lely and Kneller is evident in the appearance of such fashions as V-necklines and cross-over fronts to the gowns, short, often scallopped sleeves, pearls decorating the

The personal preferences of artists must also be considered. Francis Cotes (or his drapery painter Peter Toms), for example, seems to have liked painting his female sitters most of all in loose, often wrap-over gowns with draperies, in imitation of the antique (see pl. 224). Even when Vandyke dress might be appropriate, as in his double portrait of Thomas and Isabel Crathorne, 1767 (pl. 213), the wife wears a blue silk wrapping-gown tied at the waist with a sash, and just a touch of the seventeenth century in her Vandyke collar, whereas Thomas Crathorne wears a complete Vandyke suit and cloak. The emphasis in this portrait is on Isabel Crathorne, who fixes our attention, while her husband, set back in the canvas, gazes intently at her. It is, in fact, a posthumous image of Thomas Crathorne; Vandyke costume being used here to confer a kind of timeless dignity and, as with Eccardt's portrait of Horace Walpole (pl. 189) to draw attention to the intellectual and artistic accomplishments of sitters.

If the numbers of portraits where the sitters are depicted in Vandyke dress were to be counted (using

213 F. Cotes, *Thomas Crathorne and his Wife, Isabel*, 1767. Oil on canvas. Huntington Art Gallery, San Marino, CA.

the term here to cover all kinds of late sixteenth and early seventeenth-century costume), there would be far more women than men. Wearing such costume in real life, at a masquerade or for a portrait provided an escape from the everyday world, a chance to engage in another role – however vicariously – of Time Past. The masquerade offered women a certain amount of freedom, especially when in disguise, from their day-to-day existence, and some of the most popular costumes, namely the historical, filtered through into portraiture. The only other time when women could wear costume that was not related to their everyday fashions, was at coronations, when the wives of peers had their own distinctive dress which related to the status of their husbands. This, of course, only involved a small group of women, but it was a dignified, luxurious and historical costume (essentially, dating from the Restoration) and one in which many peeresses chose to be painted throughout the period, not just at the time of a coronation; it also provided a rare opportunity to display large amounts of jewellery. Elements of this coronation costume, notably the ermine-lined mantle, were sometimes used in portraits – alongside fashionable or even fancy dress – to indicate the status of the sitter, as in Reynolds's *Elizabeth Gunning, Duchess of Hamilton and Argyll* (pl. 27).[57]

Men, being in the world of affairs, could be portrayed in a wide range of occupational and official costumes other than their everyday dress; these included the robes of the knightly orders. The premier order was the Garter, established in the mid-fourteenth century, the costume of which was re-designed at the Restoration to emphasise its links with the past and to reinforce the historical credentials of the monarchy after the Interregnum. Beneath the vast blue velvet mantle (a medieval survival), the Knights were to wear a cloth of silver doublet and matching round breeches or 'the old trunk hose' (from the sixteenth century); in fact, as surviving examples indicate, the 'trunk hose' was either a short skirt or petticoat breeches, worn over white silk stockings. The effect of the Knights *en masse* was undeniably impressive at installation ceremonies. That of 1805 was a particularly glamorous occasion, attended by ministers of the Crown and all the foreign ambassadors; the antiquity of the ceremony was much emphasised (a riposte to Napoleon's Légion d'Honneur, inaugurated the previous year), one visitor noting of the Garter Knights, '. . . their dresses were very magnificent . . . white and silver like the old pictures of Henry VIII'.[58] The costume of the Knights of the Garter conferred status and *gravitas* on the wearer and proved an obviously popular choice for portraiture; such clothing flattered even portly Hanoverian princes, as can be seen in Hoppner's fine depiction of the Prince of Wales (*c.*1796; private collection), where he cuts an impos-

ing figure with his blue velvet mantle trailing on the ground.

One of the Prince's ancestors, Charles I, had been particularly interested in the Garter and had initiated the practice of adding the Garter star to civilian costume; it became customary for Knights of the Garter to wear the star and badge of the order as part of formal dress. This insignia can be seen, along with other intimations of rank (the fur-trimmed mantle of a peer's parliamentary robe is draped over the pedestal) in John Michael Rysbrack's posthumous portrait of Charles Seymour, 6th Duke of Somerset of 1756 (pl. 214). The Duke had been Chancellor of Cambridge University from 1689 to his death in 1748, and it is possibly in reference to his longevity that he is depicted as a young man in historic costume; Walpole rather disapprovingly noted, 'it is in a Vandyke dress, which might not be the fault of the sculptor'.[59] The costume is a slightly simplified form of Vandyke dress, without the waist-seam and overlapping tabs which early seventeenth-century doublets possess. Even so, the sculptor has gone to some trouble to depict the detail of the lace collar and cuffs; this kind of tactility was to be deplored by Reynolds (citing Bernini as an example of virtuoso skill put to ill use) in his *Tenth Discourse* of 1780. No matter if, *pace* Walpole, the

214 J. M. Rysbrack, *Charles Seymour, 6th Duke of Somerset*, 1756. Marble. Senate House, Cambridge. (Photo: Conway Library, Courtauld Institute of Art)

choice of dress was not Rysbrack's own, the sculptor has entered into the antiquarian spirit of the commission by giving his sitter a Vendyckian pose and even lengthening the curls of his wig to create a seventeenth-century hairstyle.

Historical allusions were also incorporated into the costume of the Order of the Bath, which in reality began with George I in 1725, although there are some obscure precursory references to its existence from the Middle Ages; the *London Chronicle*, reporting on the installation of new Knights of the Bath in May 1761, stated that the order dated from the reign of Henry IV in the early fifteenth century.[60] The costume comprised a crimson mantle and surcoat worn over a white silk 'doublet' and knee-breeches, white silk shoes with Vandyke 'roses' (ribbon rosettes) and an ostrich-feathered hat. One of the most theatrical of Reynolds's portraits (which almost, but not quite, teeters on the brink of a comic masterpiece) shows the Earl of Bellomont (1774; pl. 215) as a Knight of the Bath. Leaning on his sword, his banner with its emblematic coot beside him, the man known as the 'Hibernian seducer' is posed in his robes, which have faded from red to pink, thus adding to the slightly unreal image, an effect emphasised by the forest of white ostrich plumes on his satin hat. The collar of the order was a design of knots and crowns and the badge of three crowns an allusion to the union of the kingdoms of England, Scotland and Ireland.

In his depiction of the silver and rose Vandyke dress which Thomas William Coke wears in his portrait by Batoni of 1774 (pl. 216). The artist has achieved a perfect amalgamation of baroque elegance with a real costume, as worn at a masquerade in Rome in 1773. The pose is taken from van Dyck's *Earl of Warwick* (New York, Metropolitan Museum of Art), and the costume is a suit of white and silver silk, a pink cloak lined with ermine, a lace collar trimmed with a pink bow (like that on the shoes) and a hat trimmed with ostrich feathers. It is hard to discern the future agricultural reformer in this image of a glamorous youth, whose handsome appearance won him many admirers, including, reputedly, the Countess of Albany, wife of the exiled Charles Edward Stuart; it is possibly her face on the reclining sculpture of Ariadne on Naxos in the background.[61]

It was to please his English patrons that Batoni imbued his portraits with homage to van Dyck, and which – in true Renaissance manner – incorporate references to classical learning; English artists with a predominantly anti-intellectual clientèle, usually omitted this aspect of art. English artists and sitters were more interested in the dress itself to improve the status of portraiture, Reynolds even suggesting that Vandyke costume was a prop for inferior painters. He notes in his *Seventh Discourse* (1776):

215 J. Reynolds, *Charles Coote, 1st Earl of Bellomont*, 1774. Oil on canvas. National Gallery of Ireland, Dublin.

We all remember how common it was a few years ago for portraits to be drawn in this fantastick dress; and this custom is not yet entirely laid aside. By this means it must be acknowledged very ordinary pictures acquired something of the air and effect of the works of Vandyck, and appeared therefore at first sight to be better pictures than they really were.[62]

Reynolds is rather disingenuous here, for he painted a number of portraits of sitters in this costume including

216 P. Batoni, *Thomas William Coke, later 1st Earl of Leicester*, 1774. Oil on canvas. Viscount Coke and the Trustees of the Holkham Estate.

(in the very year of this *Discourse*) the moody, adolescent *Viscount Althorp* (Althorp House, Northants) in a black Vandyke suit, with long hair and a book in his hand, an image not unlike a 'melancholick' Jacobean gallant.[63] Reynolds was also, so contemporary memoirs and his sitter books inform us, fond of attending masquerades and he was also painted by Angelica Kauffman in 1767 (Saltram House, Devon) in a Vandyke costume. As a society artist, Reynolds enjoyed the social aspects of the masquerade, and, as Leslie and Taylor note, such 'a painter was especially excusable for going where he could study such living and moving pictures'.[64]

Like a number of other artists, Reynolds had an ambivalent attitude to fancy dress in portraits. The imaginative use of the work of a famous Old Master (both in pose and dress) demonstrated the artist's intellectual skills and could be picked up by the educated patron and spectator. On the other hand, Vandyke costume was perhaps too popular, too modishly part of the sophisticated world of fashion which brought artists fame (and money) but which could easily lead to the bored repetition of stale poses and uniform dress. But some sitters, it would appear, were quite happy to be painted in virtually identical Vandyke dress, as the diary of Sylas Neville reveals; in 1770 he recorded his satisfaction at finding his portrait – dressed in a dark grey and crimson Vandyke suit – so admired, that two more of the artist's sitters had elected to be painted in the same way.[65] For this sitter, as with many others, uniformity was no bar to enjoyment, but a positive confirmation of accepted taste. If we look at the work of a number of eighteenth-century artists – artists as different as, say, Hudson and Gainsborough – almost identical Vandyke costumes are repeated in their portraiture.[66] This may indicate the use of studio properties, pattern books (perhaps taken from the work of drapery painters in Hudson's case) or drawings after van Dyck (in Gainsborough's case).

Gainsborough is an interesting example of an artist who revered van Dyck but whose portraits of men in Vandyke costume often lack the conviction of similar images by his contemporaries (his portraits of young boys, on the other hand, being less formal, are more convincing with their light-hearted echoes of Titian and Watteau's Italian comedy). Gainsborough's *Charles Howard, Earl of Surrey, later 11th Duke of Norfolk* (1784–6; pl. 217) is unimaginative and pompous when set beside Batoni's *Thomas William Coke* or Angelica Kauffman's *John Simpson* (1777; pl. 219), with their sense of being at ease in fancy dress, whether real or just on the canvas. Kauffman's portrait shows a Vandyke (or Spanish) suit of red, trimmed with blue, and a matching cloak; the costume is a conventional studio work (another portrait of the sit-

ter, in the National Portrait Gallery, London, shows more or less the same suit, but with the doublet slashed on the chest), but the artist has added a distinctive touch, a collar and cuffs of fine linen edged with a border of embroidered leaves.

The pose of Gainsborough's *Duke of Norfolk* is possibly based on that of George Digby, 2nd Earl of Bristol, in van Dyck's double portrait of him with William Russell, 1st Duke of Bedford, at Althorp. His costume is a black Vandyke suit, the doublet and sleeves slashed in the correct early seventeenth-century manner; the style of the shoes with their decorative rosettes is also accurate. Intimations of the sitter's rank are lightly painted in, the coronet on the right and the parliamentary robes draped on the left. But the sitter, a well-known collector and connoisseur, looks rather stifled in his costume, as though the artist's perception is over-weighted with historical precedents; Gainsborough has tried to be more van Dyck than Vandyke. He succeeds better when he incorporates the *idea* of the historic past (rather than the fussy details of dress) into portraits, as with such images as *Hon. Frances Duncombe* (pl. 200), or when subtle motifs from the work of van Dyck appear in portraits of sitters wearing high fashion, such as *Countess Howe* (pl. 65). Gainsborough's most accomplished portraits demonstrate his wide knowledge of van Dyck (from engravings and from copies of famous paintings which he made himself after settling in Bath in 1759)[67] in an understated way – a persuasive re-interpretation of the past.

Gainsborough was not, of course, the only artist who copied van Dyck. Vertue's Notebooks record a number of artists, from the early eighteenth century onwards, who made this a practice; under the year 1745, for example, he states that the portrait painter John Robinson 'proposd the Imitations and manner of Vandykes, faces, habits &c . . . he Coppyed the double whole lengths of Vandyke Ld Russel & Digby very well – and others of this Master'.[68] The drapery painter Joseph van Aken produced a number of drawings after van Dyck, and in Jefferys's *Collection of the Dresses*, there are as might be expected, several engravings of van Dyck portraits. These include the 'habit of an English Gentleman from a capital Painting of the Pembroke Family . . . at Wilton' (this large canvas was also to be copied by Gainsborough), and a 'habit of a Nobleman of England in 1640', taken from van Dyck's *William Villiers, 2nd Viscount Grandison* (Duke of Grafton). This last-named portrait inspired the pose and costume of Richard Cosway's *William, 3rd Viscount Courtenay* (1791; Powderham Castle, Devon), who wore his masquerade dress at his coming-of-age party the previous year.

A number of Vandyke portraits relate to actual costume, as noted with regard to Batoni's *Thomas*

William Coke. Another example is Zoffany's *John, Lord Mountstuart* (*c.*1763–4; pl. 218) where the sitter's deep yellow (a van Dyck colour) costume with its liberal decoration of fake slashes and ribbon bows has the fussy theatricality of a real dress. Surviving Vandyke costumes are very theatrical, often with an *embarras de richesse* of spangles, ribbons, bows and appliquéd puffs of silk imitating Elizabethan and early seventeenth-century slashing of the fabric.[69] The quiet harmony of the plain satin doublets and knee-breeches as painted by van Dyck were not quite 'historical' enough, so the lily had to be gilded to conform to the eighteenth-century notion of the sixteenth and seventeenth centuries. In 1781 the Prince of Wales was commissioned by his brother Prince Frederick in Hanover, to order a Vandyke costume of white satin; when it appeared it was trimmed – the cloak also – with pink puffs and knots, and a similar decoration (of 'pale buff puffs & knots') adorned an accompanying Vandyke dress of 'lylock silk'.[70]

Some of the more theatrical versions of Vandyke dress (as in Reynolds's *Sir Watkin Williams Wynn and his Wife*, pl. 208) were often called Spanish. At a masquerade called a 'ridotto al fresco' at Vauxhall Gardens in 1769, there appeared a young gentleman 'habited like a Spaniard; his dress was a Pink Sattin with silver Pods, and trimmed with a narrow gold lace'.[71] Pink was a popular colour in the eighteenth century and one splendid Spanish or Vandyke suit of the mid-eighteenth century (pl. 220) is made of salmon-pink damask trimmed with silver bobbin lace; the short cloak is of blue taffeta. The description of the Vauxhall masquerade costume of 1769, as a pink suit with 'pods' (applied puffs of fabric) sounds quite like that worn by the sitter in Gainsborough's '*Pink Boy*', *Master Nicholls* (1782; Waddesdon Manor, Bucks), which is possibly a real dress. Young boys did not, of course, attend masquerades, but there was a vogue for them to be dressed in Vandyke costume and some young boys wore such costume for sport, particularly archery.[72]

This may help to account for the popularity of being painted *en famille* in Vandyke costume, which was a particular forte of the artist Zoffany. His famous group of the royal family, *George III, Queen Charlotte and their Six Eldest Children* of 1770 (Royal Collection) – which elicited Walpole's comment on seeing it at the Royal Academy, 'in Vandyck dresses, ridiculous' – shows the King in a blue Vandyke suit trimmed with silver braid and bows, the Queen in a white dress vaguely based on van Dyck's portraits of Henrietta Maria and the two eldest princes in suits closely copied from van Dyck's portrait of the Villiers brothers, which was displayed at Buckingham House. Zoffany's *Family of Sir William Young* (*c.*1766; pl. 221) shows a more cerebral group, playing and listening to

220 Vandyke costume, mid-
eighteenth century. Silk taffeta
and silver braid. Koninklijk
Oudheidkundig Genootschap,
on loan to the Rijksmuseum,
Amsterdam.

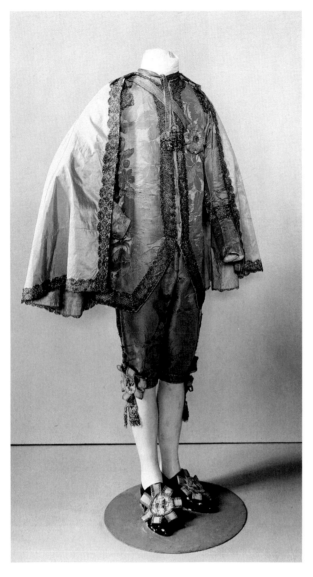

over the shoulder in imitation of a Vandyke hairstyle.
Sir William's costume is similar in flavour to the
masquerade dress worn in Reynolds's *Sir Watkin
Williams Wynn* (pl. 208), and an equally theatrical air
pervades Zoffany's painting. William Young and his
wife were friends of Garrick (from whom, apparently,
they tried to borrow theatre costume), and therefore
the choice of Vandyke dress here might be particularly appropriate.[73]

Private theatricals were very much in vogue (particularly in aristocratic circles) during the second half
of the eighteenth century and into the early nineteenth century.[74] These entertainments were mainly
undertaken by adults, but those at Holland House
from the 1760s were by young people and children.
In 1761 Walpole saw Rowe's *Jane Shore* (a highly
popular play about the mistress of Edward IV, who
was forced to do public penance for adultery after his
death) acted there, with Lady Sarah Lennox and Lady
Susan Fox-Strangways taking the female roles. Lady
Sarah, as the eponymous heroine, was 'in white with
her hair about her ears', and her dress 'taken out of
Montfaucon'; Lady Susan 'was dressed from Jane
Seymour', presumably after the Holbein portrait.[75]
Popular historical costumes could double for theatricals and for masquerades, even achieving immortality
on the canvas. Thomas Jefferys's *Collection of the
Dresses* was intended as a pattern-book for fancy dress
in art and in the flesh, being advertised alongside
accounts of masquerades and advertisements for the
theatrical costumiers who usually supplied masquerade
costume as well as stage dress. Moves towards dramatic unity in theatre productions during the second
half of the eighteenth century encouraged a similar
trend in the masquerade, with the earlier democratic
free-for-all of the public masquerade giving way to
the private fancy-dress entertainment based on a
theme. The French ambassador's ball in 1773, where
the dancers were costumed in Elizabethan and Henry
IV styles, has already been noted (see p. 193); it was
a trend, commented Walpole, to make 'romances' of
such entertainments, with an increasingly theatrical
content. One of the most famous 'romances' was
Lord Stanley's *fête champêtre*, held in the grounds of his
house near Epsom in 1774 to celebrate his forthcom-
ing marriage to Lady Betty Hamilton. The theme was
to be the pastoral and Walpole noted that
Lord Stanley 'has bought all the orange trees round
London, and the haycocks I suppose are to be made
of straw-coloured satin'; Robert Adam designed a
temporary amphitheatre for the feasting and dancing,
and professional musicians and actors dressed in rural
costumes performed minuets, masques and songs on
the theme of conjugal happiness.[76] Mrs Delany noted
that the 'master of the entertainment (Lord Stanley)
was dressed like Reubens, and Lady Betty Hamilton

music. Significantly, the dress of the female members
of the company is a mixture of the historical and the
fashionable: Lady Young, seated in the centre, wears
white satin in the style of Henrietta Maria, but with a
modish Marie Stuart cap; behind her, holding a music
score, stands Sarah wearing a loose wrapping-gown
with fresh flowers in the bosom, like a Lelyesque
pastoral nymph; only Mary, sitting on the wall wears
proper Vandyke costume with its tabbed bodice, laced
down the front. In contrast, Sir William (seated playing the cello) and all his sons wear Vandyke costume,
even the smallest boy being held up by a black page;
the artist has also taken trouble with such details as
the seventeenth-century 'bucket-top' boots worn by
Brook Young on horseback. The greatest attention is
devoted to Sir William's appearance, with his carefully
delineated lace collar and cuffs – they do look like
paper doilies, but are meant to represent the flat
bobbin lace which was worn from the 1620s to the
middle of the seventeenth century; Zoffany has also
unravelled the back hair from the wig so that it falls

221 J. Zoffany, *Sir William Young and his Family*, c.1766. Oil on canvas. Walker Art Gallery, Liverpool.

(for whom the feast was made) like Reubens' wife . . .'[77]

The romantic fever that had begun to affect women's dress in the 1770s seems to have had little influence on men's fashions: Walpole is being slightly tongue-in-cheek when he writes to Sir William Hamilton in 1774: 'If you were to come over, you would find us a general masquerade. The macaronis, not content with producing new fashions every day, and who are great reformers, are going to restore the Vandyck dress'.[78] Certainly, the light colours of some van Dyck costume – even what was perceived as the 'effeminacy' of early Stuart styles – might appeal to the macaronis, but it is more likely that Walpole has in mind some minor fashion innovation such as the calf-length breeches which these young men of mode copied from van Dyck portraits of the late 1630s. The 1770s was in fact the last time that men would wear colourful costume, and this was a taste limited to the macaronis and those who imitated their extreme fashions. As we have seen, men's dress seems to move inexorably towards dull conformity by the end of the century, the only item of clothing that could display individuality and colour being the waistcoat. During the 1780s there are references in the Prince of Wales's accounts to Vandyke waistcoats, some of which sound quite showy – for example, one 'Vandyke White Silk Waistcoat' embroidered in ribbon and silver spangles, cost £7 17s 6d,[79] quite a large sum of money; such garments clearly relate to masquerade and theatrical costume, although they would have been worn as fashionable dress, probably as evening wear.

The only other impact which the time of van Dyck made on the masculine styles of the later eighteenth century was the fashion for wearing long hair, although this was restricted to boys and young men in their teens. It was part of the move towards naturalism and informality in the clothing of boys which was so remarked on by foreign visitors, and which gave them an almost Romantic sensibility. Such young men are referred to in contemporary letters as 'Vandykes', as when, in Mrs Delany's correspondence, there is mention of Lord Warwick's 'two youngest sons . . . one eighteen, the other sixteen – the latter a beautiful

211

222 T. Barker, *Self-portrait*, c.1803. Oil on canvas. The Holbourne Museum, Bath.

Dyck. Vandyke costume in art became a somewhat stale and tired notion, related to the decline in the wearing of such dress, as masquerades fell out of favour. The great pleasure-gardens of London which had been the venue for large-scale masquerades were in decay, as was the masquerade itself, which had long been regarded by its many critics as the potential embodiment of social disorder particularly in the reversal of sexual and class roles. The French Revolution seemed to confirm these fears and hastened the demise of this public entertainment. The fancy-dress portrait, no longer related to the masquerade, became relegated to a form of artistic and intellectual self-expression, as in Barker's self-portrait, and William Hazlitt's painting of the essayist Charles Lamb (1804; pl. 223), who is dressed as Velázquez's *Philip IV*, in black and with the characteristic Spanish collar called the *golilla*. The artist has cleverly suggested Spanish dress, while at the same time giving the sitter a romantic contemporary appearance; the hair is cut short, in accordance with the fashion (whereas Philip IV's hair falls to his shoulders), and the black and white of the costume suggests the colour scheme of the early nineteenth-century Englishman.

There are also far fewer portraits of women in fancy dress by the turn of the century. This can partly be explained by the decline of the masquerade, but also because some elements of earlier costume had been assimilated into high fashion; this trend can be seen during the last quarter of the eighteenth century and it continues beyond the end of the period. In the 1820s the fashion for dress which had a high-ish waist,

Vandyke'.[80] This is maybe how the artist Thomas Barker saw himself in his *Self-portrait* (pl. 222), with long, wavy hair, and the kind of informal sleeved waistcoat or 'vest' in which seventeenth-century artists often depict themselves. The artist stands before his easel on which is displayed a view of the Temple of the Sibyl at Tivoli; the portrait must have been painted after his return from Italy in 1793 and probably at about the time of his marriage in 1803, as a companion portrait to that of his wife, also in the Holburne Museum, Bath. By this time it would have been unusual, even for an artist, to wear his hair this long, and it can safely be assumed that Barker has chosen to paint himself in this way to represent the idea of the seventeenth century, without, perhaps, any specific painter in mind, although there are allusions to artistic self-portrayals by van Dyck, Le Nain and others.

For much of the eighteenth century men's dress had not changed radically since the time of van Dyck; the knee-breeches remained the same and although (except for the costume of chivalrous orders) men had abandoned doublets, the eighteenth-century coat was not unlike the long, un-tabbed jacket that was part of informal seventeenth-century clothing. By the end of the eighteenth century, however, masculine costume was undergoing a sea-change; the dark cut-away tailcoat and pantaloons could not by any stretch of the imagination be related to dress of the time of van

223 W. Hazlitt, *Charles Lamb*, 1804. Oil on canvas. National Portrait Gallery, London.

full sleeves and jewelled fastenings, echoes the costume of the 1630s; even the ringlets in vogue recall the hairstyles of the seventeenth century. Sir Thomas Lawrence was particularly keen to paint his grand female clients in full-length poses after van Dyck; such portraits include the *Marchioness of Londonderry* (Marquess of Londonderry) in a *décolletée* dress of garnet velvet, the sleeves clasped with some of the famous family jewels, and the *Duchess of Richmond* (Goodwood House, W. Sussex) in cream satin with long sleeves full at the upper arm in imitation of seventeenth-century style. By this time portraits of women show them usually in the actual costume that they wear; the problems of determining the real from the fanciful in dress – problems exacerbated by the drapery painter, by theories of 'timeless' clothing and by the self-conscious imitation of the Old Masters – have disappeared. The task of the historian of dress in analysing costume in art thus becomes easier, with fewer challenges as to the distinctions between truth and fantasy.

★   ★   ★

Turning to the influence of the antique on costume, it is clear that there was a rather different approach in England than in France, where it had a far more profound impact on art and on dress – both fashionable and official. In theory, the English were just as interested in the civilisations of ancient Greece and Rome; the Dilettanti Society fostered the study of classical antiquity (the President wore a scarlet 'toga' – actually a cloak which fastened with a gilt clasp), young men went on the Grand Tour and collected antique statuary, and it could be said that the concept of the English gentleman with his cultivation of civic virtues was based on the Roman prototype. But, in fact, history paintings with classical themes were not appreciated in England; as Fuseli noted 'portrait with them is everything. Their taste and feelings all goes in realities'.[81] Antiquity could only flourish in the form of what Lawrence called 'half-history' pictures, that is portraits with classical dress and accessories. Such paintings were nearly always of women, the classical theme in men's costume being limited mainly to official statuary and to a mere handful of portraits.[82] Compared to France where there was a fairly extensive literature on the history of dress in ancient Greece and Rome, there was little in England; even Strutt in his *Complete View of the Dress and Habits of the People of England* (1796–9) only has the sketchiest survey of classical costume. Not until the very end of the eighteenth century did reasonably accurate classical dress enter the British theatre, when Talma's reforms were taken up by John Philip Kemble at Drury Lane.

Antique costume for women in England was more admired by dress reformers and artists than by women themselves, although by the end of the eighteenth century the Neoclassical style had begun to make an impact on fashion – not as much as in France however. Critics of contemporary fashion found it useful to hold classical costume up for admiration and emulation; a writer in *The European Magazine* (1785) attacking contemporary modes for their 'caprice . . . [and] desire of novelty', declared that only the Greeks and Romans had 'freedom and ease' in their 'loose, simple and unconfining' dress.[83] Classical dress, which was perceived as little more than loose draperies, was not practical as a masquerade costume; besides, apart from a few distinctive attributes such as Diana's bow and crescent moon, it was not easy to distinguish one mythological deity from another in terms of clothing. Diana was the only popular masquerade character (a statue of the goddess stood in one of the walks at Vauxhall Gardens), but the costume – apart from the crescent moon – was quite unlike that worn by Lady Stanhope in plate 224, being an elaborate fancy dress (this was the contemporary term to indicate a costume which was made on fashionable lines, but with a few theatrical accessories such as ribbons, scarves and flowers). The dress in Cotes's *Lady Stanhope and the Countess of Effingham as Diana and her Companion* (1765), is not real, although it may relate to the private theatricals staged in the 1760s by Lady Stanhope's brother Sir Francis Blake Delaval. Lady Stanhope's costume consists of a pink dress under a creamy-yellow gown, wrapped around at the waist with a gold-edged sash; the Countess of Effingham wears a blue dress with short scallopped sleeves (a touch of Lely, and a reference to the rank of the wearer, for the kirtle worn as part of coronation costume has sleeves of a similar design). The dress is far too undecorated and unstructured for theatre wear (Lady Effingham's right sleeve is about to fall off her shoulder); the footwear looks slightly more authentic, being gold laces worn over beige silk tights – bare legs were inadmissable on the stage even for private entertainments, although this rule seems to have been relaxed for Lady Hamilton's dramatic performances (see pl. 229).

Diana was also known for her chastity, and it was therefore perfectly proper for ladies to be painted in this way. In 1772 Angelica Kauffman painted Jane Maxwell, Duchess of Gordon (pl. 225), a celebrated Tory hostess in London and leader of Edinburgh society, as Diana, with bow and quiver at her side. The costume is a typical Kauffmanesque concoction, the full muslin over-sleeves pushed up the arm and clasped with jewelled brooches and a gold girdle round the waist; the dress is surrounded, as it were, by a red drapery, presumably a mantle which is embroidered in gold. In comparison with the gauzy

224 F. Cotes, *Lady Stanhope and the Countess of Effingham as Diana and her Companion*, 1765. Oil on canvas. York City Art Gallery.

225 (facing page) A. Kauffman, *Jane Maxwell, Duchess of Gordon, as Diana*, 1772. Oil on canvas. Scottish National Portrait Gallery, Edinburgh.

unreality of the costume, the face with its look of aristocratic hauteur has been well observed and the hair is beautifully painted with its trailing ribbon and delicate diamond crescent moon.

The whole portrait, in fact, looks more lively than most of Reynolds's attempts in this genre, paralysed as many of his sitters seem to be in the cold light of the artist's vision of antiquity and always conscious of their status in society. One of the ideas behind Reynolds's *Discourses* was to intellectualise art in Britain and one of the ways in which the President of the Royal Academy sought to do this was to promote a Grand Style imbued with the tenets of classical art and the inspiration of the Old Masters. When a portrait is 'painted in the Historical Style', he states, 'it is

neither an exact minute representation of an individual, nor completely ideal'; it follows, therefore that 'the simplicity of the antique air and attitude, however much to be admired, is ridiculous when joined to a figure in a modern dress'.[84] Reynolds pursues this argument in the *Seventh Discourse* (1776) in which he describes Greece and Rome as 'the fountains from whence have flowed all kinds of excellence . . . we voluntarily add our approbation of every ornament that belonged to them, even to the fashion of their dress'.[85] It was his view that modern dress alone in a portrait was too familiar and undignified; ideally, the 'general form' of dress should be allied to the 'air of the antique' (by 'general form' it seems that he means one based on the fashionable line, but without the details of high fashion; it was a somewhat forlorn hope, however, that such a form should remain more or less the same). The end result, in terms of costume, is often an uneasy compromise, as in his *Lady Sarah Bunbury Sacrificing to the Graces* (1765; pl. 226) with its clumsily designed, over-long, trailing gown belted with a fringed sash under the bust, the drapery of the unevenly sized sleeves pushed up the arm in a rather unconvincing manner. In its classical learning, the portrait is reminiscent of Vien (see pls 143 and 144) but without the pedantry; moreover the sitter is clearly flesh and blood,[86] in spite of Reynolds's insistence on this kind of timeless dress which Hazlitt thought so inimical to character in portraiture.[87]

In contrast, Romney – although, according to Flaxman, he was more interested in history painting than in portraiture – produced some fine portraits, as in his *Anne Verelst* (c.1771–2; pl. 227), where the classical costume is not only more realistically conveyed, but also enhances the image rather than swamping it. Painted before Romney went to Italy, the pose adopted by Mrs Verelst is taken from the statue known as the *Mattei Ceres* (Rome, Vatican Museums), which was known in England from casts and engravings. Not being constrained by Reynolds's theory (as expressed in the *Fourth Discourse* of 1771) that an 'inferior stile . . . marks the variety of stuffs', Romney paints the satin of her costume – a cream-coloured dress and a sea-green mantle – with virtuoso skill; at her breast there is a gold and ruby clasp, possibly a jewel belonging to the sitter, which adds a personal touch. Even allowing for filial pride, John Romney's comments on such portraits are apt: '. . . he was able to combine ideal grace with the realities of nature. He could impart to his female figures that indescribable something . . . which captivates the spectator without his being able to account for it. He knew how to unite Grecian grace with Etruscan simplicity'.[88]

Although classical goddesses were not popular as inspiration for masquerade costume – it would have been difficult, as Juno, to cope with a peacock, or to dance, as Hebe, with an eagle – they appear quite frequently in portraits during the later eighteenth and early nineteenth centuries. Hebe was a popular choice, being associated with youth and providing the opportunity for graceful attitudes, as cup-bearer to the gods; there was also drama (and possible sexual overtones) with the attendant image of Jupiter as an eagle. From the 1770s the subject attracted quite a number of artists, including Benjamin West, Angelica Kauffman, Romney and Gavin Hamilton;[89] one of the most familiar portraits is Reynolds's *Mrs Musters* of 1785 (Kenwood House, London), in a ravishing 'assemblage' (there is no other word for the artist's

sartorial concoctions at times) of creamy-white and pinkish-brown draperies, and with gold sandals on her bare feet.[90]

During the eighteenth century it was sometimes difficult to see what Romney *fils* calls 'ideal grace' in portraits of fashionable sitters dressed as Hebe with their hair frizzed and piled high in the styles of the 1770s and 1780s. Even Reynolds could not reform such coiffures in his portraits; although some of his admirers claimed that he did, there is no evidence for this in his painting, apart from an occasional inconsiderable lowering of the *tête*, or – as with *Mrs Musters* – a slight unravelling of stiff curls. By the early nineteenth century, under the prevailing Neoclassicism, high fashion approached more closely to the antique; portrait goddesses even began to look like fashion plates, with high-waisted and short-sleeved dresses, their hair carelessly arranged *à l'antique*. Beechey's *Lady Burrell as Hebe* of 1804 (Petworth House, W. Sussex), shows the sitter in a white dress tied under the bust, short sleeves decorated with jewels and her hair loosely knotted and garlanded with flowers. Lawrence's *Lady St John as Hebe* (c.1808; pl. 228), is also both classical and fashionable in her dress which could almost be worn at a soirée – minus, of course, the sandals and bare feet and without the eagle which is a dark, hardly visible presence at the top right of the painting. Lady St John's dress is a white pleated linen shift, the sleeves pushed up her arms in the fashionable style, and over this is a pink dress, girdled under the bust with a gold *strophion* (the band that creates the high-breasted look in classical antiquity). The sitter's red hair (red is now permissable as part of the greater individuality of the Romantic style) is bound up and knotted in the antique manner which was also *à la mode*.

Even when Lawrence paints fanciful costume, it always has a look of robust reality about it; paradoxically this is often when it is most colourful and imaginative, as in his *Lady Elizabeth Foster* (1805; pl. 230), where the prevailing theatricality of the ensemble gives the portrait an almost Ossianic look. She is painted as a Sibyl, looking out over the Roman *campagna*, but wearing a costume that is the opposite of the usual conception of classical dress as form-fitting and monochrome, usually white. So muffled is the figure that its difficult to itemise its almost gipsy-like medley. It seems to comprise a white shift under a short embroidered bodice (this is based on the fashionable spencer jacket), two skirts, one of ochre, the other black, a red scarf draped over her bust and curving round the arm which holds her Sibylline scroll and a large brown cloak, unevenly embroidered round the edge. The whole outfit ought to be preposterous as a total figment of Lawrence's imagination, but when combined with the strong character of

Greville as a 'gift' for his uncle Sir William Hamilton, who quickly became besotted with her. Romney's presents to Emma included shawls and 'some muslin dresses loose to tye with a sash for the hot weather, made like the turkey dresses, the sleeves tied in fowlds with ribban & trimmed with lace';[92] from her description, it is unclear if these are the loose chemise gowns or possibly an 'oriental' wrapping-gown, like the levite. Whatever they were, they were light, airy and sufficiently 'timeless' to be worn for her famous Attitudes, which probably began fairly soon after her installation as Sir William's mistress (they were married in 1791). The Attitudes were a form of dramatic tableaux vivants performed in a darkened room; a large golden frame was erected round an open booth lined with black velvet in which Emma represented famous paintings and statuary. Goethe's account of such an entertainment in 1787 is the most famous:

> She is very handsome and of a beautiful figure. The old knight has had made for her a Greek costume which became her extremely. Dressed in this, and letting her hair loose, and taking a couple of shawls, she exhibits every possible variety of posture, expression and look, so that at the last the spectator almost fancies it a dream . . . Standing, kneeling, sitting, lying down, grave or sad, playful . . . repentant, wanton, . . . anxious – all mental states follow rapidly one after another. With wonderful taste she suits the folding of her veil to each expression, and with the same handkerchief makes every kind of headdress.
>
> The old knight holds the light for her, and enters into the exhibition with his whole soul. He thinks he can discern in her a resemblance to all the most famous antiques.[93]

Goethe was later to modify his admiration, criticising her voice and singing ability, but she is probably the inspiration for the character of Luciane in his novel *Elective Affinities* (1809) who, although scatty and light-headed, has an Emma-like ability to perform in tableaux vivants after famous paintings, '. . . so that this living copy was beyond question inordinately superior to the original picture, and provoked universal rapture'.[94]

Men, in particular, were impressed with Emma Hamilton's performances, as her figure was so appealing, but women were more critical. Vigée-Lebrun, who painted her as a bacchante on the sea-shore near Naples, admitted that she had a good figure, but implied that she had no real dress sense and only her use of shawls gave grace to her movements. The dress that she wore for her Attitudes can be seen in the series of etchings after Frederick Rehberg (1794), of which plate 229 is one; it was a simple sleeveless shift, girdled under the bust. Lady Elizabeth Foster thought

the sitter, her face emphasised by the natural, unpowdered hair, it is a triumphant success; it is ironic that Reynolds never rises to such heights with *his* 'timeless' *grandes dames*.

One of the women associated with a theatrical interpretation of classical roles is Emma Hart, later Lady Hamilton. Born Amy Lyon in 1765, the future Emma Hamilton was one of that not inconsiderable band of lowly born women who through sheer nerve, determination (and, it must be said, luck) carved out careers in the world of the stage and from thence into society during the later eighteenth century. Her early career, which is veiled in obscurity, seems to have involved participation in 'theatricals' of one kind or another, experiences which must have made her the perfect model for George Romney, who painted her in a variety of roles during the 1780s (Circe, Medea, Ariadne, etc.) – in white draperies and scarves, sometimes in playful mood, sometimes with Greuze-like soulfulness. To Romney she was 'the divine lady', although it seems their relationship was platonic,[91] and he continued to work on portraits of her after she was packed off to Naples in 1786 by her lover Charles

she 'was draped exactly like a Grecian statue, her chemise of white muslin was exactly in that form, her sash in the antique manner, her fine black hair flowing over her shoulders...'.[95] As Emma's figure became plumper, she wore a more capacious costume 'very easy with loose sleeves to the wrist', according to the memoirs of Mrs Trench, who saw her in 1800, when she was pregnant by Lord Nelson. Mrs Trench agreed with Lady Elizabeth Foster in finding Emma Hamilton 'coarse and vulgar' as a person, but when acting out her theatrical roles, she 'becomes highly graceful, and even beautiful'; her shawls in particular were invaluable props, being disposed 'so as to form Grecian, Turkish and other drapery, as well as a variety of turbans'.[96] Inspiration for Emma's classical tableaux was easy to find, from the frescoes in Cicero's villa at Pompeii (especially the bacchantes), to the famous collection of vases owned by Sir William Hamilton.

This was Sir William's second collection of vases (the first had been sold to the British Museum after publication in four volumes in 1766–7) which was sent for sale to England in 1798.[97] Some were bought by the antiquary and collector Thomas Hope, who – almost single-handed – pioneered classical taste in interior design in England. His house, with his collec-

tion of Greek vases, some of which may appear in Adam Buck's watercolour of *Thomas Hope and his Family* (1813; New Haven, Yale Center for British Art), was open to the public.[98] In 1809 Hope published his *Costume of the Ancients*, the first book in English which dealt with classical dress and one which, the author admitted, was not scholarly; it was

230 (above) T. Lawrence, *Lady Elizabeth Foster*, 1805. Oil on canvas. National Gallery of Ireland, Dublin.

a work, stated Hope, that aimed 'not to advance erudition, but only to promote taste'. It was intended not for antiquarians but for artists, theatre designers and for members of the general public who wished to design for themselves or their houses *à la grecque* or *à la romaine* (a further book appeared in 1812, *Designs for Modern Costume*, which also depicted fashionable interiors in antique style).

Hope's introductory comments in the *Costume of the Ancients* refer to the superiority of the French with regard to classical studies, which he attributes to state support for the arts in general and the French Academy in Rome in particular. However, whereas in France ancient Rome was the main inspiration for the arts, it was Hope's intention to promote the lightness and delicacy of classical Greece, and the majority of the illustrations in his book are of Greek costume (see pl. 231) some being taken from the vases in his own collection. Like Oscar Wilde who urged the adoption of ancient Greek dress as 'the natural expression of life's beauty'[99] Hope also wished modern women would wear 'pure' draperies, uncontaminated by fussy cut and tailoring. His *Costume of the Ancients* was intended to

present to his fair model some useful hints for improving the elegance and dignity of her attire, by the dismissal of those paltry and insignificant gewgaws and trimmings that can only hold together through means of pins, sowings and other eye-rending contrivances, unknown in ancient dresses; through which the breadth and simplicity of modern female attire is destroyed and frittered away.[100]

Like so many artists and writers, Hope seems to view Greek dress as a kind of inspired drapery without 'sowings', although elsewhere he refers to the basic tunic or *chiton* as being composed of two pieces sewn together. The 'peplum' he describes as a mantle with its corners 'loaded with little metal weight or drops, in order to make them hang down more straight and even', but the *peplos* is a type of tunic with an over-hanging top, pinned on the shoulder — rather like the dress which appears to be worn by the 'Grecian female' of plate 231.[101] There is a great deal of semantic confusion over ancient Greek dress, and to be fair to Hope it was never his intention to produce a learned account of the clothing of classical antiquity but merely to inspire women's contemporary costume, so that – in the words of *Ackermann's Repository* for June 1809, 'Mr. Hope's . . . publication on *Ancient Costume . . .* will become the vade-mecum and toilet companion of every lady distinguished in the circles of fashion'. Thomas Hope used as the model for his *Costume of the Ancients* his wife Louisa, who was painted by George Dawe in 1812 (pl. 232) in a pose taken from the book. Her dress, which is not unlike that worn in Lawrence's *Lady St John* (pl. 228) – an indication of the close relationship at this time between the artist's conception of fanciful classical costume and the fashionable reality – is a low-cut high-waisted gown over a short-sleeved *chemisette* bodice. Her hair has the tight curls of late Roman style and she holds up her fashionable paisley shawl like one of the 'Grecian females' in the *Costume of the Ancients*.

Hope may only have been an amateur – in the original sense of the word as well – when it came to the study of the dress of antiquity, but his conclusions over some of the most puzzling aspects of classical clothing are sound. For example, whereas Strutt described the toga as a 'loose, long gown', Hope was much nearer the mark when he says, 'I am most inclined to think the semi-circular to have been the true form of the toga'; he was at a loss, however, to account for how it remained in place, not so much, he says, as the result of a 'spontaneous throw of the whole', but, 'like modern dresses, from some studious and permanent contrivance'.[102] He rightly noted the derivative nature of Roman dress, that the Greeks were 'the arbitri elegantiarum and the fashion-mongers of the Romans; the costume of the one insensibly confounds itself with that of the other'.[103]

His work clearly inspired Beau Brummell's *Male and Female Costume* (Hope's plates from the *Costume of the Ancients* are appropriated), which was composed in exile and in which the influence of the Greeks and Romans on modern dress is discussed. Whereas Hope is almost exclusively concerned with women's dress, Brummell's main concerns were to demonstrate the impact of classical antiquity on the modern English gentleman. 'Did any men either before or since, even look like the Greeks and Romans? and did any men ever act like them? They were the handsomest, the noblest, the most unaffected, and the best dressing; in short, the most gentlemanly people that ever were or will be'.[104] Brummell claims that 'even in the com-

233   F.-X. Fabre, *Allen Smith seated above the Arno*, 1797. Oil on canvas. Fitzwilliam Museum, Cambridge.

221

mon dress of gentlemen, the looser drapery of the trowsers, the tunic and the cloak are regular and steady approaches to the refined and elegant taste of antiquity'.[105] This might be considered wishful thinking when we look at what men actually wore, but it could be said that in the arrangement of its folds, the cloak at least might approximate to classical drapery. This is clearly the intention, for example, in Fabre's portrait of the American traveller *Allen Smith*, seated by the Arno (1797; pl. 233). The picture, obviously inspired by Johann Heinrich Wilhelm Tischbein's famous portrait, *Goethe in the Roman Campagna*, of 1786 (Frankfurt, Städelsches Kunstinstitut), shows Smith in a lightly powdered wig, a dark blue coat with a high collar, brown knee-breeches and fine white silk stockings, with a beautifully painted detail of the embroidered clocks at the ankle. The dominating feature of his clothing is a large white mantle; this is draped around the body so as to reinforce the classical ambience of the painting. In Tischbein's picture, Goethe also wears a white mantle which hides most of his costume and which gives a kind of antique grandeur to the portrait. It is possible that both sitters may be depicted in the kind of cloak that Hester Lynch Piozzi saw the men wearing in Milan in 1785, 'an odd sort of white riding coat, not buttoned together, but folded round their body after the fashion of the old Roman dress that one has seen in statues.'[106]

*   *   *

One type of costume that is linked to the antique and must now be considered, is 'Turkish' dress; used in the eighteenth-century way, this term means the clothing of the inhabitants of the Ottoman Empire (which, of course, at this time included the Greeks). On the Turkish mainland there were colonies of semi-orientalised Greeks in such cities as Constantinople and Smyrna, and their clothing was similar to that of the Turkish rulers. A kind of Turkish-Greek costume was adopted by many of the Europeans who had been resident in the area (mainly in Constantinople) from the later seventeenth century. By the early eighteenth century there was a strong western European presence in Turkey, both diplomatic and mercantile; this helped to facilitate the travels of the growing number of visitors to the Ottoman Empire, who returned to Europe with accounts (some fairly honest, some undeniably embroidered) of a mysterious and exotic *terra incognita*. Travellers' tales and embassies from the Sublime Porte to France during the early eighteenth century initiated a vogue for *turquerie* which was soon adopted by the rest of Europe; it influenced the theatre, interior design and portraiture. In 1748 the students of the French Acad-

emy in Rome organised a carnival masquerade on the theme of the 'Caravanne du Sultan à la Mecque', and dressed up as members of the Ottoman court – vizirs, pashas, imams, sultans and sultanas; some of the students, including Vien, made visual recordings of an immensely colourful occasion.[107] Some of these illustrations were used by Jefferys in his *Collection of the Dresses*, and Turkish masquerade costumes seem in England to have been second only to historical characters in popularity. Jefferys also used a number of plates from one of the most famous series of engravings of Ottoman life, the *Recueil de cent estampes représentant différentes nations du Levant*, published in Paris in 1714, after Jean-Baptiste Vanmour, one of a not inconsiderable number of European artists based in Turkey. These beautiful and detailed coloured engravings by an artist who was familiar with the costume he was depicting, became one of the major sources for Turkish costume in portraiture during the eighteenth century; even artists such as Boucher, who had never been to the Near East, were thus enabled to paint their fashionable sitters *à la turque*. One artist who specialised in this kind of portraiture was the Swiss Jean-Etienne Liotard, who had spent the years 1738–43 in Constantinople and even dressed like a Turk; some of Liotard's drawings of Greek and Turkish ladies were engraved by the assiduous Jefferys and appear in the *Collection of the Dresses*.

Lady Mary Wortley Montagu's travels in Turkey from 1716 to 1718 helped to popularise Turkish dress both as a masquerade costume and as an artistic conceit. While in Constantinople she had a dress made for herself, consisting of loose trousers (*shalwar*) of rose-coloured damask, over which were a transparent white silk gauze smock and 'a waistcoat made close to the shape' (*antery*); then there was a pink caftan, and over all a furred robe of brocade (*curdee*).[108] With this dress, we are told, elegant Turkish ladies wore a small cap of embroidered velvet or such dainty accessories as a fine silk scarf, a plume of feathers and a jewelled bouquet – all placed to one side of the head; this taste for delicate asymmetrical ornamentation recalls the Rococo style of headwear so praised by Hogarth in his *Analysis of Beauty* (1753). Another characteristic of the dress of Turkish ladies, according to Lady Mary, was their habit of looping up the caftan and tucking one end into the wide girdle at the waist, so that the smock and trousers could be seen; this feature occurs in the famous portrait of Lady Mary with her son, attributed to Vanmour (London, National Portrait Gallery), where she is depicted in an ermine-trimmed *curdee* over a gold caftan. Not only did she set the fashion in England for being painted *à la turque* (she brought back some Turkish costumes), but her portraits and letters provided inspiration for those attending masquerades. At a masquerade held for the King of Denmark in 1768, quite a few women chose to go in Turkish costume; the *Oxford Magazine* singled out the Duchess of Ancaster, 'in the character of a Sultana . . . [in] purple sattin bordered with ermine', and Mrs Delany remarked that the Duchess of Richmond went 'as the Fatima described in Lady Mary Wortley Montagu's letters'.[109] What masquerade Turkish dress looked like is not certain, but, as with the stock Turkish 'wardrobe' of the fashionable artist, it might have included such features as low-cut dresses with a cross-over bodice and short or hanging sleeves, a wide waist girdle and a fur-trimmed robe. This is the sort of dress that appears in Francis Cotes's *Elizabeth Gunning, Duchess of Hamilton and Argyll* (1751; pl. 234); an invented piece of *turquerie*, the dress consists of a very low-cut bodice of pink trimmed with gold (perhaps caftan and jewelled girdle combined), a gauzy striped scarf that acts as a kind of modesty-piece shielding the bosom, and a blue robe edged with ermine.

In terms of its relation to reality, this costume is a long way removed from the detailed depiction of actual dress that was the forte of Liotard. Elizabeth Gunning's equally beautiful sister Mary was also painted *à la turque* (*c*.1753–4; pl. 235), but in a real costume which Liotard had either brought back from Constantinople or had designed himself. Mary Gunning wears an embroidered white caftan over a modest fawn-coloured smock, with just the slightest hint of the loose *shalwar* beneath. It is an exquisite pastel which captures the dreamy self-absorption of the sitter and is imbued with the artist's affection for the decorative qualities of oriental art (Liotard must have been familiar with Persian miniatures), characterized by the delicacy of the handling of costume and furnishings.

Some years later this portrait was the inspiration for George Willison's portrait of Nancy Parsons (*c*.1771; pl. 236). As befits the sitter (the *belle amie* of a number of English noblemen), the treatment of the costume is much coarser, lacking some of the fine details of the Liotard original, such as the flower embroidery of the caftan. But it is clearly an appropriately seductive dress with its gauzy smock and the low neck and figure-revealing bodice of the white satin caftan. One rather nice detail, an individual touch by Willison, is to transfer the tiny round buttons from the bodice of Mary Gunning and attach them to the sleeve of Nancy Parsons where they can be seen by her right elbow.

From the 1770s onwards, the ornate and decorative aspects of Turkish costume, with its jewellery and fur trimming, give way to simpler styles of light silks and muslins, which are in keeping with trends in English dress towards a general informality. Angelica Kauffman, who was interested in the decorative elements of oriental costume, combined them with her

love of classical antiquity to produce a kind of Graeco-Turkish dress which is characterised by flowing graceful lines. The fabrics are usually silk gauze or muslin of the sort that ladies of fashion embroidered on the tambour frame (which entered western Europe from the 1760s); in Reynolds's *Waldegrave Sisters* (pl. 73) Anna Horatia is engaged in such a task. So also is the sitter in Kauffman's *Morning Amusement* (*c*.1773; pl. 237). Here the artist has matched the layered look of Turkish costume with the soft fullness both of classical dress and its derivative Neoclassical costume. What we see is a short-sleeved loose white silk robe (perhaps a caftan) embroidered in gold (a modern Greek or Albanian touch), a shorter embroidered gown (?*antery*) and a smock worn over the *shalwar* of embroidered muslin. It was a popular ensemble being

234 F. Cotes, *Elizabeth Gunning, Duchess of Hamilton and Argyll*, 1751. Pastel. National Portrait Gallery, London.

235 (above left) J.-E.
Liotard, *Mary Gunning,
Countess of Coventry, c.*1753–4.
Pastel. Rijksmuseum,
Amsterdam.

236 G. Willison, *Nancy
Parsons, c.*1771. Oil on canvas.
Yale Center for British Art,
New Haven, CT. Paul Mellon
Collection.

both exotic and in line with the new ideas of relaxed informality in portraits; there was also a pleasurable *frisson* of the slightly improper, as the loose trousers were only worn on the stage and in Turkish masquerade costume (in the mid-nineteenth century Amelia Bloomer's knee-length tunic and similar baggy trousers gathered in at the ankle caused a storm of protest). A number of Kauffman's sitters were painted in this stylish outfit comprising a loose caftan-robe (the true Turkish tight-fitting caftan was too structured for late eighteenth-century styles), an underdress and baggy trousers.[110] Poor imitations of Kauffman's Graeco-Turkish costume can be seen in the insipid portraits of Daniel Gardner, where a generalised version of this type of dress mingles unhappily with the influence of Reynolds.

Reynolds exemplifies the ambivalence in English dress as to which sources influence fanciful costume. In France there is a clear dividing line between *turquerie* as manifested in dress (which was a popular theme in portraiture in the middle decades of the eighteenth century), and everyday fashionable wear. In England, as already seen, orientalism in dress was also in vogue, but apart from the obvious depictions

of Turkish fancy dress in portraits, there are more subtle images of women where this may only be one of the elements behind the composition. Aspects of Turkish fancy dress (turbans, sashes, wrapping-gowns, etc.) can mingle with Neoclassical white muslin, with baroque drapery and pearls, and with the red velvet and ermine of noble status. Even gesture in portraiture can be ascribed to a number of sources; for example, the motion of holding up the fabric of the skirt with the hand on the hip is usually regarded as a van Dyckian convention, but it can also be related to the Turkish custom of hitching the caftan up at the side. Reynolds clearly liked this pose for the opportunity it gave him to vary the folds of the drapery, and it can be seen in a number of his portraits. These include *Rebecca, Viscountess Folkestone* (1761; Earl of Radnor), where the sitter's costume is quasi-oriental, with an ermine-lined overgown and a dress that is held up at one side and kept in place with the hand. Almost in spite of himself, Reynolds seems to have been attracted by the luxury and colour of Turkish costume, versions of which appear in his portraits of the 1750s and 1760s. Writing in 1770 to Sir Charles Bunbury about a portrait of the *demi-mondaine* Polly

237 A. Kauffman, *Morning Amusement*, c.1773. Oil on canvas. Private Collection.

Kennedy, Reynolds states that he had finished the face but was perplexed as to the choice of costume; the 'Eastern dresses are very rich and have one sort of dignity, but it is a mock dignity in comparison of the simplicity of the antique'.[111]

From the 1770s, in line with Reynolds's theories on timelessness in dress, nearly all the obvious ele- ments of Turkish dress disappear in his portraits, and his images of women become deliberately generalised, for example *Mrs Carnac* (c.1777; pl. 238), where no single influence predominates. This is the paradigm Reynolds's Grand Style female with beautifully painted head and ultra-fashionable hairstyle, a dispro- portionately long body (not being painted from the

225

gence behind such a handsome portrait; but it is impossible to love such images.

For most people portraits seem to work better when there is a palpable touch of humanity and reality in both sitter and costume. John Singleton Copley's portrait of Mrs Thomas Gage (1771; pl. 239), wife of the commander-in-chief of the British forces in America, is just such an example, where the slightly melancholy and abstracted pose of the sitter is reinforced by a costume that is more fashionably aesthetic than fashionably modish. As with Reynolds, there is a mixture of the seventeenth-century (the loose, wide shift sleeve and pearls as hair and dress decoration), and the oriental (the gauzy, tasselled turban and the wrapping gown with a wide girdle at the waist). But, unlike Reynolds, Copley has based what is probably an invented costume on the reality of a fashionable *déshabillé*, a wonderful vibrant pink wrapping-gown bordered in gold braid. He has given this garment the low, squarish neckline of a Turkish caftan, as in Liotard's *Mary Gunning* and Willison's *Nancy Parsons*, and a wide embroidered belt, quite like the ones they wear but without the characteristic round metal clasps. Reliant at this stage of his career on European sources, Copley weaves them with skill into his portraits. Margaret Gage's pose, her head supported by her arm, is conventional enough (see Gainsborough's *Mrs Thicknesse*, pl. 54, and Liotard's *Mary Gunning*, pl. 235), but Copley focuses attention on the gesture by causing her dark hair, unravelled from its knot or chignon at the back of her head, to fall gracefully over her shoulder.

Compared to the many portraits of Englishwomen in Turkish or quasi-oriental costume, there are relatively few of men, and those that exist mainly record real costumes usually brought back from travel abroad. Reynolds's *Captain John Foote* of c.1761 (York City Art Gallery), for example, is depicted in the embroidered muslin gown, fringed sash and shoulder mantle (or shawl, an item of clothing worn by men), and turban which he brought back with him from India. Part of the costume survives (also at York) – the gown (*jama*) and the waist-sash (*patka*) embroidered with Indo-Persian floral motifs (*buta*) of the kind that decorated the cashmere shawls imported into England from about this time. Such a costume as Captain Foote wears might have been worn at a masquerade,[112] as might the fur-trimmed long gowns worn by European men when travelling in the Near East,[113] and sometimes brought back to England with them. Edward Wortley Montagu, the eccentric son of Lady Mary (he occasionally declared that he was the illegitimate son of the Grand Sultan) adopted Turkish dress while travelling in the East in the 1760s and 1770s, and was painted in oriental costume by Romney and by Matthew William Peters. During his

238 J. Reynolds, *Mrs Carnac,* c.1777. Oil on canvas. Tate Gallery, London.

239 (facing page) J. S. Copley, *Mrs Thomas Gage,* 1771. Oil on canvas. Timken Art Gallery, San Diego.

life), and a white and gold drapery gown of indeterminate fabric. It might just be possible to discern a few faint echoes of *turquerie* in the cross-over gown and the sash at the waist – even the lifted-up overskirt, although that could recall van Dyck, just like the gauzy scarf over her shoulders. It is impossible not to respect the artist's concept and the obvious intelli-

others again were bearing refreshments or perfumes'; one lady in a caftan of gold and silver brocade was dressed as 'the beautiful Fatima described by Lady Mary Wortley Montagu whose authority had been implicitly followed'. The whole *mise-en-scène*, which was supposedly designed by de Loutherbourg, included a tribute to the newly fashionable Egyptian taste in the form of an Egyptian temple, and the host and hostess were 'habited in exact costume as a Moorish prince and princess'.[114]

The Arabian Nights element of the Orient ensured the continued success of eastern themes for entertainment, literature and interior design. With regard to costume in portraiture, it had never been an important motif for the male image (it was too removed from everyday dress) and, as for women, Turkish dress was subsumed into the Neoclassical by the end of the eighteenth-century. New areas of the world and new types of costume attracted the traveller and the artist. In the early nineteenth century, as the Ottoman empire began the gradual crumbling process that was only brought to an end by the First World War, Turkish territories such as Greece and Albania began to interest western Europe. Greece had, of course, engaged the attentions of antiquaries and archeologists throughout the eighteenth century, although it was often difficult to gain access to the sites. By the early nineteenth century English visitors were there in such quantities that a Frenchman remarked, 'there is not a classical nook unexplored by these restless wanderers'.[115] A small but influential number of travellers, however, were as interested in contemporary costume as in ancient dress. These men included *Thomas Hope*, painted by Beechey in 1798 (pl. 240) wearing Albanian or Greek dress – Hope had spent many years travelling in the Levant, Egypt and Greece. His costume comprises a white shirt, one sleeve rolled up to the shoulder, two waistcoats of gold-embroidered velvet,[116] red, baggy trousers worn to just below the knee, a red cloak lined in green and a turban – a dagger thrust through a striped sash at his waist completes this dramatic outfit. Byron, too, was painted in dashing Balkan costume; on his first visit to Greece in 1809 he bought an Albanian costume in which Thomas Phillips painted him in 1813.[117] Such brightly coloured and decorative costumes appealed to the Romantic artist, traveller and poet; like braided uniform, they also served the cause of masculine vanity in an increasingly sober sartorial world.

They were also attractive because of their nationalist implications; the modern imperative, initiated by the French Revolution, was towards liberation, and folk costume (properly speaking, regional costume) was a visible manifestation of national identity (as it remained, far more strongly than anywhere else in Europe, in the countries of the Eastern bloc under

240 W. Beechey, *Thomas Hope*, 1798. Oil on canvas. National Portrait Gallery, London.

oriental travels Edward Montagu amassed a famous collection of manuscripts which helped to inspire the young William Beckford's interest in the East. For his coming-of-age party in 1781 Beckford asked the artist and theatre designer Philippe-Jacques de Loutherbourg to transform Fonthill into a Turkish palace – another example of what Walpole referred to as 'romances', lavish thematic entertainments that had largely replaced the masquerade as a fashionable diversion by the end of the century. Beckford's oriental fantasy may have been the inspiration behind a masquerade described in the novel *A Winter in London* (1806) where the gardens of a grand house became a Turkish seraglio and young ladies 'in the dress of Grecian slaves were scattered in groups, some playing on musical instruments while others danced, and

Soviet rule). On the whole, however, political correctness without a romantic content could never be envisaged for fashionable fancy dress. When the two were combined, as with Hungarian hussar costume, the combination was irresistible. During the War of the Austrian Succession (1740–48) Hungarian hussar regiments (a kind of irregular militia) fought for Austria, Britain's ally during the conflict, and their glamorous uniform soon became familiar to the British people through newspaper accounts, and illustrations; it was a popular masquerade costume, particularly in the middle decades of the eighteenth century, featuring in Jefferys's *Collection of the Dresses* (1757). It figures also in a number of portraits, from the dashing *Lord Ludlow* of 1755 by Reynolds (Woburn Abbey, Beds) in his costume of white silk embroidered in gold, and pelisse lined with ermine; to the double portrait of *Mr and Mrs Ricketts at a Masked Ball at Ranelagh* (1757; private collection) where the couple have just un-masked, he in hussar uniform and she in the popular Rubens-wife dress.[118]

Costume with fur trimming (like hussar uniform) seems to have appealed to the English taste in fancy dress. There may be some deep psychological significance in this (maybe it is the sexuality of fur that is rejected today as well as the immorality of killing animals for their skins – fur has never been taken for granted as one of the luxuries of life in England, as it has in Italy), but the probable reason is that the English were unused to fur in everyday dress, and thus it came to be synonymous with the glamorous and the exotic. Reynolds painted his assistant Giuseppe

Marchi in 1753 (London, Royal Academy of Arts) in what was described as a 'Levant kind of dress', but which is more akin to central European costume (the confusion is understandable, as Turkish influence prevailed over much of this area). Marchi's costume consists of a gown, sashed at the waist, under a crimson coat lined with marten fur and decorated with gold frogging; his turban is composed of entwined silk scarves. Altogether the image is exotic and disturbingly androgynous.

There are a number of other rather mysterious portraits of men wearing fur-trimmed costume that may be remotely related to hussar or central European dress. Joseph Wright's *John Whetham* (*c*.1781–2; Malibu, J. Paul Getty Museum) wears a carefully observed costume of green coat trimmed with fur and a yellow waistcoat with inserted ruched slashes; a fur

242 G. Dawe, *Princess Charlotte*, 1817. Oil on canvas. National Portrait Gallery, London.

241 W. Nicholson, *Self-portrait*, *c*.1810. Oil on canvas. Scottish National Portrait Gallery, Edinburgh.

baldric holds his sword and his green fur-edged hat is not unlike a hussar's busby. Many years later the artist William Allan was painted as a Circassian archer by William Nicholson (Edinburgh, Scottish National Portrait Gallery) in a green coat and a fur-trimmed brown mantle; he cuts a rather romantic Byronic figure with his open shirt collar and knotted silk scarf. Allan had spent the years 1805–14 in Russia and brought back to Britain some Russian and Circassian costume which he lent to friends and which features in his painting.

Countries on the fringe of Europe, such as the vast Russian empire, had been brought into the centre of international politics through the web of alliances ranged against Napoleon, so by the end of the Napoleonic wars, Russian themes were *à la mode*. The vogue for 'cossack' trousers in men's fashion has already been noted (see Chapter 2), and for women the sleeveless high-waisted Russian *sarafan* was both picturesque and in harmony with the lines of contemporary dress. The rather hoydenish Princess Charlotte (described by a contemporary as a good humoured white fat girl) in her portrait by George Dawe (1817; pl. 242), is quite dignified in her Russian dress, which is also intended as a tribute to Tsar Alexander I, under whom her husband, Leopold of Saxe-Coburg-Gotha, had served; the star on her breast is that of the order of St Catherine of Russia. The dress she wears is a blue *sarafan* trimmed with braid (it is in the collection of the Museum of London) over a lace bodice; the sleeves, held together with pearl clasps, are made of fine silk blonde lace.

In spite of the attraction that remote lands and exotic places had for the Romantic spirit in the early nineteenth century, it was the passion for the historical in England that remained a constant factor in the arts. Sir Walter Scott's novels – which Hazlitt noted were based on fact, the author being 'the amanuensis of truth and history' – fed an appetite for nostalgia which was fuelled partly by a reaction against the political disruption caused by the French Revolution and wars and also by dismay among the more perceptive at the possible long-term social and cultural impact of the industrial changes. 'The taste of the times', claimed the advertisement to the third volume of the *Antiquarian Repertory* (1807–9) 'is the study and love of the writings of those who have long since been numbered with their fathers'. As historical revivalism permeated literature – even the costume historian Joseph Strutt late in life began a novel, a virtually unreadable work set in the reign of Henry VI and called *Queenhoo Hall*[119] – so it continued to affect portraiture, albeit on a smaller scale than in the eighteenth century. It still attracted artists, particularly those bored with the flat, unbroken surface of modern dress, who wished for something more dramatic, es-

pecially in self-portraits. William Nicholson painted himself in about 1810 (pl. 241) in a slashed black doublet with a high collar, tying with tassels at the front; a slightly crumpled white linen collar in the seventeenth-century Spanish style adds dramatic interest to the portrait and highlights the face with its direct challenging look and tousled short hair arranged in a fashionable style with side-burns.

Seventeenth-century dress styles, however, were less in vogue than was that of the Elizabethan period, which seemed to the early nineteenth century to be a more colourful and chivalrous period; it also, unconsciously, suited the fashion aesthetic of the time, which was based on a tight-fitting covering for the torso and an emphasis on the unbroken line of the legs. Thus, the high-collared late sixteenth-century doublet and short trunk hose could – very roughly – be approximated to the early nineteenth-century tight-fitting coat, and the Elizabethan hose could be equated with late Georgian pantaloons or trousers. Cosway's *Charles, 4th Earl of Harrington, with his Dog, Peter* of c.1805 (pl. 243) gives some idea of the elegant and romanticised view of Elizabethan costume that was to inform the coronation of George IV in 1821. Cosway gives his sitter a van Dyckian pose, but the dress, with its short-waisted slashed doublet and round trunk hose over tights, is more akin to that worn by beautiful Elizabethan courtiers in Hilliard miniatures of the 1580s.

Cosway's interest in fashion, both contemporary and historic, has already been noted, apropos of his *Self-portrait with his Wife, Maria* of 1784 (pl. 207), where the couple's dress is inspired by Rubens. Appointed Principal Painter to the Prince of Wales in 1785, Cosway's responsibilities included not just portraying the Prince and his circle, but surveying his collections. The artist was a collector of antiques, art, antiquarian relics and armour, and his taste influenced his patron's wide-ranging interests in the fine and applied arts.[120] In Pierce Egan's Regency travelogue *Life in London* (1821) Tom and Jerry visit Carlton House to see the Prince's collections of 'innumerable curiosities... boots and spurs from the time of Charles I... caps, turbans, shields, bows, dresses &c of the inhabitants of the southern hemisphere... armour & costume of the late Tippoo Saib... a Persian war dress... the war-dress of a Chinese Tartar...'[121]

The Prince of Wales's accounts from the 1780s indicate his fascination with fancy dress for masquerades and private theatricals; he orders 'fine Turkish Heron Feathers' (1786), a friar's dress with 'fine pink Silk Hose, extra long' and sandals (1802), 'a Henry 5th dress Richly Trim'd with gold Loops, Tassells & Bullions' and a scarlet 'Leontes dress Richly Trim'd with silver Spangles & Edged with Blue Velvit'

(1802), a 'Henry IV's dress in white sattin', a ghost's dress, a Sultan's dress, a 'Scelleton's' dress (?1804) and so on.[122] He was particularly interested in the romance of things Scottish, a preoccupation that lasted over many years and culminated in his visit to Scotland in 1822, orchestrated by Sir Walter Scott; on that occasion the King famously wore Highland dress, whose flowing drapery (in the form of the plaid) and general flamboyance appealed to his sense of theatre and of history, although the latter was surrounded as much with myth as fact.[123] The romantic failure of the Jacobite Rebellion of 1745 which resulted in the proscription of the kilt and plaid, excited considerable interest in Scottish culture in England and a fascination with Highland dress – the English, unique among European peoples, had no national costume and virtually nothing in the way of regional dress. The Prince of Wales's accounts show his interest as a young man in Scottish dress. In June 1789 they record the purchase of 'a Rich embroiderd Scotch Bonnet' and 'a Belted Kilt, Plaid Coat, Waistcoat'; this outfit he wore as a 'Highland Cheif' at a masquerade that same month.[124] In 1806 the Prince ordered a 'Tartan Masquerade Jacket, lin'd with green Sarsnet, green Velvet Cuffs and Collar, and 30 open work'd and studded Silver Buttons'; also some black feathers for a bonnet.[125]

All the Prince's love of fancy dress and theatre, his knowledge of art and connoisseurship and his appreciation of luxury and splendour, culminated in the lavish and elaborate pageantry of his coronation, the most expensive ever to have taken place in the country;[126] the greater part of the money came from the financial indemnity which the defeated French had to pay after the battle of Waterloo. It was thus all the more ironic that George IV – whom Talleyrand rightly saw as 'un roi grand seigneur' – was inspired by the coronations of the Bourbon kings of France and of Napoleon to create his own magnificent ceremonial which was also to be animated by a sense of the historic – specifically Elizabethan – past. It was also intended – and in this it amply succeeded – to far outshine the rather subfusc affair of his father's coronation in 1761, although, of course, the ritual and religious ceremonies remained the same.

Originally planned for the summer of 1820, the coronation was postponed for a year while the authorities wondered how to cope with the King's estranged wife Caroline of Brunswick, who had returned from racketting around Europe to claim her right to be crowned Queen and who had attracted a certain amount of public sympathy. Adverse publicity (aided by vicious caricatures) about his private life had ensured that the Prince of Wales's stock with his people had never been high; this was not to improve during the Regency when many could be found who

243 R. Cosway, *Charles, 4th Earl of Harrington, with his Dog, Peter*, c.1805. Pencil. The Trustees, The Cecil Higgins Art Gallery, Bedford.

might concur with William Hone's famous satire (after the 'massacre of Peterloo' in 1819[127]) in which the Prince is thus anathematised:

This is the Man – all shaven and shorn,
All cover'd with Orders – and all folorn;
The Dandy of Sixty, who bows with a grace,
And has taste in wigs, collars, cuirasses and lace . . .

('cuirasses' are corsets, a palpable hit at the Regent's *embonpoint*, which had to be controlled in this way).

George IV was not the first monarch who hoped to distract public attention by lavish display, and it was hoped that the coronation might restore the esteem of the people. The King threw himself with enthusiasm into the task of planning the details and in particular the design of the costume of all the participants. As one recent writer on the coronation remarks, George IV's 'delight in the unusual and exotic, his interest in the visual coherence imposed by uniform, and his pleasure in masquerades and fancy dress, should perhaps have prepared the world for an unexpected style of coronation dress'.[128] The choice of Elizabethan costume as the inspiration behind such dress gave the

244 J. P. Stephanoff (after), 'The King – His Train Borne by Eight Eldest Sons of Peers', from John Whittaker, *The Coronation of George the Fourth*, 1821–41. Hand-coloured stipple and line engraving Yale Center for British Art, New Haven, CT. Paul Mellon Collection.

processions and ceremonies the kind of visual unity that had been lacking at previous coronations. George IV's coronation on 19 July 1821 was the apotheosis of the romance of the past; it has been described as 'a gigantic fancy-dress pageant on the theme of the Faerie Queene, in which George IV played the part of a male Gloriana'.[129]

The proceedings, which took nine hours in all, began with the assembly of the coronation procession in Westminster Hall (given extra 'Gothic' imagery in the form of arches, pillars and suitable furniture), watched by such privileged spectators as the royal ladies 'attired in the most splendid dresses of white satin richly embroidered in silver, with rich bandeau head-dresses, and large plumes of white feathers', foreign ambassadors and their suites 'chiefly habited in military costume ... and profusely decorated with orders of honor' and dignitaries and courtiers in full dress.[130] The court pages wore what Sir Walter Scott described as 'Henri Quatre coats of scarlet with gold lace, blue sashes, white silk hose and white rosettes'.[131]

The basic design of the costume of the main participants was a doublet and matching round breeches (trunk hose) of silk trimmed with gold braid, a short cloak (except for the peers and members of the knightly orders who wore their traditional long mantles), a ruff, white stockings and shoes with rosettes; variations in colour differentiated one group from another, but the overall conception was red, blue, white and gold. The King's costume was the most splendid of all, and so heavy that he almost fainted (being also tightly corsetted) in the heat of Westminster Abbey; the train required eight bearers, instead of the usual six. The illustration from John Whittaker's de luxe edition of *The Coronation of George the Fourth* (pl. 244) shows the King with his train supported by eight eldest sons of peers, who wear their Elizabethan costume and Henry IV plumed hats. George IV's costume, which can hardly be seen under the vast coronation mantle, was a silver tissue doublet and trunk hose under a surcoat of crimson velvet. One contemporary account noted that the

245   T. Lawrence, *George IV*,
1821. Oil on canvas. The
Royal Collection, © 1994 her
Majesty Queen Elizabeth II.

King was 'habited in full robes of great size and richness, and wore a black hat or cap of Spanish shape, with a spreading plume of white ostrich feathers which encircled the rim, and was surmounted by a fine heron's plume. The King wore his hair in thick falling curls over his forehead and it fell behind the head in similar form'.[132] In Whittaker's illustration the King's curled peruke is clearly shown; he had begun to wear false hair in the 1790s and by the time of the coronation he was ordering hair by the yard.[133] Inordinately vain of his appearance and his public image in portraits, he wished to be painted not just as the 'first gentleman in Europe' but as 'un roi grand seigneur' in the style of Louis XIV. Lawrence was the perfect artist to produce this kind of regal grandeur, although he was sometimes lectured about flattering his royal patron with excessive enthusiasm. *The Times* ticked Lawrence off for making the Regent look a 'foppish youth' and Hazlitt remarked that the artist had accomplished on canvas more than 'wigs, powders and pomatums have been able to effect for the last twenty years'.[134] Certainly Lawrence's portrait of *George IV in Coronation Robes* (pl. 245) grossly flatters the appearance of the King, making him look twenty years younger than his real age. The coronation costume creates an image of elephantine splendour – the artist Benjamin Haydon thought him 'like some gorgeous bird of the East' – and is dominated by the huge ermine-lined mantle over which are displayed the collars (in order of descent) of the Golden Fleece, the Guelphic Order, the Bath and the Garter; the heavily embroidered velvet mantle still exists (owned by Madame Tussaud's), an incredibly sumptuous and weighty garment.[135]

After the high drama of the King's appearance in Westminster Hall in this wonderfully rich and theatrical costume, the rest of the proceedings must almost have been an anti-climax. The procession was led to the Abbey by the 'herb-women' (their office, dating from the time of Charles I, was to keep the royal apartments strewn with herbs and flowers – they made their last appearance at the coronation of George IV); in keeping with the historical theme of the ceremony, they wore white dresses with standing Medici collars and they scattered 'choice flowers' along the route. For the actual coronation service the King wore the traditional supertunica of cloth of gold and a matching dalmatic lined with ermine; afterwards the newly crowned monarch, dressed in royal purple velvet, came back to Westminster Hall where the coronation banquet was to take place as well as the presentation of gifts and the dramatic challenge of the King's Champion, a tradition dating from the late Middle Ages.

Altogether the coronation as conceived by George IV – the undoubted star of a glittering spectacle – blended real traditions with some newly minted, such as the 'Renaissance' costume. The author of *A Brief Account of the Coronation of His Majesty George IV* (1821) was not alone in admiring the 'solemn order, the variegated costume, and the excessive richness of the several parts of this splendid Procession' [which] 'conveyed to the mind an idea of all that was brilliant in feudal grandeur and superb in chivalry'; even the spectators, 'chiefly females, reminded us of the days of jousts and tournaments'.[136] The historical *mise-en-scène*, typified by the unity of the Elizabethan-inspired costume, attracted much approval. Sir Walter Scott remarked:

> Separately, so gay a garb had an odd effect on the persons of elderly or ill-made men; but when the whole was thrown into one general body, all these discrepancies disappeared . . . The whole was so completely harmonized in actual colouring, as well as in association with the general mass of gay and gorgeous and antique dress which floated before the eye . . .[137]

It was like a vast history painting which had come to life – a tableau vivant romancing the past.

Afterword

D ress is not a profound art. It is functional and it can delight the senses, but in itself it cannot express the complex human emotions that are revealed in such arts as literature, music and painting. No one would disagree with Hazlitt in his judgement that 'those who make their dress a principal part of themselves, will, in general, become of no more value than their dress'. It is easy to laugh at clothing that to our eyes looks grotesque and vulgar, and distorts the shape of the body; what we are criticising, of course, is not the dress itself, which is inanimate, but those who wear it and what we think it signifies about them – we make value judgements largely based on visual evidence. Dress can become a laughing matter when we think it departs from a sense of harmony and proportion, when we feel it becomes exaggerated and no longer related to the natural shape; this is true of certain periods in the history of dress when artifice prevails over 'classical' restraint. 'Du sublime au ridicule, il n'y a qu'un pas' was Napoleon's comment on the retreat from Moscow, but what can apply to the rapid changes of Fortune's wheel in politics can equally be relevant to costume as when, over a short period of time, the supremely elegant styles of the last years of the *ancien régime* became – under the disintegrating forces of the French Revolution – the caricatured extremes of the costume of the *incroyables* and the revealing toilettes of the *merveilleuses*. In a period of volatile political upheaval, with explicit and implicit rules about dress and manners discarded, it was perhaps natural that critics focused on such a visible sign of the times; clothing was in many ways the visualisation of political concepts and social change. Delécluze was right to point out that costume was 'un objet sérieux d'études', because 'il précède ordinairement un changement ou au moins une modification importante dans les moeurs'.[1] As has been seen, in the decade leading up to the Revolution dress was becoming simpler and more 'democratic', a tendency that political events furthered, not just in France but all over Europe. In the same way, in the early nineteenth century contemporaries noted that fashion was beginning to move from its self-denying ordinances, from its politically motivated austerity, towards greater luxury – particularly with regard to women's dress – which indicated a general revival in the fortunes of monarchy, a tendency to be confirmed by the post-Napoleonic peace congresses.

However, intelligent men and women were aware that new political ideals and the consequent years of European war had created a very different society from that of the eighteenth century. Lady Susan O'Brien, writing in her old age, recalled the changes between 1760, when 'great civility was general in all ranks', and 1818, when she discerned 'a certain rudeness or carelessness of manners affected both by men and women'; as to politics, 'the topic is become universal'.[2] How familiar this lament would be to people who had lived through any tumultuous event in history that seemed to create a sharp break with the reassurance of the past. Such a brave new world could appear so contemptuously dismissive of the complicated apparatus of etiquette, manners and dress which had evolved over a long period of time. The change from the stylish certainties of the *ancien régime* to the brashness of post-revolutionary society must have seemed startling and unnerving, particularly when coupled with the longer-term economic and social upheavals of what was beginning to be perceived by the end of the period as an industrial revolution. Taking the place of the unspoken sumptuary rules of the eighteenth century, based on a seemingly immutable system of privilege and luxury, was a new sartorial language (particularly for men), in which the worlds of ability (of all kinds) and industry were reflected. In France dress became politicised through symbolic affiliations; the State made use of costume both as propaganda and to reinforce its identity and authority in a more obvious way than had been the case before. Politics also served to make dress more 'modern', to make it relevant to a society where the *leitmotif* seemed to be constant change.

The inter-relationship between dress and art has been one of the themes in this book; their elective affinities – a mutual necessity and attraction – have been reinforced not least because both communicate by sight. Walter Vaughan pointed out in his *Essay Philosophical* (1792) that artists would 'agree that the Excellence of a Picture or Statue is more certainly proved by the Impression it makes upon the Senses than by comparing its several Dimensions'.[3] So with dress, it is through the senses, especially sight with all its interpretative connotations, that we perceive and appreciate it, rather than through the craft of its construction. A portrait represents the joint contributions of artist, sitter and costume; in this context clothes can reveal character, both heroic and mundane, and all the frailities of human nature, including vanity and pretention. A painting can take the form of an almost photographic record of the person, warts and all, with minute attention to the details of the costume, or it can be a more subtle concept in which, in the words of Fuseli, 'Historic Invention administers to Truth', that is, where the artist uses his poetic imagination rather than sticking to the reality of facts. Of course the society artist had often to compromise – flattering his clients without being too obsequiously far from the truth. When, in Venice in 1750, Nattier was asked by Casanova how he managed to make the plain Mesdames de France (the daughters of Louis XV) look like Aspasias (the beautiful mistress of Pericles), the artist replied, 'c'est une magie que le dieu de goût fait passer de mon esprit au bout de mes pinceaux'.[4]

Good taste (however defined) and the importance of rules in art contributed to the conformity of much eighteenth-century portraiture; where dress was concerned it proved quite difficult to meet the expectations of critics that the general idea should be incorporated with the particular to bring out the individuality of the sitter. When, by the early nineteenth century, the stranglehold of fanciful dress in portraits – for example, Nattier's royal and noble patrons in mythological guise, Hudson's solid English gentry as van Dyckian courtiers and Reynolds's ladies in their 'timeless' draperies – had been largely discarded, it became easier to concentrate on the character of the sitter, something facilitated by simpler styles of dress for men and women.

This book should end with a confession of sins of omission. Apart from the self-evident fact that the topic chosen is vast (my excuse would be that I have dealt with various aspects of the dress of this period elsewhere and from a somewhat different angle), I am particularly conscious that I have tended to concentrate on portraiture to the exclusion of much history painting that merits discussion from the point of view of dress. There is also a danger, at times, of treating artists as though they are being deliberately wilful in their neglect of accurate costume in history painting in particular, but also with regard to fashionable portraiture in general. *Mea culpa*. Part of the problem arises from the limited information available on the preparations and intentions of artists, and on the contribution made by their sitters to the dress in a painting.

My intention has been to try and analyse a range of works of art by looking at the different ways in which dress is depicted; 'without truth of costume', claimed Thomas Hope, 'the story cannot be clearly told . . . the picture must ever remain a riddle'.[5] While telling the story of dress, albeit in a simplified form with the image as the starting point, this book is mainly designed to aid the understanding and appreciation of costume in art, to further what Ramsay in his *Dialogue on Taste* (1755) calls, 'the discovery of truth and the just relation of things'.

Notes

Introduction

1. Vaughan (1792), p. 23.
2. Wollstonecraft (1792), p. 220.
3. The same theme occurs in Rowlandson's series *The Dance of Death*, 1814–16 (San Marino, CA, Huntington Art Gallery).
4. Vaughan (1792), p. 6. One of the few specific reforms which he advocates is the wearing of wool next to the skin, because it 'defends the body from excessive heat and cold'; he thus anticipated a similar proposal by the dress reformer, Dr Gustave Jaeger, in the late nineteenth century.
5. B.-C. Faust, *Sur le Vêtement libre, unique et national à l'usage des enfants*, Paris, 1792, pp. 1–2; quoted in Perot (1984).
6. From Rousseau's *Emile* (1762); quoted in Roche, 1989, p. 382. See also Vaughan. (1792): 'The plain Truth is, that Refinement teaches Men to dislike every Thing natural, fits them only to disguise, and disqualifies them for assuming with a manly and a liberal Air that Character which alone is truly great' (p. 29).
7. Mercier (1782–8), VII, p. 163.
8. *Holland House Papers*, British Museum, Add. MS. 51353, fol. 106v; letter from Lady Sarah Lennox to Lady Susan Strangways, 6 Feb. 1766. A pelisse in the eighteenth century was a fur-lined gown or mantle.
9. Charlton (1984), p. 155. When John Villiers visited Rousseau's tomb, which was designed by Hubert Robert, he described the sculpted imagery as '. . . a female sitting beneath a palm-tree, suckling her infant . . . on an altar before the statue of Nature is described a group of females sacrificing. A child appears to be setting fire to a heap of swaddling clothes, and bandages, whilst others are dancing round with the staff and cap of liberty'. See Villiers (1789), p. 234. See also F.A. de Boissy d'Anglas, *Quelques idées sur les arts*, 1794, in which the author suggests to the Committee of Public Instruction some ideas for national fêtes, including Rousseau among a group of mothers and children, telling the world about real liberty (p. 22).
10. Villiers (1789), pp. 214–15.
11. Bergeret (1848), p. 164.
12. Carlyle (1984), p. 181.
13. Hollander (1978), pp. 454, 452.
14. Carlyle (1984), p. 26.
15. Barker (?1780), pp. 52–3.
16. Goethe (1971), p. 164.
17. Baudelaire (1965), p. 190.
18. Combe (1777), p. 1.
19. Fuseli (1820), p. 177.
20. E. Wharton, *The Custom of the Country*, Harmondsworth, 1987, p. 112.
21. Goethe (1971), p. 159.
22. R. Campbell, *The London Tradesman*, London, 1747, p. 101.
23. Vertue (1933–4), p. 117.
24. Walpole (1888), II, p. 323. Vertue (1933–4), p. 121, notes that Hudson's portraits were 'dressd and decorated by Mr. Joseph van Aken'.
25. This pose and costume is derived from a drawing attributed to Joseph van Aken (Edinburgh, National Gallery of Scotland); the dress is a mixture of the fashionable with touches of the Vandyke, and the pose comes from Kneller's *Countess of Ranelagh* (Hampton Court Palace).
26. D. Hudson, *Sir Joshua Reynolds*, London, 1958, p. 53.
27. Whitley (1928b), quotes from a newspaper of 1766 discussing the continuation of the practice, and implying that the public are being tricked into paying for a portrait in which only the head is executed by the commissioned artist and the rest 'is generally the production of indigent excellence' (I, p. 219).
28. Whitley (1928b), I, p. 280.
29. There is a set of men's clothes from the mid-eighteenth century, including a brown coat and breeches lined with salmon-pink silk, a red wool coat trimmed with metal braid and a linen frock which has been altered probably in the 1790s. The woman's dress includes a brown linen gown, a corset, a red hooded cloak and two straw hats.
30. Hardly anything is known about this artist, except that she was apparently a pupil of the Dutch painter Jan van Rijmsdijk, who specialised in natural history drawings and who worked for the anatomist William Hunter. She exhibited at the Royal Academy in 1776, two works (one watercolour) of shells.
31. Paris (1984), p. 391.
32. Whitley (1928b), II, p. 292.
33. *The Artist's Repository and Drawing Magazine*, London, 1784–6, p. 84.
34. Ibid., p. 87.
35. Smart (1992b), p. 92.
36. Walpole (1937–83), XL, p. 370.
37. Ingres's drawing of Madame Destouches of 1816 (Paris, Louvre), for example, shows her with a feathered hat similar to one illustrated in the most fashionable journal for women, the *Journal des dames et des modes*, but the artist has turned it round slightly and made it taller. See Delpierre (1975), p. 151.
38. M. Proust, *Remembrance of Things Past*, trans. C.K. Scott and T. Kilmartin, London, 1981, I, pp. 920–21.
39. Hickey (1960), pp. 346–7.
40. Newdigate-Newdegate (1898), pp. 101–2; the Cheverels were characters based on Sir Roger and Lady Newdigate at Arbury Hall in George Eliot's *Scenes from Clerical Life* (1858).
41. *The Jerningham Letters: 1780–1843*, ed. E. Castle, 2 vols., 1896, I, p. 194.
42. Romney's Sitter Book (London, National Portrait Gallery Archives) has a few references to dress, but nothing very explicit. For example, on 26 May 1788 there is a note that 'Lady Langham desires that her Picture may be Painted in White Drapery some Impliments of Drawing introdused in the Back Ground'; on 10 June 1790 'Mrs Stephenson called desires her Pictures may be finished directly for she wants her dress' (pp. 7, 27). There are also some references to the collection and dispatch of official and occupational costume such as Garter robes, clerical vestments, etc. There is even less information in Joseph Wright's Sitter Book, also at the NPG Archives; there are a few references to the use of outside drapery painters, but the main notes on clothes concern the artist's own wardrobe and his 'hair curling'.
43. The painting from Dunbrody was offered for sale at Christie's, London, 22 April 1983, lot 83. The original, unaltered portrait by Cotes is in the National Gallery of Ireland, Dublin.
44. S. Sontag, ed., *A Barthes Reader*, London, 1982, p. xxvi.
45. Hazlitt (1843), p. 212. Baudelaire (1965), p. 190.
46. Vigée-Lebrun (1926), p. 44.
47. Roche (1989), notes that the majority of the entries on dress were written or edited by Diderot and the chevalier de Jaucourt (p. 417).
48. Diderot (1975–83), III, p. 219.
49. Quoted in Crow (1988), p. 21.
50. Diderot (1955), p. 60.
51. Quoted in Roche (1989), p. 428.
52. Diderot (1975–83), pp. 66–7.
53. See Charlton (1984), pp. 109–13, for a discussion of the concept of the noble savage apropos the discovery of Tahiti in the later 1760s, which – through the glowing account of this 'nouvelle Cythère' by Louis-Antoine de Bougainville – became held up as a 'model of Rousseauist natural society'. See also Boswell's attack on the fad for the simple life *pace* Rousseau, in his essay 'On Savages and the Mode', *London Magazine*, no. XX, 1779.
54. Hogarth (1955), p. 51. In one of the rejected passages of the *Analysis of Beauty*, however, Hogarth argues against taking the three-dimensional aspect of the rococo styles to extremes, whereby the dress is 'cut or devited into many little patches and bits like the old fashion falbelowd and flounced petticoats', and becomes 'raggs and Tatters' (p. 175).
55. Hogarth (1955), pp. 65–6.
56. Ramsay (1762), p. 21.
57. Ibid., p. 64.
58. Ibid., p. 35.
59. Boswell (1928), II, p. 11.
60. Alison (1790), p. 196.
61. Farington (1978–84), V, p. 1898.
62. David's pupil, Gérard, had to sit on a wooden horse in the studio, in order to aid the artist in his depiction of Napoleon on horseback. From Napoleon's valet Constant, David also borrowed his master's hat

and boots. Delécluze (1863), noted that David tried on Napoleon's hat and it was so large it came down to his eyes (p. 237).

63. Miette de Villars (1850), pp. 38–9.
64. Bryson (1984), p. 124.
65. Toussaint (1985), p. 8.
66. Richardson (1725), p. 194.
67. Ibid., p. 193.
68. Hogarth (1955), p. 174. Walpole claimed the practice of drapery painting arose because the dress of the early eighteenth century was so 'barbarous', artists 'clothed all their personages with a loose drapery and airy mantles, which not only were not, but could not be the dress of any age or nation, so little were they adapted to cover the limbs, to exhibit any form, or to adhere to the person, which they scarce enveloped, and for which they must fall on the least motion . . .' (1888, II, p. 260).
69. O. Goldsmith, The Vicar of Wakefield, London, 1766, p. 121.
70. Reynolds's Sitter Books (London, Royal Academy of Arts) do not reveal much about clothes, except for the occasional reference to drapery painters; these are usually un-named, although Peter Toms (who worked for Reynolds from the mid-1750s) is mentioned. There are a few references to costume in the Sitter Books, but these are not very informative, being in a form of shorthand and often indecipherable. More information can be gleaned from a book of memoranda kept by Reynolds, probably in the 1760s (private collection) where there are some notes on dress, particularly for men's portraits, and even sketches of such details as button-holes.
71. Reynolds (1975), p. 88.
72. Ibid., p. 62.
73. Conversations of James Northcote RA with James Ward on Art and Artists, London 1901, p. 211.
74. Leslie and Taylor (1865), I, p. 248.
75. Hazlitt (1843), pp. 202–3.
76. J. Dallaway, Anecdotes of the Arts in England, 2 vols, London, 1800, II, p. 478 – a manuscript note (New Haven, CT, Yale Center for British Art).
77. Woodall (1963), pp. 49–52.
78. 'Observations on the Pictures now exhibiting at the Royal Academy', 1771; quoted in W.T. Whitley, Thomas Gainsborough, London, 1915, p. 77.
79. Leslie and Taylor (1865), I, p. 249. Gainsborough was dismissive on the subject of drapery painters, although some of his portraits of the 1770s and 1780s do look so generalised that it is possible he may have used their services (as well as those of his nephew Gainsborough Dupont) to cope with the demands of his studio at the peak of his career. Payments are recorded in 1776 to the drapery painter Peter Toms (J. Hayes, Gainsborough, London, 1975, p. 27).
80. Romney (1830), pp. 195–6. Romney's Notebooks (London, Victoria and Albert Museum) include a few references to the artist's mixing of fashionable items of dress with more generalised draperies.
81. MS notes for Reynolds' Tenth Discourse, quoted in Barrell (1986), pp. 154–5.
82. Quoted in Pupil (1985), p. 380.
83. Artists on Art, compiled by R. Goldwater and M. Treves, London, 1985, p. 196.
84. Farington (1978–84), II, pp. 369–70.
85. J. Carter, 'Specimens of the Civil and Military Costume of England from the remotest period to the Eighteenth Century', 1809–11, British Museum Add. MSS 27322, fol. 9.
86. Irwin (1966), pp. 66, 68.
87. J. Dallaway, Of Statuary and Sculpture among the Antients, London, 1816, p. 131.
88. Knight (1805), pp. 5, 432.
89. Démeunier (1776), II, p. 207.
90. Boswell (1928), I, p. 161.

91. Ségur (1803), III, p. 4.
92. Quoted in Castle (1986), p. 319.
93. Rev. E. Stanley, Before and after Waterloo, ed. J.H. Adeane and M. Grenfell, London, 1907, p. 306.
94. See Black (1986).
95. See B. Behlen, 'Some Aspects of Dress in Germany 1791–1811 as Reflected in Two Contemporary Magazines', MA Report, London, Courtauld Institute of Art, 1991.
96. Delany (1861–2), III, p. 582.
97. However, Jane Austen's letters to her sister Cassandra, do refer quite a lot to fashion. See P. Byrde, A Frivolous Distinction. Fashion and Needlework in the Works of Jane Austen, Bath, 1979.
98. See Madame de Genlis, Dictionnaire critique et raisonné des etiquettes de la cour et des usages du monde, Paris, 1818.
99. Scott (1815), p. 176. English visitors noted that compared to the relative homogeneity in dress seen in London, a far greater variety was to be observed in the dress of the inhabitants of Paris: not just the more marked difference between the classes, but a range of provincial costumes that contrasted with the latest fashions of the capital. Stevenson (1817), remarked that a 'promenade through the streets of Paris [is] a source of perpetual amusement to the observant stranger. The newest stile of dress and the most antiquated cut may often be seen passing each other without the least surprise . . . In the public walks and museums . . . it is curious to mark the transition of costume from the latest nouveauté des modes displayed by le bon genre of the metropolis, down to the provincial peculiarity of the gens de peuple' (p. 231).
100. Roche (1989), p. 30.
101. A.D. Smith, '"The Historical Revival" in Late 18th-century England and France', Art History, II, no. 2, 1979, pp. 156–72.

1 The Fabric of Society

1. See Ribeiro (1984a), p. 17.
2. Thicknesse (1768), p. 67.
3. Andrews (1770), I, p. 63.
4. Ibid., p. 65.
5. Thicknesse (1770), II, p. 230, and (1766), p. 25.
6. Andrews (1770), I, p. 68.
7. Walpole (1937–83), XXXVIII, p. 237.
8. Thicknesse (1770), II, p. 155.
9. Almanach Dansant . . . , by 'Guillaume, Maître de Danse', Paris, 1770, p. 10. The simplicity and harmony of Nature was supposedly the inspiration behind dancing, just as 'the painter draws or ought to draw his copy, the actor his action, and the statuary his model, all from the truth of nature' (G.A. Gallini, A Treatise on the Art of Dancing, London, 1762, p. 146).
10. Andrews (1770), I, p. 84.
11. Chaussinard-Nogaret (1985), p. 2.
12. Elias (1983), p. 55.
13. N. Forster, An Enquiry into the Causes of the Present High Prices of Provisions, London, 1767, p. 41.
14. Vane (1753), suggested that 'the lower orders of the people' ought not to be 'permitted to wear gold or silver lace, or embroidery in gold or silver on their cloaths, or upon their hats' (pp. 121–4).
15. Wendeborn (1791), I, pp. 265–6.
16. Ibid., pp. 224–5.
17. P. Earle, The Making of the English Middle Class, London, 1989, p. 10. The term 'middle class' is difficult to define due to the complex social structure of England; it could include at one extreme the gentry and at the other the ambitious artisan or shopkeeper who aspired to a middle-class way of life. Earle estimates that about a quarter of the population of London in the early eighteenth-century

could be described as middle class.
18. Walpole (1937–83), XXXVIII, p. 2.
19. Cole (1931), pp. 345–6. Umbrellas were regarded as an effeminate novelty in England until the later eighteenth century, in spite of the brave attempts by the philanthropist Jonas Hanway to popularise their use. See A. Ribeiro, 'Men and Umbrellas in the Eighteenth Century', Journal of the Royal Society of Arts, CXXXIV, no. 5362, 1986, pp. 653–6.
20. Romney's Journal/Notebook (New Haven, CT, Yale Center for British Art), fols. 2 and 72. 'In England a man who wears a Muff is looked upon as an effeminate coxcomb . . .' states Samuel Johnson, nephew to Sir Joshua Reynolds (Sir Joshua's Nephew, Being Letters Written 1760–1775 by a Young Man to his Sisters, ed. S.M. Radcliffe, London, 1930, p. 96).
21. Mercier (1982), p. 61. The word 'bourse' here means the black silk bag into which the hair or wig is gathered at the back of the head in formal dress.
22. The Gentleman's Guide in His Tour through France, Bristol, c.1768, pp. 11–12, 109.
23. H. Decremps, Le Parisien à Londres, ou avis aux français qui vont en Angleterre, 2 Parts, Amsterdam, 1789, I, pp. 89–91.
24. Rigoley de Juvigny (1787), p. 465.
25. Black (1986), p. 176.
26. L. Sterne, A Sentimental Journey, ed. and intr. J. Sack, Oxford, 1972, p. 49. A similar theme occurs in Samuel Foote's play The Englishman in Paris, 1753, where a French perruquier states: '. . . a Perruque is a different Ouvrage, another sort of Thing here, from what it is en Angleterre; we must consult the Colour of the Complexion, and the Tour de Visage, the Form of the Face . . .' (I, i, p. 18).
27. Stendhal, Histoire de la peinture en Italie, 2 vols, Paris, 1817, II, p. 415.
28. Quoted in Roche (1989), p. 269. Roche notes that in the Encyclopédie there are 241 articles on textiles compared to 63 on fashions (p. 417).
29. Encyclopédie, ou dictionnaire raisonné des sciences, des arts et des métiers, Paris, 1762–72, XI, p. 266.
30. See M. Schoeser, 'The Barbier Manuscripts', Textile History, XII, 1981, pp. 37–58.
31. F.-A. de Garsault, L'Art du tailleur, Paris, 1769, p. 9.
32. Most of the examples of British sitters in portraits wearing fur relate to their foreign travels. A particularly sumptuous outfit is worn by Lord Mountstuart in a portrait by Liotard of 1763 (Scotland, private collection); it consists of a turquoise silk suit lined with grey squirrel. The portrait was painted while Lord Mountstuart was on the Grand Tour. See A. Ribeiro, 'Furs in Fashion. The Eighteenth and Early Nineteenth Centuries, Connoisseur, CCII, no. 804 (1979), pp. 226–31,' There are a considerable number of depictions of Frenchmen wearing silk suits trimmed or lined with fur. These include Louis Tocqué's Marquis de Marigny, 1755 (Château de Versailles), in a coat trimmed with sable, and Greuze's Comte d'Angiviller (1763; New York, Metropolitan Museum of Art), in a silk coat with elaborate frogged tassels and lined with fur. By the 1780s large fur muffs for men were in vogue in England. The Prince of Wales's Accounts (Windsor, Royal Archives) list black and blue fox and black bear (1785) and a 'fox Muff stuffed with Eiderdown' (1786).
33. See A. Ribeiro, 'The Macaronis', History Today, XXVIII, no. 7, 1978, pp. 463–8.
34. Fashion. A Poem, London, 1775, p. 20.
35. Hickey (1913), II, pp. 260–61.
36. See F. Cummings, 'Boothby, Rousseau and the Romantic Malady', Burlington Magazine, CX, no. 789, 1968, pp. 659–66.
37. Both Madame Roland (1784) and Sophie von la Roche (1786) refer with admiration in their accounts of London to the shops of Oxford Street; la Roche: 'The linen shops are the loveliest; every

kind of white wear, from swaddling-clothes to shrouds, and any species of linen can be had...' (*Sophie in London. The Diary of Sophie von la Roche*, trans. C. Williams, London, 1933, p. 262).

38. *Gentleman's Guide*, p. 109.
39. Archenholz (1789), II, pp. 114–15.
40. Before the later seventeenth century the main supply of beaver fur came from the Baltic; finding 'alternative sources of supply was a major incentive behind the exploration and settlement of North America', D. Corner, 'The Tyranny of Fashion: The Case of the Felt-Hatting Trade in the Late Seventeenth and Eighteenth Centuries', *Textile History*, XXII, no. 2, 1991, pp. 153–78.
41. Mercier (1782–8), VII, pp. 44–6. The comte de Ségur noted that during the 1780s 'Les plus grands seigneurs s'habillèrent comme leurs valets; au spectacle, dans les lieux d'assemblée, on vie parut plus qu'en bottes, en frac...' (Ségur (1803), III, p. 7.).
42. V. Cumming, *Royal Dress*, London, 1989, p. 72.
43. Karamzin (1803), III, p. 217.
44. Moritz (1924), p. 81.
45. Sobry (1786), p. 417.
46. Kimball (1943), p. 187.
47. J.N. Dufort, comte de Cheverny, *Mémoires sur les règnes de Louis XV et Louis XVI et sur la Révolution*, ed. R. de Crèvecoeur, 2 vols, Paris, 1886, I, p. 68.
48. Diderot (1975–83), II, p. 76.
49. Delany (1861–2), III, p. 605.
50. Rouquet (1755), pp. 46–7.
51. Thicknesse (1768), p. 53.
52. White lead paint continued to be used, although the dangers were now recognised; safer cosmetics included whitening washes for the face and pearl-powder. Rouge was applied in the form of impregnated papers, pads and balls of wool; it came from the red brazilwood tree or from the scarlet dye of the cochineal insect. It is worth noting how rarely, if ever, teeth are shown in portraits. Not only would this have been taken for an ungraceful grimace, but an open mouth might reveal how few teeth the sitter possessed; losses were due to illnesses and a diet over-heavy in sugar. On the general appearance of women's faces and the cosmetics used, see A. Ribeiro, *The Female Face in the Tate's British Collection 1569–1876*, London, 1987.
53. To a Frenchman, the complexions of Englishwomen often seemed too pallid due to their economy with cosmetics: 'Leurs visages ressemblent à leurs gorges, elles sont fades à force de blancheur, la brosse & le pinceau n'y ont jamais passé', G.F. Coyer, *Les Dames angloises, françisées par les soins d'un abbé*, London, 1769, p. 15.
54. E. Topham, *Letters from Edinburgh*, London 1776, p. 198.
55. Holland House Papers, British Museum Add. MS. 51353, fols. 98, 98v.
56. Traditionally known as 'Eleanor Frances Dixie', it is more likely to be an elder sister or her stepmother, who married Sir Wolstan Dixie in 1753.
57. Grosley (1772), I, p. 255.
58. Diderot (1975–83), I, p. 63.
59. D. Jeffries, *A Treatise on Diamonds and Pearls*, London, 1750. See A. Ribeiro, 'Eighteenth-century Jewellery in England', *Connoisseur*, CIC, no. 800, 1978, pp. 75–83.
60. Villiers (1789), p. 164.
61. Delany (1861–2), III, pp. 300–1.
62. Grosley (1772), I, p. 253.
63. The generally accepted dating for the portrait of Lady Howe is *c.*1763–4; an earlier date might be possible, for the Howes visited Bath (to which Gainsborough had moved in 1759) in April and May 1760. For a detailed analysis of the portrait, including her dress, see London (1988).
64. Archenholz (1789), I, p. 109.
65. Barker (*c.*1780), p. 45.

66. The *Gallerie des Modes* first refers to the *polonaise* in 1778. The origin of the term is obscure, for styles of costume *à la polonaise* in the eighteenth century usually indicate that they are trimmed with fur. Two kinds of popular *polonaise* gowns in the 1770s and 1780s, the *sultane* and the *circassian* are sometimes trimmed with fur. A not altogether fanciful suggestion is that the kilting up of the polonaise skirt into three swags of material might refer to the first partition of Poland by her three powerful neighbours, Russia, Prussia and Austria in 1772.
67. J.-M. Phlipon-Roland, 'A Trip to England', 1784, in Roland (1800), p. 184.
68. W.T. Whitley, *Thomas Gainsborough*, London, 1915, p. 231. This seems quite likely, for William Jackson also remarked that dolls were used for *The Mall* (*The Four Ages*, London, 1788, p. 167). Perhaps Gainsborough first learnt to use such dolls when he worked in the artist Gravelot's studio in the 1740s.
69. *The Gentleman's Magazine*, London, LI, 1781, p. 57.
70. *Betsy Sheridan's Journal*, ed. W. Lefanu, London, 1960, p. 58.
71. See B. Lemire, *Fashion's Favourite: The Cotton Trade and the Consumer in Britain, 1660–1800*, London, 1991.
72. Métra (1787–90), VII, p. 293.
73. *Georgiana: Extracts from the Correspondence of Georgiana, Duchess of Devonshire*, ed. the Earl of Bessborough, London, 1955, p. 91.
74. *The Jerningham Letters, 1780–1843*, ed. E. Castle, 2 vols, London, 1896, I, p. 37.
75. Archenholz (1789), II, p. 135.
76. *Lichtenberg's Visits to England, as Described in his Letters and Diaries*, trans. and ed. M.L. Mare and W.H. Quarrell, Oxford, 1938, pp. 89–90.
77. 'Was Venus ever chiselled with a high tete or was ever Euphrosyne or Thalia depicted with a cushion on either of their heads? And yet the ancient sculptors and painters were certainly as good judges of beauty as any modern connoisseurs. But if the ladies will not be satisfied with these authorities, let them consult Sir Joshua Reynolds'. From the *Town and Country Magazine*, 1779, quoted in Leslie and Taylor (1865), II, p. 227.
78. Quoted in Penny (1986), p. 388.
79. Barker (*c.*1780), pp. 17, 43.
80. Métra (1787–90), I, p. 179.
81. *Encyclopédie méthodique*, ed. J.M. Roland de la Platière, Paris, 1785, I., p. 133.
82. Mercier (1982), VI, p. 307.
83. See Ribeiro (1984a), pp. 51–2, for information on the dolls which were sent out all over Europe; the practice overlapped the early fashion magazines, but had largely died out by the end of the eighteenth century. These dolls were well used by metropolitan and provincial dressmakers and must sometimes have ended up as toys for small girls.
84. See F. Tétart Vittu, 'La Gallerie des modes et costumes français', *Nouvelles de l'estampe*, March 1987, 91, pp. 16–21.
85. Roche (1989), p. 473.
86. R. Campbell, *The London Tradesman*, London, 1747, p. 208.
87. Quoted in Williams (1831), I, pp. 124–5.
88. – Adams, *Woman. Sketches of the History, Genius, Disposition, Accomplishments, Employments, Customs and Importance of the Fair Sex*, London, 1790, p. 366.
89. A. Cunningham, *Lives of the Most Eminent British Painters, Sculptors and Architects*, London, 1833, VI, p. 163.

2 Painters of Modern Life

1. Behrens (1967), p. 126.
2. Ségur (1803), II, p. 227.
3. M. Wollstonecraft, *An Historical and Moral View of the Origin and Progress of the French Revolution*, London, 1794, p. 34.
4. Villiers (1789), p. 312.
5. Wollstonecraft, p. 437.
6. See Lee (1969).
7. Ibid., I, p. 199.
8. In fact he could be wearing knee-breeches (*culotte*) or trousers cut off above the knee; he also wears a Phrygian cap. He helps to carry an aged and infirm man in a chair, a reference which one historian has seen to an incident in Plutarch's *Lives*, when the old and blind Appius Claudius was borne through the Roman forum to the Senate House to deliver a stirring speech recalling the former glory of Rome and rejecting the peace overtures of the invading army of King Pyrrhus. See A. Kagan, 'A Classical Source for David's *Oath of the Tennis Court*', *Burlington Magazine*, CXVI, no. 856, 1974, pp. 395–6. According to the Kagan thesis, Appius Claudius, although a patrician, had attempted to expand the suffrage and could possibly be equated with those members of the Second Estate (the nobility) who had joined the Third Estate. It is a slightly far-fetched argument, which is not helped by the (wrong) identification of the old man's garment as a toga; it is, in fact, a wrapping greatcoat.
9. Duval (1841–2), IV, p. 4. Barras recalled Robespierre's 'frigid attitude, his scorn of courtesies', and likened him, curiously, to Potemkin. He describes in his *Memoirs* a visit to Robespierre who was 'wrapped in a sort of chemise-peignoir; he had just left the hands of his hairdresser who had finished combing and powdering his hair' (Barras, 1895–6, I, p. 182).
10. Duval (1841–2), I, p. 228.
11. *Journal de la Mode et du Goût*, 5 Feb. 1792, p. 3.
12. H.M. Williams, *Letters from France*, ed. J.M. Todd, 2 vols, New York, 1975.
13. J. Moore, *A Journal during a residence in France from the beginning of August to the middle of December 1792*, London, 1793, 2 vols, II, p. 430.
14. Walpole (1937–83), XXXIV, p. 164.
15. *Madame Tussaud's Memoirs and Reminiscences of France*, ed. F. Hervé, London, 1838, p. 177.
16. The Musée des Arts de la Mode in Paris has a tricolour cotton coat and tricolour striped stockings. The Musée de la Mode et du Costume in Paris has one *gilet* of cream taffeta with satin tricolour stripes and the front pieces of another with embroidered tricolour hearts and the motto 'Vaincre ou mourir'.
17. *Memoirs of the Duchesse de Gontaut*, trans. J.W. Davies, 2 vols, London, 1894, I, p. 30.
18. Nouvion (1911), p. 164. Bertin's business continued while she was abroad – it supplied the imprisoned Marie-Antoinette (see M. Delpierre, 'Le Garde-robe de la famille royale au Temple', in Paris, 1989b). In 1800 Bertin was finally granted the right to return to France, keeping her shop in the rue de Richelieu until her death.
19. *Journal de la Mode et du Goût*, 5 Dec. 1791, p. 2.
20. Dowd (1959), pp. 131–3. Dowd points out that David was ready to use his influence to protect even those of his fellow-artists with whom he disagreed politically, and he ensured that Vigée-Lebrun's name was eventually dropped from the list of official *émigrés*.
21. Tulard (1989), p. 47.
22. Quoted in Roche (1989), p. 62.
23. Mercier (1798), III, pp. 135–6.
24. *Journal des Dames et des Modes*, 9 April 1799, p. 14.
25. Quoted in Tulard (1989), p. 73.
26. *The Journals and Letters of Fanny Burney*, ed. J. Hemlow, 10 vols, Oxford, 1972–82, V, p. 290. 'Corset' here means a kind of quilted or lightly stiffened bodice, as distinct from the 'stays' which were boned.
27. Mercier (1798), IV, p. 251, and V, pp. 222–3.

28. Thibadeau (1827), p. 16.
29. Bouchot (1895), p. 147.
30. *Memoirs of the Duchess of Abrantès*, 8 vols, London, 1831–5, VII, p. 141.
31. *Journal de Paris*, May 1804, p. 1577.
32. *Journal de Paris*, Nov. 1804, p. 383.
33. A letter in the British Museum (Add. MS. 44993, fols. 23–4) from Russell to his father, dated 7 April 1810, describes his sartorial preparations for the Imperial wedding. See also S.H. Jeyes, *The Russells of Birmingham*, London, 1911, pp. 291–4. I am grateful to Helen Spencer from the Museum and Art Gallery in Birmingham who provided me with these references and sent me the details of the suit which is in her care.
34. Angelo (1828), II, pp. 447.
35. Farington (1978–84), V, p. 1849. Simond (1817), remarked on the uniformity of Englishmen who wore 'outside garments of a dull, dark cast' (I, p. 28).
36. Egan (1821), p. 148.
37. *Le Beau Monde*, London, 1808, p. 292.
38. Quoted in V. Cumming, 'Pantomime and Pageantry: The Coronation of George IV', in Fox (1992), p. 40.
39. Wilson (1825), I, p. 101.
40. Brummell (1932), p. 122.
41. Jesse (1844), I, p. 62.
42. Wilson (1825), IV, p. 208.
43. V. Woolf, *Beau Brummell*, New York, 1930, p. 3.
44. Quoted in E. Moers, *The Dandy*, London, 1960, p. 33.
45. Baudelaire (1964), pp. 26–7.
46. *The Taylor's Complete Guide*, London 1796, p. 7.
47. Egan (1821), p. 136.
48. Surr (1806), II, pp. 82–3.
49. See A. Ribeiro, 'Provision of Ready-made and Second-hand Clothing in the Eighteenth Century in England', in *Per una Storia della Moda Pronta. Problemi e Ricerche*, eds. G. Butazzi and C.A. Piacenti, Florence, 1991, pp. 85–94.
50. *Taylor's Complete Guide*, p. 7.
51. Those exempt from the tax (which was one guinea) included the royal family and their immediate servants, the army and navy, and clergy with less than £100 per annum. Those who paid the tax were known in vulgar parlance as guinea-pigs. The word may derive from an account (?apocryphal) of a tailor, who being insulted by a beau wearing '2 lbs of powder on his sconce' cut off the tail of his hair with his shears – just as piglets had their tails cut short. See the anonymous verse *New Fashions; Or a Puff at the Guinea Pigs*, 1795.
52. Wilson (1825), I, p. 224.
53. Vaughan (1792), p. 45. A French doctor, L.J. Clairian, urged on grounds of health that men should wear breeches which were not too tight-fitting but which were reasonably supportive, and they should avoid loose trousers which gave no support. See his *Recherches et considérations médicales sur les vêtements des hommes*, Paris, 1803.
54. See A. Ribeiro, 'Hussars in Masquerade', *Apollo*, CV, no. 180, 1977, pp. 111–16. It was fashionable to dress black servants in hussar costume. In Hogarth's *Harlot's Progress* (1732), Plate 2 shows the small black page in a feathered turban and a coat frogged *à la hussar*. In an equal confusion of ethnic identities, William Hickey in 1780 dressed his Indian servant Nabob 'very smart as a Hussar.'
55. There are also references in the correspondence of the Prince of Wales to the ordering of hussar pantaloons for his brother Prince Frederick in Hanover; they occur in 1781, for example, as 'hussa breeches quite down to the ancles with a strap under the foot of white ram's skin' (Aspinall, 1963–71, I, p. 53). The Prince himself might very well have worn something similar with the 'Huzzar Jacket and Waistcoat lined with cotton' listed in his Accounts

56. for 1798 (Windsor, Royal Archives).
56. *A Persian at the Court of King George 1809–10. The Journal of Mirza Abul Hassan Khan*, trans. M.M. Cloake, London, 1988, p. 137.
57. *Le Beau Monde*, 1808, p. 339.
58. *The Ton*, London, 1819, p. 77.
59. Stendhal, *Histoire de la peinture en Italie*, 2 vols, Paris, 1817, II, pp. 158, 187.
60. Nos. 867. 270 and 867. 272.
61. W.M. Reddy, *The Use of Market Culture. The textile Trade and French Society, 1750–1900*, Cambridge, 1984, p. 91.
62. F. Burney, *Camilla*, London, 1796, p. 691.
63. See *Johnstone's London Commercial Guide*, London, 1817.
64. N. McKendrick, J. Brewer and J.H. Plumb, *The Birth of a Consumer Society: The Commercialization of Eighteenth-century England*, London, 1982, p. 13.
65. Carr (1803), pp. 81, 88–9.
66. L. Hautecoeur, *Louis David*, Paris, 1954, p. 189.
67. Carr (1803), pp. 133–4.
68. Charles Blanc in his *Ingres: sa vie et ses ouvrages*, Paris, 1870, stated that he painted the lamp and the stool in David's painting of *Madame Récamier*. The Musée Ingres at Montauban possesses Ingres's drawings of the lamp and the stool, and a sketch of Mme Récamier on a chaise longue; it is thought, however, that these drawings were probably done as a record of Ingres's studies with David.
69. See the letter from Lady Mary Boyle Roche, 1793, Dublin, National Library of Ireland, MS. 5391; 'She affects the dress of a Peasant and she sometimes wears Black stockings with Red Cloacks and a Black Gown with Cocklico ribbons which we have an idea here is the Jacobin Uniform in France and when her head is bound up with a dirty handkerchief people suspect it is soiled with the Blood of Louis the 16th . . .' Quoted in M. Dunleavy, *Dress in Ireland*, London, 1989, pp. 129–30. The date of the portrait by 'Mallary' is problematical. Lady Pamela had a daughter in 1796 and another conceived before the death of her husband in 1798; if the date of the portrait is *c*.1800, it is more likely to depict the younger child.
70. *Carr* (1803), p. 89.
71. *Journal de Paris*, April 1802, pp. 1257, 1321.
72. Angelo (1828), II, p. 380.
73. *Memoirs and Correspondence of Madame Récamier*, trans. I.M. Luyster, 4th edn, Boston, MA, 1867, p. 5. An English publication on fashion and etiquette, *The Mirror of the Graces*, London, 1811, includes among its cosmetic recipes one for 'Madame Récamier's pomade', which consists of the fat of a red stag or hart mixed with olive oil and virgin wax; it was intended to be put on the limbs after exercising or dancing and claimed also to be good for rheumatism.
74. L. Bertrand, *La Fin du Classicisme et le Retour à l'Antique*, 1896, p. 365.
75. Rémusat (1880), II, p. 108.
76. 'Original Documents Relative to the Empress Josephine', 1809, Box 6, pp. 27–31 (London, Victoria and Albert Museum).
77. Grandjean (1964), p. 49.
78. In 'Original Documents', Box. 86. UU. 2.
79. Beauharnais (1927), I, pp. 68–9.
80. 'Registres des dépenses de la Cour sous l'Empire et la Restauration (Paris, Bibliotheque Nationale), MS. 5931, 1812–18.
81. This included court dresses, *robes de bal* (including one 'habit rose et argent à la François 1'), day dresses (tulle was a particularly popular fabric), redingotes of velvet and satin, *habits de chasse*, etc. See Maze-Sencier (1893), pp. 317–18.
82. Bouchot (1895), p. 226.
83. Rémusat (1880), II, p. 362.
84. Thibaudeau (1827), p. 17.

85. *Memoirs of the Comtesse de Boigne*, ed. C. Nicoullard, 3 vols, London, 1907–8, I, p. 296.
86. Simond (1817), I, p. 208.
87. *Khan*, pp. 103, 137. With the accession of George IV in 1820, hoops were abolished in English court dress which – finally – followed the French style. One lady attending court with her daughter, wrote: '. . . the Drawing-room was very full, but as hoops are abolished, it was much pleasanter and less fatiguing . . . The costumes were all the same as at the French court, and I think very pretty. Fanny and I had white net gowns prettily trimmed, and blue gros de Naples trains three yards and a quarter long'. (*An Irish Beauty of the Regency. Compiled from 'Mes Souvenirs', the Unpublished Journals of the Hon. Mrs Calvert, 1789–1822*, ed. W. Blake, London, 1911, p. 344).
88. *Journal de Paris*, Nov. 1804, p. 416.
89. *Paris in 1814. From the Journal of William Roots*, ed. H.A. Ogle, Newcastle-upon-Tyne, 1909, p. 47. Simpson (1853), p. 104.
90. Simpson (1853), ibid.
91. *La Belle Assemblée*, Feb. 1806, p. 63.
92. *The Private Correspondence of a Woman of Fashion*, 2 vols, London, 1832, I, p. 172.
93. Simpson (1853), p. 127.
94. *Mirror of the Graces*, p. 96.
95. Grandjean (1964), pp. 52–3.
96. See *A Catalogue of the Magnificent Furniture and Valuable Effects of her late Majesty Queen Caroline*, London, 1822. Examples of her taste in dress: 'a Superb Net Dress, elegantly embroidered in flowers on crimson satin, with deep flounce, trimmed with silver lace and fringe' (p. 83) and 'a beautiful black figured Gauze Dress, flounced with 2 rows of costly deep lace' (p. 86). She appears to have been particularly fond of red, and the catalogue lists, for example, a 'splendid orange colour cashmere dress' and a 'superb new crimson Velvet Dress'; the portrait by Lawrence of 1804 (London, National Portrait Gallery) shows her in a dress and hat of red velvet.
97. Brummell (1932), p. 313.
98. *Journal de Paris*, Nov. 1804, p. 2855.
99. 'Registres des dépenses', MS. 5931, fol. 206.
100. Grandjean (1964), p. 68. One of Horace Vernet's fashion plates in the series of *Merveilleuses* depicts a woman in a *witzchoura*, of cream satin lined with fox fur (1814).
101. Abrantès (1831–5), VII, p. 203.
102. *A Catalogue of the Magnificent Furniture*, pp. 85–6.
103. The portrait, in a private collection, is discussed in an article by Hans Naef, 'Un Chef-d'oeuvre retrouvé: le portrait de la reine Caroline Murat par Ingres', *Revue de l'Art*, no. 88, 1990, pp. 11–20.
104. Beauharnais (1927), II, p. 135.
105. Another study for this portrait shows the head of Caroline Murat with girandole earrings (Montauban, Musée Ingres, 867.341).

3 The Stuff of Heroes

1. Bertrand (1896), pp. 106, 108.
2. Ibid., p. 105.
3. Parker (1937), p. 62. Parker points out that not all the *philosophes* agreed on this, Condorcet, for example, believing that the ancients had 'no true notions of natural liberty, equality or the rights of man' (p. 99).
4. A.D. Smith, 'The "Historical Revival" in Late 18th-century England and France', *Art History*, II, no. 2, 1979, pp. 156–72.
5. Quoted in Bertrand (1896), p. 286.
6. See S. Eriksen, 'Marigny and Le Goût Grec', *Burlington Magazine*, CIV, no. 708, 1962, pp. 96–101; the author dates the appearance of furniture in the Greek style from *c*.1756–7.

7. Diderot (1975–83), I, p. 210.

8. See Fried (1980), p. 63.

9. E. Pilon and F. Saisset, *Les Fêtes en Europe au XVIIIe siècle*, Paris, 1943, p. 119. A number of Rose Bertin's hats in the 1770s and 1780s included classical references. In 1774 she produced a hat *à l'Iphigénie* trimmed with black flowers and the crescent moon of Diana; it was declared to be suitable for mourning (for the death of Louis XV) but it was mainly inspired by Gluck's opera *Iphigénie en Aulide*, presented in Paris in April that year. See Langlade (1913), p. 34.

10. Crow (1985), p. 176.

11. Walpole (1937–83), XXXII, p. 253.

12. Campan (1823), I, p. 49.

13. Present whereabouts unknown.

14. Reiset (1885), I, p. 159.

15. Miette de Villars (1850), p. 160.

16. See A.-C. de Tubières, comte de Caylus, *Tableaux tirés de l'Iliade et de l'Odyssée d'Homère et de l'Enéide de Virgile: avec des observations générales sur le costume*, Paris, 1757.

17. Molé (1773), pp. xiii–xiv.

18. H.F. Dandré Bardon, *Costume des Anciens Peuples*, Paris, 1722, p. v.

19. Lens (1785), p. 347.

20. See pls 120, and 121. David's studio furniture may have been inspired by the plates in Lens's book; the lamp and *chaise-longue* in the portrait of Madame Récamier (pl. 122) are fairly close in design to similar items illustrated in Lens.

21. Diderot (1975–83), III, p. 220.

22. See Y. Korshak, 'Paris and Helen by Jacques-Louis David: Choice and Judgement on the Eve of the French Revolution', *Art Bulletin*, LXIX, no. 1, 1987, pp. 102–16.

23. See the reply to this by Francis Dowley, *Art Bulletin*, LXX, no. 3, 1988, pp. 504–12.

24. See this chapter, p. ••.

25. Anninger (1982), p. 181.

26. Talma's *Reflections on the Theatrical Art*, in *Dramatic Table Talk*, ed. R. Ryan, 3 vols, London, 1825, I, pp. xvi–xviii. Although Voltaire wrote plays with classical themes, and paid lip-service to the new ideas of reform in stage dress, his idea of antique costume was very much in line with traditional baroque theatre costume. See Pentzell (1967), p. 223. The general feeling in the theatre, until the advent of Talma, was probably that of the actress Hyppolite Clairon, who says in her *Memoirs* (1800) that 'the dresses of antiquity display too much of the figure; they are properly applicable only to statues and paintings', but she wished the 'style' of classical antiquity to be indicated in theatre dress (I, p. 83).

27. L. Fusil, *Souvenirs d'une actrice*, 2 vols, Brussels, 1841, II, p. 96.

28. The Musée et Bibliothèque de la Comédie Française, Paris, has a number of togas in shades of pink and red, with gold embroidery, and a gold-embroidered red silk antique tunic that belonged to Talma.

29. Millin (1806), I, pp. 361–2. The importance of the theatre in the dissemination of accurate knowledge about the dress of antiquity is discussed in Mongez (1804); the illustrations are by his wife, a pupil of David's.

30. Malliot (1804), II, p. 308.

31. J.B.P. Lebrun, *Essai sur les moyens d'encourager la peinture, la sculpture, l'architecture et la gravure*, Paris, l'An III [1794–5], p. 9.

32. See, for example, the entry of the new Dauphine Marie-Antoinette into Châlons in May 1770; the gateway to the city was decorated with military ornaments and pictures of the Dauphin and Dauphine. Among those greeting Marie-Antoinette were six girls dressed in white, offering her flowers and declaiming verses in her honour. Various theatrical performances took place in a specially erected theatre. A full description is given in E. de Berthélemy, *Relation de l'Entrée de la Dauphine Marie-Antoinette à Châlons, le 11 Mai 1770*, Paris, 1861.

33. *Révolutions de Paris*, 22–9 Jan. 1791, p. 143.

34. A. Delrieu, 'Les Masques parisiens au dix-huitième siècle', *Revue de Paris*, Ser. 3, XIV, no. 1, 1835, p. 187.

35. *Révolutions de Paris*, 6–13 March 1790, pp. 36–7.

36. Ibid., 13–20 Feb. 1790, pp. 1–2.

37. Stendhal, *Histoire de la peinture en Italie*, 2 vols, Paris, 1817, II, p. 161.

38. Hemmings, (1987), pp. 56–7. Hemmings notes that the chariot was used again, for the *Fête de la Liberté* on 15 April 1792; the sides were decorated with effigies of Brutus and William Tell, and a life-size statue of Liberty was seated in it.

39. *Rapport et décret sur la fête de la réunion républicaine du 10 Août*, Paris, 1793.

40. There are two versions of this drawing in Paris, the one in the Carnavalet (pl. 133) and another in the Louvre.

41. Delécluze (1863), p. 8. See David's *Détails exacts des cérémonies et de l'ordre à observer dans la Fête de l'Etre Suprême*, Paris, 1794.

42. Duval (1841–2), IV, p. 356.

43. On the political role of women during the French Revolution, see H.B. Applewhite, M.D. Johnson, and D.G. Levy, *Women in Revolutionary Paris, 1789–1795*, Chicago, 1979. See also Ribeiro (1988), pp. 87–90. The general view held by the Revolutionaries (men) was that of Rousseau in *Emile* (1762), 'la dépendance étant un état naturel aux femmes, les filles se sentent faites pour obéir'.

44. *The Private Memoirs of Madame Roland*, ed. E.G. Johnson, London, 1901, p. 273. Charlotte Corday, also, wanted a Roman republic of virtue and austerity.

45. See, for example, Nicolas-Guy Brenet, *Piété et generosité des dames romaines*, 1784 (Quimper, Musée des Beaux-Arts), and Louis Gauffier, *La Générosité des dames romaines*, 1790 (Poitiers, Musée des Beaux-Arts).

46. Tulard (1989), p. 27.

47. Trahard (1967), p. 195.

48. L. Madelin, *Les Femmes de la Révolution*, Monaco, 1927, p. 27.

49. – Thérémin, *De la condition des femmes dans les républiques*, Paris, 1799, p. 84.

50. Duval (1841–2), IV, p. 147. Some churches, economically, used their statues of the Virgin as Goddesses of Reason, merely adding a *bonnet rouge* or Phrygian cap.

51. Agulhon, *Marianne au Combat*, Paris, 1979, p. 29. See also Warner (1985).

52. A. -E. Gibelin, *De l'Origine et de la forme du bonnet de la Liberté*, Paris, 1796, p. 26.

53. *Révolutions de Paris*, 17–24 March 1792, p. 534. A number of *bonnets rouges* survive in museum collections in France. They are not always red; they could be beige or blue, a colour associated with the working class.

54. There are very few surviving examples of this type of garment; one in the Musée de la Mode et du Costume, Paris, is made of a coarse red wool and cotton mixture, lined with canvas and decorated with a tricolour cockade. The *carmagnole* was a name also given to a song and a dance.

55. *Programme d'une cérémonie . . .*, Paris, l'An II [1793–4], pp. 6–7.

56. Carlyle (1984), p. 165.

57. *Révolutions de Paris*, 29 Jan.–5 Feb. 1791, p. 185. By April the following year the editor was suggesting that church vestments be used by the clergy to make dresses for their future wives.

58. *Révolutions de Paris*, 16–23 Oct. 1790, p. 81.

59. Carlyle (1984), p. 160.

60. Mercier (1772), p. 81 *et seq*.

61. The Archives Nationales, Paris, have a letter signed by Robespierre and others on the need for a revolutionary journal, to appear twice a *décade*, and to be called *Le Républicain français* (AF. II 66:484, *Comité de Salut Public*, 8 Aug. 1793).

62. Ribeiro (1988), p. 102.

63. Only Condorcet had even suggested extending the franchise to women, and that was to be limited to those with property.

64. See the discussions in *Aux Armes et aux Arts. Journal de la Société Républicaine des Arts*, 1794, ed. Citoyen Détournelle. As far as I am aware, the only designs for women's dress in this context are by P. -E. Lesueur, at the Musée Carnavalet, Paris; the styles of dress are, in fact, quite close to fashionable costume, the only quasi-classical touches being a knee-length tunic (worn over a long skirt) and a veil worn over a rigid fez-like cap on the head.

65. Tulard (1989), p. 47.

66. *Considérations sur les avantages de changer le costume français*, Paris, 1794, p. 2.

67. *Aux Armes et aux Arts*, p. 258. See also *Archives Nationales. Comité de Salut Public: Esprit Public, Arts, Caricatures, Costume national*, AF. II 489, fol. 15.

68. J. Moore, *A Journal During a Residence in France from the Beginning of August to the Middle of December 1792*, London, 2 vols, 1793, II, p. 433. The painter was probably Jean-Baptiste Isabey.

69. Arnault (1833), III, p. 369. A pamphlet published by C.-F.-X. Mercier in 1793 refers to the fact that David had been asked to design costumes for the State; clearly, he was already working on this before being given the official commission by the government in May 1794. See *Comment m'habillerair-je? Réflexions politiques et philosophiques sur l'habillement français. Et sur la nécessité d'un costume national*, Paris, 1793. It is not exactly clear what Mercier's own ideas on a national costume are, except that it should be loose and comfortable; he states his admiration for Rousseau's Armenian robe.

70. The military costume is only known by an engraving. It is not unlike the uniform of the Elèves de Mars which David designed, a frogged tunic, tight hose, a toque with tricolour and a sword with a decoration of a Phrygian cap on the hilt. The Ecole de Mars was created by the Committee of Public Safety as a kind of military academy run on Spartan lines; it lasted from June to October 1794.

71. David was rather interested in the costume of North Africa (in this he anticipated Delacroix) and one of his costume designs of 1794 the *Représentant du peuple aux armées* – includes an ornamental sabre, a copy of a Moroccan sabre which David had in his studio (see Anninger (1982), p. 198).

72. Talma based his costume on a portrait by Clouet of Charles IX, in black velvet and with a ruff. The anti-monarchical theme of the play pleased the Revolutionaries. Danton supposedly said, 'if Figaro killed the aristocracy, Charles IX will kill the royalty'. When the play was performed in July 1790 it provoked a brawl, with royalist members of the audience trying to drown out the play.

73. Delécluze (1863), p. 29.

74. Kimball (1943), pp. 4–5.

75. Delécluze (1863), p. 91. He notes that after the death of Quaï (1804), all his co-religionists cut their beards, put on stockings and 'le vil frac' which they had previously denounced as bourgeois (p. 430).

76. See H. Okun, 'Ossian in Painting', *Journal of the Warburg and Courtauld Institutes*, XXX, 1967, pp. 327–56.

77. The *fêtes* had been very expensive to create – by the spring of 1791 they were already costing 100,000 livres per month – and to house all the properties (e.g. statues, arches of triumph, chariots, standards, etc. Under the Directory the authorities allowed

some festivals to continue, although they were constantly worried that they might be a source of public disorder. By the time of the Consulate, the only remnants of such events were the celebrations for Bastille Day and military parades for Napoleon's assumption of power on 18 Brumaire (9 November).

78. Carr (1803), p. 101.
79. Sobry (1786), pp. 415–6. In the late eighteenth century the *simarre* was a long, sleeved gown worn by clergy and lawyers. For civilian costume, Sobry advocated the wearing of a short tunic or *cotte*.
80. Delécluze (1863), p. 184.
81. Lenoir (1800–6), V, p. 44.
82. The Musée de la Mode et du Costume, Paris, has a red mantle with blue embroidery in a classical design; a similar 'toga', which belonged to Jean-François Reubell, who was elected to the Ancients in 1799 (after his career as a Director) is in the Musée d'Unterlinden, Colmar. A toque belonging to the Council of Ancients' costume is in the Musée de Lunéville.
83. Hunt (1984), p. 80.
84. H. B. Grégoire, *Rapport et projet de décret . . . sur les costumes des législateurs et des autres fonctionnaires publics*, Paris, 1795, p. 3.
85. J. Grasset de Saint-Sauveur, *Costumes des représentans du peuple français*, Paris, 1795, p. 4.
86. See Paris (1982).
87. Scott (1815), p. 119. Not all British comment on such legislative costume was hostile; John Carr, for example, thought that a little finery would benefit the House of Commons, where MPs tended to dress 'in the mean attire of jockeys and mechanics' (Carr, 1803, p. 152).
88. Bergeret (1848), p. 177.
89. Delécluze (1863), p. 93.
90. In the portrait by Ingres, Napoleon is depicted in the red velvet ('velours nacarat') he wore as First Consul when he visited Liège in August 1803. He took this costume with him to St Helena.
91. Thibaudeau (1827), p. 15.
92. Farington (1978–84), V, p. 1821.
93. So deeply was the Légion d'Honneur embedded in French culture that it proved impossible to abolish it after the downfall of Napoleon, although it was so identified with his regime; there were over 37,000 members of the order by the Restoration. Under Louis XVIII the badge of Henry IV replaced that of Napoleon and the fleur-de-lis replaced the Napoleonic eagles.
94. Malliot (1804), I, p. 53.
95. See J. Chifflet, *Anastasius Childerici I, Francorum regis, sire Thesaurus sepulchralis Tornaci Nerviorum*, Antwerp, 1655. The tomb findings are discussed in A. Toplis, 'The Dress of the Merovingian Court in the Frankish Kingdom c.450–700 AD. A Study in Early Medieval Dress', MA Report, London, Courtauld Institute of Art, 1993.
96. Diderot (1975–83), I, p. 108. Madame de Genlis, who was presented at court in 1767, was impressed with Louis XV. 'Un bel extérieur dans un roi n'est nullement une chose indifferente . . . Un maintien noble, un sourire agréable . . . des manières douces et polies sont pour les princes des dons précieux'. (Genlis (1870), p. 24). The contrast between Louis XV's polished manners and Napoleon's barrack-room behaviour could not be more pointed.
97. The tunic and the fringed sash and the sword survive in the Musée Napoléon I, Fontainebleau.
98. Ingres's studies for the regalia and for the Emperor's robe are in the collection of the Musée Ingres, Montauban, nos. 867.346–51.
99. Toussaint (1985), p. 35.
100. Two paintings of the Emperor in his coronation robes were commissioned from David; both originals are now lost, although there is a sketch for one

and a partially autograph replica of the other. See P. Bordes and A. Pougetoux, 'Les portraits de Napoleon en habits impériaux par Jacques-Louis David', *Gazette des Beaux-Arts*, 6th per., CII, 1983, pp. 21–34
101. 1943.1815.12 and 13.
102. 1943.1815.12., f. 5r. Inside the front cover of this sketchbook there are a number of costume notes for the imperial princesses.
103. According to Madame de Rémusat, the Empress proposed that 'to our ordinary garments the long mantle . . . should be added, and also a very becoming ruff of blonde, which was attached to the shoulders and came high up at the back of the head, as we see it in portraits of Catherine de' Medicis (Rémusat, 1880, I, p. 313).
104. Constant (1896), III, p. 8.
105. Miette de Villars (1850), p. 186.
106. Constant (1896), III, p. 303.
107. Musée des Arts Décoratifs, Paris.
108. The Museo del Risorgimento, Milan, has the green velvet, gold-embroidered coronation robe. The Museo Stibbert, Florence, has the gold-embroidered green velvet mantle and the gold embroidered white velvet waistcoat of the *petit costume*.
109. Bertrand's costume is in the Musée de la Mode et du Costume, Paris. For the details of these court uniforms, see Paris (1982). On the imperial household, see Mansel (1987).
110. See H. Vanier, 'Les costumes de l'ordre du Saint-Esprit', *Bulletin du Musée Carnavalet*, 1972:1, pp. 2–12.
111. Pupil (1985), p. 21. The term was coined by Gautier in his *Histoire du romantisme*, 1874.
112. Elias (1983), p. 215. After Rousseau's death, the English-inspired garden at Ermenonville where he spent the last weeks of his life became a popular place of pilgrimage.
113. Paris (1984), p. 370.
114. See M.D. Sheriff, 'Invention, Resemblance and Fragonard's Portraits de Fantaisie', *Art Bulletin*, LXIX, no. 1, 1987, pp. 77–87.
115. There were thirty-three editions of *Don Quixote* published in France during the eighteenth century; Pupil (1985), p. 286.
116. In the effects of eighteenth-century artists and collectors, there are a considerable number of references to paintings of Henry IV and his life. See D. Wildenstein, *Inventaires après décès d'artistes et de collectionneurs français du XVIIIe siècle*, Paris, 1967.
117. Under the direction of the comte d'Angiviller, Louis XVI's Surintendant des Bâtiments du Roi, artists were encouraged to produce history painting with French themes, and stories from the life of Henry IV proved particularly popular. One of the most important series of paintings (six) was by François-André Vincent; they were intended as models for Gobelins tapestries. In Mercier (1772) the king of the future (more like a chief magistrate than a monarch) goes among his people on foot and is greeted by them as an equal, 'a second Henry IV'.
118. Métra (1787–90), I, p. 173.
119. Ségur (1825–7), I, pp. 40–41.
120. Pupil (1985), p. 211.
121. Rigoley de Juvigny (1787), p. 258.
122. Lanson (1926), p. 10.
123. Ibid., p. 11.
124. Ibid., p. 13.
125. Lenoir (1800–6), I, p. 11.
126. Pupil (1985), p. 395.
127. Farington (1978–84), V, p. 1829.
128. S. Owenson, Lady Morgan, *France*, London, 2 vols, 1817, II, p. 101.
129. Pupil (1985), pp. 136, 140.
130. The project never came to fruition at the time, but was eventually completed with Louis XVIII instead of Napoleon.

131. Hautecoeur (1953), p. 94.
132. See M.-C. Chaudonneret, 'Fleury Richard et le passé national; ses sources à travers quelques carnets de croquis', *Actes du Colloque International Ingres et le Néo-classicisme*, Montauban, 1975, pp. 11–19.
133. Grandjean (1964), pp. 18, 156–7. The *Catalogue des tableaux de sa majesté Joséphine dans la galerie et appartements de son palais de Malmaison*, Paris, 1811, indicates the range of the collection from Memling to David.
134. See four costume sketches at the Fogg Art Museum, Cambridge, MA; the figures, which appear to be from Swiss or German and Netherlandish sources, have notes on colours and fabrics (1965.21.53a).
135. See R. Kaufmann, 'François Gérard's Entry of Henry IV into Paris: The Iconography of Constitutional Monarchy', *Burlington Magazine*, CXVII, no. 873, 1975, pp. 790–802.
136. See, for example, nos. 867.1429 and 867.1432; the latter has notes on colour and fabric.
137. The Musée Ingres, Montauban, has a number of costume drawings related to the subject of *Paolo and Francesca*. These include studies for Francesca's dress and for Lanciotto's gown; one drawing (867.1931) shows Lanciotto in a short gown (*gonnellino*) rather like that in the version of the painting at the Musée Bonnat, Bayonne.
138. Nos. 867.378 and 867.383. There are also studies of her hands and her sleeve.
139. A preliminary drawing by Ingres (London, British Museum) varies the pose slightly and La Fornarina's sleeves are plain rather than slashed; the artist has emphasised her sloping shoulders even more than in the painting.
140. Delécluze (1863), p. 136.

4 Remembrance of Things Past

1. Walpole (1937–83), XVII, pp. 338–9.
2. See A. Ribeiro, 'Antiquarian Attitudes. Some Early Studies in the History of Dress', *Costume*, no. 28, 1994, pp. 60–70.
3. Walpole (1937–83), XVI, p. 27.
4. Ibid., I, p. 191.
5. See, for example, the volumes of material compiled by the Rev. Michael Tyson, the Rev. William Cole and the Rev. Thomas Kerrich, members of a close-knit antiquarian circle.
6. See Walpole's *A Description of the Villa of Mr Horace Walpole at Strawberry Hill*, London, 1784.
7. Walpole (1937–83), X, p. 278. The carved wooden cravat by Grinling Gibbons to which Walpole refers is now in the Victoria and Albert Museum, London.
8. Grose (1775), pp. iii–vi.
9. Grose (1807–9).
10. For 'a sketch of Hercules and Antaeus' and 'Aeneas stopped on the Threshold of the Door by Creuza', according to an unpublished typescript by R.M. Christy, 'Joseph Strutt, Author, Artist, Engraver and Antiquary, 1749–1802: A Biography', 1912 (London, British Library), ch. IV, p. 8. In the late 1770s and early 1780s Strutt exhibited again at the Royal Academy, the last time being 1784 when he showed three works, *Homer, Hesiod and Sappho Listening to the Strains of Apollo*, *King Lear when he First Remembers Cordelia*, and *Shakespeare, Milton and Spenser, with Nature Dictating to Shakespeare* (Joseph Strutt, ch. XIV, p. 12). I have not been able to discover whether any of these works survive.
11. From the Introduction to the *Complete View of the Dress and Habits of the People of England*, London, 1796, I, p. iii.
12. Stothard (1832), p. 2.
13. Ibid., p. 17.
14. Ibid., p. 20. His research was published in *Archeologia*, XIX, 1821. 1821 was the year of his

death, which, appropriately, took place while he was making drawings from the stained glass in a church in Bere Ferrers in Devon. Falling from a ladder, his head hit 'a slab on which the figure of a knight is placed in the chancel wall . . . receiving his death-blow from one of those very effigies from which, through his talents, he will receive a sublunary immortality' (Stothard, 1832, p. 22).

15. C.H. Smith, *Selections of the Ancient Costume*, London, 1814, p. vi.

16. In 1824 Meyrick produced the first serious study of armour since Grose's *Treatise on Ancient Armour and Weapons* of 1785; *A Critical Enquiry into Antient Armour* was dedicated to George IV. It became fashionable to collect armour to decorate country houses, which led to a number of fake pieces being produced.

17. *Sophie in London. The Diary of Sophie von la Roche*, London, 1933, pp. 114, 127.

18. Dayes (1805), p. 256.

19. T. Jefferys, *A Collection of the Dresses of Different Nations*, London, 1757, I, p. xiv. W.H. Pyne claimed that Garrick started the reform in theatre dress but that it was furthered by the painter P.J. de Loutherbourg who worked as a theatre designer for Garrick at Drury Lane during the 1770s. See *Wine and Walnuts*, London, 1824.

20. D.T. Mackintosh (*Times Literary Supplement*, 25 Aug. 1927) believes that the season 1762–3 brought the real beginnings of the idea that dress should be more uniform and appropriate to the period in which a play was set. He quotes from the *Public Advertiser* (4 Nov. 1762) apropos of performances of Shakespeare's *Henry IV, Part II* at Drury Lane and Ben Jonson's *Every Man in His Humour* at Covent Garden, that the 'old English habits are indeed admirably suited to the style and manners of the plays of the time'.

21. *Town and Country Magazine*, 30 April 1770, p. 237.

22. In 1823 the antiquary and future dress historian J.R. Planché was invited by Charles Kemble at Covent Garden to design the costumes for Shakespeare's *King John*; publicity for the play included 'Authorities for the Costume'. Planché's designs in the 1820s for other Shakespeare history plays made use of his research into the history of dress to create more authentic stage costume than had been the case before.

23. Walpole (1937–83), XXIII, p. 193.

24. Lowenthal (1985), p. 225.

25. Irwin (1966), p. 133.

26. Fuseli (1820), p. 109.

27. For example, James Barry who produced a drawing of *Milton Dictating Paradise Lost to Ellwood the Quaker*, *c*.1804–5 (London, British Museum), where the features of the poet bear some resemblance to those of the artist. Barry has depicted Milton in accurate mid-seventeenth-century dress.

28. Hever Castle, for example. Many large country houses in England contain galleries with portraits of English kings and queens. Some of these are more or less contemporary with the person they depict (or a copy of a lost original) but others were painted in bulk in the early eighteenth century; whatever the supposed period of the portrait, the dress is often a composite Tudor-Vandyke creation.

29. In *Mary Woffington as Mary Queen of Scots*, 1759 (Petworth House, W. Sussex), Hogarth paints the sitter in a black dress, a deep white starched ruff, and a Marie Stuart cap edged with lace and trimmed with pearls. The dress looks as though it might be copied from Jefferys's *A Collection of the Dresses*, 1757, II, pl. 204, *The Habit of Mary Queen of Scots in 1570*.

30. Quoted in Macmillan (1986), p. 69.

31. There is a small oil painting on copper by Allan showing Henry IV dressed in armour, with his mis-

tress Gabrielle d'Estrées, who wears a kind of classical shift, with one breast bare (Scotland, private collection).

32. J. Fillinham, *The Public Gardens of London*, London, British Library, 1861. *Carlisle House Collection*, p. 21.

33. Walpole (1937–83), XXXII, pp. 101–2, 110–11.

34. Woodall (1963), p. 95.

35. It was still ascribed to van Dyck in the second edition of Walpole's *Aedes Walpolianae*, London, 1752, and in his *Anecdotes of Painting*, 1762, II, p. 92.

36. *Dresses of Different Nations*, II, pl. 148.

37. See Ribeiro (1984b), chap. 3, pt I, pp. 144–57.

38. Vertue (1933–4), p. 57.

39. In the National Gallery of Scotland, Edinburgh. Some of the drawings relate to portraits by Allan Ramsay and there is still some confusion as to attribution.

40. Sale, Sotheby's, New York, 24 Feb. 1988, lot 33. The artist's daughter Sophie modelled for the picture, which derives from Samuel Richardson's novel *Clarissa Harlowe*, London, 1748. Millais clearly found the later work of Gainsborough more romantic and picturesque than that of any artist contemporary with the novel.

41. Walpole (1937–83), XXXV, p. 206.

42. *Strawberry Hill*, op. cit., p. 29. The Rubens painting inspired Romney's *Sir Christopher and Lady Sykes*, 1786–93 (Sir Tatton Sykes, Bt.).

43. See, for example, 'A Purple Satin Vandike Cloak, waistcoat, breeches, lined with yellow and trimm'd with Silver . . .' (p. 1), 'a Strip'd Satin Vandyke dress with Cloak (p. 39) and so on, in the Wardrobe Book, *c*.1784 (Wynnstay MS. 116, Cardiff, National Library of Wales).

44. Vertue (1933–4), p. 16.

45. *Elizabeth Montagu, the Queen of the Blue-Stockings. Correspondence 1720–1761*, ed. E.J. Climenson, 2 vols, London, 1906, I, p. 264. There appears to have been a complementary vogue for scarves or fichus inspired by van Dyck portraits. Lady Jane Coke in 1752 notes the new fashion for 'Vandyke handkerchiefs . . . the prettiest are those made exactly after a picture of the Queen Mother' (*Letters from Lady Jane Coke to her friend Mrs Eyre, 1747–1758*, ed. A. Rathbone, London, 1899, p. 123).

46. Hazlitt (1843), pp. 173, 176. No doubt it was the gentility of van Dyck which appealed to the eponymous heroine of Richardson's novel *Clarissa Harlowe*; when she makes her will she refers to 'my whole-length picture in the Vandyke taste that used to hang in my own parlour'.

47. *Lady's Magazine*, 1759, p. 128. The same plate from Hollar was also printed in Jefferys's *A Collection of the Dresses*, 1757, as *An English Lady of Quality of 1640* (II, pl. 216). The *Lady's Magazine* goes on to say that 'Mr. Reynolds, now at the head of portrait painting' favoured this kind of costume and the 'free dress of the hair', rather than the 'prim and close curls we have adopted from the French'. Although Reynolds is not known for the kind of detailed Vandyke costume that his master Hudson produced in quantity, historical influences were already beginning to be seen in his portraits by the late 1750s, more acceptable imagery than pure fashion.

48. Montagu, I, p. 102. Other possible Hollar sources are his *Seasons* (1641–4) and his *Theatrum Mulierum* (1643), which covers the fashionable and regional costumes of women in Europe. The most likely source, however, remains the *Ornatus muliebris anglicanus* of 1640.

49. Another portrait, only attributed to van Dyck, shows her as a shepherdess, with a large silk hat and a huge sleeve tied in at the top of her arm, allowing the chemise to puff through (Althorp House, Northants).

50. See A.M. Kettering, *The Dutch Arcadia: Pastoral Art and its audience in the Golden Age*, London, 1983.

51. Quoted in Shawe-Taylor, *The Georgians. Eighteenth-century Portraiture and Society*, London, 1990, p. 149.

52. Among the drawings by van Aken at the National Gallery of Scotland, Edinburgh, are costume studies inspired by such well-known portraits as the van Dyck three-quarter length *Henrietta Maria*, and his *Mary, Duchess of Lennox as St Agnes* (Royal Collection); also Kneller's *Countess of Ranelagh* (Hampton Court Palace).

53. S. Richardson, *Sir Charles Grandison*, London, 7 vols, 1754, I, p. 43.

54. Walpole (1888), II, p. 92.

55. Whereabouts unknown; with Leggatts, London, 1926. There are a number of portraits by Lely and his studio where the sitters wear very similar loose gowns and draperies or both. The same can be said for Kneller, and there is some confusion over attribution between the studio productions of late Lely and early Kneller.

56. The re-vamped head is probably by the hand of another artist, according to Brian Allen, Paul Mellon Centre for Studies in British Art, London. The identity of which of Hoadly's two wives, is not clear. The mask which Mrs Hoadly holds may be a reference to her husband's play *The Suspicious Husband*, first performed in 1747 at Covent Garden, with Garrick as the young rake, Ranger. Hayman's painting of the scene in the play when Ranger mistakes his cousin Clarinda for a woman of easy virtue and is horrified when she unmasks, is in the Yale Center for British Art, New Haven, CT.

57. The official costume for peeresses' coronation dress (as laid out in the comprehensive, illustrated work by Francis Sandford, *The Coronation of James II*, 1687) consisted of an embroidered skirt of white or silver, a kirtle or surcoat of red velvet bordered with miniver and fringed with gold or silver, the sleeves being short and scalloped, and a red velvet mantle with gold or silver cordons and tassels and rows of 'ermine' tails (powdering) according to the rank of the wearer; the length of the train was also regulated by the wearer's status as was the type of coronet.

58. Mansfield (1980), p. 60.

59. Walpole (1888), III, p. 39.

60. The initiation of young knights by bathing goes back at least until the twelfth century; in times of peace it was the equivalent of knighthood being bestowed on the field of battle, and by the fourteenth century it had become formalised. On the installation of new knights in 1761, see the *London Chronicle*, 26–8 May 1761, p. 505.

61. Wilton (1992), p. 120.

62. Reynolds (1975), pp. 138–9.

63. How far Reynolds initiated the vogue for young men to be painted in this kind of 'aesthetic' Vandyke style, and even to dress in this way, is not clear. John Pye in his *Patronage of British Art*, London, 1845, quotes a contemporary critic who claimed that the artist had introduced 'the Vandyke manner of wearing the hair', i.e. long and with a fringe over the eyes (p. 241).

64. Leslie and Taylor (1865), I, p. 392. Reynolds was often accompanied to the masquerade by Goldsmith, and after Goldsmith's death in 1774, by Gibbon.

65. *The Diary of Sylas Neville 1767–1788*, ed. B. Cozens-Hardy, London, 1950, pp. 70–71. The artist was called 'Sykes, a pupil of Hudson'.

66. For example Gainsborough's portraits of the brothers Bartholemew and William Henry Pleydell-Bouverie of 1773–4 (Earl of Radnor, Longford Castle, Wilts) show virtually the same imaginary Vandyke doublet with an eighteenth-century stock and shirt ruffle. Gainsborough's *Jonathan Buttall*, *c*.1770 (San Marino, CA, Huntington Art Gallery), better known as the '*Blue Boy*' (a portrait inspired by Titian and also by van Dyck's George Villiers in the double portrait of the Villiers brothers in the Royal

Collection) wears a suit similar to that worn by Paul Cobb Methuen in his portrait of *c.*1776 (Corsham Court, Wilts) except that the latter's sleeves are formed of strips of fabric and the braid is slightly different.

67. These included his copy after the large group, *The Earl of Pembroke and his Family* at Wilton, Wilts, and the double portrait, *Lords John and Bernard Stuart*, then at Cobham Hall, and now in the National Gallery, London.

68. Vertue (1933–4), p. 124.

69. The Royal Museum of Scotland, Edinburgh, has two Vandyke suits of *c.*1780. One is of pink silk trimmed with applied cream-coloured slashes edged with black and with silver sequins; there is a cream waistcoat with fake slashes of pink and with silver sequins. The other suit comprises a doublet and breeches of ruched cream silk trimmed with silver lace.

70. Aspinall (1963–71), I, pp. 51, 62.

71. 'Vauxhall Gardens Scrapbooks', 5 vols, London, British Library, I, p. 77.

72. See Ribeiro (1988), pp. 213–6. Also J.L. Nevinson, 'The Vogue of the Vandyke Dress', *Country Life Annual*, 1959, pp. 25–7. One of the most famous archery portraits is Ramsay's *John, Lord Mountstuart, later first Marquess of Bute*, 1759 (Marquess of Bute) winner of the Silver Arrow, the annual prize given for archery at Harrow. He wears a pink suit with braid and fringes, a Vandyke collar and cuffs and shoe rosettes.

73. Webster (1976), p. 42.

74. See S. Rosenfeld, *Temples of Thespis. Some private Theatres and Theatricals in England and Wales 1700–1820*, Society for Theatre Research, London, 1978.

75. Walpole (1937–83), IX, p. 335. The costume of Jane Seymour might have been similar to the one described in Mrs Montagu's correspondence, at the Countess of Moira's masquerade in 1768, a 'stiff bodice and farthingale with silver gauze beads and ermine made of black and white Persian' (*Mrs Montagu, 'Queen of the Blues': Her Letters and Friendships from 1762–1800*, ed. R. Blunt, 2 vols, London, 1923, I, p. 47).

76. See the account in the *Gentleman's Magazine*, June 1774, pp. 263–5. The event inspired a play by John Burgoyne, *The Maid of the Oaks*, performed at Drury Lane in 1775, with Mrs Abington in the main role. It also inspired a masquerade put on by the Scavoir-Vivre Club (ancestor of Boodles) at the Pantheon in May 1775; see the account in the *Town and Country Magazine*, May 1775, p. 230.

77. Delany (1861–2), II, p. 1.

78. *Walpole* (1937–83), XXXV, pp. 418–9. Walpole declares that the style would not suit his figure, so he proposes to wait 'till the dress of the Druids is revived, which will be more suitable to my age'.

79. Royal Archives, Account No. 29228; the same account includes a 'superfine short green Vandyke waistcoat' which cost £3, 13s, 6d.

80. Delany (1861–2), IV, p. 110. The date is 1767.

81. See above, n. 25.

82. There are four Dilettanti portraits by George Knapton of sitters in Roman dress; these include the Duke of Dorset as a Roman consul (1741) and Viscount Barrington as a Roman general (1745) (Society of Dilettanti, Brooks's Club, London). There is an interesting portrait by the American artist Charles Willson Peale (in London 1767–9) of William Pitt, Earl of Chatham, in Roman dress (Maryland Department of General Services, Hall of Records and Artistic Property Commissions), a knee-length tunic, cloak and buskins; he stands before an altar of peace and in the background is a figure of Liberty with a Phrygian cap on a pole. Pitt championed the cause of the American colonies and the portrait was commissioned by a Virginia busi-nessman then in London.

83. *The European Magazine*, London, 1785, p. 25.

84. Reynolds (1975), p. 88.

85. Ibid., p. 138.

86. Mrs Thrale claimed that Lady Sarah 'never *did* sacrifice to the Graces; her face was gloriously handsome, but she used to play cricket and eat beefsteaks on the Steyne at Brighton'; quoted in London (1986), p. 224, entry by D. Mannings.

87. Hazlitt's essay 'On Certain Inconsistencies in Sir Joshua Reynolds' Discourses', in Hazlitt (1959) discusses the way in which Reynolds's theory 'limits nature and paralyses art'; it 'consists too much of negations, and not enough of positive, prominent qualities. It accounts for nothing but the beauty of the common Antique, and hardly for that . . .' (p. 144).

88. Romney (1830), p. 162. The author claims that his father was responsible for the classical simplicity in dress which later artists take for granted: 'The succeeding painters have enjoyed all the advantage of this reform in female attire, which gives to their portraits much elegance, without their being obliged to have recourse to fancy designs' (p. 196).

89. See, for example, Benjamin West's *Mrs Worrell as Hebe, c.*1770 (London, Tate Gallery) in a white gown with an emerald brooch on the shoulder and a striped silk scarf; and Gavin Hamilton's *Emma Hamilton as Hebe c.*1786 (Stanford, CA, University Museum and Art Gallery) where the diagonal drapery of her costume reveals her bare bosom, and a menacingly large eagle drinks out of a cup held out in her hand. (The problem of what to do about the eagle when appearing at a fancy-dress ball was solved when, at the Devonshire House Ball in 1897 for Queen Victoria's Diamond Jubilee, the Countess of Westmoreland came as Hebe in a vaguely art-nouveau dress of white muslin, with a stuffed eagle perched on her shoulder).

90. Unlike many other portraits by Reynolds, this portrait – recently cleaned – looks better in the flesh than it does in reproduction.

91. Romney (1830), p. 183.

92. Jaffé (1972), p. 30.

93. J.W. von Goethe, *Travels in Italy*, trans. A.J.W. Morrison and C. Nisbet, London, 1892, p. 199. Walpole waspishly refers to 'Sir W. Hamilton's pantomime mistress – or wife – who acts all the antique statues in an Indian shawl . . . people are mad about her wonderful expression, which I do not conceive, so few antique statues having any expression at all . . .' (Walpole, 1937–83, XI, pp. 337–8.).

94. Goethe (1971), pp. 191–2.

95. D.M. Stuart, *Dearest Bess: The Life and Times of Lady Elizabeth Foster, afterwards Duchess of Devonshire*, London, 1955, p. 59.

96. *The Remains of the late Mrs Richard Trench. Being Selections from her Journals, Letters and other Papers*, ed. the Dean of Westminster, London, 1862, p. 107.

97. The first collection – see a *Collection of Etruscan, Greek and Roman Antiquities from the Cabinet of the Hon. William Hamilton*, P.F.H.D. D'Hancarville, [P.-F. Hugues] 4 vols, Naples, 1766–7; the second collection – see a *Collection of Engravings from Ancient Vases discovered in the Two Sicilies during 1789 and 1790*, 4 vols, Naples, 1791–5.

98. None of the vases here has been identified except two from Hamilton's first collection sold to the British Museum in 1772; the artist uses the vases generally to indicate Hope's taste and connoisseurship, although there may be some that he owned.

99. In an article, 'The Relation of Dress to Art', *Pall Mall Gazette*, XLI, no. 6230, 1885; see R. Ellman (ed.), *The Artist as Critic: Critical Writings of Oscar Wilde*, London, 1970, p. 19.

100. T. Hope, *The Costume of the Ancients*, London, 1809, p. 12.

101. The *peplos* is a tunic with an over-fold, the ends of which can usually be seen in Greek art, even when the over-fold is so long that it is tied round at the waist. The *chiton*, on the other hand, has no such fold, although folds can be created by the length of the material being drawn up through girdle(s). What Hope's *Grecian Female* wears is a short mantle, an Ionic *himation*, over her dress, although it looks a bit like a *peplos*.

102. *Costume of the Ancients*, p. 43.

103. Ibid., p. 13.

104. Brummell (1932), p. 123. Brummell urged the formation of a 'Club of Costume, in which no gentleman should be admitted as a member who is not well versed both in its Grecian and Roman progress, and in its principles as a fine art' (p. 129).

105. Ibid., p. 3.

106. H.L. Piozzi, *Observations and Reflections made in the course of a Journey through France, Italy and Germany*, London, 1789, 2 vols, I, p. 93.

107. J.M. Vien produced a set of drawings of his fellow students dressed up *à la turque* and it was engraved as the *Caravanne du à la Mecque*, 1748 (London, Victoria and Albert Museum). There are also some paintings by another artist participant, Jean Barbault, of the various Turkish characters in this masquerade (Paris, Louvre).

108. See Ribeiro (1979). Apart from the word *shalwar*, Lady Mary's spelling has been retained, although *antery* should be *anteri*, and *curdee*, *kurk* or *kirk*. However, the spelling and the terminology of these dress terms is open to a number of interpretations and names could change, for example according to the length of a particular garment. What Lady Mary calls a 'waistcoat' (*antery*), is possibly a short gown (*yelek*), whereas the *anteri* probably refers to the long gown, often looped up into the girdle and which, for convenience, is referred to as a caftan.

109. *Oxford Magazine*, Oct. 1768, p. 161. Delany (1861–2), II, p. 185.

110. See, for example, *Mary, Duchess of Richmond*, 1775 (Goodwood House, W. Sussex) in gold and white *shalwar*, an overdress of white lined in green, and a velvet robe edged with ermine. A similar costume can be seen in the portrait of *Theresa Parker*, 1773 (private collection), except that the robe is of white silk lined with pink.

111. Leslie and Taylor (1865), I, p. 398. It is not clear which portrait is referred to here, but two surviving portraits of the sitter (Michael Astor Collection) show her in vaguely 'oriental' dress; one shows her in a cross-over gown with a Greek key pattern along the hem and a scarf in her hair and the other shows her in a flowered dress under an ermine-trimmed gown, wearing a cone-shaped headdress decorated with pearls.

112. At a masquerade for the King of Denmark in 1768, 'Lord Clive appeared in the dress of a Nabob very richly ornamented with diamonds' (*Oxford Magazine*, Oct. 1768, p. 160); at a masquerade at Carlisle House in 1772, there appeared a masquerader as 'a nabob, the dress an actual present from a nabob to the wearer and estimated beneath its worth at five hundred pounds (*Town and Country Magazine*, May 1772, p. 238).

113. See Knapton's Dilettanti Society portraits of Lords Bessborough and Sandwich, who were painted in the Turkish dress they wore when they travelled in the Near East (Society of Dilettanti, Brooks's Club, London). On Englishmen dressed *à la turque*, either as travellers or as masqueraders, see Ribeiro (1984b), pp. 217–25.

114. Surr (1806), II, pp. 217–20.

115. Simond (1817), II, p. 194.

116. The National Portrait Gallery, London, has the green waistcoat, and the front of the red one.

117. Government Art Collection; the National Portrait Gallery, London, has a cut-down head and shoulders version. The artist has added a moustache for an extra touch of Balkan verisimilitude. The costume is at Bowood House, Wilts, the collection of the Earl of Shelburne.

118. See A. Ribeiro, 'Hussars in Masquerade', *Apollo*, CV, no. 180, 1977, pp. 111–16. The Harris Museum and Art Gallery, Preston, has two miniature hussar suits used by Devis for a doll/layman; one is a blue silk jacket and breeches trimmed with gold braid and tassels, and the other is a jacket of pink silk trimmed with gold, and a matching conical hat.

119. The novel was unfinished at his death and completed by Sir Walter Scott, an acknowledgment of his 'merits as an excellent artist and a sedulous antiquary'. It was published in 1808, Scott claiming, generously, that it inspired him to write *Waverley* (1814).

120. See S. Lloyd, 'Richard Cosway, RA. The artist as collector, connoisseur and virtuoso', *Apollo*, CXXXIII, no. 352, 1991, pp. 398–405.

121. Egan (1821), p. 270. The Prince of Wales's accounts refer to a payment of £52. 10s. for 'a suit of Chinese equestrian armour and a mandarin of war's court dress', 1818 (Windsor), Royal Archives, No. 29577).

122. Windsor, Royal Archives, Accounts, Nos 29232, 29315, 29320 and 29414.

123. See H. Trevor-Roper, 'The Invention of Tradition: The Highland Tradition of Scotland', in *The Invention of Tradition*, eds. E. Hobsbawm and T. Ranger, Cambridge, 1983, pp. 15–41.

124. Windsor, Royal Archives, Account No. 29234. Betsy Sheridan found the costume 'Ellegant (and) becoming', see *Betsy Sheridan's Journal*, ed. W. Lefanu, London, 1960, p. 168.

125. Windsor, Royal Archives, Account No. 29415. The same account refers to altering, i.e. widening, a belted plaid.

126. The cost was £238,238; that of William IV cost £42,298 and Victoria's cost £69,421. See D. Cannadine, 'The Context, Performance and Meaning of Ritual: The British Monarchy and the "Invention of Tradition", c.1820–1977', in *Invention of Tradition*, p. 163.

127. A demonstration in St Peter's Fields, Manchester, in the summer of 1819, was dispersed by the mounted yeomany, resulting in several deaths and numerous injuries to the demonstrators.

128. V. Cumming, 'Pantomime and Pageantry: The Coronation of George IV', in Fox (1992), p. 45. The present, necessarily simplified account of the coronation, relies on Valerie Cumming's work in this respect, particularly her study of the costumes. I am indebted to her for her help.

129. Girouard (1981), p. 27. A rather more jaundiced view, held by Cannadine, op.cit., is that the coronation was so 'overblown that grandeur merged into farce' (p. 117).

130. *A Brief Account of the Coronation of His Majesty George IV*, London, 1821, pp. 4–5.

131. J. Whittaker, *The Coronation of His Most Sacred Majesty King George IV*, London, 2 vols, London, 1821–41, n. p.

132. *A Brief Account*, p. 8.

133. Windsor, Royal Archives, Account No. 29597, 2 May 1821: '24 yards of hair' and bottles of gum.

134. Whitley (1928b), p. 247.

135. It is deliberately quite different in style from the traditional coronation mantle of his predecessors, and with a longer train. It is still in good condition, apart from some fading on the front. Lined with real ermine, it is in two separate pieces, and was probably stitched lightly on one shoulder, the other being held with a clasp. The Museum of London has a copy of George IV's coronation suit of cloth of silver trimmed with gold lace, a crimson velvet surcoat embroidered in gold, and accessories – a crimson velvet sword belt embroidered in gold, silver ribbon garters with gold lace rosettes and a pair of white kid shoes with red heels and gold lace rosettes. It was owned by the Earl of Ancaster, and possibly made for the King as a copy, but not worn by him.

136. *A Brief Account*, p. 13.

137. *Coronation . . . of George IV*.

Afterword

1. Delécluze (1863), p. 136.

2. *The Life and Letters of Lady Sarah Lennox 1745–1826*, ed. Countess of Ilchester and Lord Stavordale, 2 vols, London, 1901, II, pp. 291–3.

3. Vaughan (1792), p. 22.

4. Quoted in Paris (1984), p. 334.

5. T. Hope, *Costume of the Ancients*, London, 1809, p. 5.

Select Bibliography

NOTE: Exhibition catalogues are listed under city unless by a single or main author, when they appear in alphabetical sequence.

Abrantès, L., duchesse d', *Memoirs*, 8 vols, London, 1831–5

'A.J.', *Essay sur le beau*, Amsterdam, 1767

Alison, A., *Essays on the Nature and Principles of Taste*, Dublin, 1790

Allen, B., *Francis Hayman*, Iveagh Bequest, Kenwood, and Yale University Press, 1987

Andrews, J., *An Account of the Character and Manners of the French; with Occasional Observations on the English*, 2 vols, London, 1770

Angelo, H., *Reminiscences*, 2 vols, London, 1828

Anninger, A., 'Costumes of the Convention: Art as Agent of Social Change in Revolutionary France', *Harvard Library Bulletin*, XXX, 1982, pp. 179–203

Anstey, C., *The New Bath Guide*, London, 1766

Archenholz, J.W., *A Picture of England, Containing a Description of the Laws, Customs and Manners of England*, 2 vols, London, 1789

Arnault, A.V., *Souvenirs d'un séxagenaire*, 4 vols, Paris, 1833

Aspinall, A. (ed.), *The Letters of King George IV, 1812–1830*, 3 vols, Cambridge, 1938

——— *The Correspondence of George Prince of Wales 1770–1812*, 8 vols, London, 1963–71

Baillio, J., *Elizabeth-Louise Vigée Le Brun 1755–1842*, exh. cat. Fort Worth, TX, Kimbell Art Museum, 1982

Barker, W., *A Treatise on the Principles of Hair-Dressing*, London, c.1780

Barras, P.J.F.N., comte de, *Memoirs*, ed. G. Duruy, trans. C.E. Roche, 4 vols, London, 1895–6

Barrell, J., *The Political Theory of Painting from Reynolds to Hazlitt*, New Haven and London, 1986

Baudelaire, C., *The Painter of Modern Life and Other Essays*, trans. and ed. J. Mayne, London, 1964

——— *Art in Paris 1845–1862. Salons and Other Exhibitions Reviewed by Charles Baudelaire*, trans. and ed. J. Mayne, London, 1965

Beauharnais, H. de, *Mémoires de la Reine Hortense*, ed. J. Hanoteau, 3 vols, Paris, 1927

Beaunier, M.M.F., and Rathier, L., *Recueil des Costumes Français . . . Depuis Clovis jusqu'à Napoléon I*, Paris, 1809–1813

Behrens, C.B.A., *The Ancien Régime*, London, 1967

Bergeret, P.-N., *Lettres d'un artiste sur l'état des arts en France*, Paris, 1848

Bertrand, L., *La Fin du classicisme et le retour à l'antique*, Paris, 1896, repr. Geneva, 1968

Black, J., *Natural and Necessary Enemies. Anglo-French Relations in the Eighteenth Century*, London, 1986

Boswell, J., *The Hypochondriack . . . Essays in the London Magazine, 1771–1783*, ed. M. Bailey, Stanford, 1928

Bouchot, H., *La Toilette à la cour de Napoléon*, Paris, 1895

Boudier de Villement, P.J., *L'Ami des femmes*, Paris, 1758

Brighton, *Angelica Kauffman*, see Roworth (1992)

Brookner, A., *David*, London, 1980

Brownlow, E.S., Countess, *The Eve of Victorianism. Reminiscences of the Years 1802 to 1834*, ed. B. Porcelli, London, 1940

Brummell, G.B., *Male and Female Costume, Grecian and Roman Costume, British Costume from the Roman Invasion until 1822, and the Principles of Costume Applied to the Improved Dress of the Present Day*, ed. and intr. E. Parker, New York, 1932

Bryson, N., *Word and Image. French Painting of the Ancien Régime*, Cambridge, 1981

——— *Tradition and Desire. From David to Delacroix*, Cambridge, 1984

Campan, J.L.H., *Memoirs of the Private Life of Marie-Antoinette*, 2 vols, London, 1823

Carlyle, T., *Sartor Resartus*, London, 1984

Carr, J., *The Stranger in France*, London, 1803

Carré, H., *Jeux, sports et divertissements des rois de France*, Paris, 1937

Castle, T., *Masquerade and Civilization. The Carnivalesque in Eighteenth-century English Culture and Fiction*, London, 1986

Chadwick, W., *Women, Art and Society*, London, 1990

Chapman, R.W. (ed.), *Jane Austen's Letters to her Sister Cassandra and Others*, 2 vols, Oxford, 1932

Charlton, D.G., *New Images of the Natural in France: A Study in European Cultural History, 1750–1800*, Cambridge, 1984

Chaussinard-Nogaret, G., *The French Nobility in the Eighteenth Century*, trans. W. Doyle, Cambridge, 1985

Cherry, D., and Harris, J., 'Eighteenth-century Portraiture and the Seventeenth-century Past: Gainsborough and van Dyck', *Art History*, V, no. 3, 1982, pp. 287–309

Cleveland, OH, *Style, Truth and the Portrait*, see Saisselin (1963)

Cole, W., *A Journal of my Journey to Paris in the Year 1765*, ed. F.G. Stokes, London, 1931

Colley, L., *Britons. Forging the Nation, 1707–1837*, New Haven and London, 1992

Combe, W., *A Poetical Epistle to Sir Joshua Reynolds*, London, 1777

Constant [Louis Constant Wairy], *Memoirs*, trans. P. Pinkerton, 4 vols, London, 1896

Crow, T., *Painters and Public Life in Eighteenth-century Paris*, New Haven and London, 1985

Dayes, E., *Essays on Painting*, London, 1805

——— *Professional Sketches of Modern Artists*, London, 1805

Delany, M., *Autobiography and Correspondence of Mary Granville, Mrs Delany*, ed. Lady Llanover, 6 vols, London, 1861–2

Delécluze, E.J., *Louis David. Son Ecole et son temps*, Paris, 1863

Delpierre, M., 'Les Costumes de cour et les uniformes civils du premier Empire', *Bulletin du Musée Carnavalet*, no. 2, 1958, pp. 2–23

——— 'Ingres et la mode de son temps'. Actes du Colloque International Ingres et le Néo-classicisme, *Bulletin des Amis du Musée Ingres*, 1975, pp. 147–56

——— *Modes à l'antique et modes romantiques*, Tours, Musée des Beaux-Arts, 1981–2, pp. 3–16

Démeunier, J.N., *L'Esprit des usages et des coutumes des differens peuples*, 3 vols, London, 1776

Detroit, IL, Institute of Arts, *French Painting, 1774–1830. The Age of Revolution*, 1975

Diderot, D., *Pensées détachées sur la peinture, la sculpture, l'architecture et la poésie*, intr. J. Pierre and ed. R. Desné, Paris, 1955

——— *Salons*, ed. J. Seznec and J. Adhémar, 3 vols, Oxford, 1975–1983

Dowd, D.L., *Pageant-Master of the Republic. Jacques-Louis David and the French Revolution*, University of Nebraska Studies, Lincoln, NB, 1948

——— 'Jacobinism and the Fine Arts', *Art Quarterly*, XVI, 1953, pp. 195–214

——— 'The French Revolution and the Painters', *French Historical Studies*, I, no. 2, 1959, pp. 127–48

Dreyfous, M., *Les Arts et les artistes pendant la période révolutionnaire*, Paris,? 1906

Duval, G., *Souvenirs de la Terreur de 1788 à 1793*, 4 vols, Paris, 1841–2

Edinburgh, Scottish National Portrait Gallery, *Van Dyck in Check Trousers. Fancy Dress in Art and Life, 1700–1900*, 1978

——— *Allan Ramsay*, see Smart (1992a)

Edwards, E., *Anecdotes of Painters who have resided or been born in England*, London, 1808

Egan, P., *Life in London: or the Day and Night Scenes of Jerry Hawthorn Esq., and his elegant friend*

Corinthian Tom, London, 1821

Egerton, J., *Wright of Derby*, exh. cat., London, Tate Gallery, 1990

Elias, N., *The Court Society*, trans. E. Jephcott, Oxford, 1983

Farington, J., *Diary*, eds. K. Garlick, A. Macintyre and K. Cave, 16 vols, New Haven and London, 1978–1984

Fort Worth, TX, *Vigée Le Brun*, see Baillio (1982)

Fox, C. (ed.), *London: World City, 1800–1840*, exh. cat. Essen, Villa Hügel, 1992

Fried, M., *Absorption and Theatricality. Painting and Beholder in the Age of Diderot*, Los Angeles, 1980

Fuseli, H., *Lectures on Painting*, London, 1820

Gaudriault, R., *Répertoire de la gravure de mode française des origines à 1815*, Paris, 1988

Genlis, S.F., comtesse de, *Mémoires sur la cour, la ville et les salons de Paris*, Paris, 1870

Girouard, M., *The Return to Camelot*, New Haven and London, 1981

Goethe, J.W. von., *Elective Affinities*, trans. and intr. R.J. Hollingdale, Harmondsworth, 1971

—— *Goethe on Art*, trans., intr. and ed. J. Gage, London, 1980

Gould, C., *Trophy of Conquest. The Musée Napoléon and the Creation of the Louvre*, London, 1965

Grandjean, S., *Inventaire après décès de l'impératrice Joséphine à Malmaison*, Paris, 1964

Gronow, Captain R.H., *Reminiscences and Recollections. Being Anecdotes of the Camp, Court, Clubs and Society, 1810–60*, 2 vols, London, 1892

Grose, F. (ed.), *The Antiquarian Repertory*, 6 vols, London, 1775, 1780, 1807–9

Grosley, P.J., *A Tour to London: or New Observations on England and Its Inhabitants*, trans. T. Nugent, 2 vols, London, 1772

Haskell, F., *Rediscoveries in Art: Some Aspects of Taste, Fashion and Collecting in England and France*, London, 1976

—— *Past and Present in Art and Taste*, New Haven and London, 1987

Haskell, F., and Penny, N., *Taste and the Antique*, New Haven and London, 1981

Hautecoeur, L., *L'Art sous la Révolution et l'Empire en France, 1789–1815*, Paris, 1953

Hayes, J., *The Portrait in British Art*, London, 1991

Hazlitt, W., *The Spirit of the Age, or Contemporary Portraits*, London, 1825

—— *Criticisms on Art*, ed. W. Hazlitt, London, 1843

—— *Table Talk*, London, 1959

Hemmings, F.W.J., *Culture and Society in France, 1789–1848*, Leicester, 1987

Hickey, W., *Memoirs*, ed. A. Spencer, 4 vols, London, 1913: ed. P. Quennell, London, 1960

Hilles, F.W. (ed.), *Letters of Sir Joshua Reynolds*, Cambridge, 1929

Hogarth, W., *The Analysis of Beauty*, ed. and intr. J. Burke, Oxford, 1955

Hollander, A., *Seeing Through Clothes*, New York, 1978

Honour, H., *Romanticism*, London, 1979

Hunt, L., *Politics, Culture and Class in the French Revolution*, Berkeley, CA, 1984

Irwin, D., *English Neoclassical Art. Studies in Inspiration and Taste*, London, 1966

Jacobs, E., Barber, W.H., et al., *Woman and Society in Eighteenth-century France. Essays in Honour of John Stephenson Spink*, London, 1979

Jaffé, P., *Lady Hamilton in Relation to the Art of her Time*, exh. cat., London, Kenwood, Iveagh Bequest, 1972

Jesse, W., *The Life of George Brummell*, 2 vols, London, 1844

Karamzin, N.M., *Travels from Moscow through Prussia, Germany, Switzerland, France and England*, 3 vols, London, 1803

Kimball, F., *The Creation of the Rococo*, exh. cat. Philadelphia Museum of Art, 1943

Klingender, F.D., *Art and the Industrial Revolution*, rev. ed., London, 1968

Knight, R.P., *An Analytical Inquiry into the Principles of Taste*, London, 1805

Langlade, E., *Rose Bertin. The Creator of Fashion at the Court of Marie-Antoinette*, trans. H.S. Rappoport, London, 1913

Lanson, R., *Le Goût du moyen age en France au XVIIIe siècle*, Paris, 1926

Le Camus, A., *Abdeker, or The Art of preserving Beauty*, London, 1754

Lee, V., *Jacques-Louis David: The Versailles Sketchbook*, *Burlington Magazine*, CXI, no. 793, 1969, pp. 197–208; CXI, no. 795, 1969, pp. 360–69

Lee, V., *The Reign of Women in Eighteenth-century France*, Cambridge, MA, 1975

Leith, J.A., *The Idea of Art as Propaganda in France 1750–1799*, Toronto, 1965

Lenoir, A., *Musée des monumens français*, 5 vols, Paris, 1800–1806

Lens, A., *Le Costume des peuples de l'antiquité*, Dresden, 1785

Leslie, C.R., and Taylor, T., *The Life and Times of Sir Joshua Reynolds*, 2 vols, London, 1865

Levey, M., *Sir Thomas Lawrence, 1769–1830*, exh. cat., London, National Portrait Gallery, 1979

—— *Rococo to Revolution*, London, 1984

London:
P. & D. Colnaghi, *The British Face. A View of Portraiture, 1625–1850*, 1986
Hazlitt, Gooden and Fox, *Horace Vernet*, see Ribeiro (1991b)
Heim, *The Painted Word, British History Painting, 1750–1830*, 1991
Kenwood, Iveagh Bequest, *Lady Hamilton*, see Jaffé (1972)
  Thomas Hudson, see Miles (1979)
  Pompeo Batoni (1708–87) and his British Patrons, 1982
  The Earl and Countess Howe by Gainsborough. A Bicentenary Exhibition, 1988
National Portrait Gallery, *Johann Zoffany*, see Webster (1976)
  Sir Thomas Lawrence, see Levey (1979)
  Archives, Sitter books for George Romney, Joseph Wright, James Northcote
Royal Academy of Arts, *Reynolds*, see Penny (1986)
Tate Gallery, *Wright of Derby*, see Egerton (1990)
  The Swagger Portrait, see Wilton (1992)
Victoria and Albert Museum, Barbier Letters
  'Original Documents Relative to the Empress Josephine', 1809
Romney papers and notebooks

Los Angeles, County Museum of Art, *An Elegant Art. Fashion and Fantasy in the Eighteenth Century*, exh. cat., 1983

Lowenthal, D., *The Past is a Foreign Country*, Cambridge, 1985

Macmillan, D., *Painting in Scotland. The Golden Age*, Oxford, 1986

Malcolm, J.P., *Anecdotes of the Manners and Customs of London*, London, 1808

Malliot, J., *Recherches sur les costumes, les moeurs, les usages réligieux, civils et militaires des anciens peuples d'après les auteurs célébrés et les monuments antiques*, 3 vols, Paris, 1804

Mansel, P., *The Eagle in Splendour. Napoleon I and his Court*, London, 1987

—— *The Court of France, 1789–1830*, Cambridge, 1988

Mansfield, A., *Ceremonial Costume*, London, 1980

Marquiset, A., *Une Merveilleuse. Madame Hamelin, 1776–1851*, Paris, 1909

Marriott, T., *Female Conduct: Being an Essay on the Art of Pleasing*, London, 1759

Masson, F., *Livre du sacre de l'Empereur Napoléon*, Paris, 1908

Maza, S.C., *Servants and Masters in Eighteenth-century France*, Princeton, 1983

Maze-Sencier, A., *Les Fournisseurs de Napoléon I et des deux impératrices*, Paris, 1893

Meister, H., *Letters written during a residence in England*, London, 1799

—— *Souvenirs de mon dernier voyage à Paris*, Paris, 1910

Melbourne, National Gallery of Victoria, *The Great Eighteenth Century Exhibition*, 1983

Mercier, L.S., *L'An deux mille quatre cent quarante, rêve s'il en fut jamais*, Amsterdam, 1770, trans. W. Hooper as *Memoirs of the Year 2500*, London, 1772

—— *Parallèle de Paris et de Londres*, c.1780, ed. C. Bruneteau and B. Cottret, Paris, 1982

—— *Tableau de Paris*, 12 vols, Amsterdam, 1782–88

—— *Le Nouveau Paris*, 6 vols, Paris, 1798

Métra, F. (ed.), *Correspondance secrète, politique et littéraire*, 18 vols, London, 1787–90

Miette de Villars, –., *Mémoires de David*, Paris, 1850

Miles, E., 'Thomas Hudson (1701–1779): Portraitist to the British Establishment', Yale University, PhD diss., 1976, microfilm, Ann Arbor

—— *Thomas Hudson, 1701–1779*, exh. cat. London, Iveagh Bequest, Kenwood, 1979

Miller, J. (ed), *The Don Giovanni Book. Myths of Seduction and Betrayal*, London, 1990

Millin, A.L., *Dictionnaire des beaux-arts*, 3 vols, Paris, 1806

Molé, G.F.R., *Histoire des modes françaises*, Paris, 1773

Mongez, A., *Recueil d'antiquités*, Paris, 1804

Montfaucon, B. de, *L'Antiquité expliquée et représentée en figures*, Paris, 1719–24

—— *Les Monumens de la monarchie françoise*, 5 vols, Paris, 1729–33

Moritz, C.P., *Travels in England in 1782*, intr. P.E. Matheson, London, 1924

Nayler, Sir G., *The Coronation of His Most Sacred Majesty King George the Fourth*, London, 1837

Newdigate-Newdegate, Lady, *The Cheverels of Cheverel Manor*, London, 1898

New York, Metropolitan Museum of Art, *The Age of Napoleon. Costume from Revolution to Empire, 1789–1815*, 1989

Nivelon, F., *The Rudiments of Genteel Behavior*, London, 1737

Nouvion, P. de, *Un ministre de modes sous Louis XVI. Mademoiselle Bertin, marchande de modes de la reine, 1747–1813*, Paris, 1911

Paris:
Bibliothèque Nationale, Registres des dépenses de

la cour sous l'Empire et la Restauration, 1812–21

Hôtel de la Monnaie, *Diderot et l'art de Boucher à David. Les Salons, 1759–1781*, 1984

Musée du Louvre, *Jacques-Louis David*, 1989 [1989a]

Palais Galliéra, Musée de la Mode et du Costume, *Uniformes civils français. Cérémonial circonstances, 1750–1980*, 1982

——— *Modes et révolutions, 1780–1804*, 1989 [1989b]

Parker, H.T., *The Cult of Antiquity and the French Revolution*, Chicago, 1937

Paulson, R., *Emblem and Expression. Meaning in English Art of the 18th century*, London, 1975

——— *Representations of Revolution, 1789–1820*, New Haven and London, 1983

Penny, N., *Reynolds*, exh. cat. London, Royal Academy, 1986

Pentzell, R., 'New Dress'd in the Ancient Manner. The Rise of Historical Realism in Costuming the Serious Drama of England and France in the Eighteenth Century, PhD diss., Yale University, 1967, Microfilm, Ann Arbor

Peppiatt, M., and Bellony-Rewald, A., *Imagination's Chamber: Artists and Their Studios*, London, 1983

Percier, C., and Fontaine, F.L., *Livre du Sacre*, Paris, 1807

Perot, P., *Le Travail des apparences*, Paris, 1984

Philadelphia, PA, *The Creation of the Rococo*, see Kimball (1943)

Prudhomme, L., *Révolutions de Paris*, 17 vols, Paris, 1790–1794

Pupil, F., *Le Style troubadour, ou la nostalgie du bon vieux temps*, Nancy, 1985

Ramsay, A., *A Dialogue on Taste*, 2nd edn, London, 1762

Reiset, G.A.H., comte de, *Modes et usages au temps de Marie-Antoinette. Livre-journal de Madame Eloffe, marchande de modes, couturière lingère ordinaire de la Reine et des dames de sa cour*, 2 vols, Paris, 1885

Rémusat, C.E., comtesse de, *Memoirs, 1802–8*, ed. P. de Rémusat, trans. C. Hoey and J. Lillie, 2 vols, London, 1880

Reynolds, Sir. J., *Discourses on Art*, ed. R.R. Wark, New Haven and London, 1975

Ribeiro, A., 'Some Evidence of the Influence of the Dress of the Seventeenth Century on Costume in Eighteenth-century Female Portraiture', *Burlington Magazine*, CXIX, no. 897, 1977, pp. 834–40

——— Turquerie. Turkish Dress and English Fashion in the Eighteenth Century, *Connoisseur*, CC I, no. 807, 1979, pp. 16–23

——— *A Visual History of Costume. The Eighteenth Century*, London, 1983

——— *Dress in Eighteenth-century Europe, 1715–1789*, London, 1984 [1984a]

——— *The Dress Worn at Masquerades in England, 1730 to 1790, and its Relation to Fancy Dress in Portraiture*, New York and London, 1984 [1984b]

——— *Fashion in the French Revolution*, London, 1988

——— 'Fashion in the Eighteenth Century: Some Anglo-French Comparisons', *Textile History*, XXII, no. 2, 1991, pp. 329–45 [1991a]

——— *Horace Vernet, 1789–1863. Incroyables et Merveilleuses*, exh. cat. Hazlitt, Gooden and Fox, London, 1991 [1991b]

Richardson, J., *An Essay on the Theory of Painting*, 2nd edn, London, 1725

Rigoley de Juvigny, J.A., *De la Décadence des lettres et des moeurs depuis les Grecs et les Romains jusqu'à nos jours*, Paris, 1787

Roche, D., *La Culture des apparences. Une Histoire du vêtement XVIIe–XVIIIe siècle*, Paris, 1989

Roland [Phlipon-Roland], J.-M., *Works*, London, 1800

Romney, J., *Memoirs of the Life and Works of George Romney*, London, 1830

Rouquet, J.-A., *The Present State of the Arts in England*, London, 1755

Roworth, W.W. (ed.), *Angelica Kauffman. A Continental Artist in Georgian England*, Brighton, Royal Pavilion, Art Gallery and Museums, exh. cat., 1992

St. John, J., *Letters from France to a Gentleman in the South of Ireland*, 2 vols, Dublin, 1787

Saisselin, R.G., *Style, Truth and the Portrait*, exh. cat. Cleveland Museum of Art, OH, 1963

Scott, J., *A Visit to Paris in 1814*, London, 1815

Ségur, A.J.P., comte de, *Les Femmes, leur condition et leur influence dans l'ordre social*, 3 vols, Paris, 1803

——— *Memoirs*, 3 vols, London, 1825–7

Séguy, P., *Histoire des modes sous l'Empire*, Paris, 1988

Shawe-Taylor, D., *The Georgians. Eighteenth-century Portraiture and Society*, London, 1990

Simond, L., *Journal of a Tour and Residence in Great Britain during the years 1810 and 1811*, 2 vols, Edinburgh, 1817

Simpson, J., *Paris after Waterloo*, Edinburgh, 1853

Smart, A., *Allan Ramsay, 1713–1784*, exh. cat., Edinburgh, Scottish National Portrait Gallery, 1992 [1992a]

——— *Allan Ramsay: Painter, Essayist and Man of the Enlightenment*, New Haven and London, 1992 [1992b]

Smith, J.T., *Nollekens and his Times*, 2 vols, London, 1828

Smollett, T., *Travels through France and Italy*, London, 1766

Sobry, J.F., *Discours sur les principaux usages de la nation françoise*, London, 1786

Steegman, J., *The Rule of Taste from George I to George IV*, London, 1936

Stevenson, S.W., *Journal of a Tour through France, Flanders and Holland, including a Visit to Paris*, Norwich, 1817

Stothard, C.A., *The Monumental Effigies of Great Britain; Selected from our cathedrals and churches, for the purpose of bringing together and preserving correct representations of the best historical illustrations extant, from the Norman Conquest to the reign of Henry the eighth*, intr. A.J. Kempe, London, 1832

Strutt, J., *A Complete View of the Manners, Customs, Arms, Habits &c of the Inhabitants of England*, 3 vols, London, 1774–6

——— *A Complete View of the Dress and Habits of the People of England*, 2 vols, London, 1796–9

Surr, T.S., *A Winter in London*, 3 vols, London, 1806

Sydney, Art Gallery of New South Wales, *French Painting: The Revolutionary Decades, 1760–1830*, 1980

Thibaudeau, A.C., *Mémoires sur le Consulat, 1799 à 1804*, Paris, 1827

Thicknesse, P., *Observations on the Customs and Manners of the French Nation*, London, 1766

——— *Useful Hints to Those who make the Tour of France*, London, 1768

——— *A Year's Journey through France and Part of Spain*, 2 vols, Bath, 1777

Tours, *Modes à l'antique . . .* , see Delpierre (1981–2)

Toussaint, H., *Les Portraits d'Ingres: peintures des musées nationaux*, Paris, 1985

Trahard, P., *La Sensibilité révolutionnaire*, Geneva, 1967

Tulard, J., *Les Salons de Peinture de la Révolution française, 1789–1799*, Paris, 1989

Vane, L., *Letters to a Gentleman of Fortune*, London, 1753

Vaughan, W., *An Essay Philosophical and Medical concerning Modern Clothing*, London, 1792

Vaughan, W., *Romantic Art*, London, 1978

Vertue, G., 'Notebooks', *Walpole Society*, XVIII (1929–30), XX (1931–2), XXII (1933–4)

Vigée-Lebrun, E.L., *Memoirs*, trans. G. Shelley, London, 1926

Villiers, J. (Earl of Clarendon), *A Tour through Part of France*, London, 1789

Wakefield, D., *French Eighteenth-century Painting*, London, 1984

Walpole, H., *Anecdotes of Painting in England*, ed. R.N. Wornum, 3 vols, London, 1888

——— *Letters*, ed. W.S. Lewis and others, 48 vols, New Haven and London, 1937–83

Warner, M., *Monuments and Maidens: The Allegory of the Female Form*, London, 1985

Webster, M., *Johann Zoffany*, exh. cat., London, National Portrait Gallery, 1976

Wendeborn, G.F.A., *A View of England towards the Close of the Eighteenth Century*, 2 vols, London, 1791

Whitley, W.T., *Art in England, 1800–1820*, London, 1928 [1928a]

——— *Artists and their friends in England, 1700–1799*, 2 vols, London, 1928 [1928b]

Williams, D.E., *The Life and Correspondence of Sir Thomas Lawrence, Kt.*, 2 vols, London, 1831

Wilson, H., *Memoirs*, 4 vols, London, 1825

Wilton, A., *The Swagger Portrait*, exh. cat., London, Tate Gallery, 1992

Windsor, Royal Archives, Accounts for George IV, 1783–1830

Wollstonecraft, M., *A Vindication of the Rights of Woman*, London, 1792

Woodall, M. (ed.), *The Letters of Thomas Gainsborough*, London, 1963

Index

Figures in *italic* type refer to pages on which illustrations appear.

254

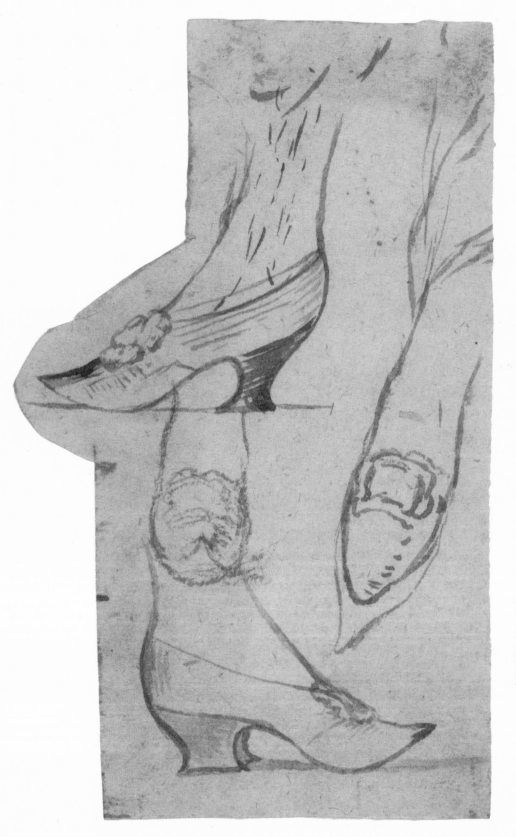